Mountain Biking Adventures:

Multi-day routes in northern Britain

Disclaimer

The authors have taken all reasonable effort to ensure that the information herein is accurate, however the authors accepts no responsibility if it is not, nor if unforeseen circumstances occur while doing the routes. We would also advise that in planning your route you check local transport, accommodation and please be aware that some paths and rights of way may be affected by changes such as forestry work or weather. We would appreciate any information regarding changes. You can do this by contacting the Publisher in the first instance.

Tony Wragg and Hugh Stewart

2QT Limited (Publishing)

Mountain Biking Adventures:

2QT Limited (Publishing)
Settle, North Yorkshire BD24 9RH
www.2qt.co.uk

Copyright © 2017 Tony Wragg & Hugh Stewart.
All rights reserved.

The rights of Tony Wragg & Hugh Stewart to be identified as the authors of this work has been asserted by them in accordance with the Copyright, Designs and Patents Act 1988

Ordnance Survey Maps is reproduced by permission of Ordnance Survey
on behalf of HMSO © Crown Copyright 2017.
All rights reserved. Ordnance Survey Licence number 100050133

All rights reserved. This book is sold subject to the condition that no part of this book is to be reproduced, in any shape or form. Or by way of trade, stored in a retrieval system or transmitted in any form or by any means, electronic, mechanical, photocopying, recording, be lent, re-sold, hired out or otherwise circulated in any form of binding or cover other than that in which it is published and without a similar condition, including this condition being imposed on the subsequent purchaser, without prior permission of the copyright holder.

Cover design & typesetting by Dale Rennard

Photographs © 2017 Hugh Stewart and Tony Wragg except as below.

Illustrations copyright © 2017 accorded to Quentin Harding and Paul Tynan for additional photographs, and to the following who supplied photographs directly or via http://wwwgeograph.org.uk/ which are Licenced under Creative Commons Attribution for Collaborative Statistics (http://creativecommons.org/licences/by-sa/2.0/), with kind permission: (Author's titles in brackets). Images: Strath Dionard (Track in Strath Dionard) p15 adapted © Alan Reid; Moine Path p18 adapted © Colin Bennett; The Flow near Cnoc Maol Donn (A boggy depression in the Flow) p22 © John Lucas; Liathach from Loch Clair (Loch Clair and Liathach) p45 © Bob Jones; Bridge over A'Ghairbhe. Beinn Eighe (Bridge over A'Ghairbhe river) p52 adapted © Bob Jones; Sublime singletrack to Carnmore (Path to Carnmore) p57 © Russel Wills; The causeway to Carnmore p59 © Russel Wills; Achneigie, Strath Sealga (Achneigie and Beinn Dearg Mor) p59 adapted © Tom Richardson; Viewpoint above Invermoriston along Loch Ness (Viewpoint along Loch Ness) p117 © Lis Burke; Ford across the Feshie: one of potentially many (Ford across the Feshie) p133 © Jim Barton; The superb track descent to Glen Mark (Track on the ridge of Couternach) p137 © Alan Reid.

Printed in Malta by Latitude Press Ltd.

A CIP catalogue record for this book is available from the British Library

ISBN 978-1-912014-87-3

Cover image: Descending from Mam Barrisdale to Inverie, Knoydart.

Multi-day routes in northern Britain

ACKNOWLEDGEMENTS

Our thanks to Mark Worthington for improvements to some photographs, to Andy Paton for some corrections, and to Dave Knowles for help with the bike and tyre section. Thanks also to the following for companionship and support on the rides, no matter how ridiculous: Adam Fennel, Mike Fisher, Quentin Harding, Geoff Hodgett, Dave Knowles, David Lavelle, Sean Murphy, Andy Paton, Simon Penson, Joao Pontes, Duncan Sherman, Mark Smith, Andrew Tynan, Paul Tynan and Andy Vickers.

HEALTH WARNING

Mountain biking is inherently dangerous!

Falling off carries the minimum risk of bruising, through fractures to the collar bone and ribs (common, due to landing on chest or shoulder), fractures of the hip, lower legs and pelvis, serious spinal fractures of back and neck, head injuries, and finally (in most cases), death!

This much is obvious: what is less obvious, and which took one of us fifteen years to learn, is that falling down a slope off your bike is not like falling from a standing start, like walking, but has a catapulting action, which can lead to a roll, which in turn is truly and unbelievably difficult to stop. Therefore, when considering the seriousness of a runout, take care of what lies beyond the immediate ten to fifteen metres. One author is lucky to be alive when, having lost concentration, came off on what he considered a safe slope, but only stopped rolling, by chance, a couple of metres from a precipice.

Therefore, it makes sense not to go alone and to have some first-aid skill within your party. Naturally, if you value solitude on your bike, ride more conservatively than you would in company, and always let someone know your route and estimated time of arrival.

You have been warned.

Mountain Biking Adventures:

INTRODUCTION

We came to mountain bikes from the mountains. With earlier outdoor adventures in the 70s inspired by walking Wainwright's English Coast-to-Coast we made up our own Scottish and Welsh coast-to-coast walks, setting out a stall for multi-day themed adventures.

Our Scottish coast-to-coast walk inevitably led to Munro bagging, so that through the 80s and 90s we came to know the Highlands well. More than a handful of Munros were accomplished in two or three day expeditions, bivouacking or using bothies.

Towards the end of the Munro bagging we began to use bikes to get to more remote mountains. When the Munros were done and also, to some extent, were our bodies, we looked to what we imagined might be less taxing adventures.

These began with three-day tours along well-known through routes with barely the need to put a foot down. Thereafter, we quickly settled on a four-day format and broadened our concept of 'through routes' to include passes previously restricted to those on foot. Some will say that they still should be, because, from time to time, this occasioned us to use our bikes as rather expensive zimmer frames for a kilometre or two. But it has readmitted us to wilderness and adventure.

Over the last two decades, mountain biking has developed enormously as a 'sport'. We are full of admiration for the technical and athletic capabilities of modern day mountain bikers and recognise that many excellent mountain biking guides have been written and custom-built trails set up.

In this guide, however, we try to reopen a sense of adventure and wilderness, providing routes with a continuity and 'arc' missing from modern guides, which focus on day and half day outings. It is important to check each route to see whether the remoteness and grade are for your level, and if in doubt, go for an easier one first.

From the Highlands we expanded our attention to the Yorkshire Dales and the Pennines and to the chalk trails of the south.

We've not managed to come up with an outing with the same scale and continuity in Wales. We regret this and, when challenged, often responded, 'Well you put something together then!' This invitation still stands.

USING THE BOOK

All routes are three or, mostly, four days. They are listed in the ROUTE LIST, in order from the north of Scotland down to the South Downs of England. The list shows the number of days, the total distance and percentage off-road, the total ascent, and the grade of the hardest day, the crux grade. The distances are to the nearest 0.5km, and ascent to the nearest metre. Both were obtained from Memory-Map™

GRADING

Here we have tried to give the best indication at a glance of what the route involves. The grade for each day is indicated with a letter and a number, for example, M2.

Multi-day routes in northern Britain

PHYSICAL DIFFICULTY

The letter, E (easy), M (moderate), or H (hard) indicates the Physical Difficulty of the route, the amount of work and, therefore, fitness required. The length, and total ascent, given for each day of each route, are obvious factors. This is, of course, significantly modified by the conditions on the ground indicated in the following table:

Physical difficulty	Conditions on the ground include one or more of			
	Rough stuff	**Path**	**Track**	**Tarmac**
E	none	some good, wholly rideable, singletrack	well-metalled forest track or estate roads	up to half
M	a few kilometres of pathless bushwhacking over grassy or heathery ground	a few km of indistinct singletrack requiring some pushing	mixture of rutted or stony and well-metalled tracks	less than half
H	up to 10km of bushwhacking through rough and rocky terrain	sustained indistinct singletrack requiring some pushing	deeply rutted and/or boggy tracks	less than one third

SERIOUSNESS

The number 1, 2 or 3 indicates the Seriousness of the route. This encompasses risks due to: remoteness, river crossings, runouts, weather and navigation as indicated in the following qualitative table.

	Risk factors include one or more of				
Seriousness	**Remoteness**	**River crossing**	**Runouts**	**Weather**	**Navigation**
1	never more than one hour's ride on a good surface to main road, village or telephone	only easily rideable fords of smaller side streams	no runouts	low-lying routes where bad weather is merely inconvenient	straightforward, way-marked or unambiguous paths and tracks
2	high pass(es) more than one hour's ride to main road, village or telephone	crossings of significant rivers involving some wading	some steep runouts from good non-technical singletrack	high mountain passes, but with some shelter from wind and rain	good map reading and navigation skills required
3	parts of the route are up to half a day of challenging mountain country from main road, village or telephone	river crossings that could entail a significant detour or retreat if in spate	steep and or rocky runouts from narrow and/or technical singletrack	routes which spend some time in high altitude unsheltered country where low temperature, high wind and/or rain could risk exposure/ hypothermia	excellent navigation skills requiring use of map and compass in poor visibility are critical to safety.

Mountain Biking Adventures:

Of course what is physically hard for one person is not for another. The differentiation between the first (1) and second (2) Seriousness element of the grade may also be debated with considerable amusement. We feel, however, that there is little argument about the top Seriousness grade (3).

The 'Crux' grade – the grade of the hardest day – is given in the introduction to each route.

Note that an easy, less serious day can be transformed into a hard, and very serious one by foul weather, often occurring in Scotland and the north of England. For this reason we have not given any times. If unsure about what you're getting into, we reiterate our suggestion that you start with an easy one and gauge for yourselves subsequently.

TEXT ABBREVIATIONS

Left and rights are written L and R, compass directions N, S, E, W etc, kilometres km, metres m, and the national routes, walking and cycling, are also abbreviated after the first mention, ie Pennine Way is PW.

MAPS

The maps in the book are of the largest useful scale: mostly 1:250,000 for tarmac sections and 1:50,000 for off-road. They are at a high level of 'zoom out' to conserve space and, therefore, are to be used with the route descriptions. Map references are National Grid, the system for which is explained at the edge of each OS map. Most GPS devices and apps can be set to operate in this mode.

LEGEND

The following symbols are used in the maps:

Symbol	Description
▬	Route
○→	Direction of travel (indicated where the route enters a map)
▷	Start
🛏	Overnight
◎	End

PLANNING AN EXPEDITION

For some this is a tiresome, but necessary, part of the process. Others, like us, find it a joy and an integral part of the pleasure of a trip. We hope that as well as enjoying the rides presented, you will be inspired to create your own and/or join up parts of these routes in your own way.

There are four key steps to this. They all need to be done well in advance. They are presented sequentially, but you may have to go through the loop a couple or three times to get everything to work together.

Multi-day routes in northern Britain

Firstly, decide when to do your ride.

Any time from May to September has its pleasures. Because of their length, remoteness and exposure we don't recommend any of these routes in winter or in early spring, where heavy precipitation and meltwater can make even small burns hard to cross. Theoretically, the best time is midsummer, when days are long, important for some of the harder routes, and when deer stalking issues can be completely avoided. The downside in Scotland, and less so in northern England, is the midge, or rather millions of them. They pose no problem when riding, but are very tiresome when pushing, carrying or stationary. Because of statistically lower rainfall, lack of midges, good availability of accommodation and reasonable day length, late September has been our favoured time.

Next, determine whether everyone in your group is physically capable of doing each planned day. This involves careful scrutiny of the exact route, the length and height gained, and the grade given. Look at the route and see if there are any points to take a road, either to shorten or make easier, or escape to shelter. It's good to have ridden with members of the party before such a trip. This applies particularly to the remote Scottish routes. We cannot stress too much that some of these routes are really wild and arduous.

If that step is passed, check and book the accommodation. This is particularly important in remote areas where there is little choice and a crucial establishment may become unavailable seasonally or for refurbishment or change of ownership. Ask about payment method. You may need to take cheques or cash. It's worth checking availability of secure accommodation for your bikes. Ask about the possibility of an early breakfast, especially early or late in the season where a good getaway is crucial on a big day. Ensure they serve dinner, or that there is a restaurant nearby, and warn them if you're likely to be late in from a big day.

Lastly, check availability of, and book transportation to the start and finish of your route. There are several specific bike carrying companies in Scotland, like Bike Bus and Tim Dearman Coaches. Increasingly, taxi companies have a bike transportation trailer or van, or will help you find one. Cycle spaces on trains, especially in the Highlands, are limited and precious. Book them early. Booking typically opens 100 days in advance. Don't panic if you can't get a reservation. Most train operators in the Highlands are quite flexible in practice. If you're really worried, take a big, sturdy binbag and a bit of gaffer tape so you can dismantle and pack your bike and take it on as luggage. Cycle policies on trains from the south (and Europe) also vary a great deal. Check early and book early for great deals. The sleeper services from London have a lot of bike space and are very attractive: disembarking in the Cairngorms at 7am, taking breakfast at a local hostelry and being on your road by 8:30 is such a joy compared to half a day – or more – of gruelling motorway journey. The 'early bird' deals cost barely more than a night's accommodation.

Finding appropriate boat operators can be more problematic and demands a more creative approach. Tourist Information and the web are useful. Hotel keepers often have contacts. A particularly profitable approach in remote areas is to speak to the Post Office or village store. The local Postmistress or Postmaster will know everyone and be happy to point you in the right direction to bring work to the community.

Mountain Biking Adventures:

EQUIPMENT

The routes in this book pass through very remote country, often 10km from tarmac, 20km from the main road and a 100km or more from a bike shop. It's important, therefore, to minimise the risk of breakdown and have the skill and wherewithal to do critical repairs. Remember that repairs that are simple and easy in the warmth of your bike shed can be very tiresome in the wet and cold, mud and grit of a remote singletrack.

BIKE AND SPARES

The key to avoiding issues is to set out with a good quality well-maintained mountain bike with recent proven good function.

Many of the routes have been done on bikes without any suspension, though that is rare recently. The choice between hardtail and full-suss is entirely personal. More 'senior' members of these tours have tended to favour hardtails on account of their lightness, simplicity and ease of handling where they need to be carried or lifted over obstructions. Full-suss bikes definitely perform better on technical downhill and the young and fit seem to value this more.

Tyres should be in good condition. Check the walls as well as the tread. A larger party might consider taking a spare tyre. Take at least one spare inner tube per bike and ensure that you have at least two for each wheel size in the party. Tubeless technology does reduce the risk of pinch punctures and enables lower running pressures, and, therefore, better traction on technical sections. Fixing them in remote, dirty, wet and cold terrain needs thinking about. The simplest thing is to take a spare tube, which can be used if the trail conditions are poor. Tubeless function can then be restored in the evening. The authors tend to use grippy cross-country treads run at pressures that prioritise traction and security on the rougher and more remote sections and consequently accepting slightly higher than necessary rolling resistance on the tarmac. Each member should carry a repair kit and pump as it is easy to get separated from the pack when you have a flat. A pump with integral pressure gauge would enable pressure to be adjusted according to conditions.

Brake pads and blocks can wear alarmingly quickly in wet and gritty terrain. Start the trip with a new set (you can always re-use the part worn pads on short routes nearer home) and have a full spare set with you.

It's easy to snag a spoke on rocky singletrack. You can store them easily down the seat tube. Have a couple of each length. Check the lengths, they are often different front and rear and on the drive side.

Modern aluminium and carbon frames often have a 'sacrificial' rear derailleurs hanger. This is a small length of aluminium which fixes to the dropout and to which the derailleur is attached. It's a good idea to each take a spare one of these. They are really easy to bend on rocky singletrack and it's a lot quicker and far less risky to swap one over than to try to straighten it with a rock! You can almost always borrow tools at your accommodation to straighten it at your 'leisure'.

Take a few links of chain, ideally taken from the chain when fitted. One author always fits a new chain for these trips. Take some oil and lube the chain and jockey wheels each night.

Lastly, to effect these repairs, make sure you carry a multitool which covers the range of Allen keys and Torxs tools on your bike, and a chain tool, and have practised using them.

A pair of small pointed pliers, a penknife and an assortment of zip ties amongst the party can often permit invaluable improvisation.

Multi-day routes in northern Britain

NAVIGATION AND MOUNTAIN CRAFT

Some of the days in this guide are long and hard and remote. As emphasised above, ordinary mechanicals can take up time. It's important not to lose more time with a navigation error. Sometimes weather, river and mountain conditions will require you to make an adjustment to your route.

Make sure that within your party you have 1:50,000 maps covering the route (and any diversion you may be forced to take) and a compass, and the knowhow and experience to use them. You can lighten maps by taking off the cover or you can print out sections of map from mapping systems like OS Maps and the commercial Memory-Map™. Whatever map you use needs to be weather proof. You can get pre-laminated maps or you can store map sections in a waterproof map holder. One author laminates Memory-Map™ printouts.

A GPS unit that can upload preprogrammed routes is very useful. It permits much of the difficult navigation to be done in one's armchair. We urge you, however, not to rely on them: they can fail, they are easily lost from cycle mounts and require assiduous attention to battery life.

It is wise to carry lights, in case, for whatever reason, you find yourself finishing your ride after dark. Even if you are confident, a light and a whistle are useful for signalling should rescue be sought. Mobile coverage is very patchy.

LUGGAGE

A rucksack. Our experience is that panniers and other substantial bike mounted luggage make pushing in rough terrain, lifting over fences and stiles difficult, and river crossing awful. Seat post mounted bar systems (other than small saddlebags) can damage or break the seat post when used in rough terrain. A small saddle mounted bag for your spare tube, tools and repair kit and a small crossbar mounted pouch for snacks, are useful to avoid opening your sack in bad weather.

Within the rucksack waterproof bags and containers are needed to keep evening wear and sundries dry.

CLOTHING

Gear that will keep you warm in foul weather. You will be in remote, high places much of the time. After considerable trial, and error, we recommend a cycling shirt, a decent soft shell, and a light waterproof with hood, and down below bike shorts and a pair of light 'Ron Hills' or long lycra tights. Some recommend waterproof overtrousers for waiting off the bike. We have never used them and much of the advice above is focused on not having occasion to. Waterproof or thick woollen socks worn inside stout mountain biking boots with recessed cleats to facilitate pushing on steep and/or pathless sections.

Gloves are recommended for comfort, warmth and protection.

Helmet and a light inner cap for ear/scalp warmth.

Consider a small first-aid kit. If, like us, you are of a 'certain age' take painkillers and anti-inflammatories.

For the evenings, the absolute minimum: lightweight, midge-proof clothing and 'Crocs' or flip-flops.

Mountain Biking Adventures:

SUNDRIES

Again, the absolute minimum. A toothbrush, a pack of tissues or some toilet paper, sanitary ware, a small antibacterial rub or a few sterile wipes. Small amounts of Vaseline and/or DoubleBase Gel for sore crotches. Essential medicines, including inhalers.

FOOD AND DRINK

Many of the routes require that you take enough food for the day. Don't rely on village shops or cafes without telephoning to confirm opening times, days and seasons (web information can be unreliable).

A few high-energy bars/gels can be a comfort.

Take plenty of water. In most of these areas it's safe to take water from medium-sized side streams. Take some sterilising tabs if you're not confident.

MONEY

Whilst most places take debit/credit cards, check with your hosts and take plenty of cash as there may be no cashpoint on the entire trip.

ACCESS

In England bridleways and byways are fine to ride on, and our routes do not stray from them. Cycling on routes designated as footpaths is not (yet) permitted.

Our Scottish routes are mostly following those in 'Scottish Hill Tracks', a publication of the Scottish Rights of Way and Access Society, (SRWAS): in total 91% of all the Scottish cycling is on roads, National Cycle Routes or numbered Scottish Hill Tracks.

In Scotland access has always been more relaxed. In over forty years of mountain activity on foot and bicycle we have found the vast majority of landowners and their staff to be cooperative, helpful and even welcoming. However, it is worth knowing your rights and responsibilities before you sally forth.

Access in Scotland was formalised by the Land Reform Act of 2003. The Act confirms a right of access to most land and inland water, 'if exercised responsibly,' respecting the owner's privacy, safety, livelihoods and the environment. Prior to 2003 we had some 'interesting conversations' on expeditions during the stalking season. On one occasion we did turn back when the manager, with whom we had a previous oral agreement to use a track, alleged that the landowner had threatened him with dismissal were he to let us through. By contrast, on another well known through route, a Factor very politely asked us if we would mind waiting for half an hour whilst grouse beaters worked the area directly ahead. We took an early lunch, and in twenty minutes went on refreshed.

The Act is interpreted in 'The Scottish Outdoor Access Code', available to read on the internet. The general message with regard to riding is to dismount if meeting horses or walkers on narrow tracks, not to churn up soft ground, and to heed any signs in forests about alternative routes if felling is in progress. Thus far this is obvious common sense.

The real problem for riding is with deer stalking/shooting. This takes place for stags from 1st July, (although practically 1st August) to 20th October. The Code avoids the actual word 'stalking' until page 69. It suggests you avoid areas where stalking is taking place, and use the

Multi-day routes in northern Britain

Hillphone Service (outdooraccess-scotland.com), which should at least tell you how to contact the manager. There are, however, some areas on which there are no details! A further problem is illustrated by one manager near Kinlochewe, who, when asked about stalking on a particular day, stated, 'there is stalking every day so keep out'. This is not 'reasonable' and was, we feel, reasonably ignored.

The guidance requires landowners not to lock gates on paths or tracks unless there is reasonable cause, and, if it is necessary to lock a gate, to provide an alternative. Most provide a pedestrian gate or stile. Look carefully, because the alternative may be a few metres away. If none can be found it is reasonable to climb over or round the gate.

Annex 1 of the Code states that it is a criminal offence to intend to intimidate and deter in order to obstruct the activity (cycling in this case).

It is up to you how to interpret the Code and the above. Since 2003 we have not been materially impeded on rides during the stalking or shooting season. We have been challenged and there have been a very few free and frank exchanges of view. However, where we have been polite and firm in communicating our understanding of the Act and the Code we have always been able to go on. We have, on occasion waited a few moments whilst a specific activity is completed or taken a short diversion around the curtilage of a dwelling.

CODE OF CONDUCT

This follows on from the above.

Respect all other track/path users. Give way to pedestrians and horses. Try not to spook the latter (or the former). Dismount where necessary. Give clear, early, warning of your approach to all users (including other cyclists) with your bell or a hearty 'good morning/good afternoon'.

Take away all litter. Leave gates in the state you found them. Avoid churning up soft ground. Bury any faeces.

Be polite to all you meet, even, or perhaps especially, difficult managers or landowners.

Mountain Biking Adventures:

LIST OF ROUTES

Working north to south.

		Days	Start
1	Moine Thrust. Overscaig to Helmsdale	4	Overscaig
2	Sutherland and Ross and Cromarty Circular	4	Helmsdale
3	Aultguish Circular, Easter and Wester Ross	3	Aultguish Inn
4	Contin Circular via Torridon and Fisherfield	4	Contin
5	Applecross, Monar and Torridon Circular	4	Craig, Achnashellach Forest
6	Affric Circular via Kintail and Torridon	4	Tomich, Strathglass
7	Scottish Coast to Coast 1: Glenelg to Dundee	4	Glenelg
8	Knoydart and Lochaber	4	Cluanie Inn
9	Monadhliath Circular from Spean Bridge	3-4	Spean Bridge
10	Scottish Coast to Coast 2: Ardnamurchan to Montrose	4	Acharacle
11	Cairngorm Circuit from Kingussie, via Braemar and Tomintoul	3	Kingussie
12	Cairngorm circuit from Braemar via Aviemore and Blair Atholl	3	Braemar
13	Cairngorm and Monadhliath circular from Blair Atholl	4	Blair Atholl
14	Cairngorm circular from Ballater via Tomintoul, Kincraig and Blair Atholl	4	Ballater
15	Dalwhinnie to Dunkeld	4	Tulloch, Glen Spean
16	Perth to Fort William	4	Perth
17	English Coast to Coast: Whitehaven to Sunderland	4	Whitehaven
18	Dales Circular from Settle	4	Settle
19	High Cup/Teesdale Circular	4	Lancaster

Bonus Route

20	South Downs and Ridgeway	4	Eastbourne

Multi-day routes in northern Britain

Finish	Distance (km)	Off road (%)	Ascent (m)	Crux day grade
Helmsdale	261	62	4832	H3
Ardgay	280	48	5127	H3
S+F	210.5	52	4101	M2
S+F	250	47.5	5822	H3
S+F	246	45	5973	H3
S+F	229.5	56	5195	H1
Dundee	341.5	49	7264	H2
Taynuilt	203.5	63.5	5645	H3
S+F	239	38.5	4688	H2
Montrose	297.5	53	5322	H3
S+F	155	74	3003	E3
S+F	204.5	60	3881	H2
Kinloch Rannoch/Rannoch Moor Station	249	62	5016	H3
S+F	238	62	5448	H3
Dunkeld	235.5	70	3882	M3
Fort William	259.5	61	5259	H3
Sunderland	224	67	5554	H3
S+F (or Finish Lancaster last day)	183.5	62	4887	M1
S+F	231	37	4850	M1
Goring/Princes Risborough	398	68	6816	H1

1. MOINE THRUST. OVERSCAIG TO HELMSDALE

Total route (days):	Four days			
Start:	Overscaig Hotel, Loch Shin			
Finish:	Helmsdale			
Total Distance:	261km (162.5miles)			
Total Off-road (%):	62%			
Daily distance (km):	64	65	60	72
Daily off-road (%):	54%	50.5%	52%	75%
Ascent:	4832m (15,859ft)			
Crux day grade:	H3			

Multi-day routes in northern Britain

OVERVIEW

The first day of this route runs more or less along the line of the Moine Thrust. Here the sudden shift in topography and geology along the line where continents once collided was central to the understanding of plate tectonics in late 19th century. We can be curious about this too, or simply enjoy the stupendous 'Torridonian' mountain landscape. Subsequent days enjoy the spectacular scenery of the North Coast (and its beaches if you are very keen) and the interesting Flow Country, a once barren peat desert almost ruined last century by greedy planting and draining. The last day is almost 'downhill all the way', past eerie Gothic lodges, to the North Sea.

Access is by train and taxi. Finding accommodation other than at Durness is difficult. At the end of the second day the Bourgie Hotel is the only accommodation for miles. The author used The Forsinard Hotel at the end of the third day. This hotel is not open at the time of writing, but fortunately there are convenient trains from Forsinard Station to Halkirk or Wick where accommodation is relatively plentiful.

DAY 1.

Start:	Overscaig Hotel, Loch Shin
Finish:	Smoo
Distance:	64km (39.5miles)
Off-road:	*34.5km (21.5miles) 54%*
Ascent:	1225m (4021ft)
Descent:	1294m (4246ft)
Grade:	H3

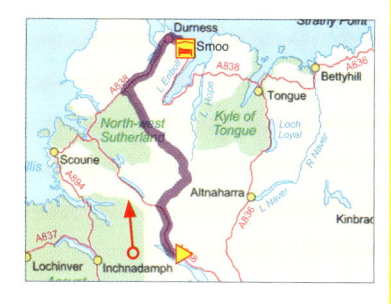

OVERVIEW

The route is described from the Overscaig. If you begin from the station at Lairg, you must add 24km of tarmac and a little ascent. If you elect to take a taxi from Lairg you could take it all the way to West Merkland and take 11km off the route. On a light summer evening the ride from Lairg to accommodation at Overscaig is a delight. Good tracks and paths take you into the heart of the Foinaven/Arkle massif. An easy 1.5km of bushwhacking is needed to join up the tracks.

ROUTE 1. MOINE THRUST, OVERSCAIG TO HELMSDALE

13

Mountain Biking Adventures:

ROUTE

Take the A838 N for 11km past Loch A' Ghriama and most of Loch Merkland. Immediately before a bridge over the Allt Albannach turn R and follow the well-made track north-easterly through the Beallach nam Meirleach and past a series of lovely small lochs. The way swings northerly and begins to steepen towards Gobernuisgach Lodge.

Take in the views and then the second good track to the L, about 200m before the Lodge. Cross the Allt a'Choire Ghrainde and then in about 300m the Abhainn Srath Choire an Easaidh, both on good bridges. In about a further 100m join the track (shown as a path on OS maps) coming up from the Lodge and follow it NW into and along Glenn Golly. This is a delight, but it gets better as the good path steepens along the E ridge of Meall Horn. Some will ride this. Most will push in places. But soon, avoiding a less strong path to the L, you pass Lochan Sgeireach and a number of smaller lochans to reach the summit of the day on Creag Staonsaid.

If the day is clear you will not need to be cautioned to stop and gawp here. Foinne Bhein (Foinaven) lies before you in shattered quartzite splendour. To its L, Arkle can just be seen round the corner of Meall Horne. These mountains, like those of Canisp and Inverpolly Forests, Torridon and Applecross are made of younger quartzite and sandstone and share their dramatic shape. As you will see at Smoo there is also, unusually in Scotland, limestone. To the E, these younger rocks were driven, somewhat counterintuitively, under the old basement rocks along the

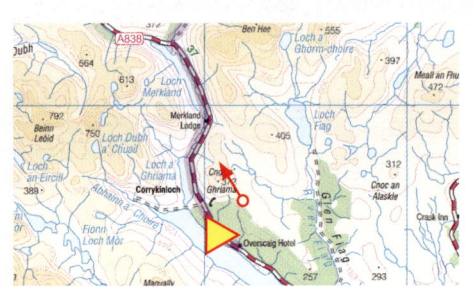

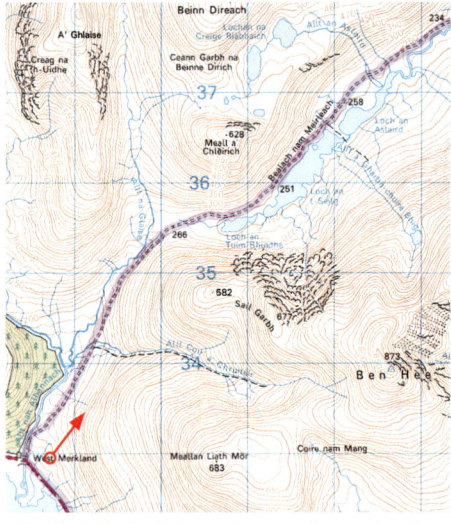

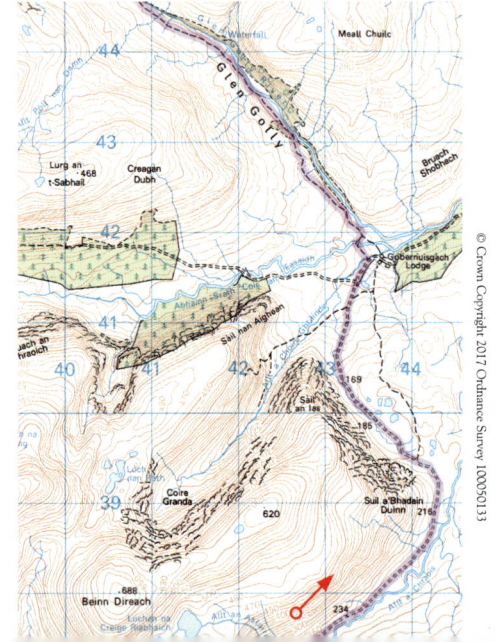

ROUTE 1. MOINE THRUST, OVERSCAIG TO HELMSDALE

14

Multi-day routes in northern Britain

aforementioned Moine Thrust. This landscape is dominated by the rolling Flow Country, a peat desert characterised by older Lewisian gneiss, from which emerge residual mountains like Ben Hope and the granite intrusion of Ben Loyal to the NE.

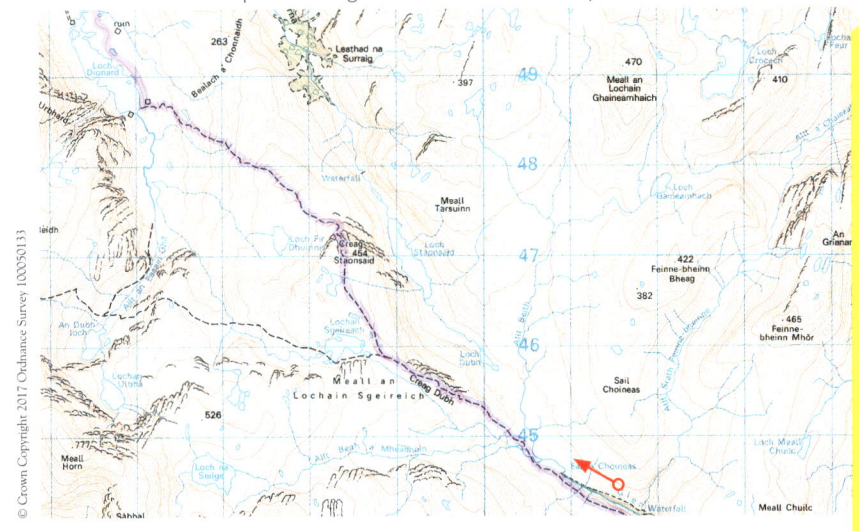

Having drunk your visual fill, descend, technically, on a good but rocky track to a fishing shack at the head of Loch Dionard. From here you must bushwhack around the loch to pick up the good track along Strath Dionard. This author took the W bank but it was rough and rocky and involved a lot of lifting of the bike. It may well be worth risking the bog on the more open country on the E side and a potentially trickier river crossing.

Strath Dionard.
Adapted from original photo © Alan Reid (cc-by-sa/2.0)

ROUTE 1. MOINE THRUST, OVERSCAIG TO HELMSDALE

15

Mountain Biking Adventures:

Take the track 10km NW to the main road, pausing from time to time to fully take in the magnificent corries and buttresses of Foinaven. Turn R and tootle down to the Kyle of Durness and the village itself. Continue on the A838, cutting off the corner on a minor road at the delightful Sango Sands beach. Wonder at the greenness of this little outcrop of limestone country and in less than a km you will be at Smoo Cave. Its magnificent zawn is worth a look. There is accommodation back in the village or at the eponymous Smoo Cave Hotel a little further on.

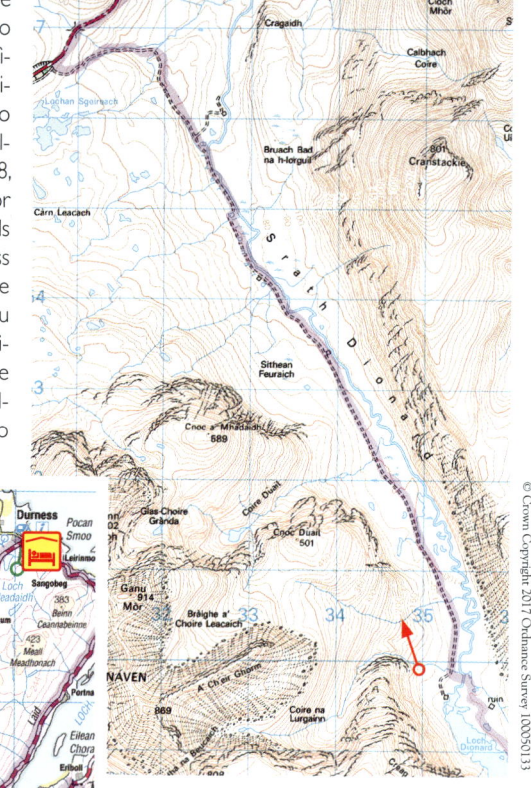

DAY 2.

Start:	Smoo
Finish:	Borgie
Distance:	65km (40.5miles)
Off-road:	33km (20.5miles) 50.5%
Ascent:	1254m (4115ft)
Descent:	1245m (4088ft)
Grade:	M1

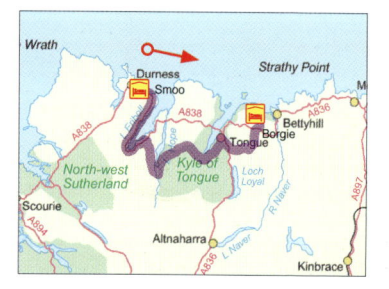

OVERVIEW

There is, necessarily, a lot of tarmac in this day but the coastal scenery is wonderful and the off-road sections are, each in their own way, 'interesting'. The ancient Moine Path, though recorded on maps dating from the 19th century, is, surprisingly, not included in the Scottish

Multi-day routes in northern Britain

Rights-of-Way Society's 'Scottish Hill Tracks'. It is, however, a great walk and much of it can be ridden. A few km of easy bushwhacking are needed to join things up later in the day or if the Cashel Dhu ford needs to be avoided.

ROUTE

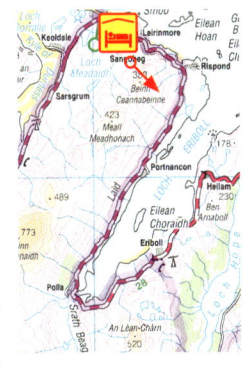

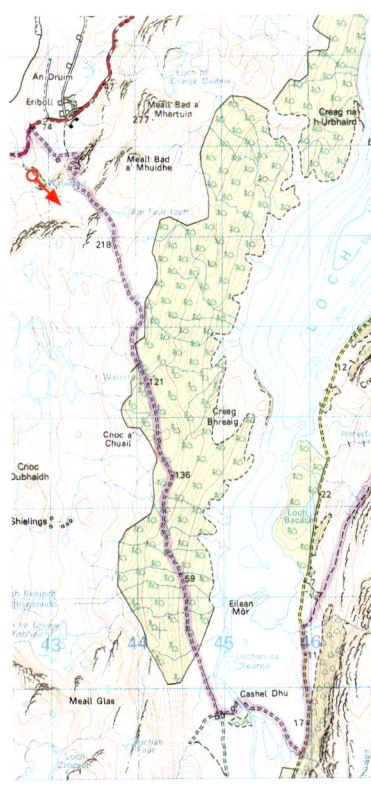

Leave Smoo/Durness on the A838 and follow it round the bottom of Loch Eriboll. About 3km up the E side, just before the hamlet of Eriboll, as the road suddenly steepens, a good track goes off R, SE. Take it, past the farmstead, where the surface improves, surprisingly, to tarmac and climbs steeply on zigzags. The track remains well metalled to the summit at about 220m. There are glorious views to the NW over Loch Eriboll, and to the W back towards Foinaven and Arkle. To the S and E both Loch Hope and Ben Hope can be seen. The descent is a delight. At the foot the track curves briefly E and then N round a building to the ford at Cashel Dhu. This is wide, but usually shallow. (If there is a lot of water, there is a bridge 4km to the S at Alltnacaillich, so return to the foot of the descent and follow the continuation of the track S for 1km and then make your way, as best you can for another 3km along the grassy bank of the river. Return N on the minor road.)

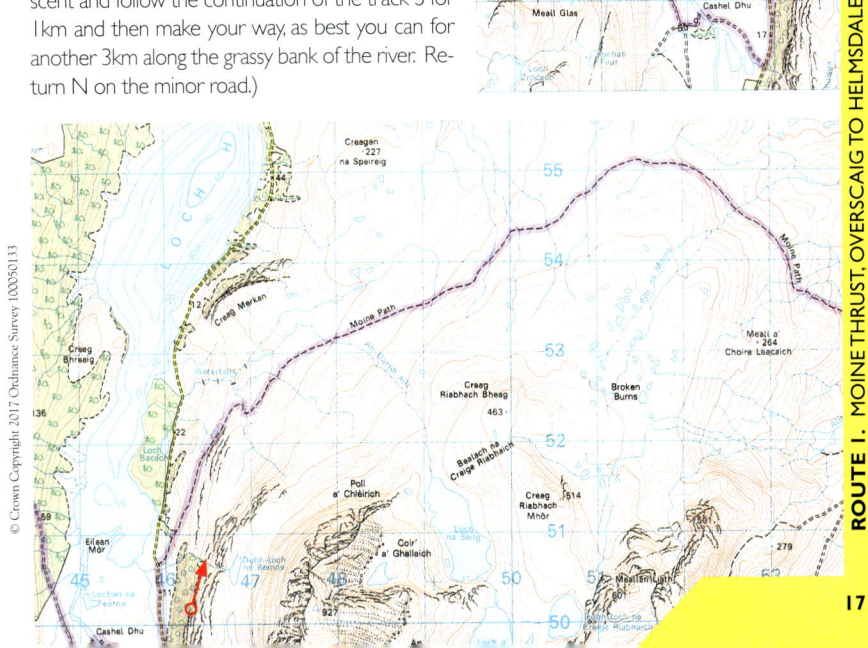

ROUTE 1. MOINE THRUST, OVERSCAIG TO HELMSDALE

17

Mountain Biking Adventures:

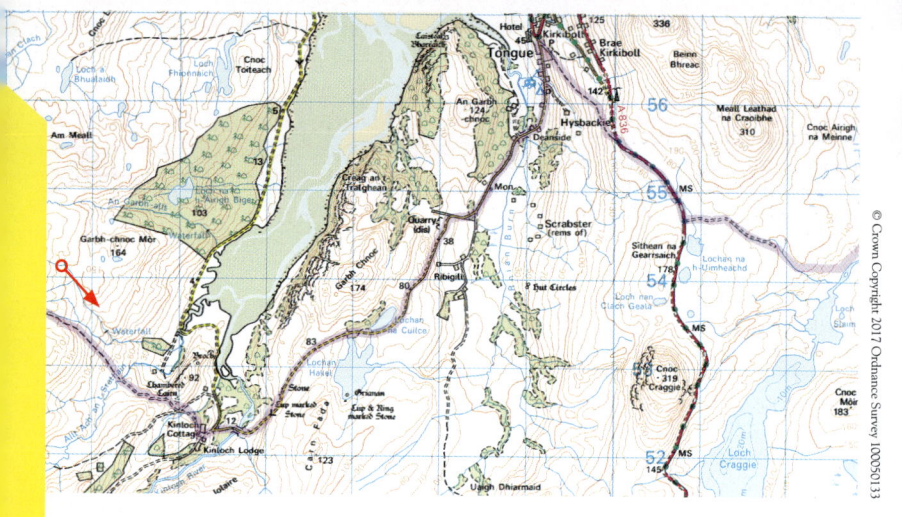

Once across the Cashel Dhu the track joins a minor road in about 800m. About 1300m N of here, some 20m after crossing the very small Allt Dubh Loch na Beinne, an indistinct grassy path rises to the R. This is the Moine Path. Follow it, as it climbs gently NE to a summit of about 280m after 6km. It's very grassy and not easy-going, but it does reward with fine views of this marvellously desolate countryside and with the eerie way that first Ben Hope and then Ben Loyal seem to rear up out of nowhere. The descent is better, but only because it is downhill. Soon after a final grassy stretch you are on a better track, a few m before an obvious junction. Take the R hand track and, in about 300m, just before Kinloch Lodge turn L and then go out past Kinloch Cottage to join the minor road at a sharp bend.

ROUTE 1. MOINE THRUST, OVERSCAIG TO HELMSDALE

Moine path, with Creag Riabhach Bheag.
Adapted from original Photo © Colin Bennett (cc-by-sa/2.0)

© Crown Copyright 2017 Ordnance Survey 100050133

18

Multi-day routes in northern Britain

Turn R and follow this minor road for about 7km to Tongue. On entering the village take the first R, Loyal Terrace, which turns back sharply just before the junction with the A838. Tarmac gives way to a rough, grassy, slightly overgrown track shown as path on the OS 1:50,000. Follow it till it emerges on the A836. Turn R and follow this road SE for 1km until you come to a track to the L with the attractive sign 'Tongue Landfill Site'. Follow it for about a km until it peters out and then keep going without track or path on an ESE bearing until you find yourself on the banks of the River Borgie. Pick up sheep and deer tracks as best you can and follow the riverbank for 2km until you come to an old sheiling where the winding Allt Ach' a BhaidSaraich joins the river. From here a patchy path, not shown on the map, takes you eastwards another 1.5km to join a good track by weirs opposite the abandoned farmstead at Dalness. The good forest track curves N and then just under 5km brings you to the main road again at Borgie Bridge. Turn R and in 200m turn L on the minor road to Borgie and its eponymous hotel.

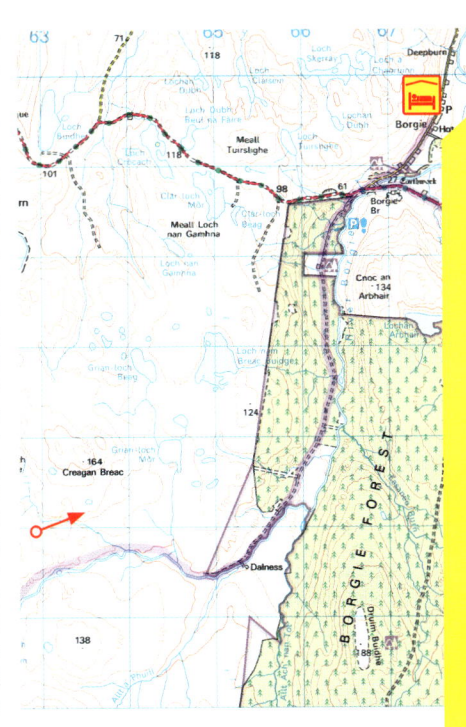

DAY 3.

Start:	Borgie
Finish:	Forsinard Station
Distance:	60km (37.5miles)
Off-road:	31.5km (19.5miles) 52%
Ascent:	1146m (3763ft)
Descent:	1024m (3360ft)
Grade:	M1

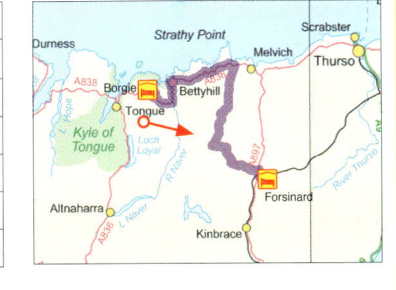

OVERVIEW

Again, there is a lot of tarmac, along an ostensibly main road, to start with. However, the views to your L of craggy coves and sandy bays are a delight and there is no shortage of exercise as the road dips in and out of them. About halfway along there is a superb outlook point over the bleakly mysterious flow country between Strathnaver and Strathalladale, through which you will pass in the second half of the day. There is also, again, a few km of easy bushwhacking.

ROUTE 1. MOINE THRUST, OVERSCAIG TO HELMSDALE

19

Mountain Biking Adventures:

ROUTE

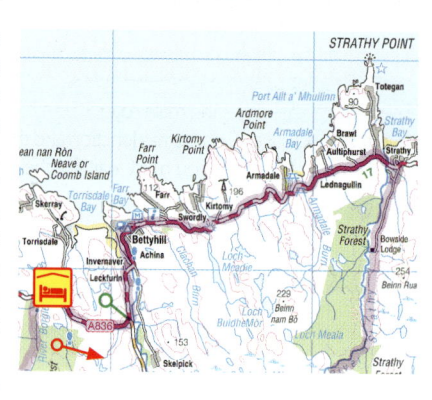

Regain the A836 and follow it for 27km to Strathy. If you haven't taken a packed lunch, stop for supplies at the Store in Betty Hill or take refreshment at the eponymous Inn at Strathy. About 500m after the bridge take the first R and follow it SSW, firstly on tarmac and then on a well-metalled track for about 20km. It starts through open country, and then passes, for the last few km, through forest. At its most southerly point the track comes out into a clearing a few hundred m across and doubles back on itself to the building at Lochstrathy. Leave the track and continue in the same general direction for 200m along the banks of the infant Strathy until you find the gate through the forest fence.

Out in the open, since there is a 2.5m high fence around the whole of the next forest complex including Loch Dhu, which fence is not shown on the 1:50,000 map but is on the 1:25,000, you are best to aim for the N end of Loch Nam Breac. To do this take a bearing 105° true for about 3km. The bushwhacking is not as tricky as the map suggests. At the loch go due S between the loch and the forest fence. Stay with the fence as it turns SW and soon crosses The Cutting (called Allt Loch Crocaich further upstream), then the allegedly Dry Burn just over a km further.

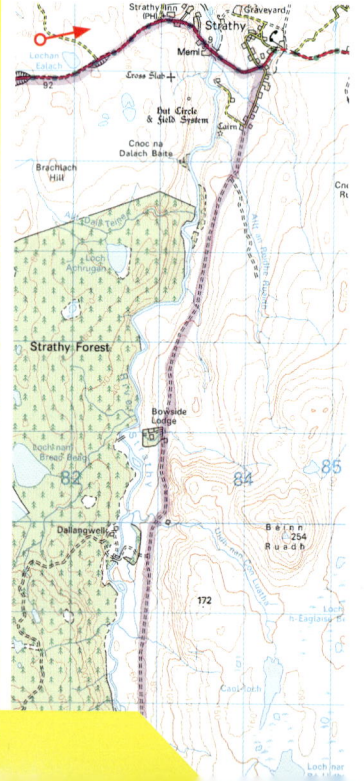

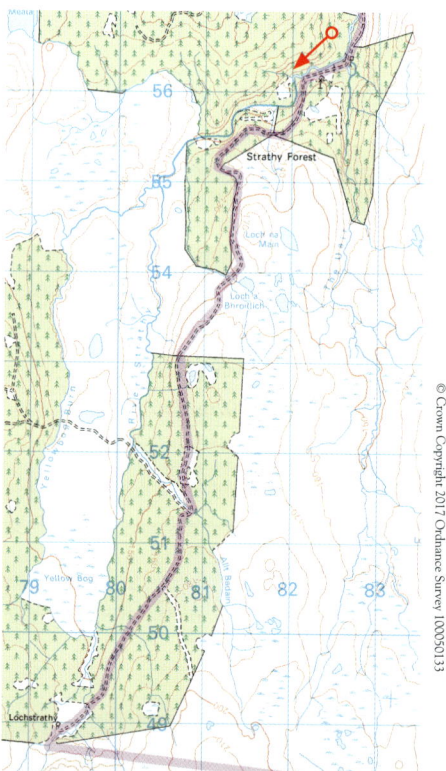

ROUTE 1. MOINE THRUST, OVERSCAIG TO HELMSDALE

© Crown Copyright 2017 Ordnance Survey 100050133

20

Multi-day routes in northern Britain

At the next corner, NC822472, as the fence turns SW you go SSW to meet a good forest track in the shortest distance, about 500m at a disused quarry. Follow this track more or less easterly through the next patch of forest. At the edge of the forest, what the locals call the Pony Track becomes much more patchy and grassy, but continues for a further 3.5km to Forsinard Lodge. Take the main road S 1km to the station. If you have timed your day right you can get the 17:12 to Georgemas Junction and then in 2-3km you can be in your accommodation in Halkirk. If you didn't, you must wait for the 21:42 and may have to sing for your supper.

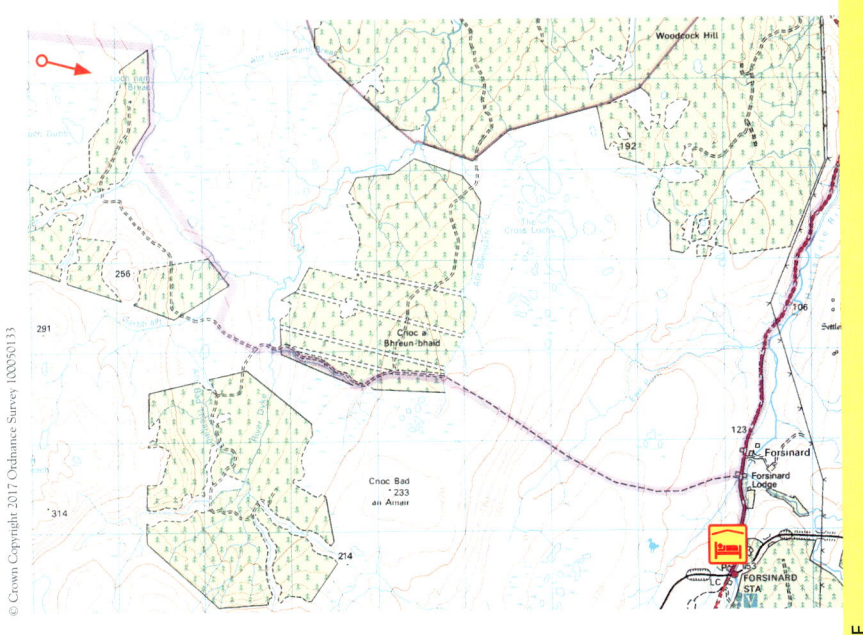

DAY 4.

Start:	Forsinard Station
Finish:	Helmsdale
Distance:	72km (45miles)
Off-road:	54km (33.5miles) 75%
Ascent:	1207m (3961ft)
Descent:	1343m (4409ft)
Grade:	M1

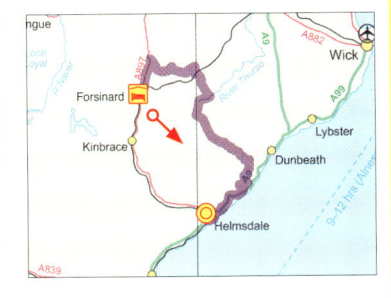

OVERVIEW

Apart from a few tarmac km at the beginning and the end, this route consists entirely of good forest and estate tracks. It was a slight fib at the start to say it's downhill all the way, but it feels like it, and there's no need to put a foot down.

ROUTE 1. MOINE THRUST, OVERSCAIG TO HELMSDALE

21

Mountain Biking Adventures:

ROUTE

Tootle back to the station, and get the 07:03 or the 08:47, according to taste, back from Georgemas Junction to Forsinard. Be sure to have ordered a packed lunch (and if the early train, a packed breakfast as well) as there is no refreshment en route.

From Forsinard Station take the A897 N for 6km. Opposite the car park on the L take the track which immediately crosses the Halladale River. Once across the river turn R and, in 200m, R again to cross Forsinain Burn. In a further 800m enter a forest on a good track in a broad firebreak. Ignore the first R but bear R on the next, stronger track in a clearing about 1km in. Follow this track S and then ESE until you leave this section of forest and contour around the southern end of Sletill Hill. Continue easterly, bearing R where you can, except by the small mound of Cnoc Maol Donn, NC979455, where you take the stronger track NE.

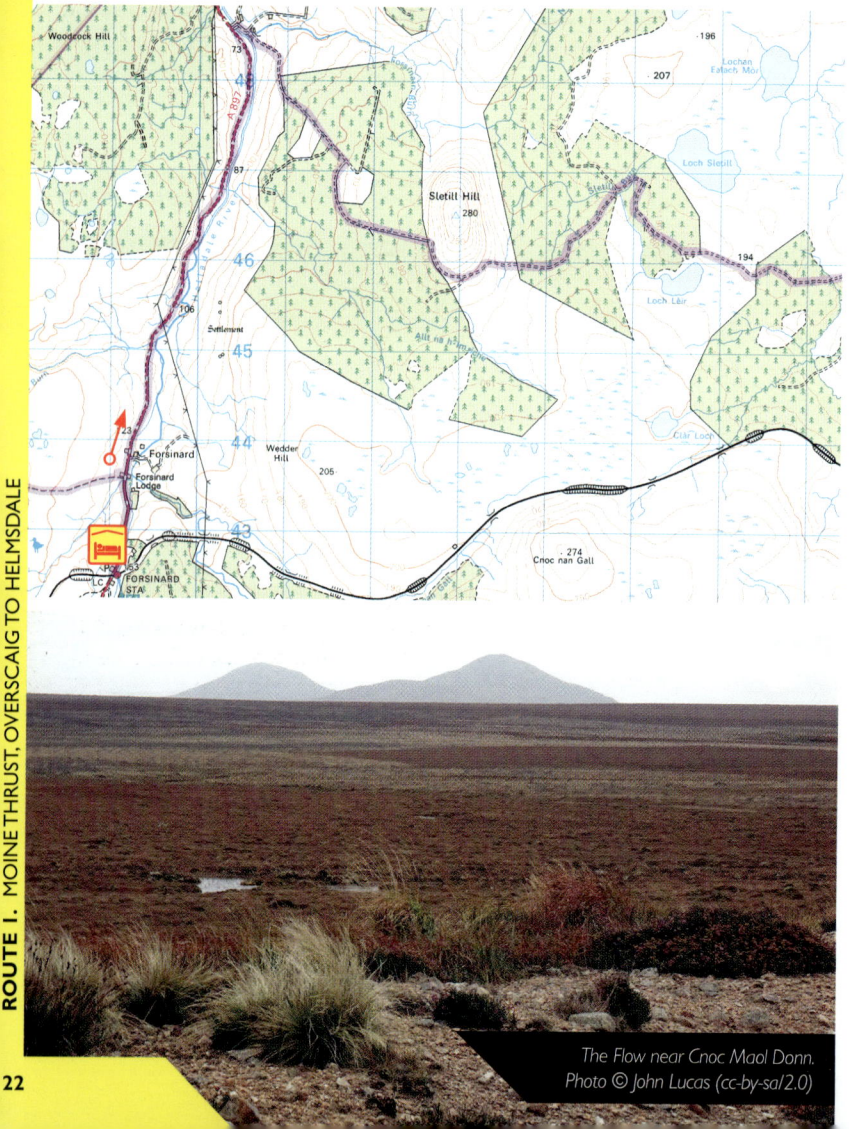

The Flow near Cnoc Maol Donn.
Photo © John Lucas (cc-by-sa/2.0)

ROUTE 1. MOINE THRUST, OVERSCAIG TO HELMSDALE

22

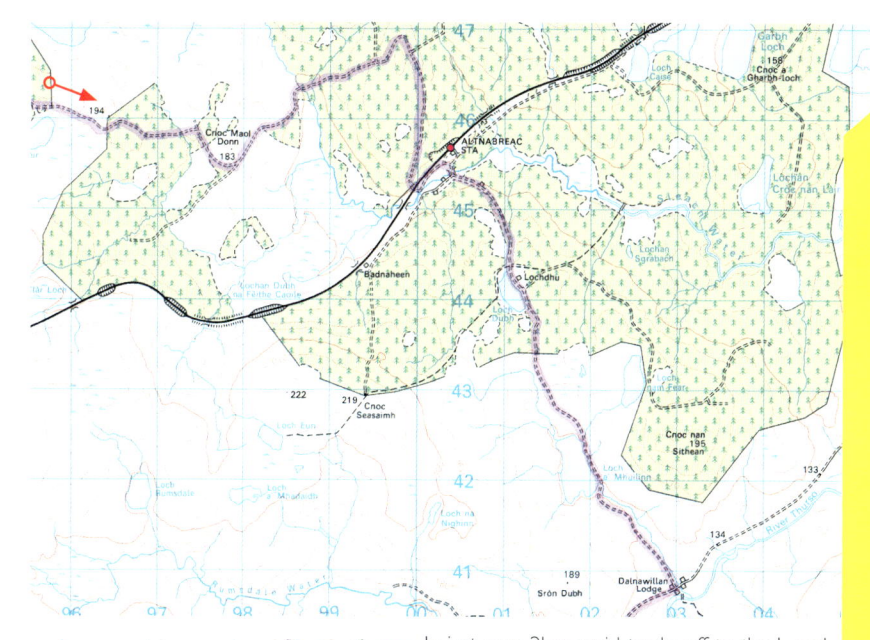

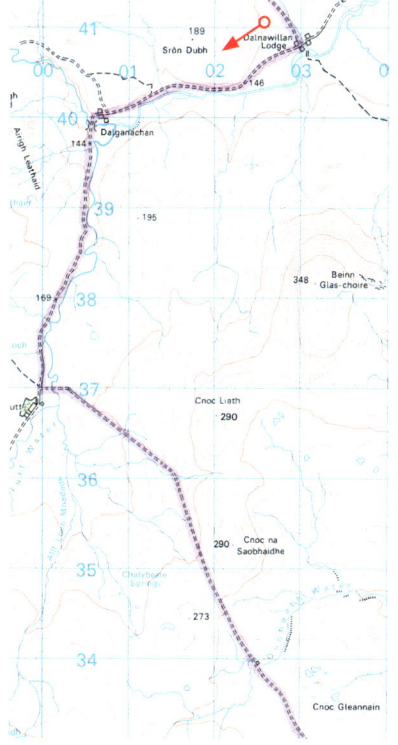

Multi-day routes in northern Britain

In just over 2km avoid tracks off to the L and follow the stronger track as it curves round to the S into another forest area, then crosses the railroad at a 'private' crossing. Continue NE, beside the railroad, avoiding two L turns to Altnabreac Station, until you cross Sleach Water by bridge, where turn L, and in about 1500m pass the marvellously Gothic Lochdhu House beside Loch Dhu. Another 3km brings you to Dalnawillan Lodge, just as imposing but less Transylvanian. Turn R and continue more or less westerly for 2.5km until the track curves sharply S at Dalnagachan. Follow the track S for 3km until, at a crossroads about 200m before Glutt Lodge, turn L. Continue south-easterly for 10km until you arrive at a tarmac road at a gate beside a phone box. If you are in a hurry take the tarmac down stream to Dunbeath and brave the A9 to Helmsdale (or call a taxi).

If your off-road appetite is not sated, turn R, take the bridge over Berriedale Water, and take the first L. Follow this track, keeping L, close to the river past several farmsteads to the R. The track, grassy and patchy in places runs beside or slightly above the river for 10km to Langwell House.

ROUTE 1. MOINE THRUST, OVERSCAIG TO HELMSDALE

23

Mountain Biking Adventures:

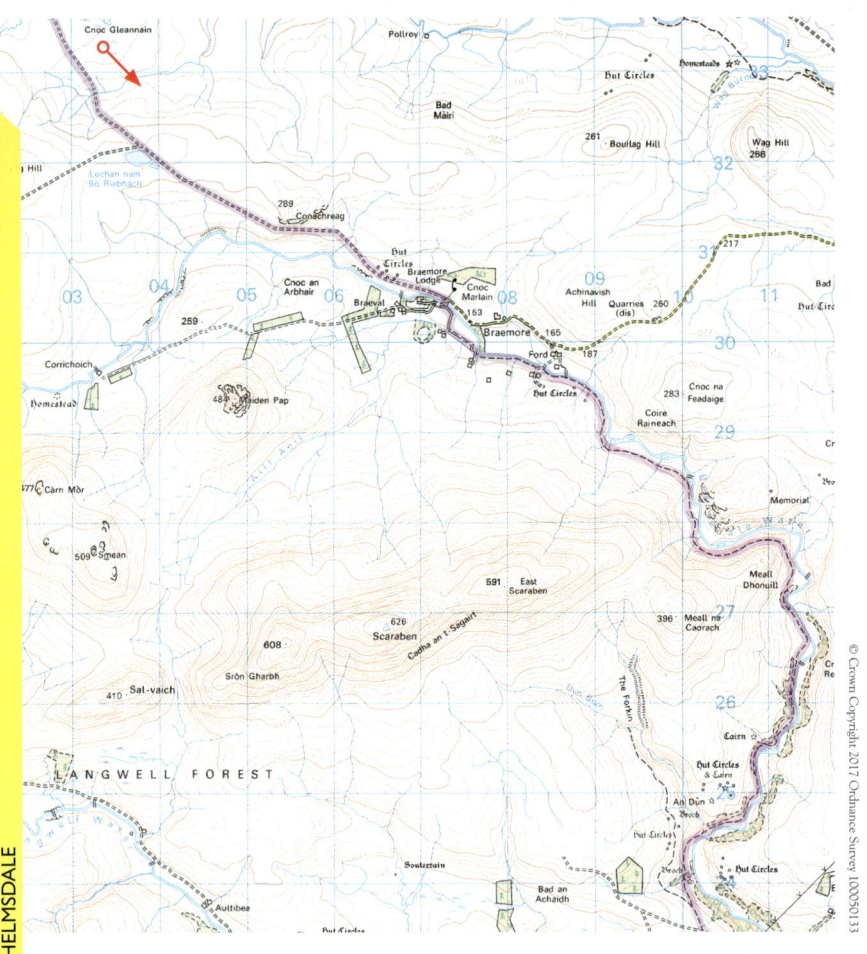

When you finally emerge from the Berriedale valley and start to descend towards the sea with Langwell House before you, turn R along the edge of woods about 200m before a windmill. At the end of the woods zigzag down to the banks of Langwell Water and go W for 600m to a bridge. Cross the bridge and follow the track N and then through a hairpin bend S to emerge, in a couple of km, at the A9. Brave the traffic and press on S to Helmsdale and the train, or rendezvous with vehicular support at the parking place for Badbea Historic Clearance Village, 1.5km down the road.

ROUTE 1. MOINE THRUST, OVERSCAIG TO HELMSDALE

Multi-day routes in northern Britain

ROUTE 1. MOINE THRUST, OVERSCAIG TO HELMSDALE

25

2. SUTHERLAND AND ROSS AND CROMARTY CIRCULAR

Total route (days):	Four days			
Start:	Helmsdale			
Finish:	Ardgay			
Total Distance:	280km (174miles)			
Total Off-road (%):	48%			
Daily distance (km):	106	60.5	54	59.5
Daily off-road (%):	30%	80%	20.5%	71%
Ascent:	5127m (16,826ft)			
Crux day grade:	H3			

Multi-day routes in northern Britain

OVERVIEW

This coast to coast to coast begins in Helmsdale with a long but gentle westward journey over the lower reaches of Sutherland's 'Flow Country', a weird undulating desert where mountains seemed to appear from nowhere. The second day sneaks over the shoulder of Ben More Assynt and then between the magnificent residual giants, Canisp and Suilven, on rough terrain. Day three is a mixture of delightful minor roads by sea and loch and 6km of madness along the Postman's Route. Finally, there is a one day coast-to-coast (or tidal to tidal at least) romp.

Whilst not a closed loop you can get to the start and finish by train.

DAY 1.

Start:	Helmsdale
Finish:	Overscaig Hotel
Distance:	106km (66miles)
Off-road:	33km (20.5miles) 30%
Ascent:	1156m (3795ft)
Descent:	1049m (3443ft)
Grade:	M2

OVERVIEW

A long road section westwards leads to a moor with track and path cycling, and a lowish col, finishing with more road in lonely surroundings.

ROUTE

From the centre of Helmsdale take the A897 N into Strath Ullie and continue on this road NW for 28km to Kinbrace. Don't be put off by the fact that this is on an 'A' road. 'Helmsdale' suggests you might be North Yorkshire and the terrain suggests the same for the first 15km or so. Gradually, you rise from this green valley until you find yourselves in the lonely weirdness of the flow country. (You could take the equally delightful 09:47 train).

At Kinbrace turn L on to the B871 and follow it for 7.5km. One km after the end of Loch Achnamoine take a L fork on to a well-metalled track as the road sweeps from WNW to NW and Badanloch Lodge. Follow this track W for 15km, avoiding turns to L and R until you arrive at Loch Choire House.

Turn R and in 250m cross the Mallart River by bridge, continuing W around the foot of Loch Choire and taking the track S along its western shore. (The route along the eastern shore may be better, but means a greater impingement on the curtilage of the lodge.) The track becomes grassy in places.

ROUTE 2. SUTHERLAND AND ROSS AND CROMARTY CIRCULAR

27

Mountain Biking Adventures:

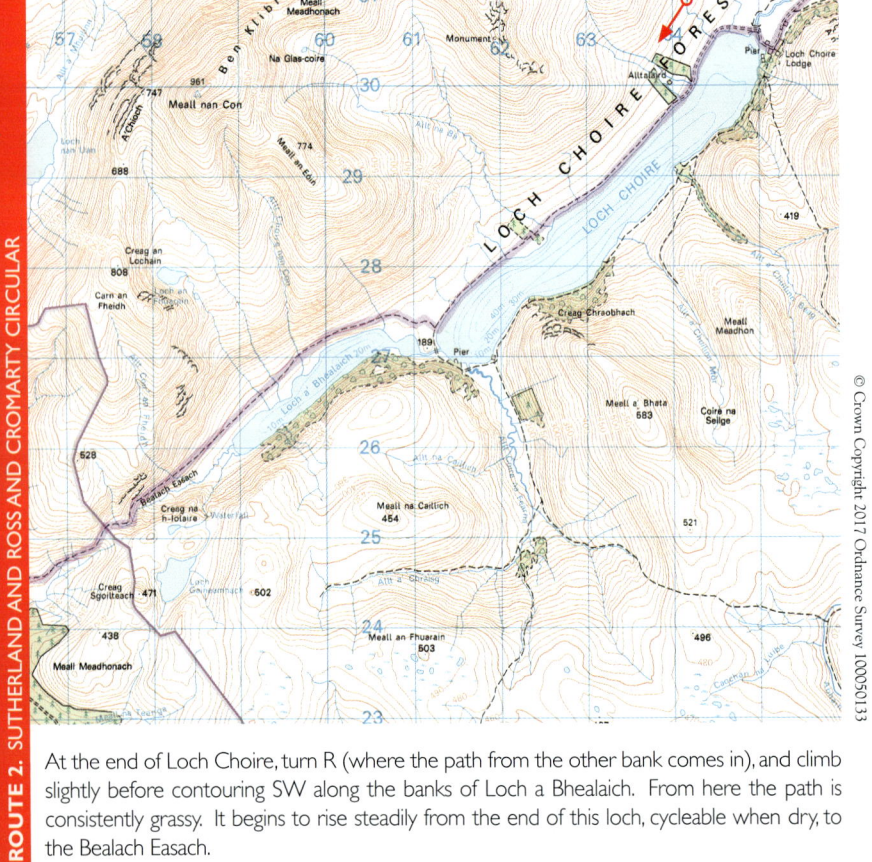

ROUTE 2. SUTHERLAND AND ROSS AND CROMARTY CIRCULAR

© Crown Copyright 2017 Ordnance Survey 100050133

At the end of Loch Choire, turn R (where the path from the other bank comes in), and climb slightly before contouring SW along the banks of Loch a Bhealaich. From here the path is consistently grassy. It begins to rise steadily from the end of this loch, cycleable when dry, to the Bealach Easach.

Multi-day routes in northern Britain

Approaching Bealach Easach by Loch a Bealaich

From the col, the, track descends for about 1km, and then very gently along the banks of the Tirry, where it becomes a little patchy. Join the A836 just S of the Crask Inn, where welcome refreshment can be taken.

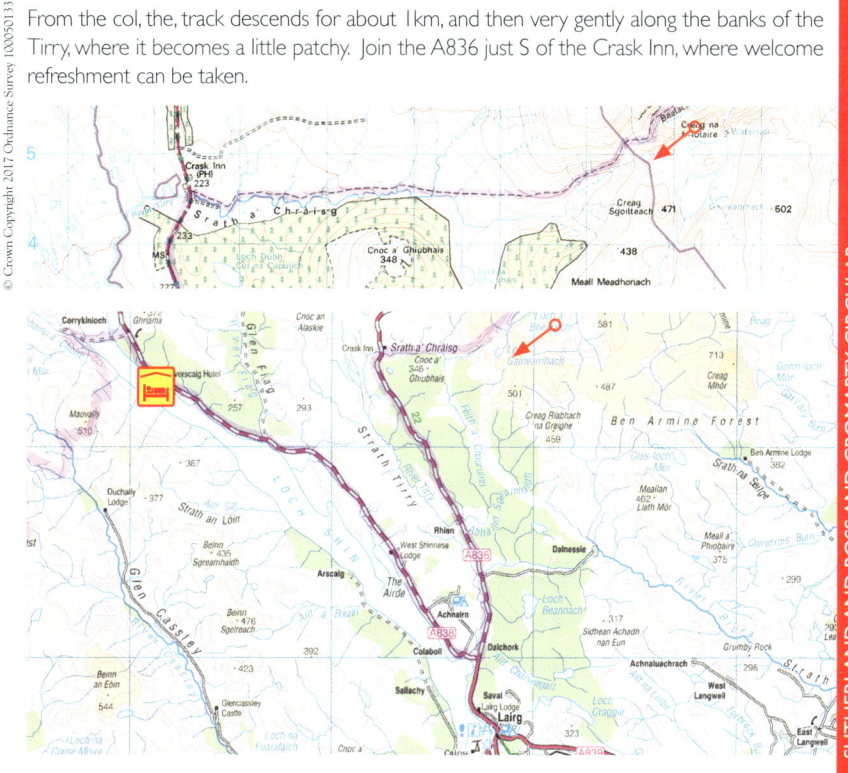

Head S on the A836. After 2km, at a gap in the forest, decide whether to bushwhack 4km SW to pick up the A838 to tonight's lodgings at the Overscaig Hotel or, like the authors, take a 28km road trip to the foot of and then along Loch Shin.

ROUTE 2. SUTHERLAND AND ROSS AND CROMARTY CIRCULAR

Mountain Biking Adventures:

DAY 2.

Start:	Overscaig
Finish:	Lochinver
Distance:	60.5km (37.5miles)
Off-road:	48.5km (30miles) 80%
Ascent:	1375m (4513ft)
Descent:	1483m (4869ft)
Grade:	H3

OVERVIEW

A long, hard day, with a major push across the Inverpolly National Nature Reserve. Good riding near the huge massif of Ben More Assynt, and near the end on a track, the certainty of which will help those who think they may be benighted. Stunning scenery in the Reserve.

ROUTE

From the Overscaig Hotel head N on the A838 for 3km until you emerge from the forest or where an unsigned road turns off L beside a couple of bungalows. Take this road. About 100m down the road there is a gate marked Hydro. Follow this road W towards Corrykinloch. Two km past the bridge at the foot of Loch a Ghriama, turn L, initially S, then SW along the head of Loch Shin. After 1.5km the road starts to climb. Keep climbing, avoiding L and R turns until zigzags have you climbing more steeply by a radio mast and contouring briefly around Maovally and you drop by further hairpins into Glen Cassley. After the last hairpin, keep L (straight on) and go past a power station in the valley bottom. At the next broad crossroads go straight on and cross the bridge over the Cassley. Climb steeply up a couple of zigzags and turn L, S when you face a pipe, about 1.5m in diameter. Follow this water capture pipe for about 1.5km where a good track (shown as a path on some maps) goes up to the R. Follow this track WNW for 2km as if you are heading for the summit of Ben More Assynt. From the turning circle, where the good track ends, pick out the path S. It is not totally distinct but some of it can be ridden. Follow it, more or less contouring, round the foot of Loch Carn nan Conbhairean and round the SE spur of Ben More Assynt.

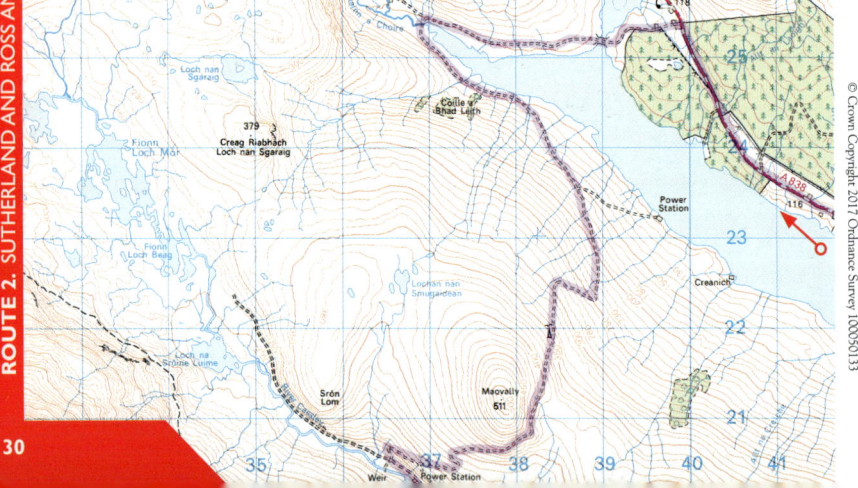

Multi-day routes in northern Britain

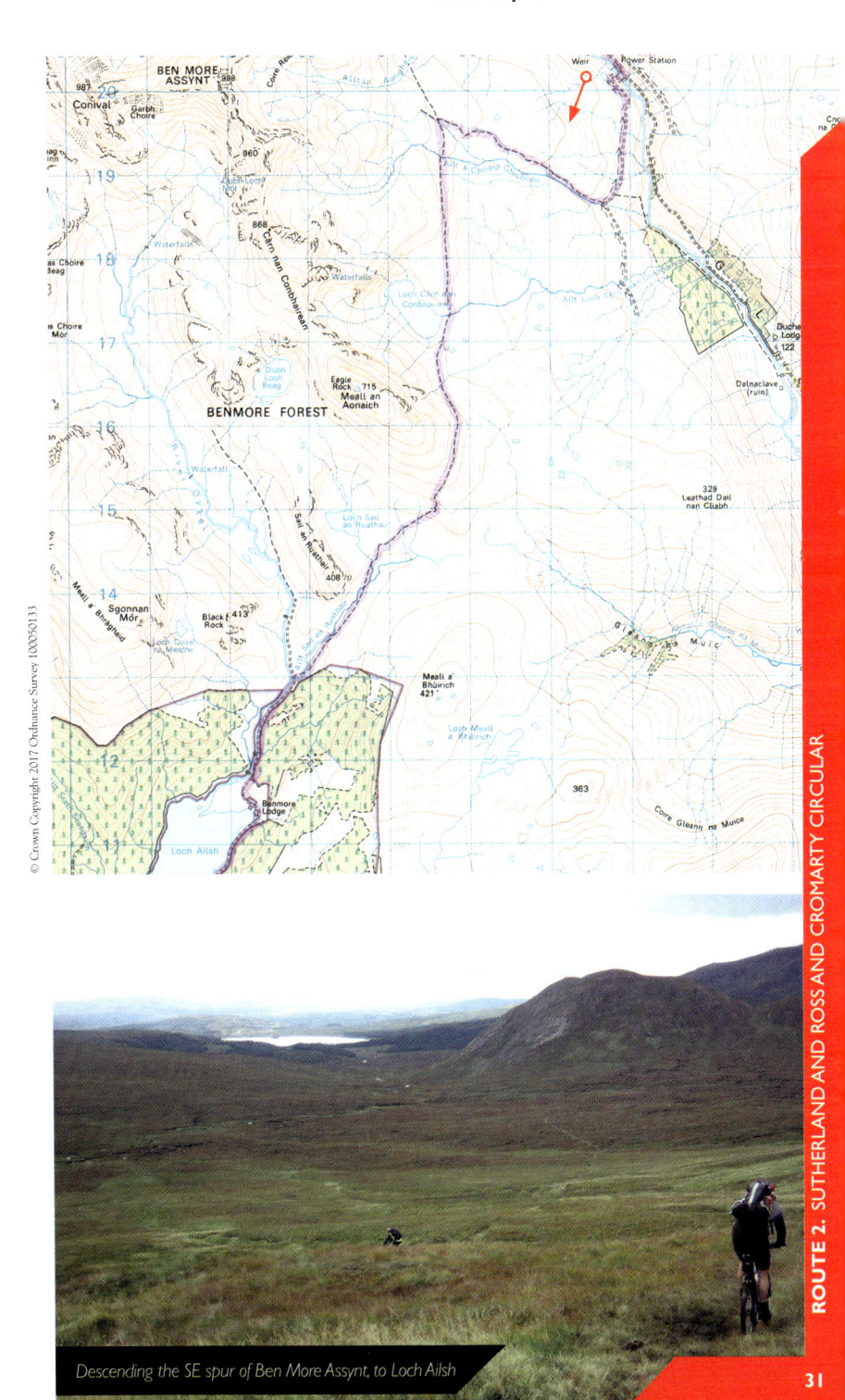

Descending the SE spur of Ben More Assynt, to Loch Ailsh

ROUTE 2. SUTHERLAND AND ROSS AND CROMARTY CIRCULAR

31

Mountain Biking Adventures:

The ground steepens and you may enjoy much of this descent if you are brave. Past Loch Sail an Ruathair the path is not so steep and is a little patchy, but can mostly be ridden. After 2km and 150m after a second fording of the Allt Sail an Ruathair you'll arrive at a well-metalled track. Turn L and ford the Allt Sail an Ruathair again. If you are canny, you will see a footbridge just before the intersection, which you can take to avoid the final ford. Continue S on this good track past Benmore Lodge and Loch Ailsh, occasionally gawping over your shoulder at the magnificent mountain behind you, until you come to the A837. Turn R and follow this road for 6.5km to Ledmore junction and turn L on to the A835. In 500m a bridge carries you over the Ledbeg River. After 800m there is a small pull in on the right-hand side of the road. Cross into it and look for a vague path going NW. It may be simpler just to take a bearing and bushwhack for about 500m until you come to Cam Loch. (The path marked on the map leaves immediately before the next bridge, but is even more indistinct and the authors have never found it.) Whichever way you go, pause at the wonder of the view from the higher ground along Cam Loch to Suilvan and Canisp, between which your route will take you.

Near Lochan Fada, Suilven looming

Once at the loch's edge a slightly more distinct path can be found which follows the shape of the loch slightly more closely than is shown on the map. It drops back to the loch's edge and becomes cycleable, if spoke snappingly technical. After just over 1km, and fording a stream, the path continues on the same bearing for 800m which takes it away from the edge of the loch. It then heads N for 1km over a shallow ridge before resuming its NW direction to pass along the banks of Lochan Fada. This, and the section which follows, is on very rough ground. It is, mercifully, exactly as shown on the map. Cross the stream at the head of Lochan Fada. The path is very indistinct here. Head NW through the steep defile of the aptly named Gleann Dorcha. The path is consistently about 50m from the stream until the 'dark glen' opens out at the foot of Loch na Gainimh. The path improves a little as it continues NW on the NE shore of this loch and joins a grassy track just by the head of the loch. An undulating descent sweeps you down past Glencanisp Lodge and on to a tarmac road which will deliver you to the centre of Lochinver. Do look over your shoulder from time to time.

Multi-day routes in northern Britain

ROUTE 2. SUTHERLAND AND ROSS AND CROMARTY CIRCULAR

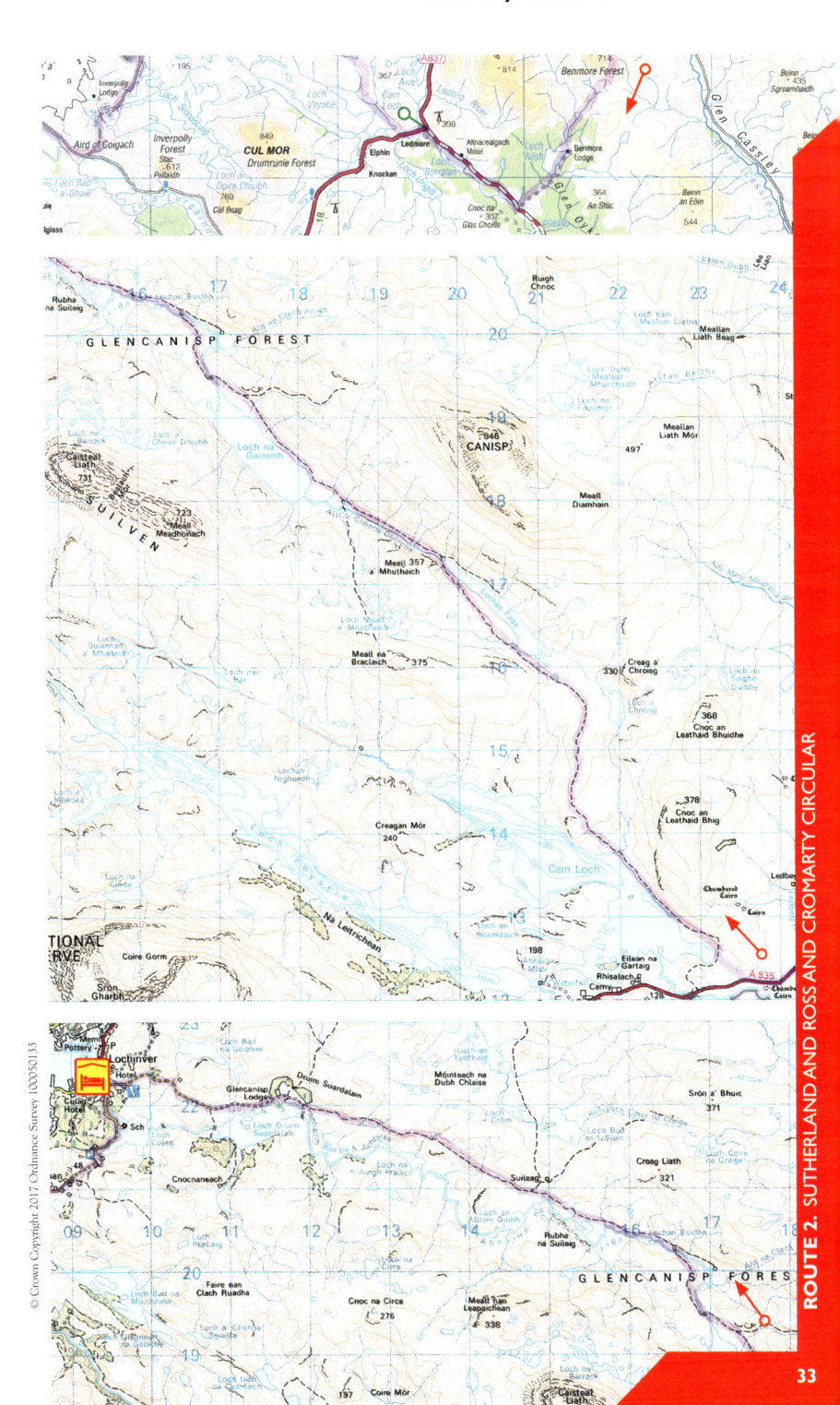

Mountain Biking Adventures:

DAY 3.

Start:	Lochinver
Finish:	Ullapool
Distance:	54km (33.5miles)
Off-road:	11km (7miles) 20.5%
Ascent:	1540m (5055ft)
Descent:	1540m (5055ft)
Grade:	H3

OVERVIEW

A scenic road leads to the maddest place you could possibly take a mountain bike, although on a visually superb path, hence a truly excellent adventure.

ROUTE

Take the unclassified road sign-posted 'Achiltibuie 16' and follow it for 26km over a deceptive 750m of ascent and descent as it twists and turns through this fabulous West Coast country with incomparable mountain, sea and island views.

Take refreshment at the Summer Isles Hotel and contemplate whether or not you want to attempt the Postman's Route, which is rough and strenuous even by yesterday's standards, and, to be frank, does not involve much cycling though you may use your bike occasionally as an impromptu stepladder. If the answer is 'No', retrace your steps to Aird na Coigach and take the R fork leading to the banks of Loch Lurgainn, which is not without its delights, and then take the main road S to Ullapool.

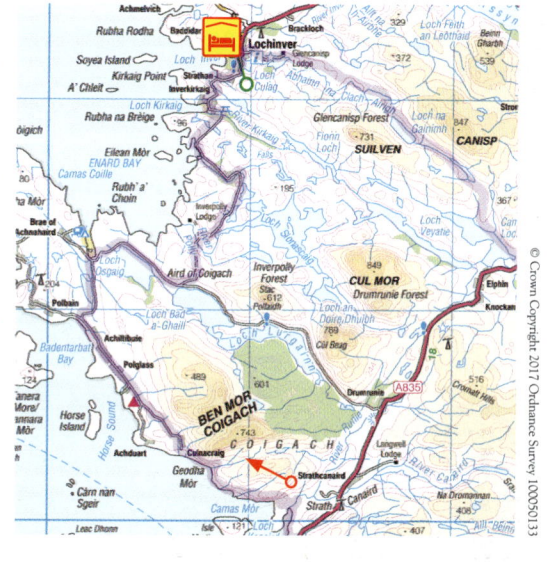

If you are on for 6km of pushing and carrying amidst some of the most spectacular coastal scenery, continue, straight on, SW from Achiltibuie for 5.5km until you approach the hamlet of Culnacraig. The tarmac ends at a sign saying 'NO PARKING. Turning place only.' A track continues to the R. Follow it, S, for almost 500m until, just after a building on your L, you take the much weaker track S as the main track curves L round the building.

About 200m down this track, after a loose hairpin bend, and before you get to the burn, the path goes off to the L. It is quite indistinct to start with but improves in 2-300m.

ROUTE 2. SUTHERLAND AND ROSS AND CROMARTY CIRCULAR

Multi-day routes in northern Britain

It has to be admitted that where the path is cycleable, the runouts are unattractive and for the rest it is a push and, at times, a carry. The views, and the position, however, are unparalleled. Where the way is most unclear, the path is fairly well way marked with posts about 1.5m high. The ground is very rough and you should allow three to four hours. Eventually, you are delivered into the estuary of Strath Canaird. When you get to flat ground, do not follow the path to the L, but turn R and go WSW along the banks of a burn until you come to a track raised on a levee.

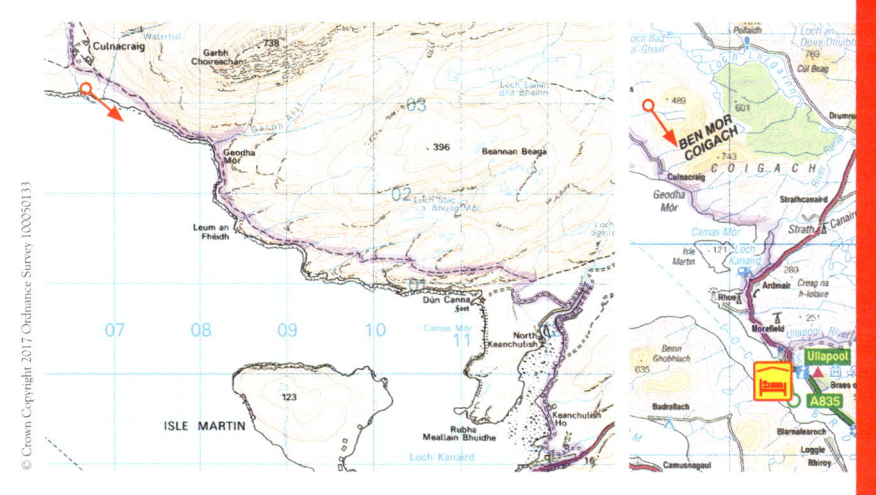

Turn L on the track and follow it to a bridge. Cross the bridge and turn R. In 2km this track delivers you to the A835. Turn R and in 7km you are in Ullapool.

The Postman's Path: Hard going but glorious scenery

ROUTE 2. SUTHERLAND AND ROSS AND CROMARTY CIRCULAR

35

Mountain Biking Adventures:

DAY 4.

Start:	Ullapool
Finish:	Ardgay
Distance:	59.5km (37miles)
Off-road:	42km (26miles) 71%
Ascent:	1056m (3467ft)
Descent:	1056m (3467ft)
Grade:	E3

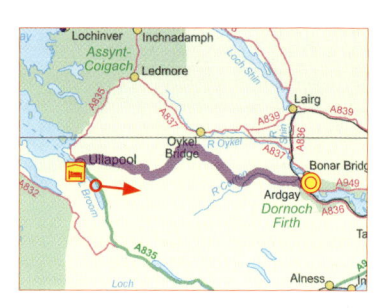

OVERVIEW

Mostly good off-road across northern Scotland, an easier day to finish.

ROUTE

Leave Ullapool on the A835 N and turn R just before the bridge over Ullapool River on a wide unsigned track. Follow this path past two quarry workings. Keep bearing L after the second quarry and the cross the first bridge over Ullapool River. The second bridge shown on the OS map is no longer there, though a cautionary sign on the N bank still warns you that it is dangerous. Across the river, keep R and follow the good track along the edge of Loch Achall and past Rhidorroch House.

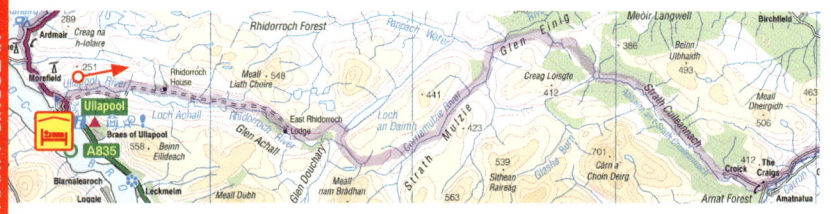

Five km after the end of the loch you pass East Rhidorroch Lodge over the river. Two km after this a good path strikes off to the L and in 300m there is a fork in the track. Take the R fork (The L fork is a good track, but shown as a path on the map. Be sure to avoid it.) Your track descends to the head of Loch an Daimh. On the OS map it is shown as crossing a stream about 150m from the fork and then a second one in a further 500m. Do not cross the stream. When you get to the beach at the head of the loch, and having crossed a small burn, head SW looking for the vestige of a good stalking path striking up the hillside. The path is wholly grassed over, but slightly terraced, though nowhere clear. It divides in about 100m. Take the L fork SSW and as it curves round SSE rise along the bank of the Allt nan Caorach. Continue SE along the

ROUTE 2. SUTHERLAND AND ROSS AND CROMARTY CIRCULAR

© Crown Copyright 2017 Ordnance Survey 100050133

Multi-day routes in northern Britain

edge of the ravine where the path becomes progressively stronger. There is a narrow lochan about 300m long, but barely 20m wide, in the upper reaches of the gully not shown on the OS map, but is on Memory-Map™. After the end of the lochan, the track curves round to the E on to more open ground and, in about 1km, meets a good track heading ENE.

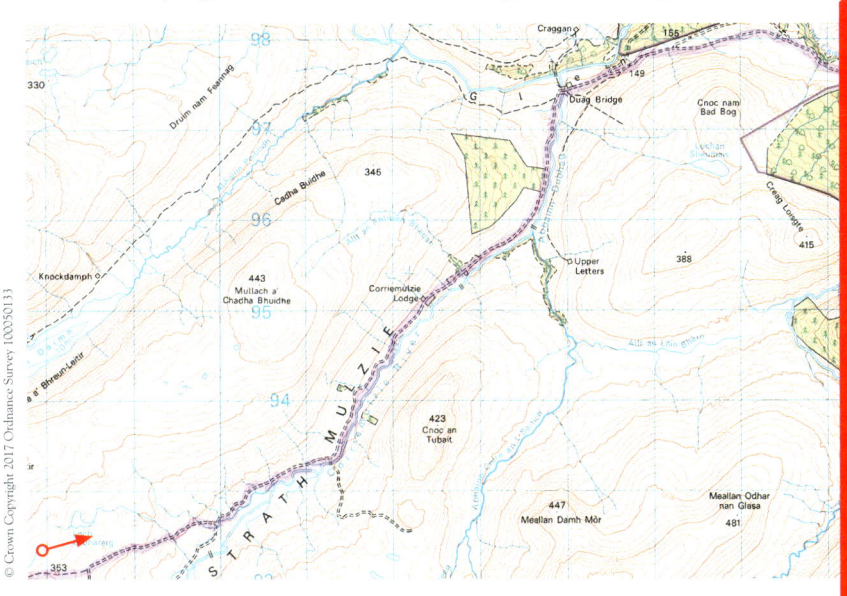

Enjoy the gentle descent into Strath Mulzie for 8km to Duag Bridge. In 600m fork R, not L. Even though the L one is a better track, it would add nearly a further km. In a further 800m, again take the weaker track to the R. If you miss it, a better track to the R 1km further on brings you to the same place. As you approach a patchy forest avoid the spur to the R and yet again take the weaker trail which continues to the L, crosses a stream, and curves up into the forest itself. Follow this track SE into Strath Cuileannach.

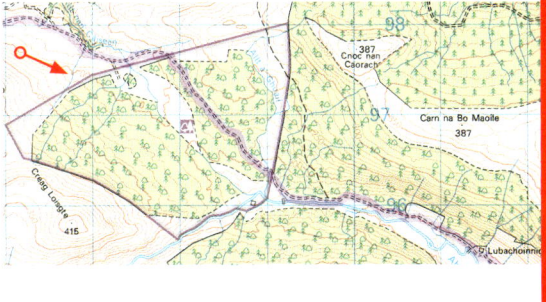

Tootle 9km to Croick to meet tarmac which will carry you down to The Craigs and Strathcarron and, in a further 14km, Ardgay and the station.

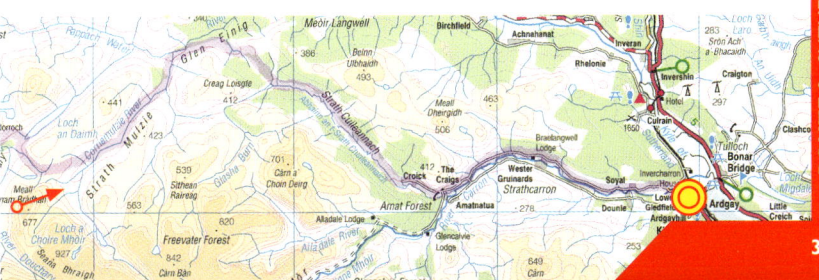

3. AULTGUISH CIRCULAR, EASTER AND WESTER ROSS

Total route (days):	Three days			
Start & Finish:	Aultguish Inn, Ross and Cromarty, on the A835 Inverness to Ullapool road		
Total Distance:	210.5km (131 miles)		
Total Off-road (%):	52%		
Daily distance (km):	84	77.5	48.5
Daily off-road (%):	62%	42%	52%
Ascent:	4101m (13,462ft)		
Crux day grade:	M2		

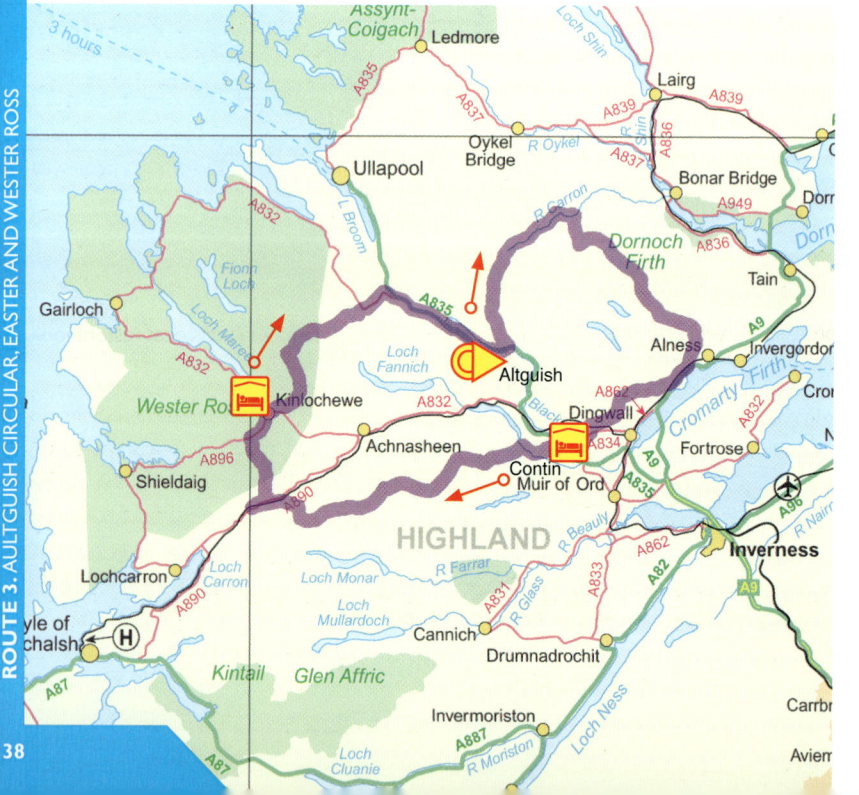

Multi-day routes in northern Britain

OVERVIEW

Remote days through wild and rugged territory, with five star mountain scenery, increasing from day one through the glens of Easter Ross, to day two towards the big Munros S of Glen Carron then the Torridon Hills, then on day three, the utter grandeur of the Fisherfield Forest. The only 'off-piste' is on day three and is only 8km.

DAY 1.

Start:	Aultguish Inn
Finish:	Strathpeffer
Distance:	84km (52.5miles)
Off-road:	52km (32.5miles) 62%
Ascent:	1495m (4907ft)
Descent:	1661m (5454ft)
Grade:	M2

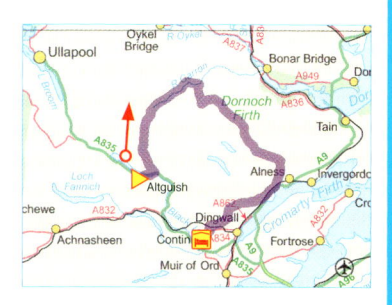

OVERVIEW

A long, remote day till Strath Rusdale, with much ascent, although this is all rideable on Landrover tracks. Passes through the edge of an interesting rewilding project of Alladale Estate, although wolves and bears are not expected as part of this adventure. Some road then leads to a short, rough track and then road down to Strathpeffer. No refreshments till Evanton. A grand Highland day.

INFORMATION

The Alladale Estate was bought by Paul Lister in 2003 and became a wilderness and rewilding area, the largest in the UK. Deer, which eat young trees, are being reduced, the ultimate idea for this is to introduce their predators, wolves and bears, although this has not been allowed yet. However, in 2014, 800,000 young local trees were planted. Other projects are: wild boar research, you should see some by the track in pens; peat restoration by drainage disturbance; and red squirrel, wildcat, elk and forest bison introduction. Unfortunately, Mr Lister's plans seem to include a high fence for what amounts to a zoo, with charges to enter. Worth looking online before starting off to see latest developments.

Strathpeffer is a Victorian spa town, based on sulphurous springs. The Strathpuffer 24hr mountain bike endurance event takes place each January just east of here in the forest, the 10km circuit being rated moderate (in summer conditions!).

ROUTE

Downhill from the Inn on the A835, turn L just after Black Bridge on to a good track, but R after about 3km just before another bridge. There may be a locked gate here. Keep L at the next junction, go over a small hill and along Loch Vaich. A low pass, ignoring a R then a L turn, leads to Deanich Lodge.

ROUTE 3. AULTGUISH CIRCULAR, EASTER AND WESTER ROSS

39

Mountain Biking Adventures:

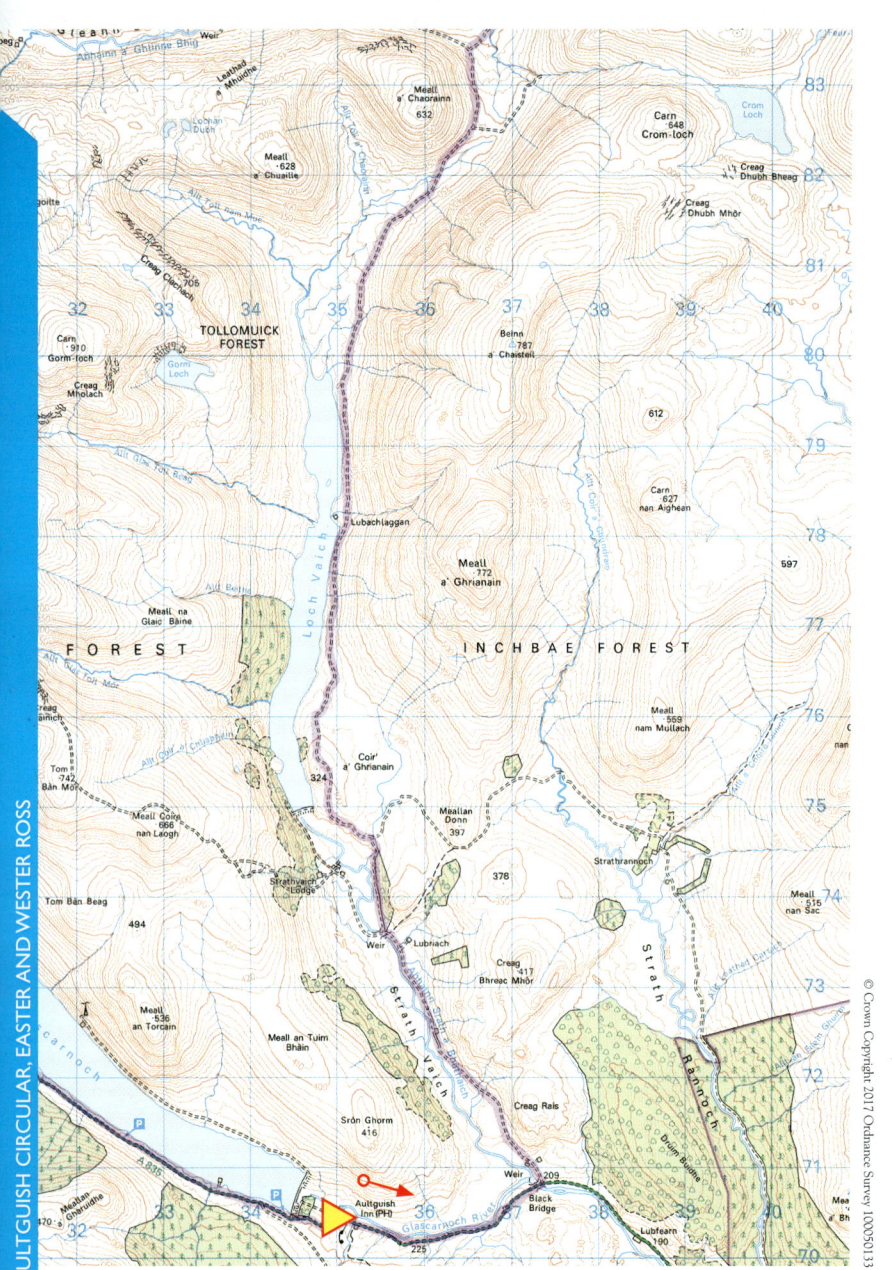

ROUTE 3. AULTGUISH CIRCULAR, EASTER AND WESTER ROSS

A long easy track down Gleann Mhor goes past woods of Scots pine, and you may see wild boar enclosures by the track. Over the Alladale River turn R and continue down stream to cross the River Carron by Glencalvie Lodge, to access Glen Calvie by the signed route indicated inside the Lodge grounds. Do not be put off by any 'Private' signs outside the grounds.

© Crown Copyright 2017 Ordnance Survey 100050133

40

Multi-day routes in northern Britain

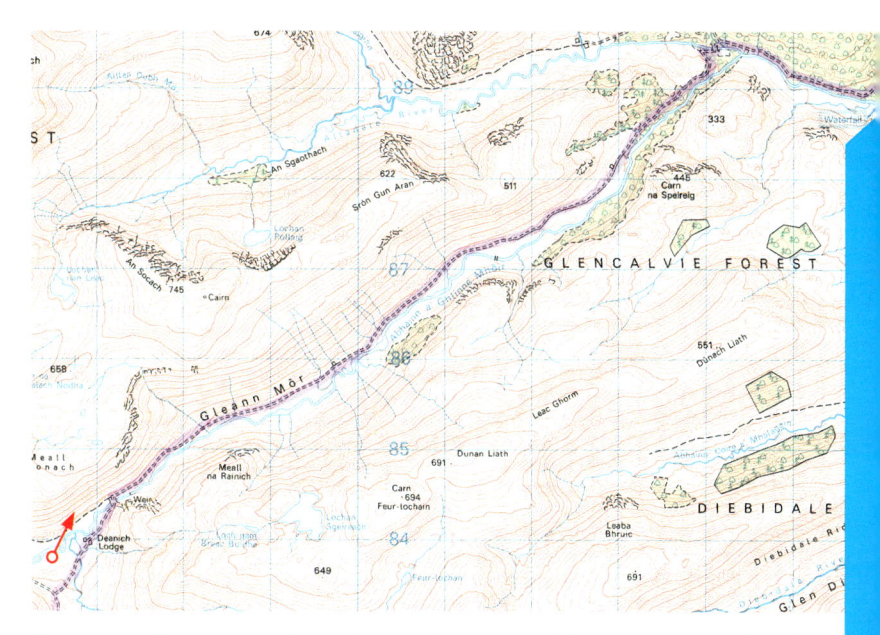

Continue up Glencalvie until the track curves L, eastwards. Follow the track out of the Glen and over to Lochan a' Chairn. There follows an unusual mile of totally straight track, followed by some blocking boulders just before the forest edge. Five km on the forest track leads to a minor road leading down to the B9176, turn R and head on to Evanton for tea.

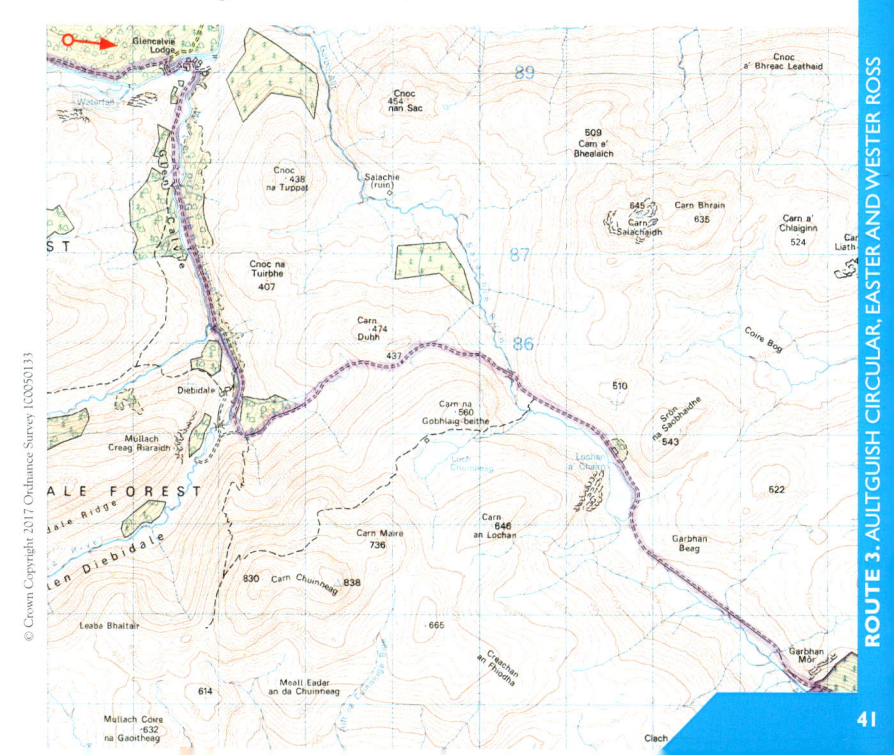

Mountain Biking Adventures:

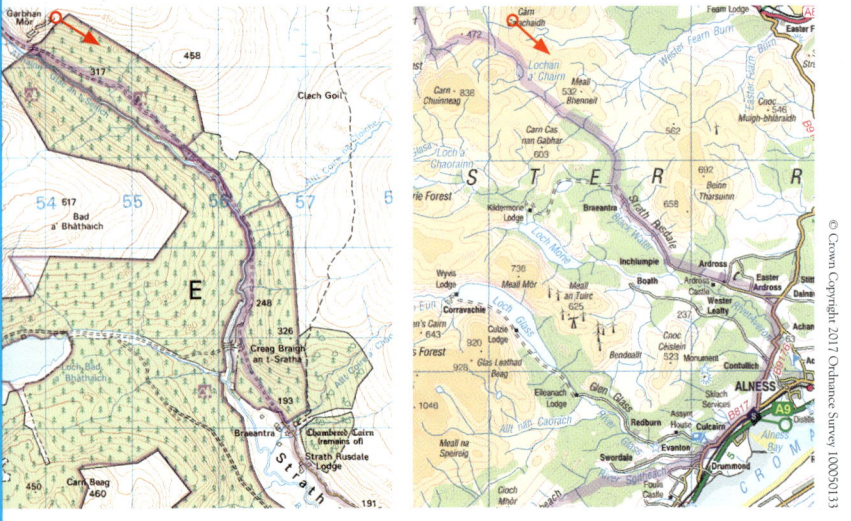

Ascent from Glen Diebidale.

© Crown Copyright 2017 Ordnance Survey 100050133

Take the R turn after crossing the Sgitheach River, then R again to follow the valley up, past Knockancurin and by a forest. Before the Achleach ruin turn L through the forest, keeping on WSW at a junction on a muddy path/track, to rejoin the Sgitheach valley. This joins a minor road, and you turn R off it at the second turn, heading along the hillside then L, S at the end and double back under the railway, down to the main road and R to Strathpeffer.

ROUTE 3. AULTGUISH CIRCULAR, EASTER AND WESTER ROSS

42

Multi-day routes in northern Britain

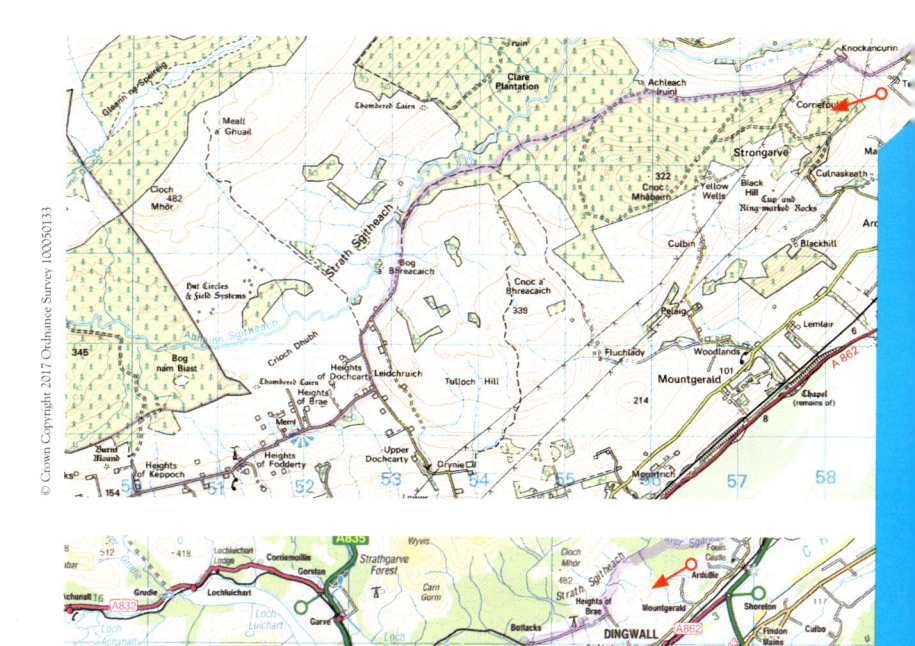

DAY 2.

Start:	Strathpeffer
Finish:	Kinlochewe
Distance:	77.7km (48.5miles)
Off-road:	32.5km (20miles) 42%
Ascent:	1607m (5275ft)
Descent:	1639m (5382ft)
Grade:	M2

OVERVIEW

A long through route up Strathconon, basically from one side of Scotland to the other here, with over 19 remote km offroad, the last part a good descent on track. A short ascent on forest tracks leads to another good descent down from the Coulin pass to Torridon and Kinlochewe. Views of the Torridon Giants are excellent from the pass onwards. No refreshments, although you could try at 'Gerry's' Hostel if desperate.

ROUTE 3. AULTGUISH CIRCULAR, EASTER AND WESTER ROSS

43

Mountain Biking Adventures:

INFORMATION

A Crannog, which you will see on maps in some local lochs, but probably not in the flesh, was an Iron Age loch dwelling, or an artificial, or modified natural, island. A Crannog centre exists by Loch Tay.

Craig, or 'Gerry's' hostel, is Scotland's oldest independent hostel. Originally two semis for railworkers, Gerry Howkins opened it in 1964. Many tales testify to his idiosyncratic character, and he will be missed by all who stayed there, as he sadly died in 2014.

Coulin is pronounced 'cowlin'. The pass was an old drove road.

ROUTE

Carry on the main road to turn R on the A835, through Contin and turn L 400m after crossing the river on to a minor road. Follow this up the Strath for 30km, criss-crossing the River Meig, to Corrievuic, just past Scardroy Lodge.

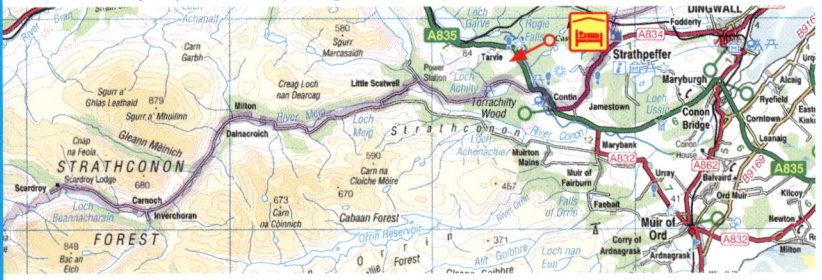

There is now 11 rough km till the track starts just before the watershed at Glenuaig Lodge, although most is rideable. The path becomes boggy after a gate by the Allt na Criche, but the really rugged mountain scenery makes up for it.

Gleann Fhiodhaig.

Multi-day routes in northern Britain

The track down to Craig is fast and straightforward. Turn L down the A890 for just over 3km and then R up a track to Achnashellach station. Climb up to cross the railway line carefully, and continue uphill. Turn R at a forest track by a sign for Coulin Road and carry on through the forest on the main track to the summit at 287m, a climb of 240m. You are now truly in God's country, with Beinn Eighe ahead, and as you descend on a fast track into upper Torridon, mighty Liathach appears to the NW. Keep L at Coulin farm as R involves pushing by Loch Coulin, and pass the Lodge and by Loch Clair now on tarmac.

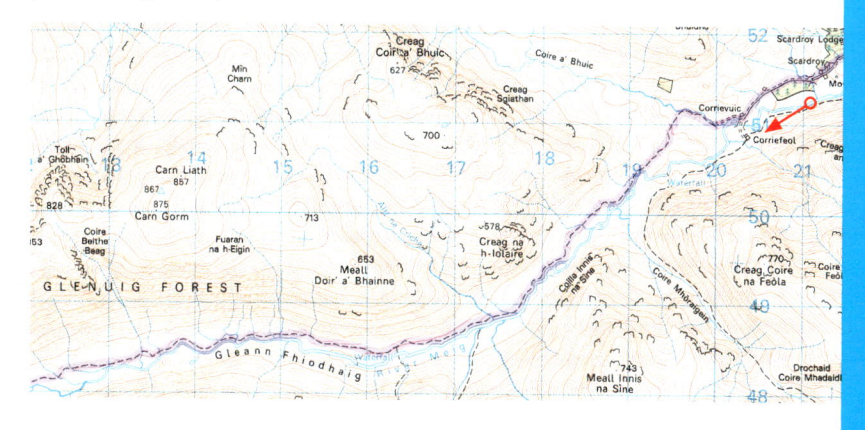

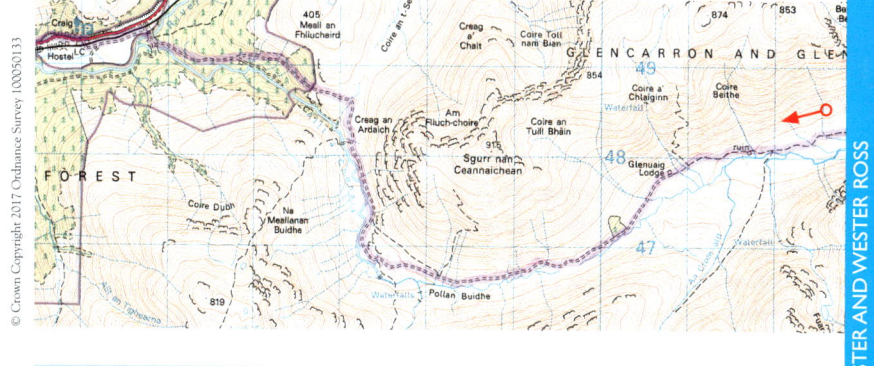

Liathach from Loch Clair. Photo © Bob Jones (cc-by-sa/2.0)

ROUTE 3. AULTGUISH CIRCULAR, EASTER AND WESTER ROSS

45

Mountain Biking Adventures:

Turn R and enjoy your 5km descent to Kinlochewe on a narrow 'A' road with passing places.

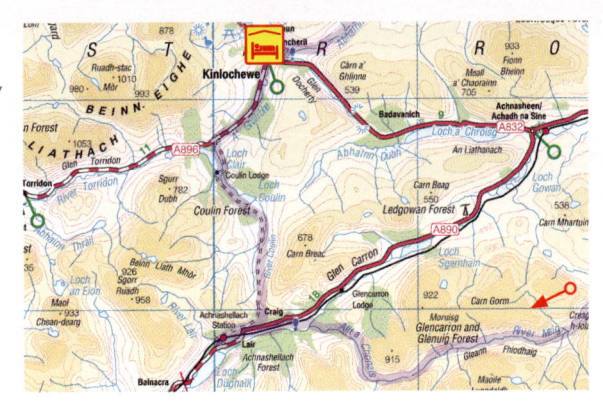

DAY 3.

Start:	Kinlochewe
Finish:	Aultguish Inn
Distance:	48.5km (30.5miles)
Off-road:	25km (15.5miles) 52%
Ascent:	999m (3280ft)
Descent:	800m (2627ft)
Grade:	M2

OVERVIEW

A hard day due to 8km pathless or with a difficult path, but through really wild country with stunning views of rugged mountains, the best yet. The last half is all on 'A' roads but is easterly. No refreshments en route.

INFORMATION

The line of the route from Lochan Fada over Bealach na Croise down towards Loch an Nid is the line of part of the Moine thrust, which extends from Skye to the north coast. The thrust is basically westward movement of a plate of metamorphic rocks over Lewisian and Cambrian rocks, the metamorphic rocks deforming into something called mylonite.

As you look towards Sgurr Ban approaching Loch an Nid you can see the largest single exposed bedding plane in the British Isles, of quartzite, with the curious knob of Lewisian gneiss of Meallan an Laoigh above it.

Corrieshalloch Gorge is an impressive box canyon caused by glacial meltwater, worth a short diversion to walk down to a viewing point if you have time and haven't seen it.

Loch Glascarnoch is a reservoir built in the fifties as part of the Conon, (seen on day 2) scheme of six dams and seven power stations, in this case the station, Mossford by Loch Luichart, is 8km away and the water is tunnelled. When the level drops the old road can be seen.

Multi-day routes in northern Britain

ROUTE

Head from Kinlochewe on the A832 and soon turn L over the river to Incheril, continuing to a car park. Go R on a Landrover track up the valley to fork L at the Heights of Kinlochewe. There may be a locked high gate here, in which case a ladder stile is perhaps an easier obstacle to manage.

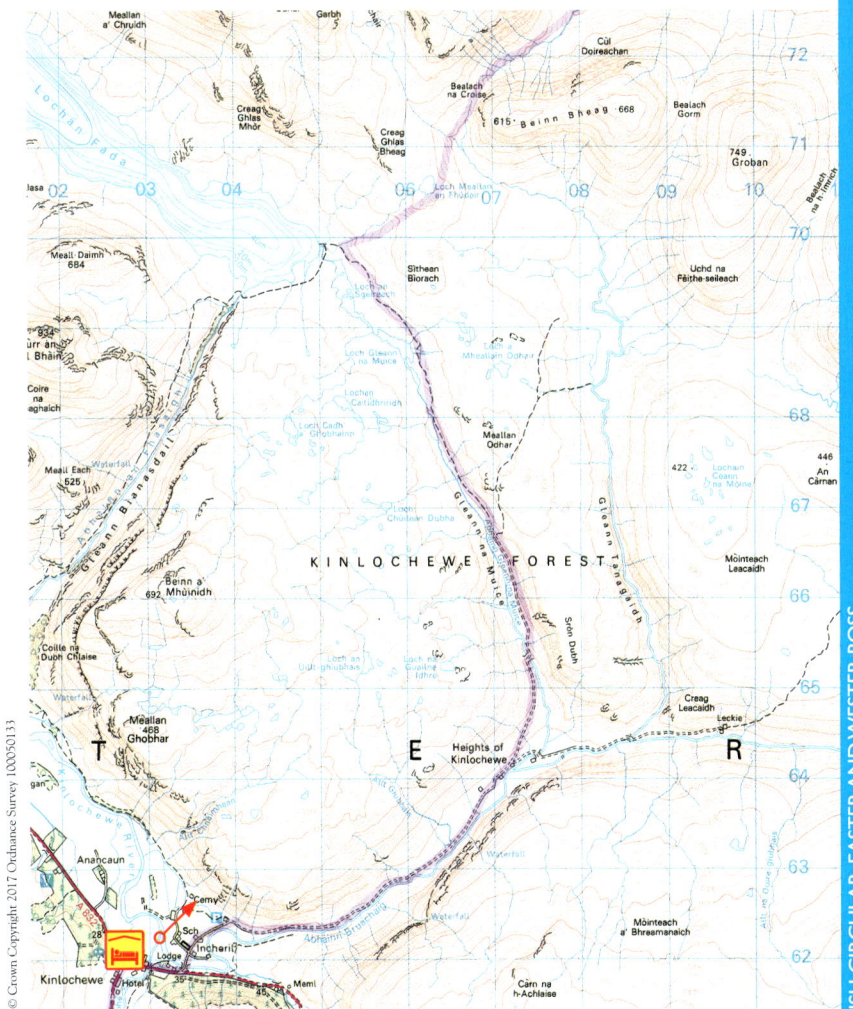

In 1.5km after crossing the river ignore the signed path R and carry on to Lochan Fada. The signed path, although well made, leads to horrible peat hags.

Now pathless, but not too bad underfoot, push upwards alongside the E side of the outflow burn from Loch Meallan an Fhudair and round it on the E side, to find an indefinite path, rideable in part, contouring towards the Bealach na Croise.

ROUTE 3. AULTGUISH CIRCULAR, EASTER AND WESTER ROSS

47

Mountain Biking Adventures:

Bealach na Croise.

From the Bealach find a rough path, initially contouring round the slopes of Sgurr Dubh on the W of the burn, to cross this lower down when you can see a good way to the path on the hillside leading E to a watershed by a ruin. Past this, the path is reasonable till the burn is crossed, when it turns rough, but now it's only 1.5km to Lochivroan, where, as it has recently been improved as a holiday home, a decent track leads beside Loch a Bhraoin to the A832. Be sure, however, to turn L at the forest corner to get there.

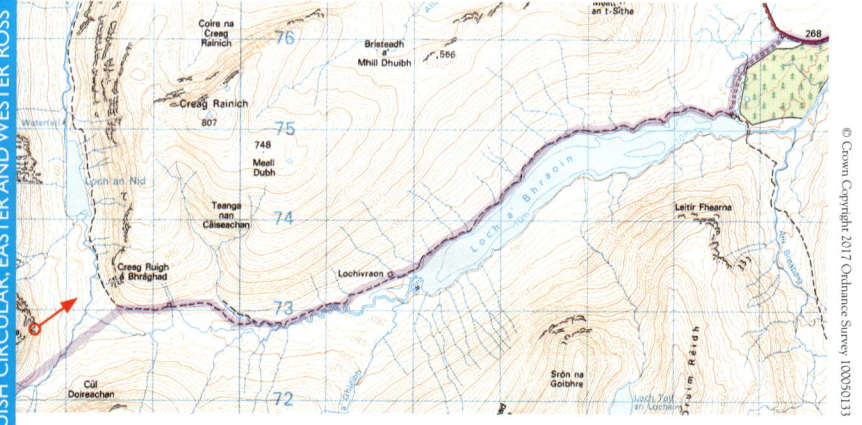

Go down the main road to the Braemore junction (see information about Corrieshalloch Gorge), turn R and a 90m ascent in 4km leads to a level run alongside Lochs Droma and Glascarnoch and home.

Multi-day routes in northern Britain

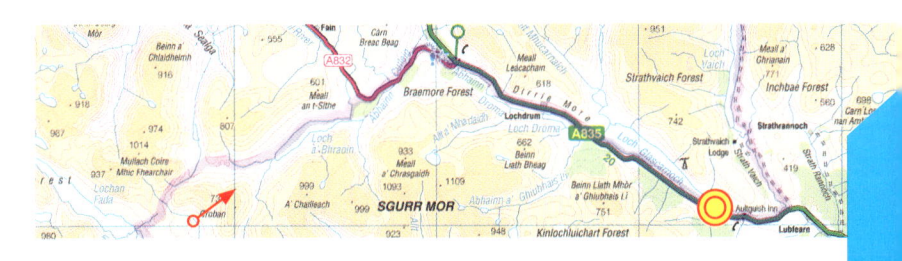

Day 1 - Heading into wilderness by Loch Vaich.

Day 1 - Deanich Lodge, Gleann Mor

ROUTE 3. AULTGUISH CIRCULAR, EASTER AND WESTER ROSS

4. CONTIN CIRCULAR VIA TORRIDON AND FISHERFIELD

Total route (days):	Four days				
Start & Finish:	Contin				
Total Distance:	250km (155miles)				
Total Off-road (%):	47.5%				
Daily distance (km):	80	59	45	65	
Daily off-road (%):	28%	37%	79%	58%	
Ascent:	5822m (19,108ft)				
Crux day grade:	H3				

Multi-day routes in northern Britain

OVERVIEW

This four day route starts with a slight variation on the classic Strathconon through route taken on Day 2 of Route 3 into Strathbran/Strathcarron and then the Coulin Pass to Torridon. The second day takes in superb West Coast scenery on minor roads and some technical singletrack to Poolewe before a massive 45km Day 3 takes you through Fisherfield to Dundonnell. Our return has one grunt to 553m then it's downhill (nearly) all the way back to Contin.

DAY 1.

Start:	Contin
Finish:	Torridon
Distance:	80km (49.5miles)
Off-road:	22km (14miles) 28%
Ascent:	1407m (4620ft)
Descent:	1407m (4620ft)
Grade:	M1

OVERVIEW

An easy tarmac warmup through Strathconan and low moorland carries you into Strathban then the magnificent Coulin Pass delivers you to the foot of the Torridon Giants.

ROUTE

Take the A835 North from Contin and after about 1km turn L on a minor road past Loch Achilty and, in a total of 6km just after a power station, take the bridge L towards Little Scatwell. In 2km cross the dam at the head of Loch Meig and turn R. Follow this minor road for about 18km until, at the head of Loch Beannacharain, the tarmac ends.

Take the track R leading WNW above Scardroy Lodge and follow it into, through, and out of the forest, fording numerous side streams. Continue on the same line, fording further streams. As you get higher up the way begins to deteriorate and is rutted and boggy in places, particularly over the watershed. It does not improve enormously on the descent but it is more rideable downhill. Keep L at NH167542 to avoid the dead end path to the R, and at NH149551

ROUTE 4. CONTIN CIRCULAR, VIA TORRRIDON AND FISHERFIELD

51

Mountain Biking Adventures:

take the R fork, which, though increasingly faint, can be followed around beside the Allt Mhartuin and then follows the stream under the railway. Once under the railway keep close to the edge of the stream until, just as it kinks L into Loch Gowan, it improves dramatically and leads you to a footbridge over the narrows in the loch to the main road.

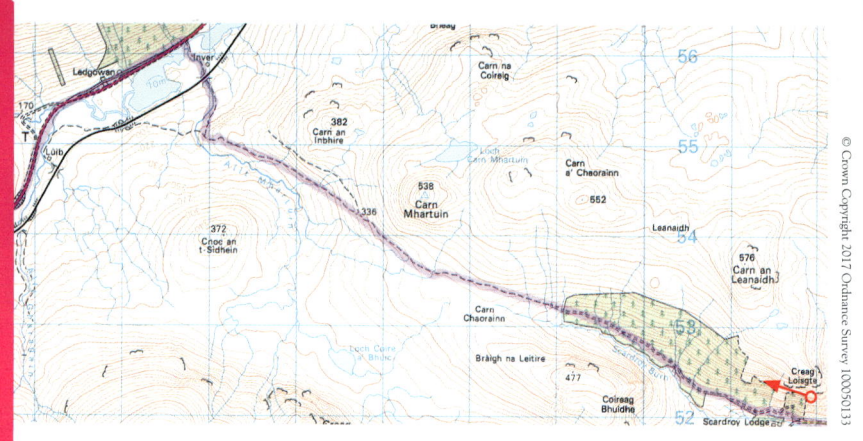

Turn L on the A890 and head WSW for about 14km, then 400m before the road goes under the railway turn R on to the track immediately after the bridge height limit signs. Keep L and follow this track above and parallel to the railway and main road until, at a crossroads just above the station, the well-made track sweeps round in a hairpin. Take the hairpin and continue to climb, steadily at first, ENE until, in a further 2km your track curves N through a couple of bends to the Coulin Pass. Enjoy the descent and, at the bridge over the Easan Dorcha, turn R and tootle out past Loch Coulin and Coulin Lodge.

Bridge over A'Ghairbhe. Beinn Eighe.
Adapted from original Photo © Bob Jones (cc-by-sa/2.0)

Multi-day routes in northern Britain

When you come out of the trees at the Lodge and turn L alongside Loch Claire, be sure to look up at the Beinn Eighe massif and, as you go along the shore, look out for the classic view of Liathach emerging to your L.

At the road turn L and drift down to Torridon amidst mountain splendour.

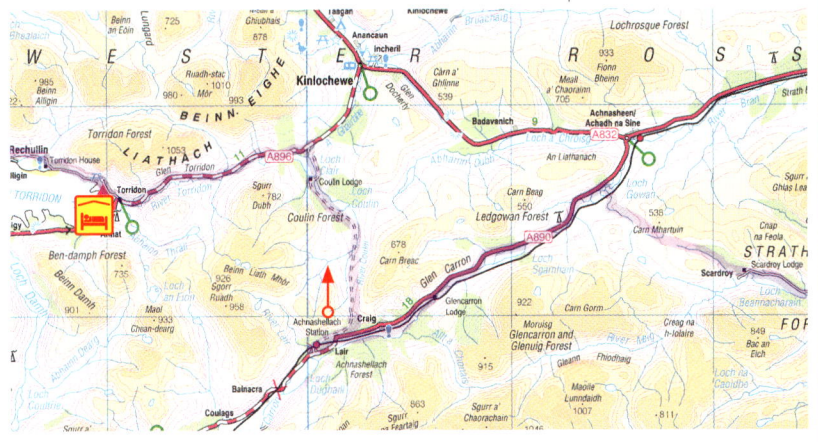

DAY 2.

Start:	Torridon
Finish:	Poolewe
Distance:	59 km (37miles)
Off-road:	23.5km (14.5miles) 37%
Ascent:	1730m (5680ft)
Descent:	1730m (5680ft)
Grade:	M1

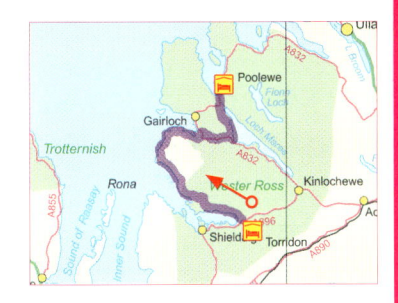

OVERVIEW

A truly delightful West Coast outing on minor roads and fairly good paths.

Sea-light and sunshine if you're lucky, no shortage of up-and-down and some great technical singletrack.

ROUTE

Leave Torridon on the minor road, WNW along the northern bank of Loch Torridon with a bit of up-and-down and stupendous views of Applecross until, in about 12km, you pass Loch Diabaigas Airde and drop into Lower Diabaig. In the middle of the

ROUTE 4. CONTIN CIRCULAR, VIA TORRIDON AND FISHERFIELD

53

Mountain Biking Adventures:

hamlet turn R and keep R. Your path rises to the R again 50m before the last house on the tarmac road. Just before the path a track cuts back sharply to the R. Take this, and in 50m cut back equally sharply to the L. The track now contours and picks up your path. More of it can be ridden than you imagine. Ignore internet tales of woe based on a traverse with touring bike and panniers. Enjoy the scenery as the island of Rona and, behind it, Skye come into view. Enjoy a short rest at Craig if you wish, then press on for more of the same to Redpoint Farm. Shortly after the farm you arrive at the B8056.

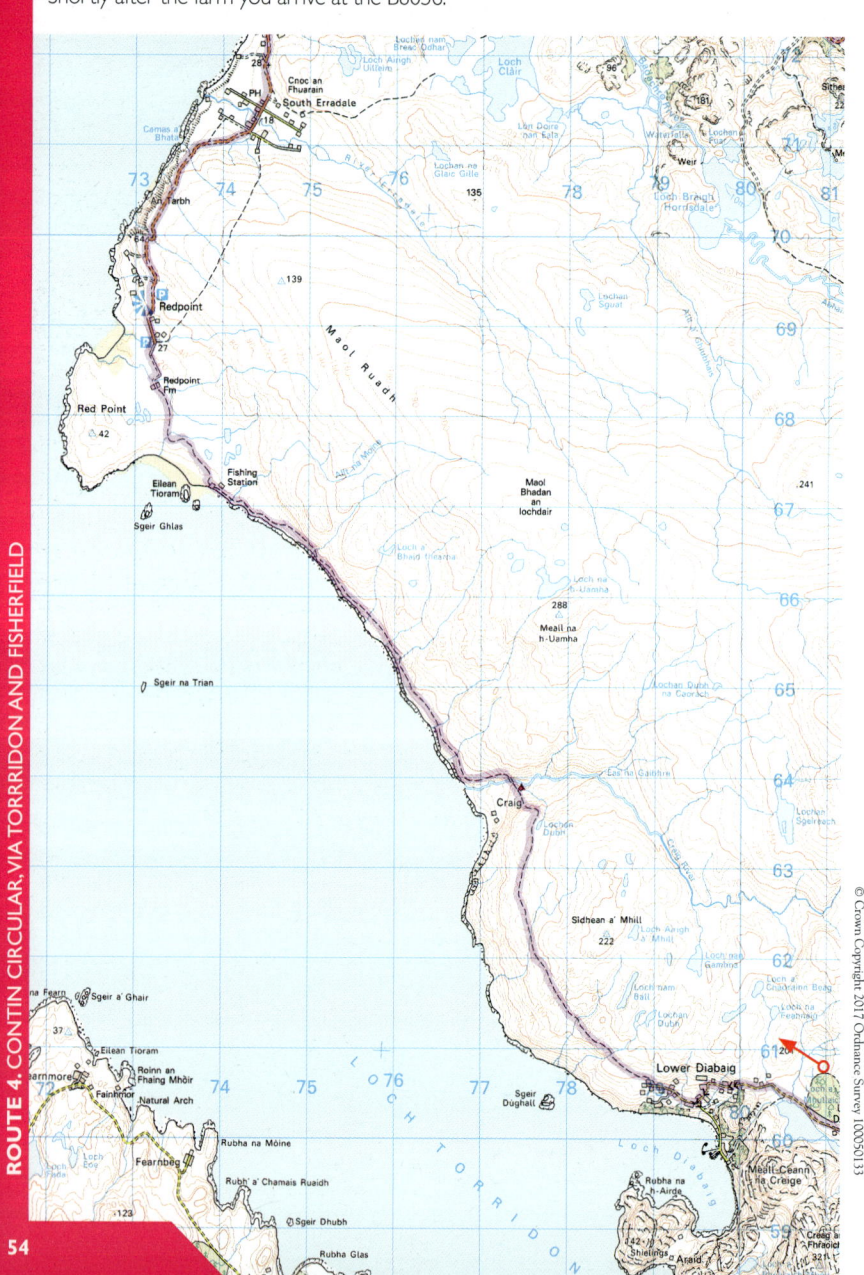

Multi-day routes in northern Britain

Beinn Alligan across upper Loch Torridon.

Follow this as it curves N and E through the hamlets of Badachro and Sheildaig to join the A832. Here turn L and follow this 'main road' N for 300m to Kerrysdale. Just after the bus stop take the first R, E, past buildings, following the well-metalled track as it turns first S and then SE. Follow it for 2.5km until you regain the main road and turn L past Loch Bad an Scalaig. About 2km into the next forest, as the road curves S, ignore tracks to L and R but take the next L in a further 200m. Tarmac soon gives way to a track and then, in 400m turn L, on to tarmac, and follow the track past Slatterdale to the picnic site. At the end of the road carry on along the obvious path signposted to Poolewe. Follow this path N to the A832. Turn R and in a couple of km you are in Poolewe.

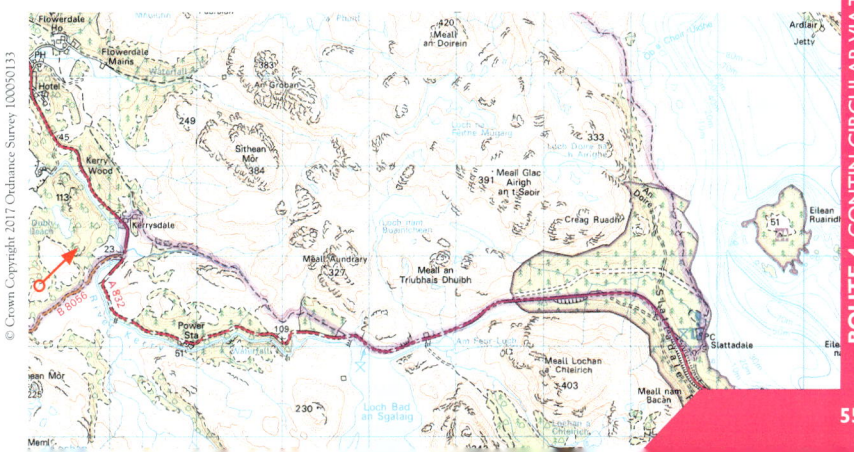

ROUTE 4. CONTIN CIRCULAR, VIA TORRRIDON AND FISHERFIELD

55

Mountain Biking Adventures:

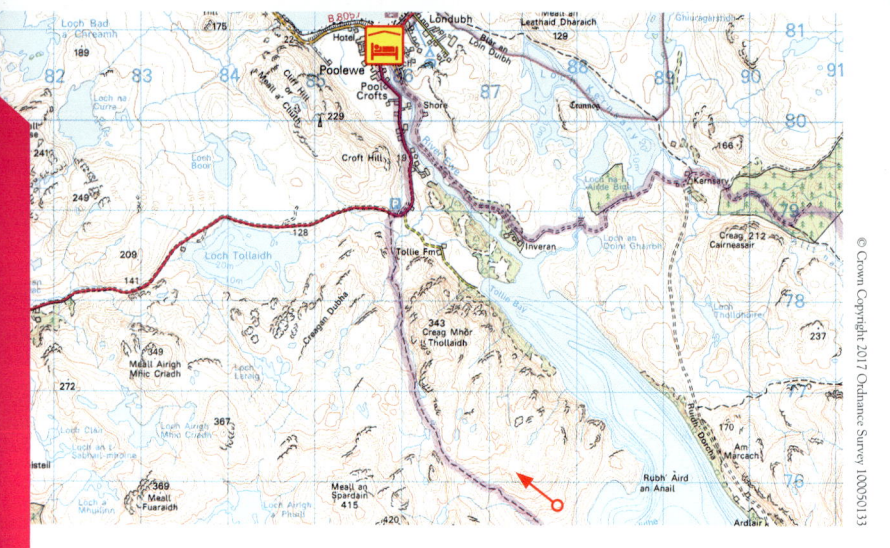

DAY 3.

Start:	Poolewe
Finish:	Dundonnell
Distance:	45km (27.5miles)
Off-road:	35km (22miles) 79%
Ascent:	1328m (4360ft)
Descent:	1328m (4360ft)
Grade:	H3 (crux day)

OVERVIEW

A stunning day through the heart of some of the most sublime mountain scenery to be found anywhere, with, for an aperitif, a 10km piece of unparalleled singletrack. It is, however, remote, and apart from said 10k stretch, unremittingly hard and unforgiving, despite the statistics suggesting the easiest day.

ROUTE

Cross the River Ewe on the northbound A832 and turn immediately R. Pass the church and school and continue SSE on a well-metalled track which curves eastwards past Inveran to Kernsary. Go L here, across the bridge and, having passed in front of the main house bear round to the R and, in about 500m be sure to take the R turn into the forest. The road snakes about a bit inside the forest, but about 200m before the end of the track, on a L hand curve your path continues SE into open country above Fion Loch and many shining lochans. It is

Multi-day routes in northern Britain

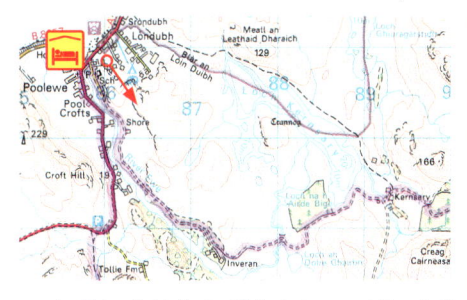

unsurpassed singletrack, narrow, gravelly and well drained, albeit with the occasional harshly spaced drainage channel. Follow it SE until you turn S up, briefly, into Strathan Buidhe, cross a couple of footbridges and turn N again to pick up your original line. Your way curves around the foot of Fionn Loch and between that body of water and Dubh Loch on a narrow causeway.

Now your work really begins. Just before the bothy at Carnmore take the R hand fork and climb steeply E on an excellent stony path. Most will push. From the diagonal climb, the path curves NE into a steep defile, before opening out on to a plateau by a group of lochans, where it is easily rideable for 2km. If the weather is fine, do take time, however, to gawp around you at the nearby Fisherfield giants, A'Mhaigdean and Ruadh Stac Mor and behind them glimpses of Sgurr Ban, Mullach Coire Mhic Fhearchair, and Beinn Tarsuin. At the head of Gleann na Muice Beag the path plunges steeply N.

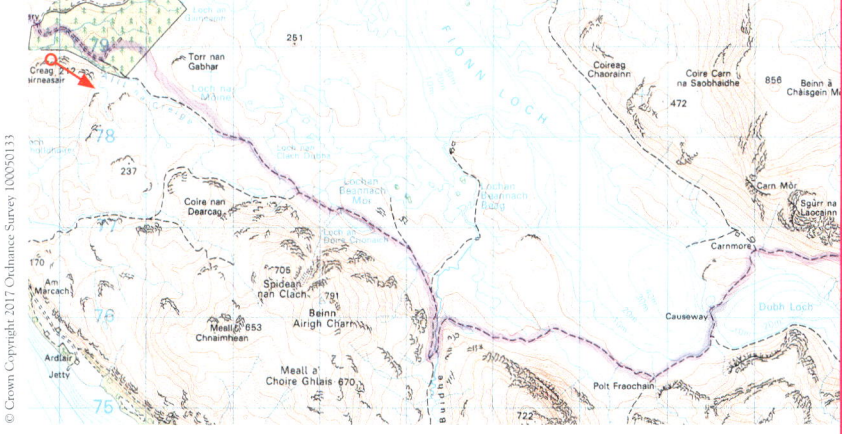

Sublime singletrack to Carnmore. Mist on Beinn Lair.
Photo © Russel Wills (cc-by-sa/2.0)

ROUTE 4. CONTIN CIRCULAR, VIA TORRIDON AND FISHERFIELD

57

Mountain Biking Adventures:

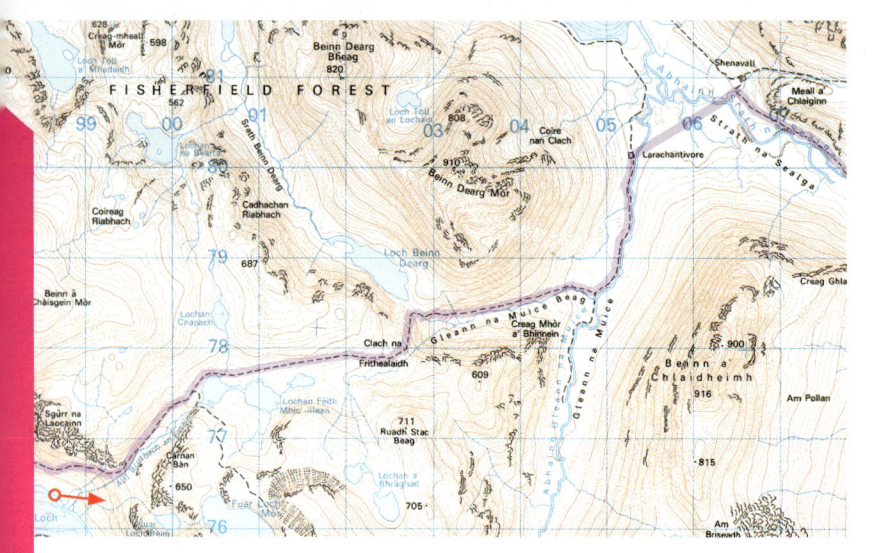

The young and brave may ride the hairpins (not shown on the 1:50,000 map) and the old will use their bikes as expensive zimmers on the rocky descent. The more easterly path along the foot of this glen is more rideable, until it enters Gleann na Muice, where the gradient eases but the track has been chewed up by multi-wheel drive vehicles. If you are reduced to walking use the opportunity to admire An Teallach and its outliers towering above Shenavall. The ground around the head of Loch na Sealga is very boggy, so it's best to leave the path at Larachantivore, wade the river where you can and take a bearing for a point just S of the bothy at Shenavall. It has to be acknowledged that this is boggy too. After about a km ford the Abhainn Strath Na Sealga, again, where you can. In another 200m on the same bearing pickup a mostly rideable path and follow it R, SE to where it turns into a good track at Achneigie and continue in the same direction. As the valley turns S, so does the track, less distinct in places, but then turns steeply N, a stiff climb on a better surface, and carries you over another lochan strewn plateau before plunging into the superb descent towards Dundonnell River.

At the main road turn L and proceed on 4km

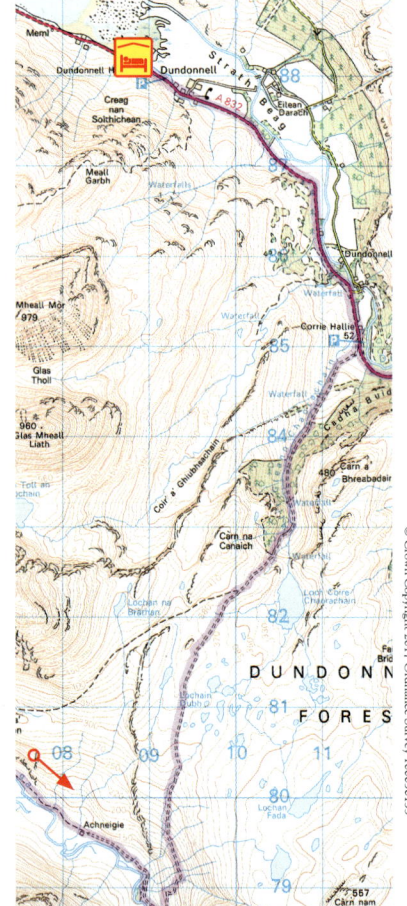

ROUTE 4. CONTIN CIRCULAR, VIA TORRRIDON AND FISHERFIELD

Multi-day routes in northern Britain

to the hotel.

The causeway to Carnmore.
Photo © Russel Wills (cc-by-sa/2.0)

Achneigie, Strath Sealga. Beinn Dearg Mor behind.
Adapted from original Photo © Tom Richardson (cc-by-sa/2.0)

ROUTE 4. CONTIN CIRCULAR, VIA TORRRIDON AND FISHERFIELD

Mountain Biking Adventures:

DAY 4.

Start:	Dundonnell
Finish:	Contin
Distance:	65km (40miles)
Off-road:	37km (23miles) 58%
Ascent:	1357m (4454ft)
Descent:	1357m (4454ft)
Grade:	M3

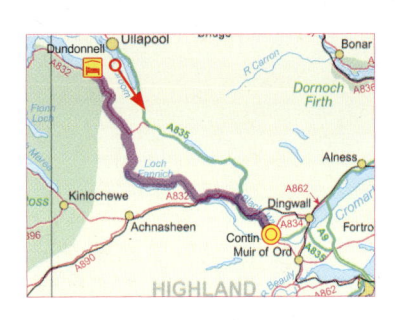

OVERVIEW

Seventeen km of tarmac gain about half the height of an 'interesting' col from the summit of which it is 'downhill all the way' back to your starting point on a challenging path, estate roads, a bit more tarmac and nominated cycleways.

ROUTE

From Dundonnell, retrace your steps SE on the A832 and continue climbing gently from sea level to 332m over 12km. From this high point the road dips slightly for 2km until, on a long left hand curve, there is a track to the R about 200m before the start of a small wooded area. Take it W and, in about 1km, as the track curves to the S, 200m before the boathouse beside the loch, turn L and immediately cross a bridge. The track, not shown on the OS map continues through a small wood and emerges about 150m from a second bridge, over the outflow from Loch a Bhraoin.

A distinct path goes up the hill towards the Allt Breabaig which it later fords (and so do you) and continues with a little riding and some easy pushing up its E bank to a boggy col. We have missed this path after the ford twice, as it rises away from the stream. It is much better, believe me, to find it.

From this bealach between Sgurr Breac and Sgurr nan Clach Geala, a grassy path descends SSW to the head of Loch Fannich. Some have described it as cycleable: we slithered, as it descends into bog in places. In any case, about 1km after joining the loch the path turns to a good track. Follow the track for 12km past Fannich Lodge and slightly beyond the dam before curving SE beside the River Grundie to emerge in a further 7km on to the A832.

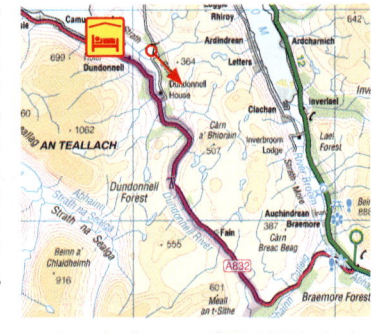

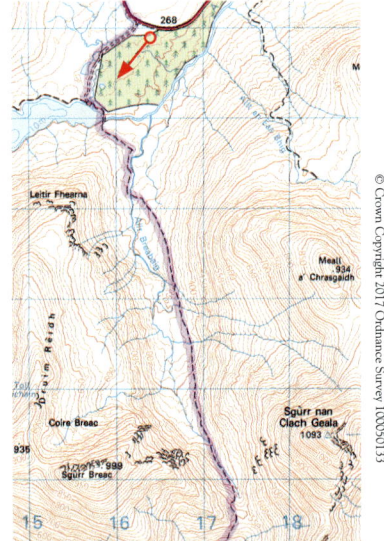

ROUTE 4. CONTIN CIRCULAR, VIA TORRIDON AND FISHERFIELD

© Crown Copyright 2017 Ordnance Survey 100050133

60

Multi-day routes in northern Britain

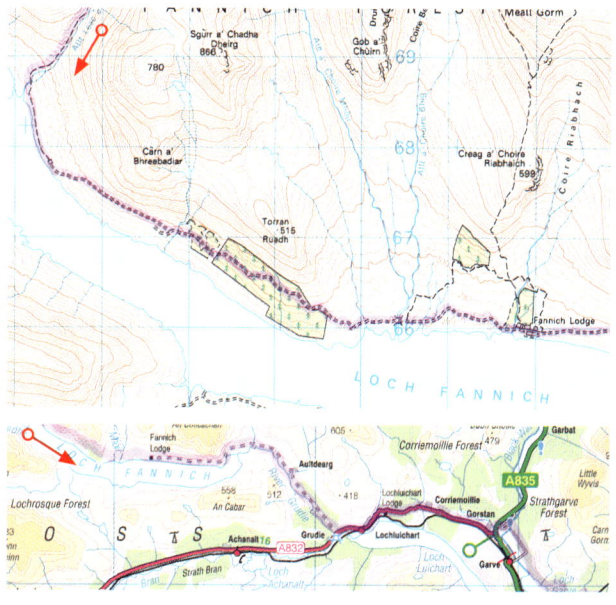

Turn L and follow this road E for about 8km until you arrive at the A835. If you are in a hurry turn R and scurry down the main road to Contin. If you have more time for tracks and byways, turn L, and in about 300m turn R on the tarmac road signposted Gairbh Beag (Little Garve). Go straight on, cross the lovely Little Garve Bridge (now pedestrian only) and turn S on the tarmac road. The tarmac stops just before Strathgarve Lodge. Here, take the rightmost of three tracks and bypass the Lodge being sure to keep L as you emerge from among some industrial scale buildings. Continue through the forest on a good track to the railway at the bottom of Loch Garve. Go R, under the railroad, and follow what is now advertised as a cycle trail until, if you spot the sign, it's worth the slight detour to the R to view Rogie Falls from a footbridge. Return to the track the way you came. If you don't spot it you land up in Contin anyway.

ROUTE 4. CONTIN CIRCULAR, VIA TORRIDON AND FISHERFIELD

61

5. APPLECROSS, MONAR AND TORRIDON CIRCULAR

Total route (days):	Four days			
Start & Finish:	Craig, Achnashellach Forest			
Total Distance:	246km (153miles)			
Total Off-road (%):	45%			
Daily distance (km):	80	64.5	33	68.5
Daily off-road (%):	49%	53%	24%	45%
Ascent:	5973m (19,603ft)			
Crux day grade:	H3			

Multi-day routes in northern Britain

OVERVIEW

A slightly contrived route in order to experience Applecross and the Monar wilderness in one trip. The remoteness and wildness of the latter nicely contrasted by the ancient sanctuary of Applecross. Two hard days with plenty of good off-road followed by two relatively easy days, although after cresting the alpine Bealach na Ba by road on Day 3 you might not agree. The Torridon mountain scenery on Days 3 and 4 is superlative.

DAY 1.

Start:	Craig, Achnashellach Forest
Finish:	Struy Bridge
Distance:	80km, (50miles)
Off-road:	39km, (24miles) 49%
Ascent:	1589m (5215ft)
Descent:	1634m (5363ft)
Grade:	H3

OVERVIEW

A long day, almost across Scotland. The first two thirds is the reverse of Route 3, Day 2. The Gleann Fhiodhaig path is boggy in places, but at least 70% rideable, and the remoteness and big mountain scenery are good. A long road section down Strathconon leads to an uphill pull on tarmac to Orrin Reservoir, then a good track, winding round and down to Strathglass.

INFORMATION

There is no car park at Achnashellach Station, thus we have started the route by a good one, off the road, in the forest opposite the track across the railway, NH040493. See Route 3 for information about Craig. The Conon Valley hydroelectric system has six dams and seven power stations, some of which you pass. The Loch Meig water is diverted to Loch Luichart and used by the eponymous Station; the Orrin Reservoir water travels to the Achilty Station by Loch Achonachie, the last loch before the climb to Orrin. The pipeline you travel alongside, which the track services, obviously feeds the reservoir.

ROUTE

Cross the main road then the railway at the crossing, follow the track E by the line, then cross the river and start the climb through the forest, keeping uphill, L, at any junction. This is all rideable. There is a descent and ascent before the end of the track at Glenuaig Lodge. The start of the path is rocky from storm debris, but thereafter for 9km is mostly rideable, although boggy in places, especially where the vehicle track has taken over from the old path. A good descent to Corrievuic leads to the start of a long road section down Strathconon.

Mountain Biking Adventures:

The descent to Corrievuic, Strathconon.

ROUTE 5. APPLECROSS, MONAR AND TORRIDON CIRCULAR

© Crown Copyright 2017 Ordnance Survey 100050133

64

Multi-day routes in northern Britain

One km past Loch Achonachie turn right up a road, the long climb to Orrin. Take care to fork R and up at Fairburn house, not on the main road turning L. Then L at the 'T' junction, R at the next junction by the house, L after 300m, and at the 'crossroads' turn R then immediately L to descend and cross the river and up, on tarmac, to the reservoir.

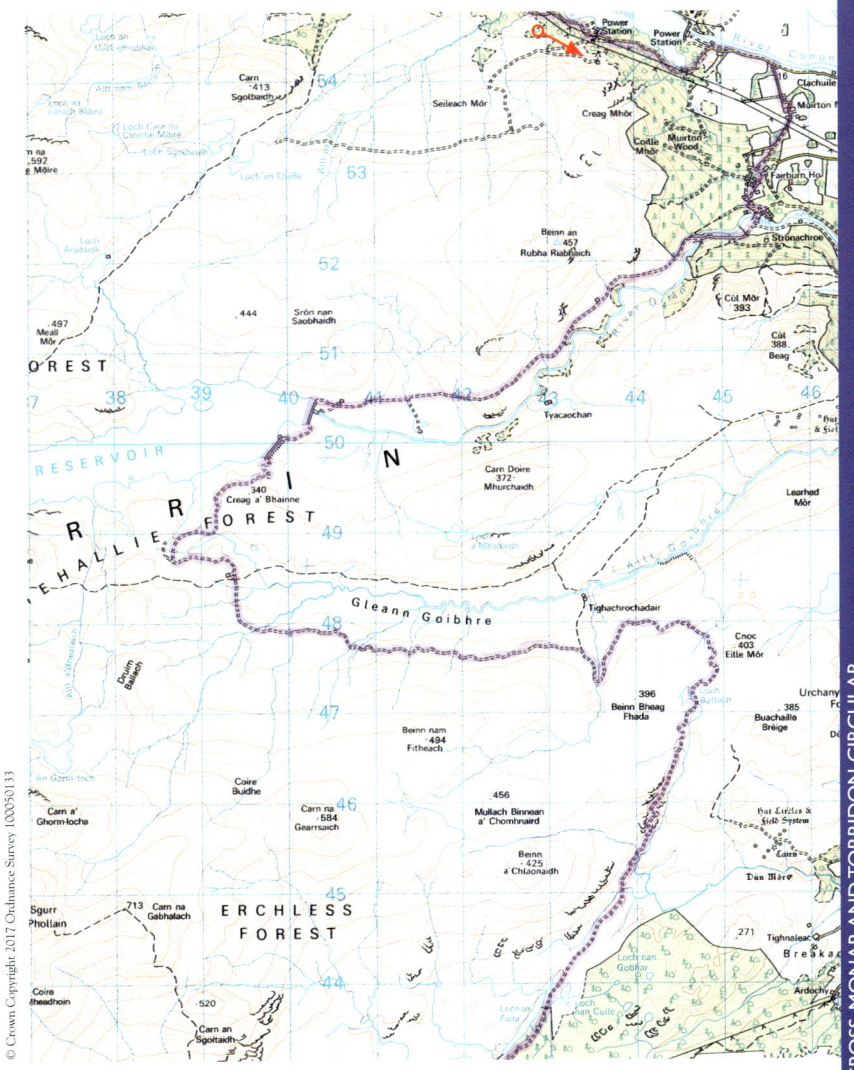

The tarmac ends at the end of the second dam, but the vehicle track is good, climbing again, and you must turn L at the top at a 'T' junction, to follow the pipeline for 5 or 6km. Although a good track, when wet there may be murky deep puddles in every depression, all of which are rideable. Eventually the track curves round to the S and descends intermittently, with at least one high stile to carry over, through mainly harvested plantation down to the main road at Erchless Castle. Turn R for Struy Bridge.

ROUTE 5. APPLECROSS, MONAR AND TORRIDON CIRCULAR

Mountain Biking Adventures:

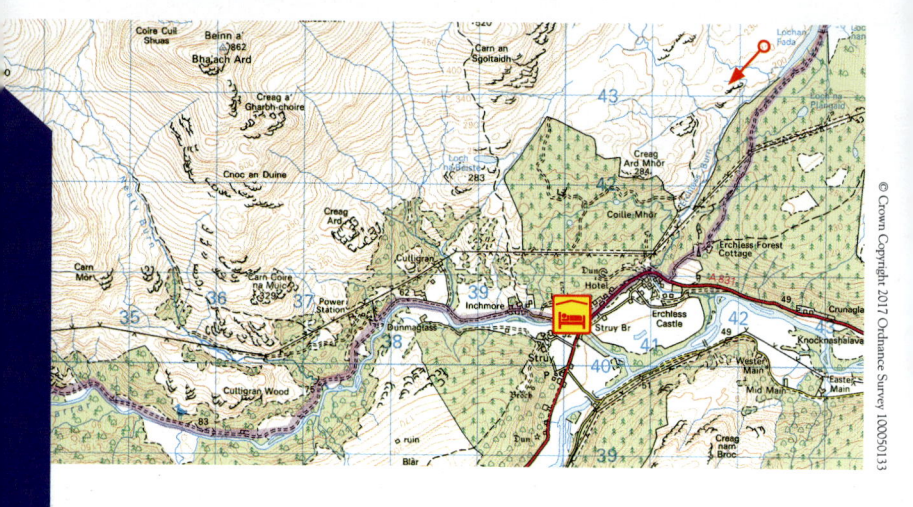

DAY 2.

Start:	Struy Bridge
Finish:	Strathcarron
Distance:	64.5km (38miles)
Off-road:	Off-road 34.5km (21.5miles) 53% of which 5km (3miles) is pathless.
Ascent:	1485m (4871ft)
Descent:	1526m (5004ft)
Grade:	H3

OVERVIEW

A long hard day with 5km bushwhacking; it took us nine hours, but could take longer! There is no escape route and it's wild country once the Monar Dam has been passed. Strathfarrar is lovely, the middle third wilderness, and the ending has recently been messed about by a new hydroelectric scheme, with new bridges to help and a new dirt road, but at the expense of the scenery. A good track descent to finish at the coast.

INFORMATION

The middle part of the day is on an old coffin road from Glenstrathfarrar to Kintail, which kept S past what is now Iron Lodge. The Monar Dam is the largest concrete arch dam in Britain, and is a beautiful horseshoe structure. When completed in 1962 it doubled the length of Loch Monar. Water from it travels by pipe to Deanie Station which you pass en route. A diversion off the route below, rejoining later on, allows a view of its grandeur: from the ford this would

Multi-day routes in northern Britain

add 0.8km and about 120m ascent, but it's all on tarmac. Flows in the rivers are regulated to help Atlantic Salmon on their way, and there are lifts for this at strategic points. Pait Lodge is maintained, and alleged to be a (very remote) holiday home.

Traffic is limited up the glen, but not for you.

ROUTE

At Struy Bridge turn up Glen Strathfarrar and continue through its loveliness on tarmac till 1.3km beyond Braulen Lodge, where an easily rideable ford crosses what is still the River Farrar. The bridge, marked on some maps before that, has gone. A track now curves round to continue W, becoming metalled as the track from the Dam joins, and ends in a cirque by some minor water-works. The path now becomes a push by the stream, then is rideable to a junction: ahead and leftish the path continues over a high col; R, a vehicle track heads for the low col 'twixt Meallans Buidhe and Odhar, but you have to leave the track soon to get there. The walking wisdom is to take the latter, (to the R), a boggy, rough push. Over the col contour W and then descend, NW to NH124391 where a vehicle track leaves the side of the Allt Riabhachain. At present, this is where the footbridge is hidden, not further upstream. The river is strong here, find the bridge. Turn R past it on a rough and boggy vehicle track to Pait Lodge. Passing respectfully through the grounds, pick up the track, L, by the Garbh-uisge, the outflow from An Gead Loch till past the second loch, Loch an Tachdaich. From here, choose a suitable line to cross the boggy ground round the end of the loch towards the junction of Allt Loch Calavie and Allt a Ghraigh-fhear. The greatest difficulty in the rough traverse is the connecting channel between Loch an Tachdaich and Lochan Gobhlach, not wide, but very deep. Cross the Allt Loch Calavie and ascend the flank of the hill beside Allt a Ghraigh-fhear to meet the marked path, a Landrover track. Head W. This made track does not, unfortunately, go further E as shown on the OS Map.

Fording the Farrar.

Mountain Biking Adventures:

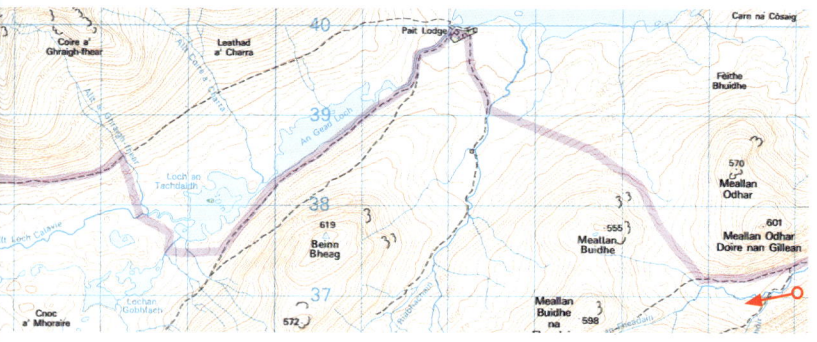

Pathless wilderness above Loch Monar.

Now you're riding again, continue round to and beside Loch Calavie, and down pleasantly to the Black Water, where a ford and a new bridge are being constructed to cross the side stream to access Bendronaig Lodge, a poor man's lodge. The new hydroelectric scheme road straightens out the southerly 'v' by a new bridge, and due to the confusion of new tracks, check you go the right way, up WSW, and up again. The descent has been straightened out in places by the new dirt road, but is welcome. At a new, temporary, machinery park as the strath widens out, take the Attadale House track N of the river, if you can find it, or continue to the main road on a new road to the S of it. A short road section with an unwelcome hill leads to Strathcarron.

Multi-day routes in northern Britain

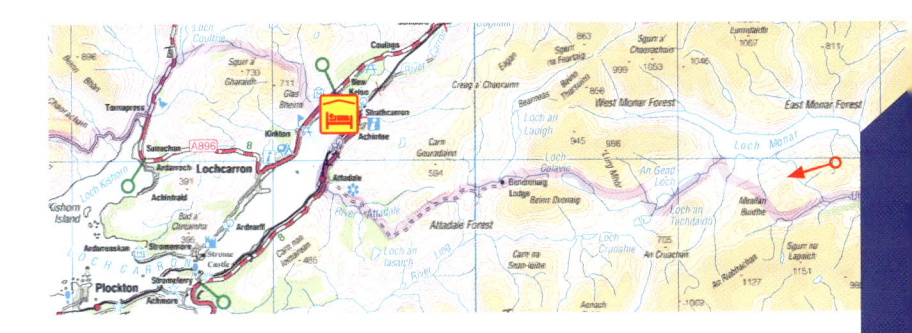

DAY 3.

Start:	Strathcarron
Finish:	Applecross
Distance:	33km (20.5miles)
Off-road:	8km (5miles) 24%
Ascent:	1191m (3910ft)
Descent:	1191m (3910ft)
Grade:	M1

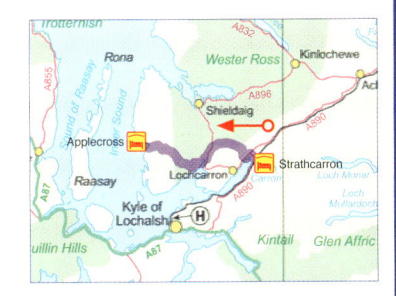

OVERVIEW

The 8km start off the main road is for hardcore adventurers only, and ones who haven't yet done the Bealach na Lice route, which is an alternative and a classic MTB route (see Route 6, Day 2. This would add 24km and 470m of ascent to the given figures). The adventure route involves a 3km, mostly pathless, push to a col, and a slithery descent on a boggy track unless very dry.

The Bealach na Ba is a classic road cycle, and is not as steep as the map indicates.

INFORMATION

The Wester Ross Tourist Guide states that the 8km start from Tullich is an excellent walk! Around the Bealach a Ghlas Chnoic is certainly very scenic. There is a splendid café at Tornapress, shut on Mondays. The Applecross Hotel is eternally busy, book meals well ahead, and if accommodation is not available there, an exceptional Hostel, Hartfield House, is 2.4km away, used to filthy bikers and, as an extra, an outstanding café and restaurant, Applecross Walled Garden, is en route to it. That garden is over 300 years old, restoration after disuse started in 2001.

The Bealach na Ba, (Pass of the Cattle), was a route for cattle from the peninsula to the mainland markets. It is the largest ascent, 626m, of any road in the UK, and is on the Motorcyclist's popular 'North Coast 500' route, so be careful.

Mountain Biking Adventures:

ROUTE

Take the main road across the Strath and turn L on the A896. In the wood turn R to Tullich, and as the track swings R a marked path carries straight on. This continues, marked but unrideable, round the hamlet and, by the river, becomes a bit more definite. Now you will see later a track on the opposite hillside which ends at about NG916440. This would help progress, although I cannot satisfactorily tell you how to get to it. Passage back across the river at the top end is possible by a narrow concrete dam. The 'path', disappears often, and later on does not really exist. Press on, seeking the best line, noting the true bealach is to the N, away from the cliffs on the L. Near the obvious quartzite cliff at the bealach the path starts, a boggy vehicle track. Slither down 2km to where a bridge (not shown on OS Map) crosses the Allt a Giuthais. Cross it and a tempting 50m of good track over this leads to 1.5km of horrible squelchy forest track, before a very good descent on made track at the end.

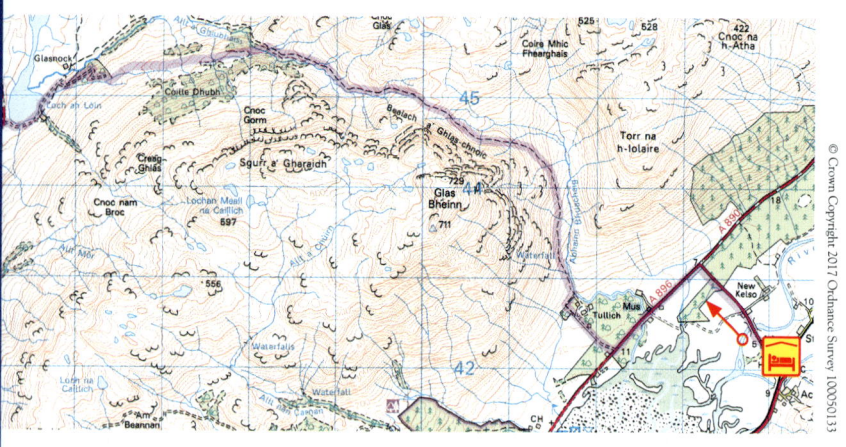

A tarmac track then leads to the main road and a short ride S to a welcome café at Tornapress. The Classic Bealach now beckons, 9.5km to the summit, a true alpine pass, but nowhere near as bad as the Lakeland passes. Wind and motorbikes are the only worries; we were blown off at one point. A similar distance of descent brings you down to the sea and the sylvan pastures of another world.

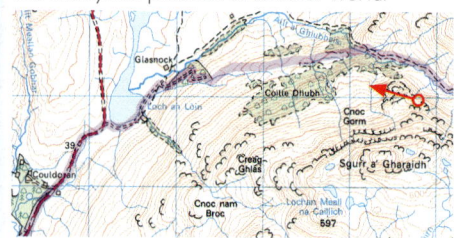

Multi-day routes in northern Britain

DAY 4.

Start:	Applecross
Finish:	Craig
Distance:	68.5km (42.5miles)
Off-road:	30.5km (19miles) 45%
Ascent:	1708m (5608ft)
Descent:	1606m (5272ft)
Grade:	M1

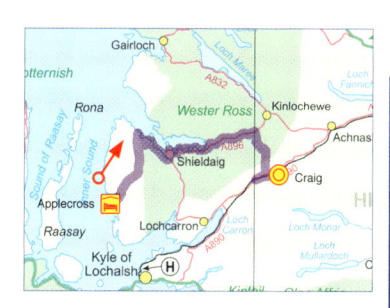

OVERVIEW

The stats suggest this could be the hardest day: it's not, and the excellent and scenic riding more than makes up for them. The superb single track leads north to Kenmore, where you join the switchback Applecross Coastal Road. A short off road approaching Torridon relieves the road soreness, but road continues up the grand Torridon Glen, and then a good track takes you over a relatively low pass and down to finish.

INFORMATION

Applecross looks and feels like a sanctuary, which it was, as Scotland's second most important Christian centre was established here around AD675, where the Clachan church is today. If you have time, a Heritage centre is close by the church. The Kenmore track is an old coffin road for the northern Applecross community to allow burials at the church. It has cairns and milestones, maintained by a local Trust.

The Northern Coastal Road was not finished till 1975.

Refreshments exist at Shieldaig, the Torridon Inn which you pass right by, and the Torridon café and stores, although that is 1.2km off route.

The Coulin Estate track to the station was made for access to it, but not open as a right of way till 1930.

ROUTE

Take the road N till it swings L, then carry straight on towards Applecross House, which is bypassed on the L. Across the river turn up the glen, firstly on a road, then track for 2.5km, where a good singletrack starts. A push up a gorge leads to a superb 8km ride over a rock and lochan strewn landscape, always with the lovely West Coast vista lurking over the next brow. The Northern Coastal Road then takes you on a roller coaster course to the A896, where you continue L past Shieldaig and a large enclosed bay. Just past the River Balgy turn L up a track, which leads you in and out by the coast, with Liathach looming ahead, and in 5km to the Torridon Inn. Back on the main, but singletrack, road, ride up the Torridon Glen in awe of your majestic companion, Liathach, till past the Loch Clair Wood, turn R to Coulin Lodge. Follow the track across the river at the loch end, and past the lodge on its R, continuing on the good track, tarmac till past Coulin, then improved (2016) for hydroelectric up the Easan Dorcha Glen. Keep on up the glen by the River Coulin, but make sure to turn

Mountain Biking Adventures:

L over the river just before a bifurcation. The climb to the col becomes somewhat rutted. As you're doing this classic ride the wrong way round, stop at the top to look back at the contrasting (Torridonian) quartzite front of Beinn Eighe, before descending through recently harvested forest easily to the station and a short road section back to Craig.

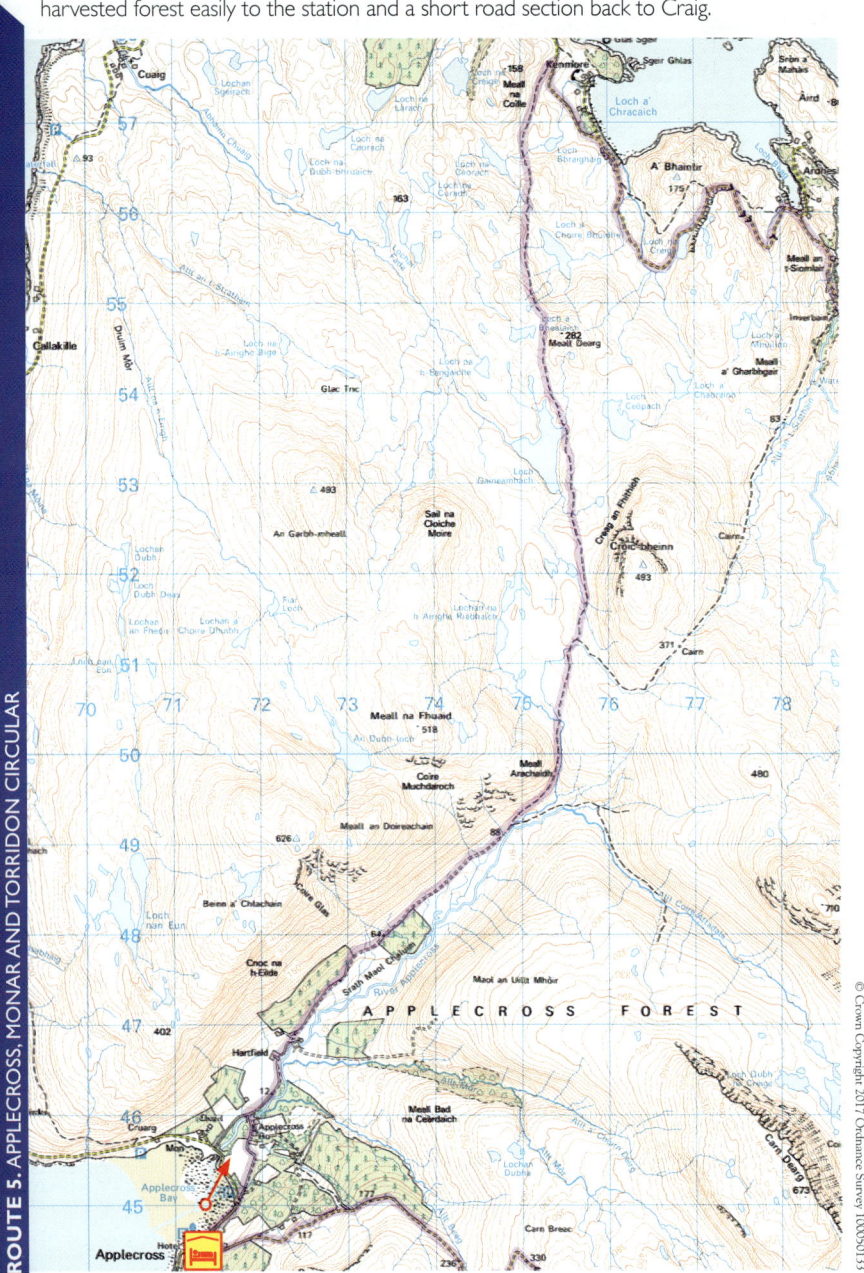

Multi-day routes in northern Britain

The Kenmore single track.

The Bealach na Ba road.

ROUTE 5. APPLECROSS, MONAR AND TORRIDON CIRCULAR

6. AFFRIC CIRCULAR VIA KINTAIL AND TORRIDON

Total route (days):	Four days			
Start & Finish:	Tomich, Strathglass			
Total Distance:	229.5km (142miles)			
Total Off-road (%):	56%			
Daily distance (km):	46	51.5	77	55
Daily off-road (%):	90%	61%	50%	34%
Ascent:	5195m (17,050ft)			
Crux day grade:	H1			

Multi-day routes in northern Britain

OVERVIEW

Beautiful Affric leads to the grandeur of Kintail, then on to further grandeur in Torridon via one of the best descents in Scotland. Some wilderness with possible adventure around Loch Fannich, then eastern moors back to the start.

DAY 1.

Start:	Tomich, Strathglass
Finish:	Shiel Bridge, Kintail
Distance:	46km (28.5miles)
Off-road:	*41km (25.5miles) 90%*
Ascent:	1028m (3374ft)
Descent:	1107m (3632ft)
Grade:	M3

OVERVIEW

A 90 percent off-road day on one of the 'great cross country routes in Scotland'. Forest tracks lead up and over to the lovely Glen Affric and the remote Alltbeithe Youth Hostel. Mixed singletrack then leads through a magnificent big mountain flanked pass and gorge, and a track takes you down to the sea.

INFORMATION

After the initial forest plantation, you pass through one of the original Caledonian Forest remnants, of Scots Pine, Birch, Rowan and Juniper. 'Trees for Life', a charity aiming to protect and restore this Caledonian Forest in alliance with several other organisations, works here. We heard of replanting and fencing areas west of Alltbeithe nearly ten years ago, when, it has to be said, the glen was bare and lifeless, so there's hope for the future here.

ROUTE

Go SW from Tomich and branch right to cross the river. The road soon becomes track. Two km later turn sharp right back on yourself and start a long climb, into the forest and up W after a 'T' junction. After the summit a short descent leads to Loch Beinn a Mheadhoin. Continue by the loch on the good track through woodland, then by Loch Affric, soon climbing a little way above it.

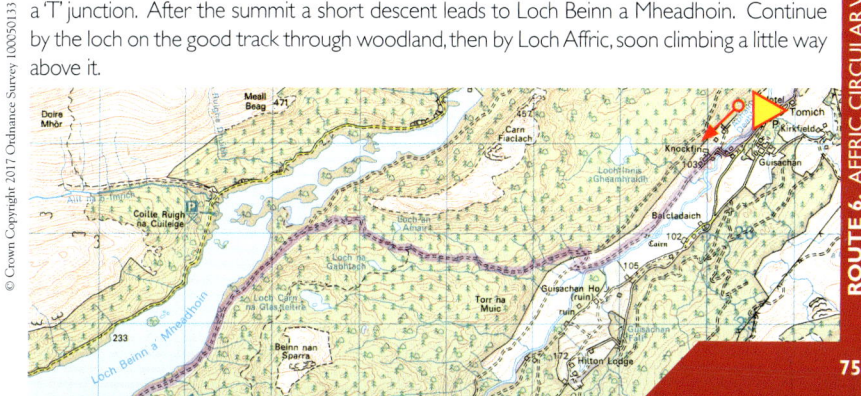

Mountain Biking Adventures:

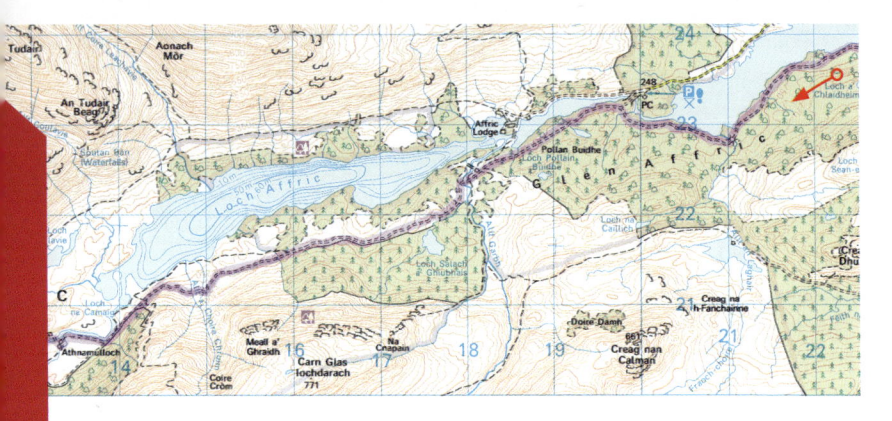

At Achnamulloch, cross the footbridge and press on to the remote Youth Hostel at Alltbeithe, on a track which deteriorates but is passable for Landrovers. After a chat and, possibly, tea, keep on the double track N of the river, cross the Allt Beithe Garbh by footbridge and then either ford the wide, but manageable, Allt Gleann Gniomhaidh, or divert 200m upstream to a bridge.

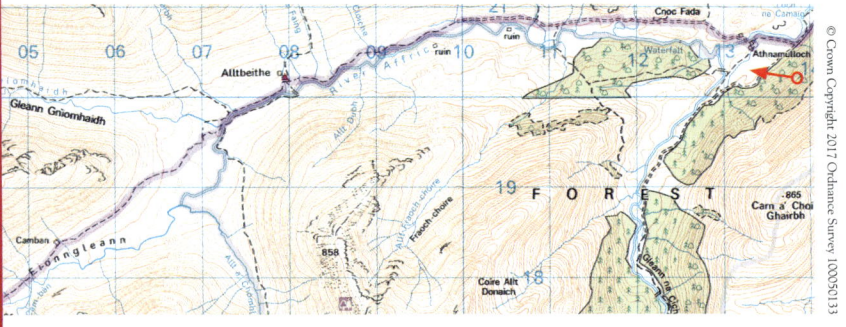

© Crown Copyright 2017 Ordnance Survey 100050133

The path is now singletrack all the way to Glenlicht House, passing Camban bothy, through big mountain country, Beinn Fhada to the N and the 'Brothers' then the 'Five Sisters' ridge opposite. The going is reasonable until around the impressive gorge of the Allt Grannda, when it becomes rough and rocky, and with a 300m descent.

ROUTE 6. AFFRIC CIRCULAR VIA KINTAIL AND TORRIDON

Approaching the Allt Grannda gorge, the Five Sisters behind.

Multi-day routes in northern Britain

As the valley opens out go S over two bridges and turn R to get to Glenlicht House, which is maintained and served by a good Landrover track, which takes you down Gleann Lichd to Morvich. The minor road loop leads L to the main road and Shiel Bridge.

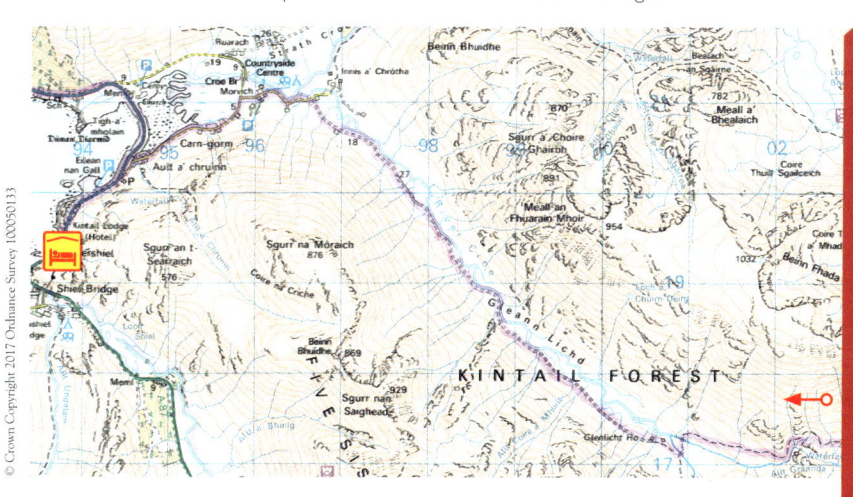

DAY 2.

Start:	Shiel Bridge
Finish:	Torridon
Distance:	51.5km (32miles)
Off-road:	31.5km (19.5miles) 61%
Ascent:	1747m (5735ft)
Descent:	1747m (5735ft)
Grade:	H1

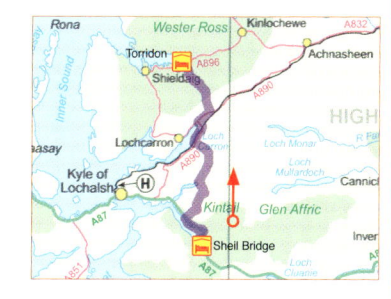

OVERVIEW

From sea to sea thrice! The highest and hardest ascent first, followed by a gentler middle with riding, ending with probably the best through route and descent, both scenically and to ride, in the country.

INFORMATION

Refreshments at Attadale gardens café, as you hit Loch Carron, and the Strathcarron Hotel.

ROUTE

Head round the head of Loch Duich on the A87 and fork R on to a minor road 700m after the Inerinate filling station. Cross the river and head up a steep hill, just after which

ROUTE 6. AFFRIC CIRCULAR VIA KINTAIL AND TORRIDON

77

Mountain Biking Adventures:

turn sharp R on a track, and over a locked gate by a building. There is now a 430m ascent to the pass over to Camas-Luinie, starting with this good track, which becomes a path a couple of hundred metres before the Allt a'Mhaim. The path is now a push to the col, where it is imperceptible but allegedly cairned; it appears again to the W of the Allt Mor. Initially some is rideable, but this deteriorates, and it is quicker to take the shortest route, descending to Camas-Luinie. Head N on the road, cross the River Ling and turn R up the glen on the track to Nonach Lodge. The path starts beyond a large out-building. Keep to the riverside until after the footbridge over the first major tributary, when climbing starts, heading for the forest E of Loch an Lasaich. A power line accompanies you on your R. The ascent is 230m from here, but the path is now surprisingly good.

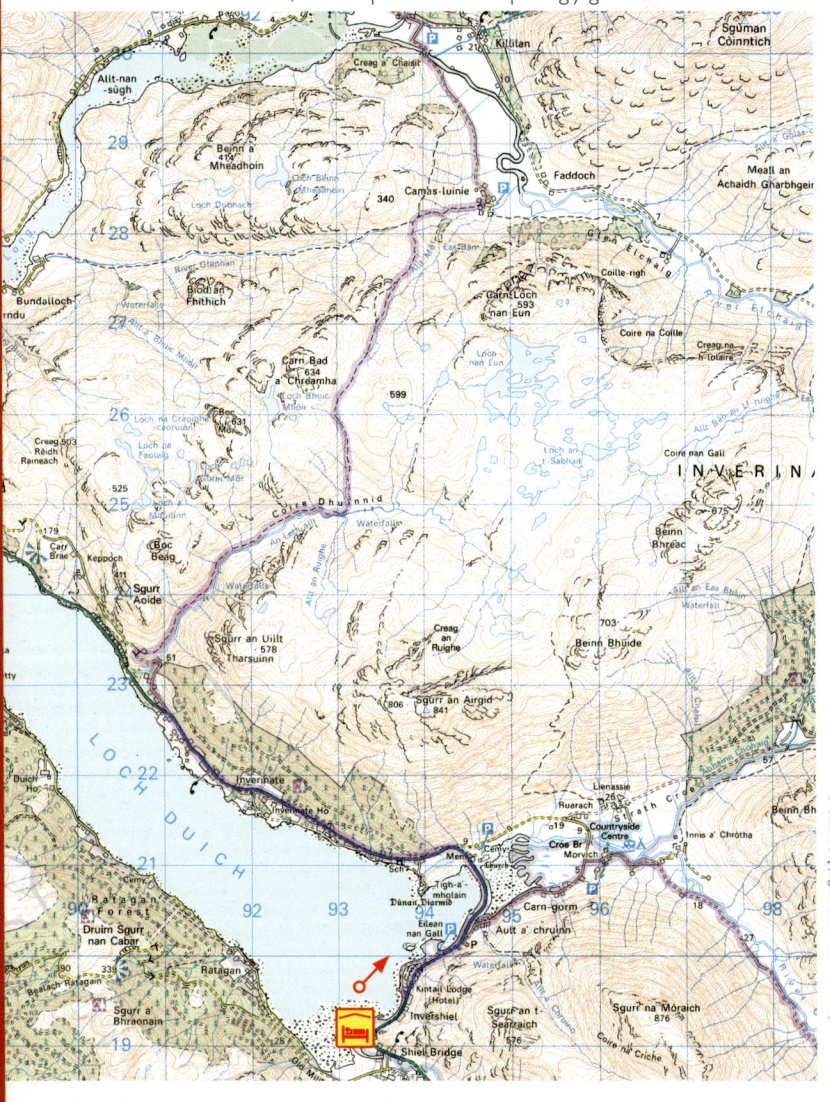

Multi-day routes in northern Britain

A forest track soon starts, keep going N then NNE, joining a large hydroelectric access track at NG957366. Descend to Attadale and then R on the A890 to Strathcarron.

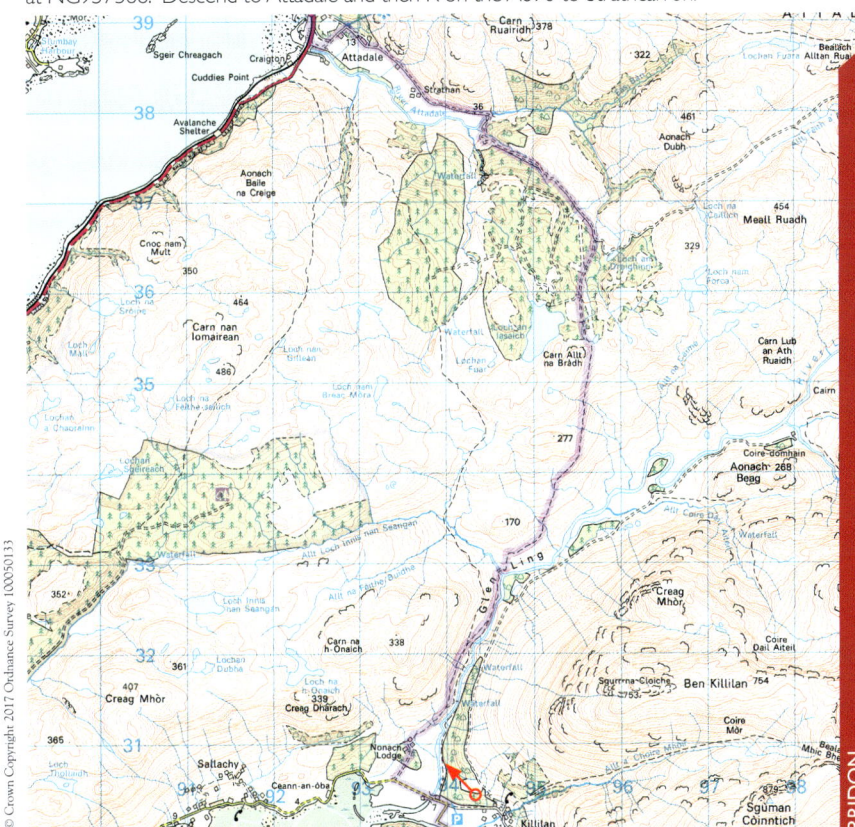

Continue on the main road over the River Carron and turn R up the Strath. At Coulags turn off L up a track signed 'Public Right of Way to Torridon', then L again on to a path before a cattle grid. You are now on one of the best routes in Scotland, for walking or biking: a good 13.5km singletrack all the way, with an ascent of 390m, amongst the rocks and hills of ancient brown/pink Torridonian sandstone and quartzite. Only the steep last bit to the Bealach na Lice requires a push for mortals, allowing further scenic appreciation. You might find it hard to believe on crossing the Alltan Odhar, quite near Coulags, that I was once almost carried away here by water up to my chest. The descent is beyond superlatives, a constructed path to start, curving round Loch an Eoin, stepping stones, huge sandstone slabs to career over, and a technical steeper finish to Annat.

ROUTE 6. AFFRIC CIRCULAR VIA KINTAIL AND TORRIDON

Mountain Biking Adventures:

Torridonian sandstone slab on the descent to Torridon.

ROUTE 6. AFFRIC CIRCULAR VIA KINTAIL AND TORRIDON

© Crown Copyright 2017 Ordnance Survey 100050133

Multi-day routes in northern Britain

Final descent to Loch Torridon.

DAY 3.

Start:	Torridon
Finish:	Contin
Distance:	77km (48miles)
Off-road:	38km (23miles) 50%
Ascent:	1280m (4200ft)
Descent:	1280m (4200ft)
Grade:	M3

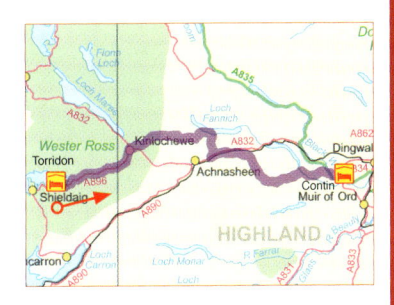

OVERVIEW

An inevitable anti-climax in terms of riding after yesterday, although scenically the initial road up Glen Torridon, around Kinlochewe, and of the Fannichs over Loch Fannich are top class. The Lochrosque Estate, traversed north of the A832, is secretive and unwelcoming. There is no entry regarding stalking in the 'Heading for the Scottish Hills' website (Fionn Bheinn), see the Access section. This means we cannot find out whether, from August to February, we can act responsibly in regard to any stalking. The decision is yours, therefore, whether to go through this wild, and in the case of Strath Chrombaill, somewhat dreary, land with a high locked gate at the end to negotiate. A 200m climb on good track and 17km on road finish.

INFORMATION

Kinlochewe is so named as Loch Maree used to be Loch Ewe. From the 1600s iron ore was sent from England by sea to be smelted near here, as charcoal from the extensive woods was available. The woods have mainly gone as a result. As a major droving route

ROUTE 6. AFFRIC CIRCULAR VIA KINTAIL AND TORRIDON

81

Mountain Biking Adventures:

passed this way there has always been an inn, and now a shop and post office, and there also used to be inns at Babinluchie and Dalnacroich, as that route was also a drovers' route. Note: there is no road access over the Achonachie Dam.

ROUTE

Take the road up Glen Torridon to Kinlochewe, through magnificent scenery of layered Torridonian sandstone. Turn R and soon L after the Lodge, to Incheril. Through the car park and past the Great War Memorial turn R on the track to the Heights of Kinlochewe, where fork R, cross two bridges on the track and continue till it ends, just before Leckie.

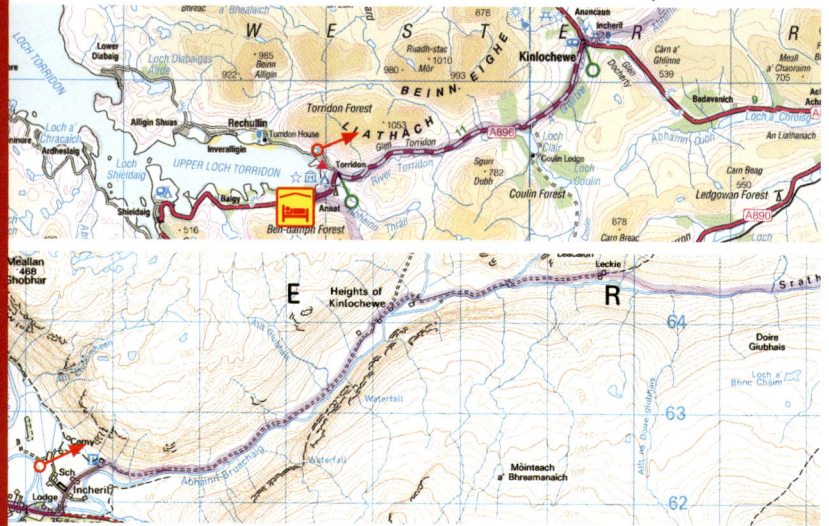

Head towards the river and follow it by an old fence, on a possible path. Cross the wide but usually shallow river after the Allt a' Chlaiginn has joined, and bushwhack up to the good pipeline track. This leads to Loch Fannich, for a short while beside it, before heading S over the hill and descending nearly 300m to Strath Bran. Just before the road a high gate or, easier, an adjacent wooden fence may have to be negotiated.

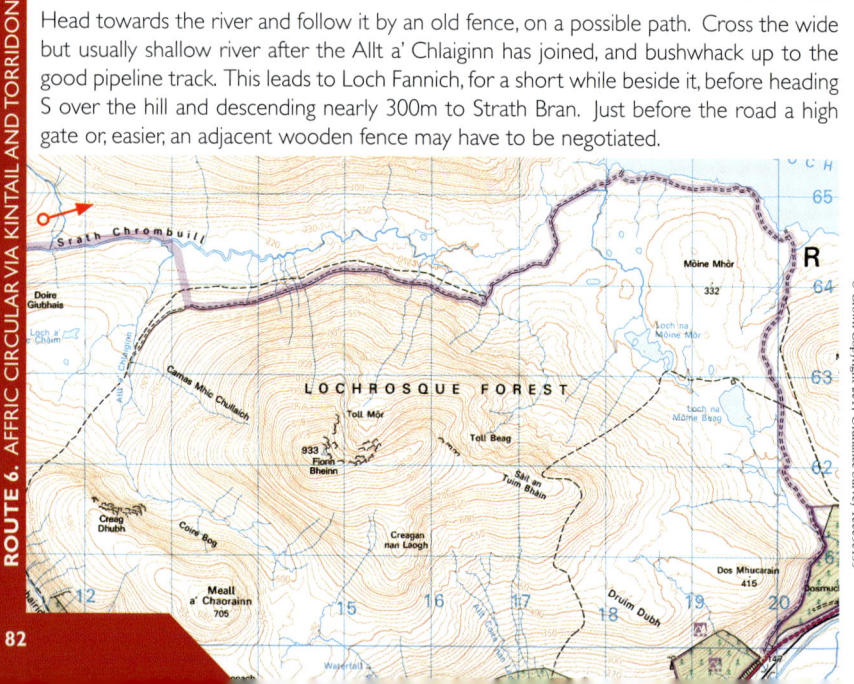

Multi-day routes in northern Britain

Track S from Loch Fannich; The Fannichs behind.

Continue E on the A832 for a long 3km, then turn R on a track over the railway and river. Turn L and go through a forest on a track which is, initially, quite interesting, then straightforward. Keep on to the ruins of Badinluchie, fording the usually quiet burn. A ruined bridge is up stream, and a footbridge is shown on Google Earth near the loch if in spate conditions. A good track now climbs nearly 200m over the col, and descends SE through a forest. Turn sharp R near the road, by a group of huts. Turn L down Strathconon on the minor road for 6.5km and turn over the Loch Meig Dam. Turn R again after crossing the River Conon and continue past Loch Achilty to Contin.

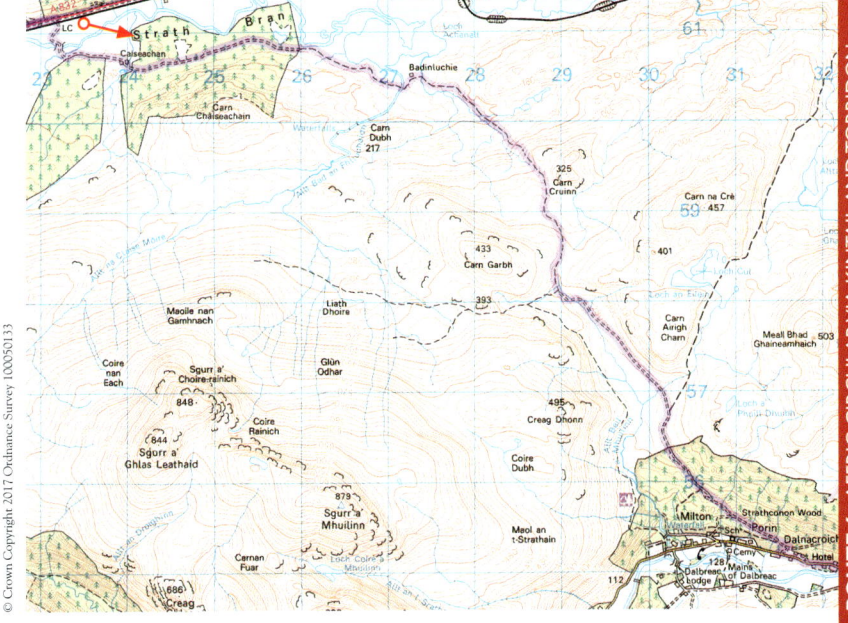

ROUTE 6. AFFRIC CIRCULAR VIA KINTAIL AND TORRIDON

Mountain Biking Adventures:

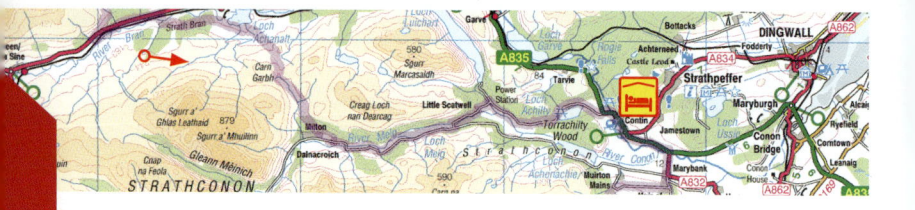

DAY 4.

Start:	Contin
Finish:	Tomich
Distance:	55km (32.5miles)
Off-road:	18.5km (11.5miles) 34%
Ascent:	1140m (3640ft)
Descent:	1038m (3408ft)
Grade:	E2

OVERVIEW

A fair climb on tarmac to Orrin Dam, then a good track traversing the moor and with a good descent to Strathglass, and 18km home on road. Information as for Route 5.

ROUTE

Head S down the A835 and turn R over the Moy Bridge to Marybank. Continue up the hill and turn first R on a straight road to Fairbairn house, just after which turn L and join the course of Route 5, Day 1 (p65), continuing down Strathglass at Erchless Castle. It is pleasanter to turn soon after over the river and continue to Tomich on the E bank on a minor road.

ROUTE 6. AFFRIC CIRCULAR VIA KINTAIL AND TORRIDON

© Crown Copyright 2017 Ordnance Survey 100050133

84

Multi-day routes in northern Britain

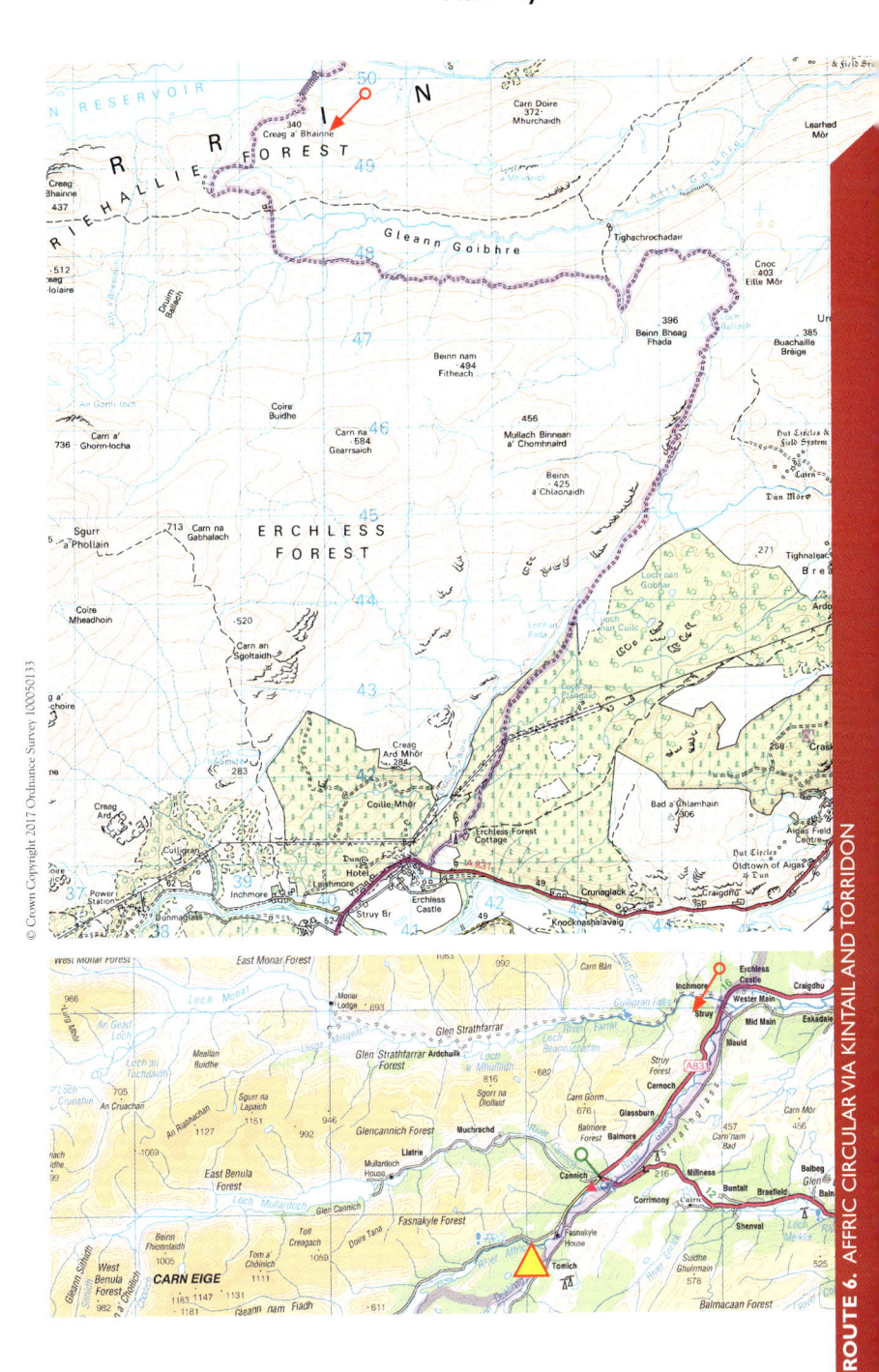

ROUTE 6. AFFRIC CIRCULAR VIA KINTAIL AND TORRIDON

85

7. SCOTTISH COAST TO COAST 1: GLENELG TO DUNDEE

Total route (days):	Four days			
Start:	Glenelg			
Finish:	Dundee			
Total Distance:	341.5km (212miles)			
Total Off-road (%):	49%			
Daily distance (km):	77.5	80.5	92.5	91
Daily off-road (%):	38%	48%	79%	29%
Ascent:	7264m (25,021ft)			
Crux day grade:	H2			

Multi-day routes in northern Britain

OVERVIEW

This is a monstrous route that does not follow the line of least resistance and should not be undertaken lightly. It is presented as a four-day tour. It may be judicious to break it up with an extra day or two. There are several places where a road alternative will relieve tired legs without spoiling the route.

It begins in Glenelg on the Sound of Sleet overlooking Skye with a rough and mountainous traverse to Kinloch Horn followed by a minor road through dramatic scenery by Loch Quoich and Glen Garry, before tracks and forest roads deliver you to Fort Augustus. From here the Corrieyairack Pass takes you to Strathspey. The third day does not boast a high pass, and you have no need to put a foot down, but it still tops up to 90km and about 2000m of ascent to take you to Ballater via Rothiemurchus, Abernethy, Glen Avon, Loch Builg and Glen Gairn. Finally, you pass over the apex of the Brechin Angus Hills to Glen Doll and Glenn Clova before tootling out to the Firth of Tay at Dundee. There is a final off-road coda over the Sidlaw hills, should you choose it.

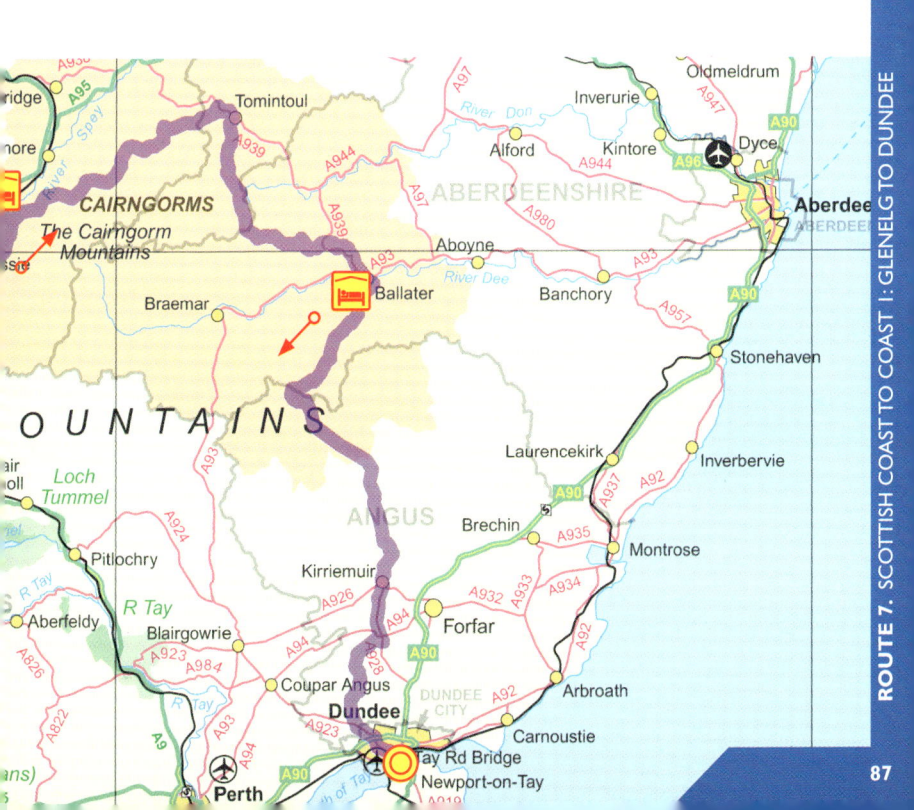

Mountain Biking Adventures:

DAY 1.

Start:	Glenelg
Finish:	Fort Augustus
Distance:	77.5km (48.5miles)
Off-road:	29.5km (18.5miles) 38%
Ascent:	2053m (6741ft)
Descent:	2043m (6705ft)
Grade:	H2

OVERVIEW
See the whole route overview.

ROUTE
From Glenelg take the unclassified road S along the coast to Eilanreach. As the road curves R to cross the river to the village, bear L for Glen Beag. Tootle up the tarmac being careful to take in the two magnificently preserved ancient Brochs, Dun Telve and Dun Trodden, on the R and L respectively, about 2.5km in. The tarmac gives way to a well-metalled track just before the farmstead of Balvraid. In a further 2.5km, about 200m after a patch of forest on your R enclosed by a bend in the Abhein a Ghlibbe Bhig turn R, S, on a grassy track (shown as a path on the map). Ford the small burn and head SE, gawping up at Ben Sgritheal before curving round to ESE and joining the power lines which will be your travelling companions for the next 30 or 40km.

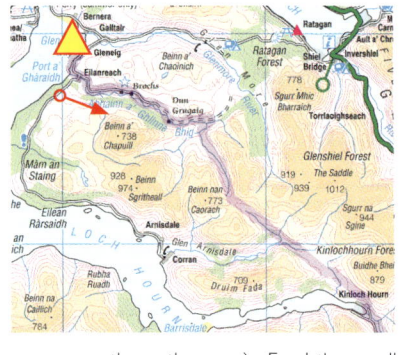

Glen of the Abhain Dubh Lochan, Bealach Aoidhdailean centre.

Multi-day routes in northern Britain

Over the next 2km the track deteriorates to path, though some of it can be cycled, until you are in the head of the corrie where you face a steep push up to Bealach Aoidhdailean and the direction turns SE. The path is indistinct at the col, but stick to the pylons on the L side of the burn and it will quickly become apparent, if not cycleable. At a 'T' junction just before a lightly wooded area, turn R where the track improves considerably. Follow it, consistently SE, to Kinloch Hourn.

If you want to avoid this very rough section, continue on the unclassified coast road S from Eilanreach and round to Arnisdale in Loch Hourn (you will not be disappointed by the mountain and island views, or climbing). Just after the village turn L on a good track and follow it up Glen Arnisdale. Though shown on the map as a path after the first 2km, it remains a good track. You will be obliged to ford the Arnisdale just before the Dubh Lochs but you will soon find yourself beneath the pylons and on the right track.

The path is stony and rough until, after the final rise, a push for most, you can see your way straight down to Kinloch Hourn. Watch out along the way for glimpses of the Rough Bounds of Knoydart across Loch Hourn. Descend with enthusiasm – you have earned it – to the edge of and down through the forest.

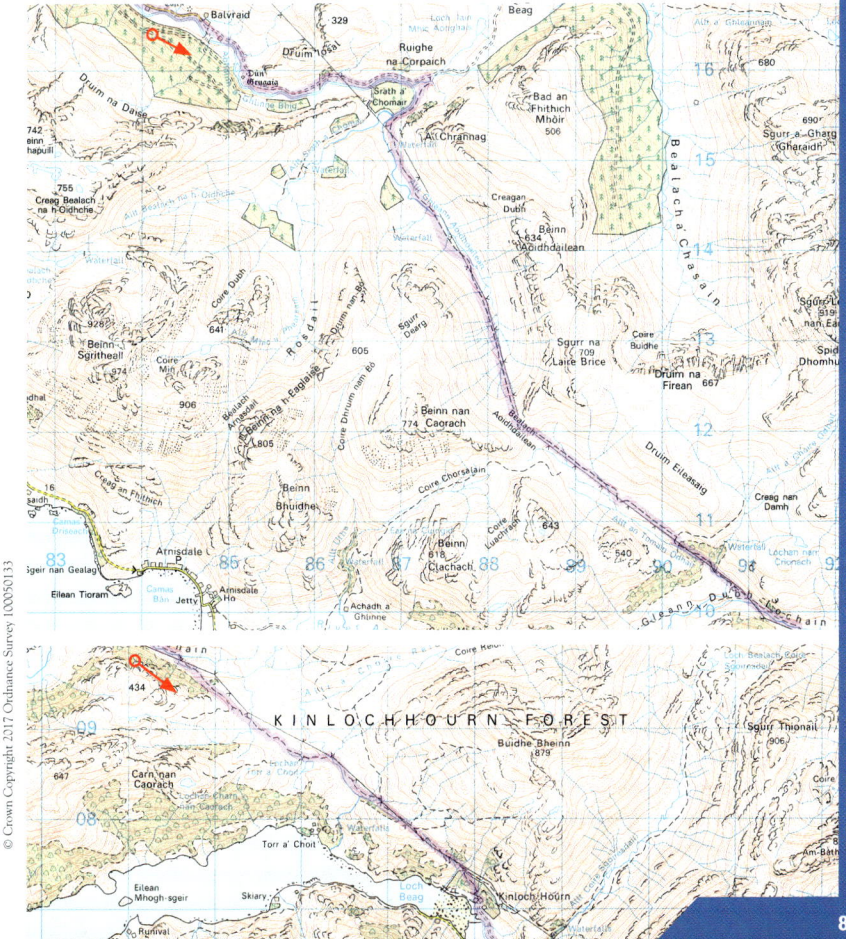

Mountain Biking Adventures:

View over Loch Hourn to Ladhar Bheinn.

At the foot of the forest take the track SE to a bridge and cross it. The tearooms are about 500m to the W on the tarmac road.

The route now follows the unclassified road SE, then E for about 30km, past Loch Quoich and further potential refreshment at the Tomdoun Hotel. Halfway along Loch Garry, you join the A87.

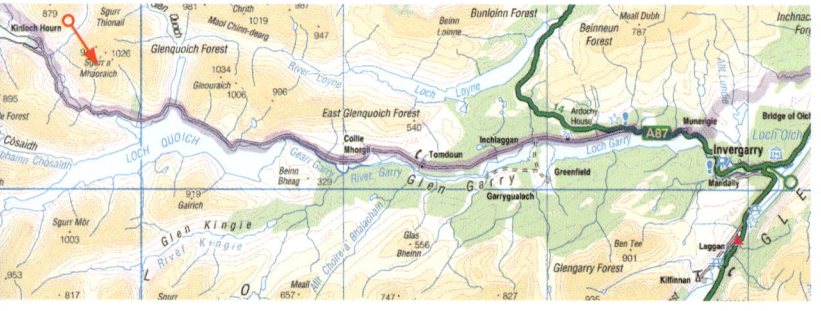

After 2km take a L turn signposted for Leachan Dubha and follow to the R. Keep straight on through the few houses at Munerigie and, as the road deteriorates from tarmac to grassy track, through the eponymous wood. On emerging from the wood turn L, almost back on yourself and take the mostly distinct track N and then NE around Loch Lundie. Go straight on at the junction with the track coming up the other side of the loch and stick with the improving road as it goes first E then NE and then E again. The track parallels just S of Invervigar Burn, itself the boundary of a large forested area, and forks just before a large grassy clearing. Go L, cross the burn by bridge and follow the forest track avoiding a R turn until, in 2km you come to the Burial Ground.

Go L, then immediately R, around a rectangular walled clearing. The tarmac road takes you, in 4km, to Fort Augustus.

Multi-day routes in northern Britain

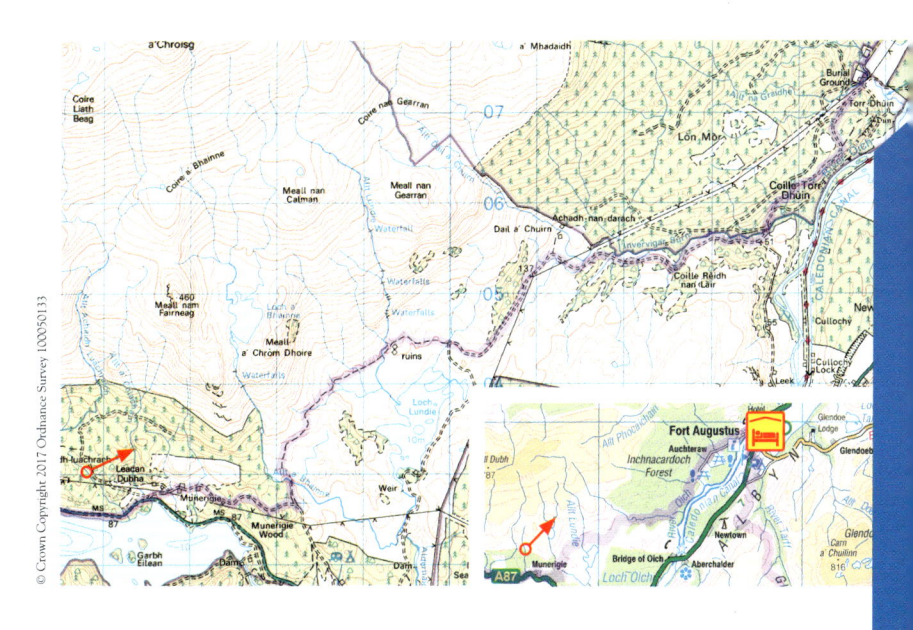

DAY 2.

Start:	Fort Augustus
Finish:	Kincraig
Distance:	81km (50miles)
Off-road:	*38.5km (24miles) 48%*
Ascent:	1733m (5687ft)
Descent:	1516m (4976ft)
Grade:	H2

OVERVIEW

The classic pass of the Corrieyairack, although the riding is not so classic, followed by pleasant easy riding over moor and through forest on good tracks.

ROUTE

Depart Fort Augustus on A82. Just after the golf club on your R, turn L following signs for the Burial Ground. Go round it and continue S to the unclassified road where turn R. In about 500m General Wade's Road rises to the L, on a stony track, beside a wall, just after a new 'industrial' gateway and immediately before the drive to a cottage. Climb along 11km and up 750m. Fortunately the track is mostly very good. Rejoin your travelling companions from yesterday, the electricity pylons. From the summit descend steeply into Corrie Yairack, on less good track. Once on the corrie floor a good, stony, gently descending track whisks you down to Melgarve.

Mountain Biking Adventures:

Tootle 13km down to Spey Dam, across the Spey and in a further 3km you are in Laggan, where you may take refreshment at the Laggan Stores, but you may not stop. Turn R on to the A86 and follow it S for just over 0.5km before turning L on the A889 signposted for Dalwhinnie. In a further 2km turn L on an unclassified road signposted Glentruim and follow it for 4km. Just after passing the Clan Macpherson Memorial on your L, turn R on to a good track and follow it S for 1300m. The track emerges from forest passes through a scrubby area, and then runs alongside a wall on the L side. About 100m along the wall go L through a gap and skirt round the ruins of a complex enclosure before going E, downhill through a grassy field to Crubenbeg.

The Corrieyairack track.

© Crown Copyright 2017 Ordnance Survey 100050133

ROUTE 7. SCOTTISH COAST TO COAST 1: GLENELG TO DUNDEE

92

Multi-day routes in northern Britain

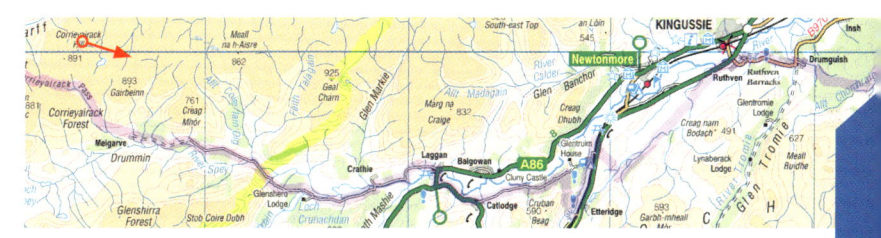

Follow the tracks S around the buildings, to Truim Bridge. Cross the bridge and turn L on to the minor road which brings you, in about 200m, to the A9. Turn L on the cycleway and go along beside the road for 3.5km until you come to a minor road passing under the A9. Go through the tunnel and take the well-metalled track SE to Phones. Curve R around the first building here, and then L over a burn. About 50m over the burn turn L (more or less straight on) on a grassy track and follow this NE for just under 7km avoiding all temptations to L and R, particularly around Lochan Odhar, until you once more reach the A9. Cross the A9 carefully, go along it to the R for 50m and take a track off to L, which soon admits on to tarmac. Follow the tarmac to the R for 500m until it passes through a tunnel under the A9 and, in another 500m, meets the B970 at Ruthven.

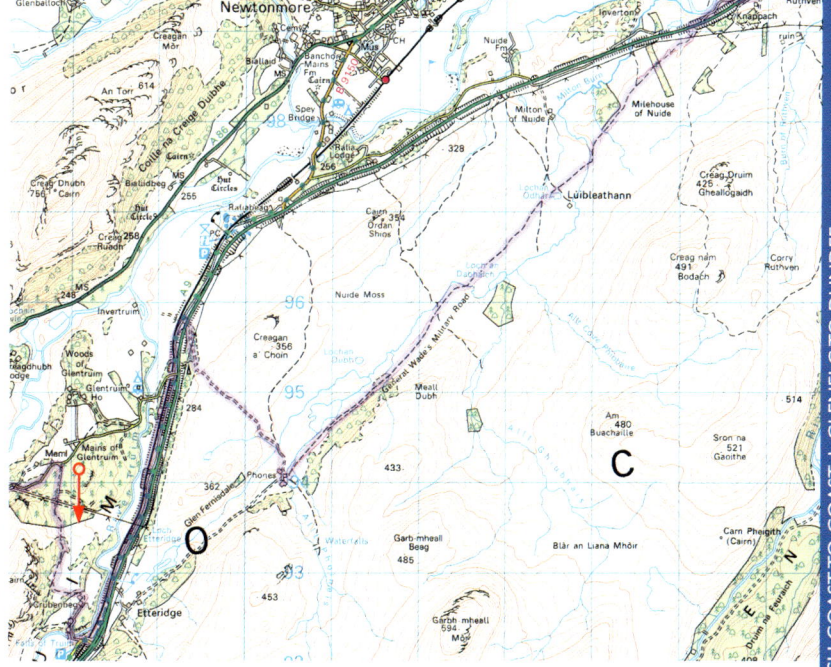

Follow the B970 E for 3km to Tromie Bridge. If you are tired, and you may well be, you may elect to continue on this road until you get to Kincraig. If you're up for more delightful forest track, turn R just after the bridge. In 50m turn L and ascend for about 0.5km and turn R at the crossroads following the sign 'Right of Way via Glenfeshie to Linn of Dee and Braemar, or to Glen Tilt and Blair Atholl'. The track goes E for 2km and then NE for a similar distance to join the tarmac road up Glen Feshie. If your off-road appetite is sated take this road N for 4km to the B970. Turn R, and then, in less than a km, L on the unclassified road to Kincraig.

Mountain Biking Adventures:

If it isn't, you can be delighted by a path along the Feshie. 1.5km along the tarmac road turn R where a brown sign says 'Public footpath to Feshie Bridge'. In less than 100m you are directed to the L again, not along the path shown on the map, to Ballintean, where a circuitous but reasonably well signed path takes you round the back of the buildings and rightwards, E, to join the original path. Follow this grassy path, with great views of the magnificent Feshie, N to Feshie Bridge and the B970. Turn L for about 1km and then R at the unclassified road to Kincraig.

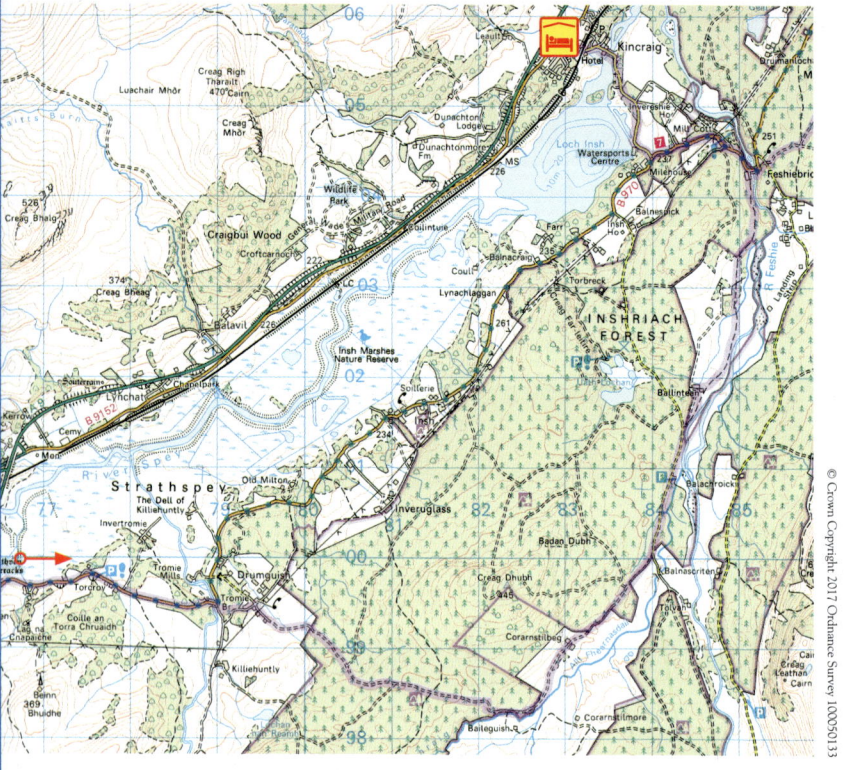

DAY 3.

Start:	Kincraig
Finish:	Ballater
Distance:	92km (57.5miles)
Off-road:	73km (45.5miles) 79%
Ascent:	1916m (6290ft)
Descent:	1960m (6423ft)
Grade:	H2

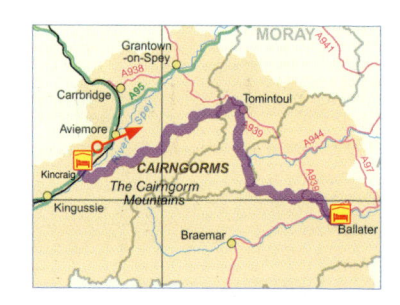

ROUTE 7. SCOTTISH COAST TO COAST 1: GLENELG TO DUNDEE

94

Multi-day routes in northern Britain

OVERVIEW

Apart from the traverse of Glen Gairn from Loch Builg, this day's route is inevitably, and unashamedly, a reversal of elements of the Cairngorm Circuits. It is inevitable because any traverse of this part of the country has to pass through the Cairngorms. It is unashamed because, though not boasting massive climbs or fearful descent, it consists of fabulous, no-need-to-put-a-foot-down, mountain biking through the Rothiemurchus and Abernethy Forests, traverses a wild moor with dramatic views of the Cairngorm massif and takes a classic glaciated through route. And climbs almost 2000m in over 90km.

ROUTE

Return to Feshie Bridge and cross it. The road rises in a hairpin curving to the L and about 20m out of the bend there is a track to the R blocked off to vehicular traffic. Take it and at the crossroads go straight on, on good track, into the forest. Take the first L in about 500m and then the first R in a further km. Avoid further lefts and rights until you emerge from the planted forest at NH879056, into a brief clearing before the track ends at a small cabin. This exit point is important: if you miss it and exit the forest by Loch Gamhna, as many have done, there is a very muddy section to cross, then a further chewed-up path E. Take the L hand path here at the forest exit point and enjoy a fabulous bit of shrubby singletrack until you emerge at Loch Gamhna. Continue N until you meet the track around Loch an Eilein. Normally, one would recommend a full circuit, but you have a big day so turn R and in just over 1km turn R again, away from the loch and go E on a fabulous track for 2km to the Cairngorm Club Footbridge. Cross it and bear R, SE and then climbing slightly ENE until in 2.5km you reach a large forest track. Turn L, follow it to the tarmac at the end of Loch Morlich, and turn R. In a few minutes you will be succumbing to the temptation to stop for refreshment at the Glenmore Shop Cafe Restaurant.

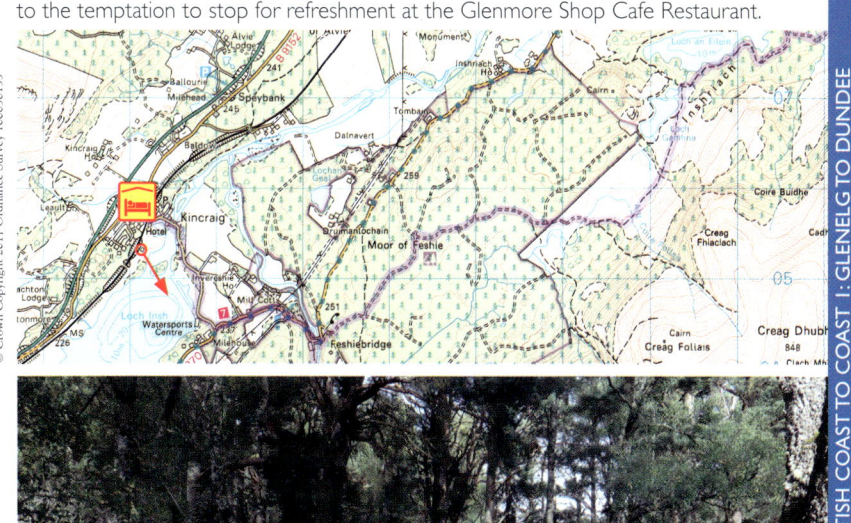

Easy riding round Loch an Eilein.

95

Mountain Biking Adventures:

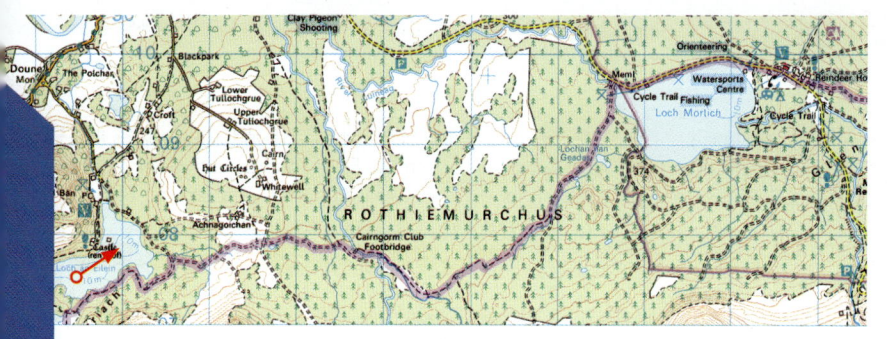

After the shop, in about 250m, take the second L, signposted Glenmore Lodge, and bear R on the tarmac in front of the Reindeer Centre. Very soon, turn off on to the cycle and walkway, which runs parallel to the road to the end of the tarmac just beyond the Lodge. As it goes round to the NNE it passes Lochan Uaine. Ignore the R turn for the track to Bynack, optimistically signposted for Braemar, and continue N, past Ryvoan Bothy, and into Abernethy Forest. Continue straight on as the track curves E and descends to a ford across the Nethy. Rising from the ford the track comes obliquely to a crossroad, go across and continue straight on, E. After a clearing by Loch a Chnuic, go straight on at the edge of the next bit of forest and cross another, smaller ford. The path is now less distinct and easy to lose, but, leaving the forested area, passes through more scrub ground, trending NE for 0.5km towards an obvious defile of Eag Mhor.

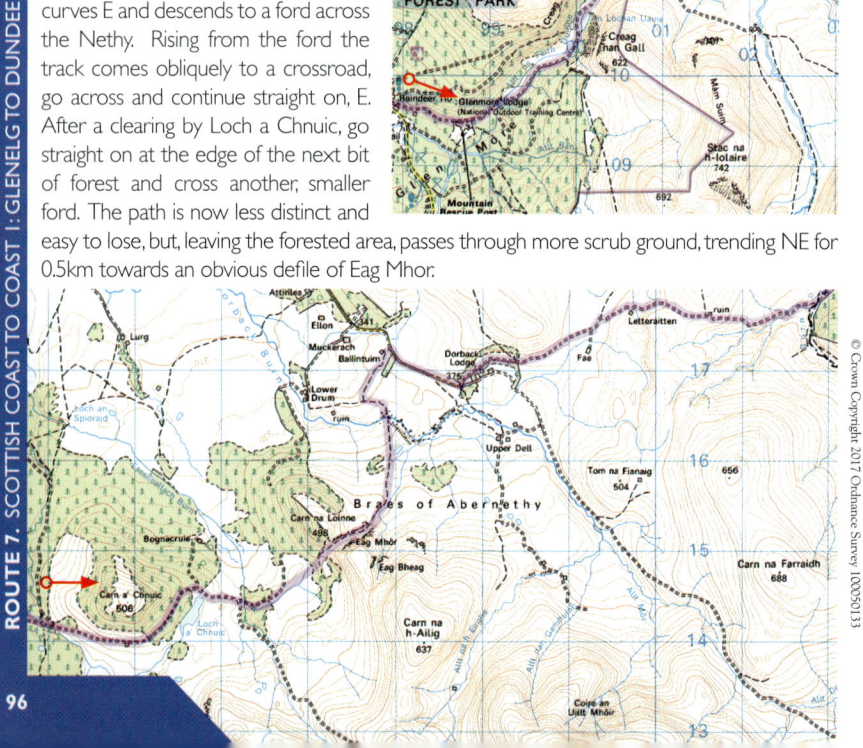

Multi-day routes in northern Britain

As you approach the gap the path becomes more obvious, takes you through the gap, and heads N to ford Dorbach Burn in a further 1km. Rising from the other side of the burn a grassy track curves W before a R turn takes you NNE past a strip of forest to the tarmac road. Turn R, and in 1km, at the end of the tarmac, arrive at a large turning circle with industrial scale sheds on the L. Just past the sheds and immediately before the cattle grid which guards the road to Dorbach Lodge, a gate admits you to a grassy track. Follow this round the back of the lodge and continue on a good track E for 4km until you drop into Glen Brown. Before enjoying this descent look back over the Abernethy Forest and the Cairngorm massif.

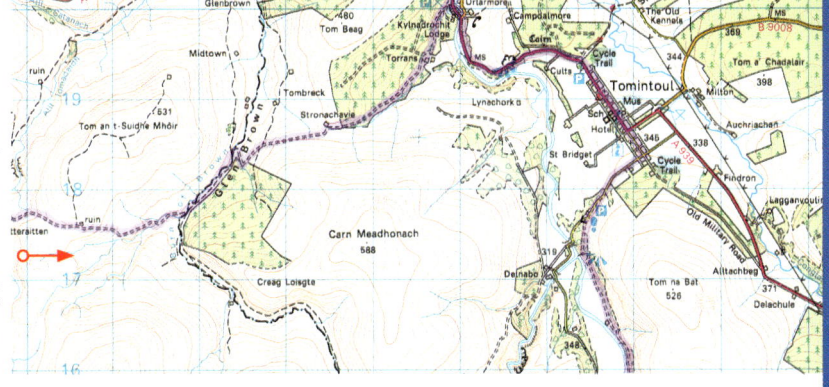

Rothiemurchus Forest.

At the foot of the descent, immediately after a ford take the grassy track to the L which, in less than 100m, fords the burn again, and descend more gently to Burn of Brown. Cross this burn where you may and then go NE between the burn and the forest as best you can. Just past the end of the forest on your R look out for a gate in the fence to your R. Go through it and pick up a track, grassy at first, which ascends eastward by the end of the forest before improving and climbing gently NE, then descending to join the A939 at Bridge of Avon. Turn R and then in 2km pass through Tomintoul on Main Street. Turn R on Delnabo Road (the third road after the A939 turns L).

Mountain Biking Adventures:

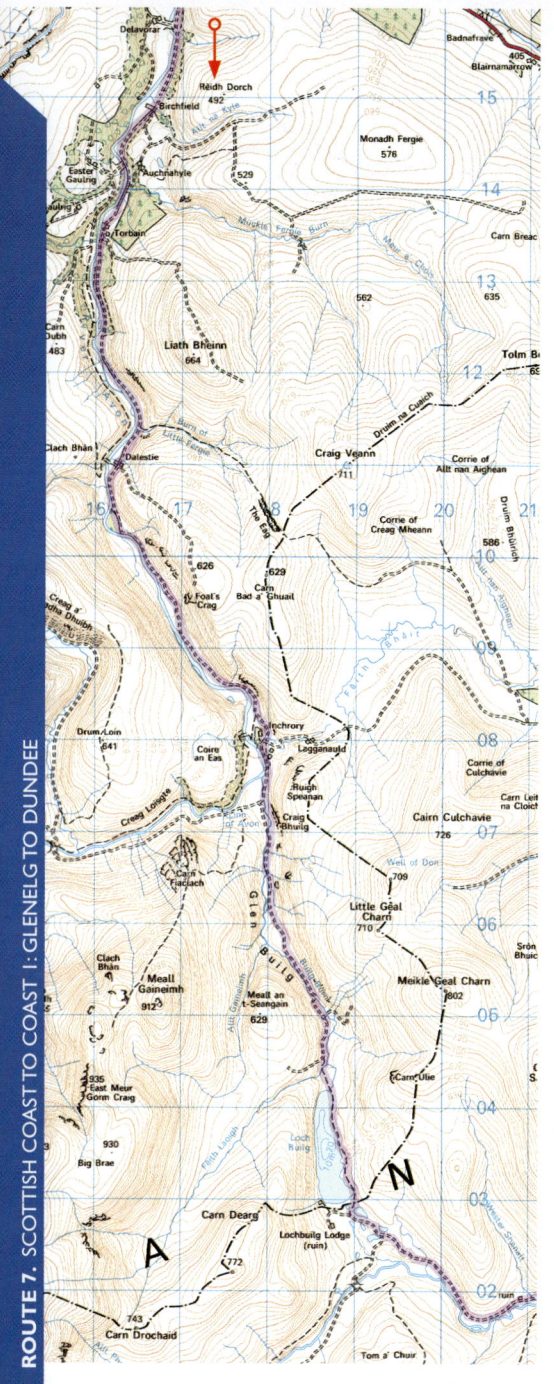

About 1km out of town, where the tarmac bears sharply R, a track goes straight on following signs for 'Car park.'

Take it, S for 10km. Just less than 1km after Inchrory where the Avon comes in from the W, the stronger track sweeps around to the R and crosses Builg Burn. Do not cross the bridge, but continue S, on a poorer, but good track on the E side of Builg Burn (not as shown on the OS map). In 2km ford the burn and then, in a further 1km, avoiding both L and R turns, ford the Feith Laoigh. The track becomes path at this point. In 200m ford the Builg for the last time at the foot of Loch Builg and follow the delightful singletrack along the E bank of the loch. At the head of the loch emerge on to a good track amidst a group of small ponds and turn L. Go straight on for 12km down Glen Gairn until you emerge on to the B976. Turn L and in 1.5km arrive at the A939.

If you're tired, and you should be, turn R and follow this road and the A93 for a total of 10km to Ballater. If you're still feeling frisky, turn L, cross the Gairn and in about 500m take the track on the R to Glengairn church. Follow it E for about 1.5km past Tomnavey until it rises from the farmyard, turns sharply R, and joins a better track on which you turn R and keep R to find the track along the bottom edge of the wood past Balno. In a total of 2km arrive at the farmstead of Inverenzie. The track improves and in 700m arrives at a 'T' junction. Turn R, through the gate, and you're on tarmac again. Tootle down this lovely minor road to the A93 and turn L for Ballater.

Multi-day routes in northern Britain

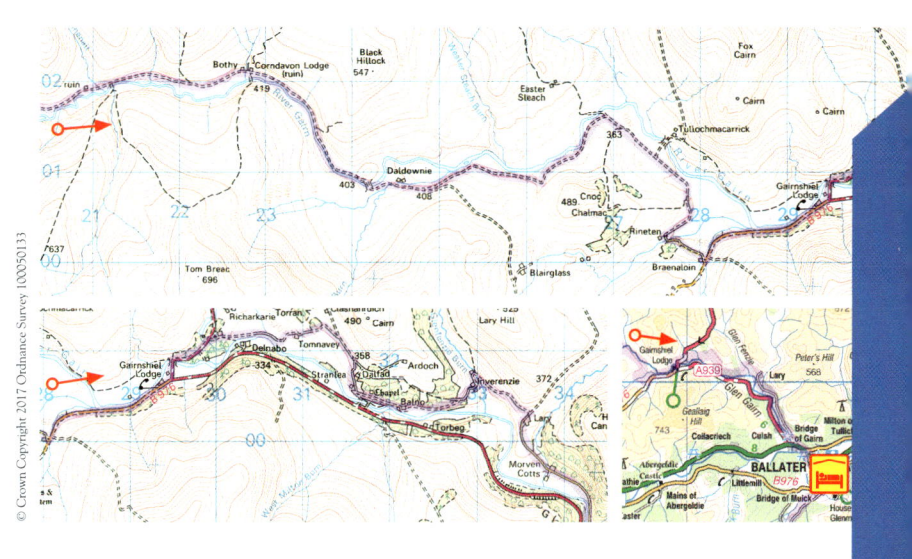

DAY 4.

Start:	Ballater
Finish:	Dundee
Distance:	91km (56.5 miles)
Off-road:	26.5km (16.5 miles) 29%
Ascent:	1562m (5128ft)
Descent:	1758m (5771ft)
Grade:	H2

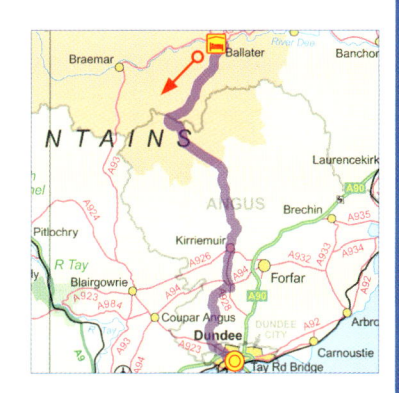

OVERVIEW

A long day with an ascent to 710m at the height of the Eastern Cairngorms (formerly the Brechin Angus), followed by a steep descent and a long descent, mostly on minor roads, down lovely Glen Clova, to finish, if still with energy, over the Sidlaw Hills.

ROUTE

Leave Ballater on Bridge Street and cross the eponymous bridge. Turn R and follow the B976 to Bridge of Muick. Just as the road curves toward the bridge take the road on the immediate R of the memorial bench, signposted 'Glen Muick'. Follow it

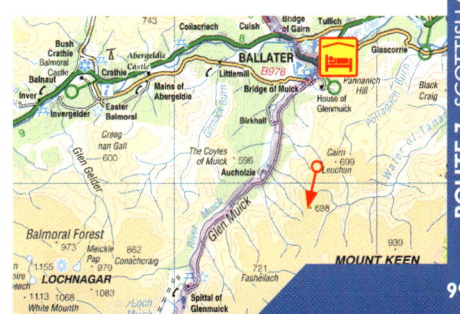

ROUTE 7. SCOTTISH COAST TO COAST 1: GLENELG TO DUNDEE

99

Mountain Biking Adventures:

for 10km to Spittal of Glenmuick, occasionally gawping up at Lochnagar. Past the car park, keep straight on keeping R on the good track along the edge of the steep sided Loch Muick. In 2km from the bottom of the loch, just after a bridge, the path splits. Take the L hand fork climbing 150m in less than 500m of track. Your reward is a glorious path along the edge of the corrie with magnificent views in all directions.

Ascending above Loch Muick.

At the shallow col between Sandy Hillock and Broad Cairn take the path L, S, by a small hut. It is narrow and technical, rocky and with uncompromising drainage ditches. Most will walk the steeper sections. In a patch of forest, cross the headwater of the South Esk and in 100m turn L to head ESE on improving track. In 2km the valley turns S and just round the corner is a footbridge. If the water is low continue on the good track and take your chances at the ford through the South Esk just N of Moulzie. Otherwise, cross the footbridge and take the grassy path S. It runs along the western edge of the patch of woodland, not through it, as shown on the OS map. Rejoin the track just E of the ford. In 2km of improving track you're gazing up at the magnificent corries above Glendoll Forest to the R, and on the tarmac road heading down Glenn Clova to the eponymous hotel. You can take the B955 down either side of the glen from here.

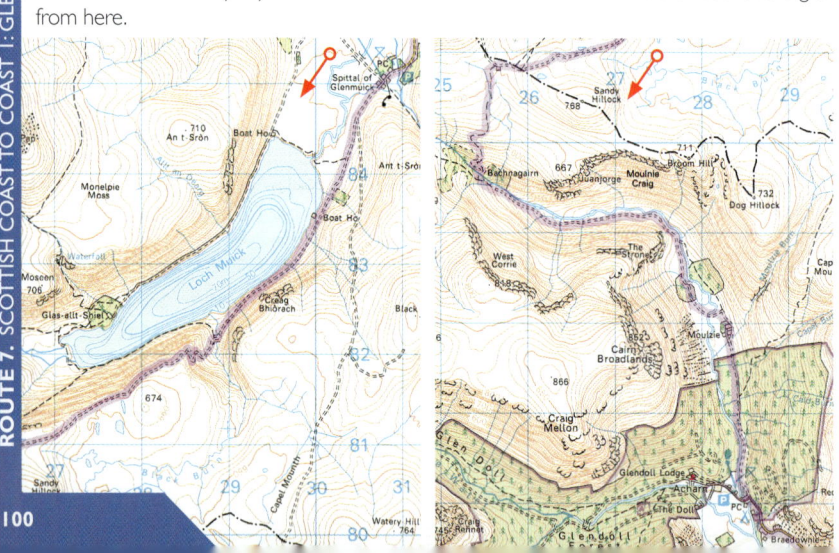

ROUTE 7. SCOTTISH COAST TO COAST 1: GLENELG TO DUNDEE

© Crown Copyright 2017 Ordnance Survey 100050133

100

Multi-day routes in northern Britain

Enjoy this lovely green bottomed, steep sided, valley for almost 20km until, after Dykehead, you begin to emerge into more open country. Keep going on the B955 to Kirriemuir. If you want refreshment there, carry straight on at the golf course rather than taking the 'ring-road'. In either case keep going S following signs for the A928. Follow that road S a further 4km to Glamis. Fans of 'The Scottish Play' will be disappointed by any detour on that account. At the junction with the A94 turn R and then immediately L. In 465m (the precision is necessary because there is no signage) take the easy to miss R on a forest track. Follow it W, crossing an unclassified road more or less straight on and continue W and then WSW through further forest for 2km to emerge again at a minor road and turn L. Follow this road without deviation for 3km as it curves S through Easter Denoon until the tarmac ends at Wester Denoon. Continue on the good track due S for about 1km where it curves sharply SE. In 650m after the bend, be sure to take the R fork, staying on the same side of Denoon Burn, and heading S again. Continue to climb towards Auchterhouse Hill, bearing R again to skirt it to the W. Enjoy the view over Dundee and the Firth of Tay for a moment and then plunge towards a circle of new, rather posh, houses. Turn R at the bottom and, when you emerge in about 600m on to tarmac, turn L. Follow this road S. Pass through the hamlet of Kirkton of Auchterhouse and, just after the road has curved to the W, turn L, S, and continue downhill, S, without deviation to Dronley. Turn R and immediately L. Continue until you meet the A923 on the outskirts of Dundee and follow this road into the centre and on to Discovery Point.

ROUTE 7. SCOTTISH COAST TO COAST 1: GLENELG TO DUNDEE

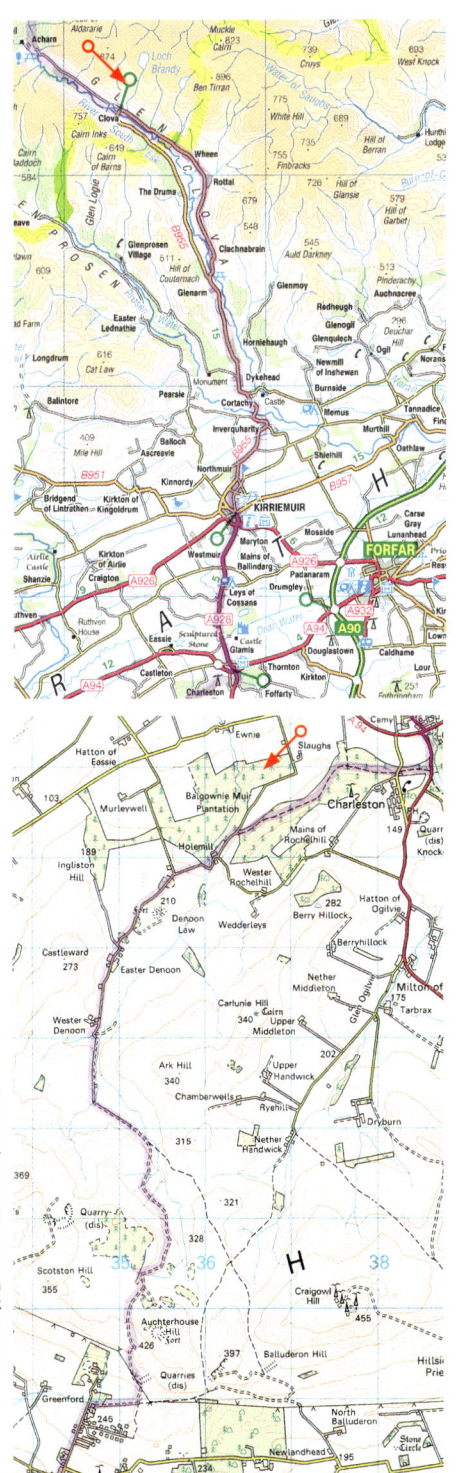

101

8. KNOYDART AND LOCHABER

Total route (days):	Four days			
Start:	Cluanie Inn			
Finish:	Taynuilt			
Total Distance:	203.5km (126miles)			
Total Off-road (%):	63.5%			
Daily distance (km):	57.5	34.5	66	46
Daily off-road (%):	79%	97%	45%	44%
Ascent:	5645m (18,527ft)			
Crux day grade:	H3			

Multi-day routes in northern Britain

OVERVIEW

A true adventure to the Knoydart peninsular and back, with a boat trip to get there and another to reach an even wilder and remote part of the 'Rough Bounds'. Perhaps a night in a converted railway carriage is followed by a contrasting day with a distinct feeling of civilisation after the first two, ending with the Devil's Staircase. A relatively short, but rough, trip by a sea loch to finish. We left our cars at the finish and arranged transport to the start the night before.

DAY 1.

Start:	Cluanie Inn
Finish:	Inverie
Distance:	57.5km (35.5miles)
Off-road:	*45.5km (28miles) 79%*
Ascent:	1757m (5768ft)
Descent:	1971m (6471ft)
Grade:	M3

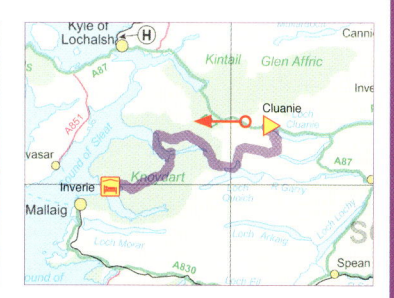

OVERVIEW

An exhilarating and adventurous day, which does, however, depend on a boat trip from Arnisdale. Our informal arrangements were made with the fish farm, through a contact of the Post Mistress. Persist with any necessary negotiation: it is worth it. A track and path lead through the Cluanie and Quoich hills down to the isolated hamlet of Kinloch Hourn and the sea, then a climb and wild riding through remote country leads back to the sea, a short boat trip over Loch Hourn (Loch of Heaven, traditionally, despite Wikipedia) to the Knoydart ('Canute's Bay') peninsular and then a big climb and grand descent to Inverie.

INFORMATION

'A pint and a heaped plate of seafood, with rain lashing on the windows and the sound of waves crashing outside.' That sums up Inverie and the splendid Old Forge Inn. Why anyone would keep the monument to Lord Brocket, a Nazi sympathizer who tried to evict the 'Seven men of Knoydart', who claimed land here on return from WW2, is a mystery. A cairn in memory of the men is in the village. The area is now owned by the Knoydart Foundation, a community buy-out.

Cluanie and Loch Quoich are regularly recorded as the wettest places in Britain; however, after a night of non-stop rain at Cluanie, we managed the major river crossing OK.

The tea shop at Kinloch Hourn is usually open, opposite the car park.

ROUTE 8. KNOYDART AND LOCHABER

103

Mountain Biking Adventures:

ROUTE

Go S down the track starting 200m from the inn. This crosses the loch at an isthmus and ascends 200m round the eastern end of the South Kintail Ridge. After descending for 1km, just before it crosses the river, branch R up a good singletrack and ascend, and over to the River (sic) Loyne. In a couple of km this becomes a Landrover track, which leads you to Alltbeithe, and after a L turn here to a northern limb of Loch Quoich, and then a minor road at the main loch.

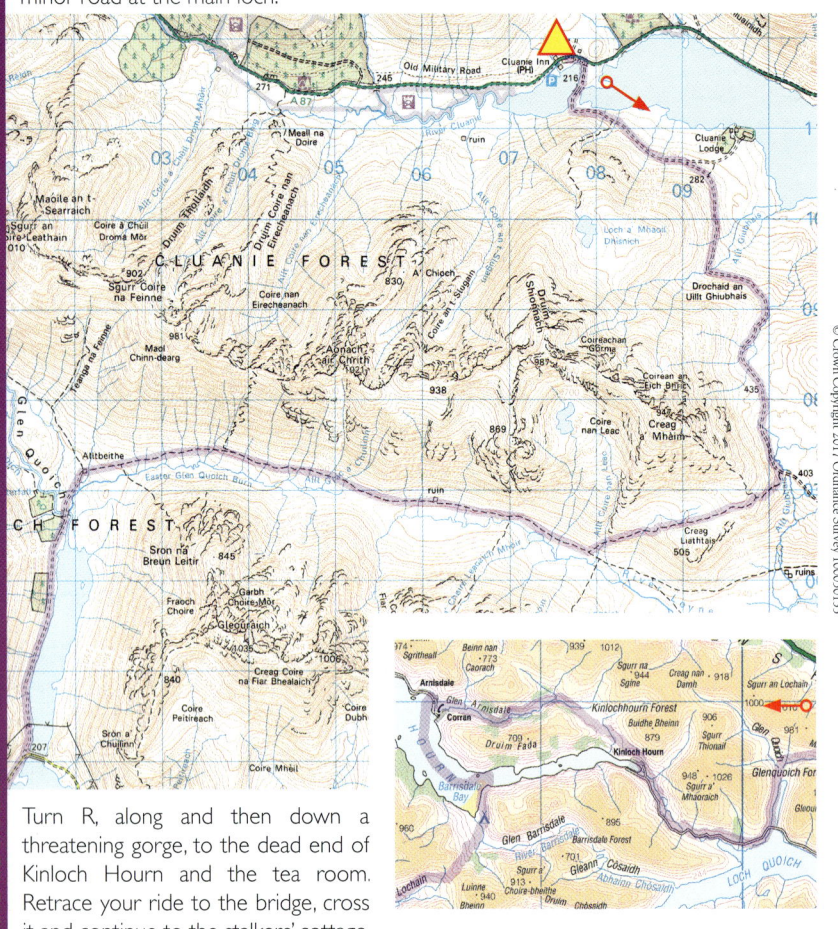

Turn R, along and then down a threatening gorge, to the dead end of Kinloch Hourn and the tea room. Retrace your ride to the bridge, cross it and continue to the stalkers' cottage, where a path R leads up through a natural and rhododendron forest. Through a gate at the top join a track by a pylon line and continue up a steep push NW to 270m. The track descends and becomes a path, and from here to the sea is mostly rideable and always interesting. Cross a river by a bridge, a further vision of the sea loch soon appears and, after a short ascent, descend to the Abhain Ghleann Dubh Lochain. This has to be forded to gain a boggy vehicle track. Follow the Abhain round W as the path splits, and cross the next river by a bridge. Enter the narrow, wild, gorge past the two lochans, the track getting

Multi-day routes in northern Britain

quite rocky just before the last bridge. A short ascent leads to a steep tricky descent, then 1.5km later on the reasonable track, crosses the Arnisdale River, curves round Glenfield and joins the minor road N to Arnisdale, whence you must make your arranged crossing of Loch Hourn. Hopefully this will give you ample time to take in the magnificence of Ladhar Bheinn and its Coire Dhorrcail.

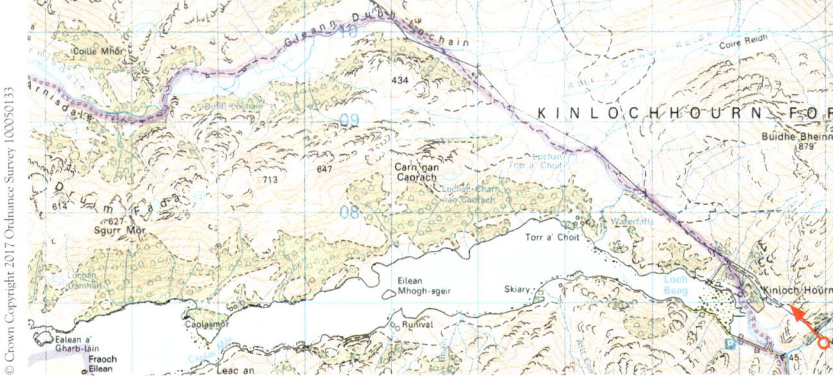

Gleann Dubh Lochan.

Alighting from the boat near the Boat House, gain the good track to Barrisdale and the Bothies, cross the Barrisdale River by bridge and continue initially up a good track then a good path towards Mam Barrisdale, the pass you see to the SW, do not take a path L going S. It's mostly a push to 450m in 5km from the bridge, in wild mountain country. The descent is on good singletrack, only walking for steep bits. Past yet another Black Lochan and a monument to Lord Brocket on a hillock, there is a final short climb. At a clearing in the next forest keep L on a track and finally descend to the sea and Inverie.

Mountain Biking Adventures:

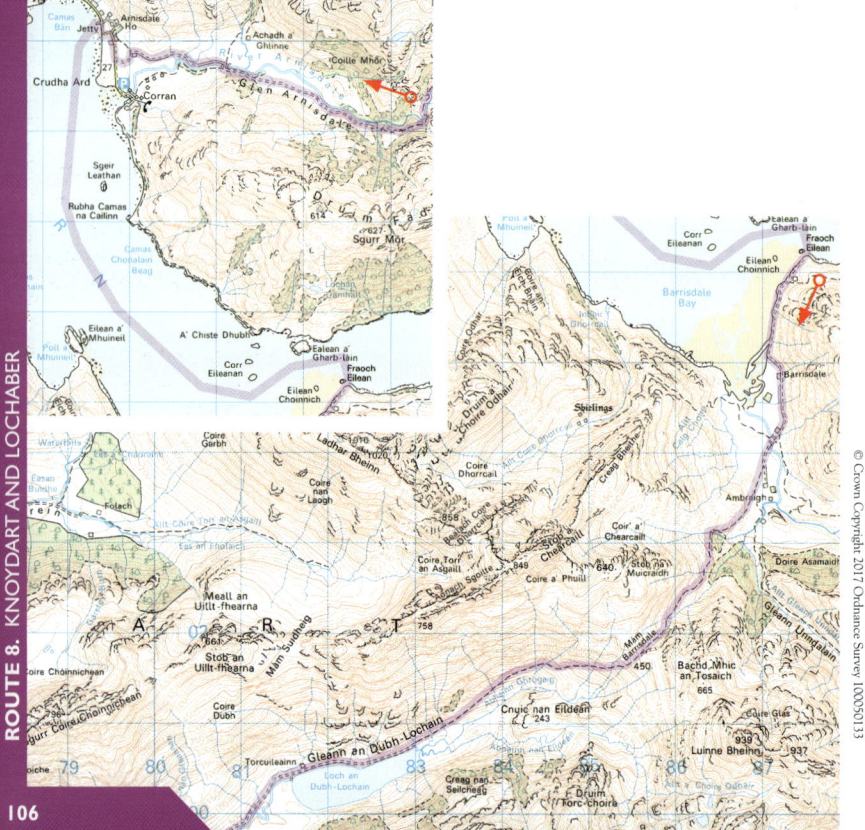

The Dubh Lochan gorge.

ROUTE 8. KNOYDART AND LOCHABER

© Crown Copyright 2017 Ordnance Survey 100050133

106

Multi-day routes in northern Britain

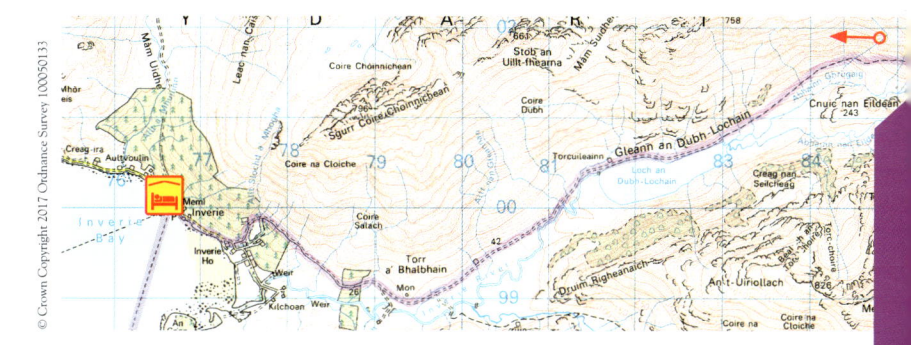

DAY 2.

Start:	Inverie
Finish:	Glenfinnan
Distance:	34.5km (21.5miles)
Off-road:	33.5km (20.5miles) 97%
Ascent:	1202m (3945ft)
Descent:	1147m (3765ft)
Grade:	H3

OVERVIEW

Just 34km and modest ascent, easy day! No. Although all on 'path' or track, the boggy nature of the 'Rough Bounds' is the problem. Indeed, if the night has been very wet, and notwithstanding the fact that there is only one river to be forded near the Mam na Cloiche' Airde which, in theory, could be bushwacked past, it would be best to take the ferry to Mallaig and bike to Glenfinnan. Tributaries can be torrents. The planned boat trip should not be a problem to arrange.

The wild and rugged nature of the surrounds should compensate for the hard going, if seen. There are two pushes of 300 and 400m, the first interesting, the second dreary, separated by boggy forest and glen, and followed at last by a good descent.

INFORMATION

Glenfinnan is where Bonnie Prince Charlie raised his standard in 1745, before his failed bid for the combined English and Scottish crown. A large monument commemorates this, erected after a road here built in 1812. The Fort William to Mallaig railway came later, in 1897, giving us the photogenic curved and entirely concrete viaduct so loved by film producers, especially the ones of H. Potter. A 1958 sleeping carriage at the station is available for accommodation: we recommend it.

ROUTE 8. KNOYDART AND LOCHABER

Mountain Biking Adventures:

ROUTE

The boat from Inverie will take you up the 'Loch of Hell', Nevis, to the pier at Torr Cruinn. From here a good track leads into Glen Carnach, with a view of shapely Ben Aden (Aodainn), and a slatted footbridge over the Carnach. A 'path' then goes through boggy ground to the promontory and round, partly on the shingly beach, to Sourlies Bothy. Ahead is a push and some manhandling to 310m beside the Finiskaig river, on a definite but wet path. We soon met some lads who'd stayed there overnight. We passed and repassed them until after the bealach, which indicates how tough the going was. The river has to be forded before the Lochans a'Mhaim, after which it's only a km to the bealach. On the way down the path splits just before the forest: take your pick.

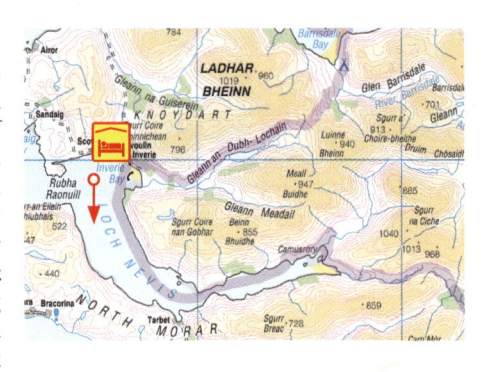

Carnach bridge.

ROUTE 8. KNOYDART AND LOCHABER

© Crown Copyright 2017 Ordnance Survey 100050133

108

Multi-day routes in northern Britain

We chose the R hand one straight into the forest, a horrible squelch, but at least partly, if frustratingly, rideable. The L hand path is reportedly no better. After the A' Chuill bothy just off to the L, you will be pleased to hear that the track, obviously used by Landrovers, improves immensely and you can ride properly round Monadh Gorm. A km after a track has joined on the L from Strathan turn L on a path to the bridge over the River Pean. There is now a dreary trudge of 5km with a 400m ascent before the promise of a decent descent. Best to keep to the E of the Allt on a quad track, despite what the map shows. This can be followed to the bealach, after which a path appears which descends on the R of the stream and, after about a km, becomes a good ride, and a proper track after the bridge. This leads down the forested Glen Finnan, under the iconic viaduct for the Mallaig to Fort William railway, to the main road. Since we did this, hydroelectric work has been carried out in the glen, and to what extent that has changed the scenery we cannot say; the route is unchanged.

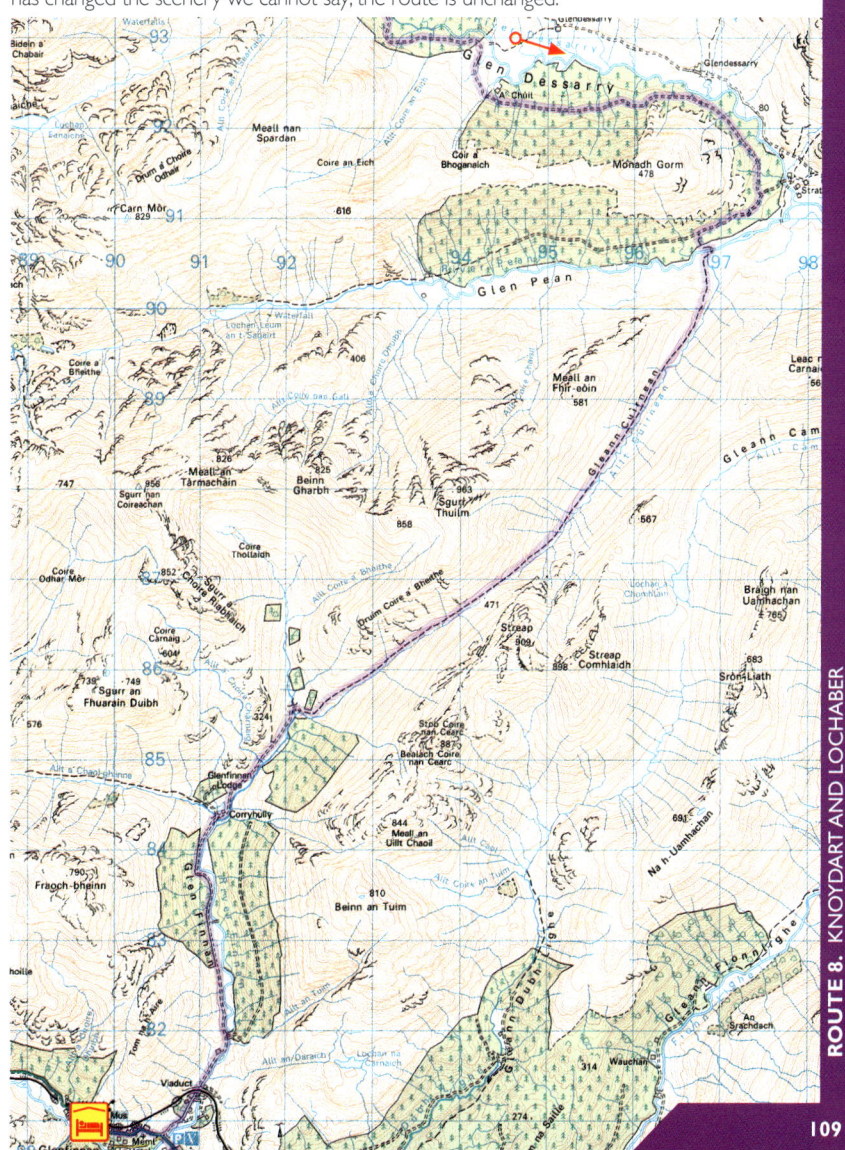

ROUTE 8. KNOYDART AND LOCHABER

109

Mountain Biking Adventures:

DAY 3.

Start:	Glenfinnan
Finish:	Kings House Hotel
Distance:	66km (41miles)
Off-road:	30km (18.5miles) 45%
Ascent:	1820m (5974ft)
Descent:	1650m (5417ft)
Grade:	M1

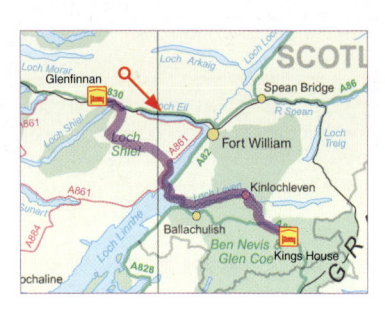

OVERVIEW

A complete change from yesterday: no bogs, and slightly more on road than off. A track, then path, to 390m leads to a good descent and a long glen to the sea again and a ferry this time. More road to Kinlochleven, then General Wade's track/path to 548m, going against the flow of pedestrians on the West Highland Way, and a tricky descent of the Devil's Staircase to the Glencoe road.

INFORMATION

Kinlochleven is dominated by relics of the old Aluminium smelting industry, from 1909 when the navvy-built Blackwater Dam was finished, carrying water in huge pipes down to the factory. This closed in 1996 and the water is now used for hydroelectric production, the old factory converted to an indoor climbing centre, including an ice wall: the Ice Factor.

The 154km West Highland Way is a very popular long distance path from Milngavie to Fort William, opened in 1980.

Refreshments are at Corran, pubs both sides of the loch, and at Kinlochleven, including a café at the Ice Factor.

ROUTE

Take the A830 for 2.5km until a break in the forest on the S caused by the Allt na Cruaiche, where a track leads R, into the glen. The track continues past the power station and becomes a path after about 2km, rideable in part to the col at 390m, where take a L fork and descend for just over a km on a better surface into Cona Glen. A track now takes you gently down the glen for 13km to the A861, turn R and after 7km of seaside down Loch Linnhe you arrive at the Corran ferry.

On the West Highland Way from Kinlochleven

ROUTE 8. KNOYDART AND LOCHABER

Multi-day routes in northern Britain

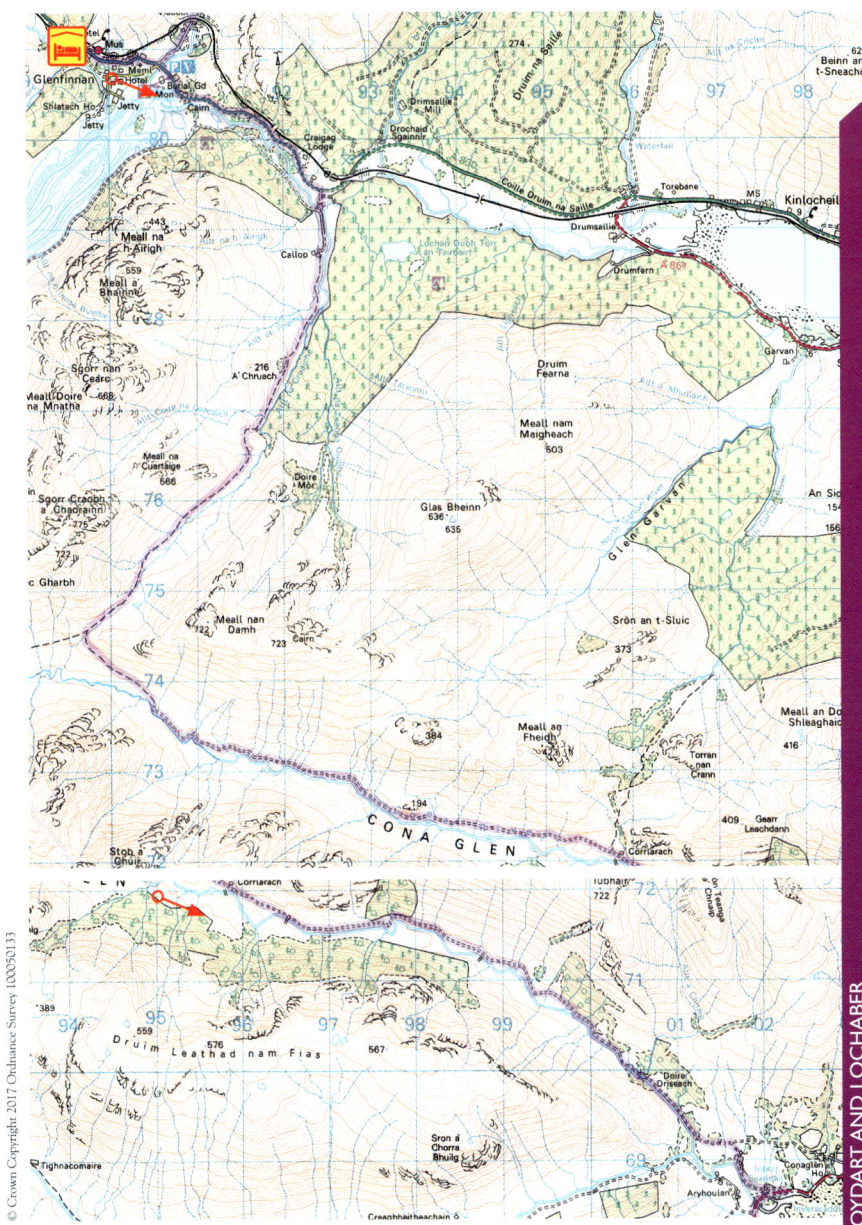

On the E side gain the busy A82 and turn R. For 13km you cycle on road by sea lochs, becoming pleasantly wooded after turning L on the 'B' road at North Ballachulish to Kinlochleven. If you are calling for tea at the Ice Factor Centre cafe, cross the bridge to it. Then carry on round the perimeter, past the campsite and curve round at the end of the sheds to join the West Highland Way crossing under the huge pipes. A pleasanter way is to turn L

ROUTE 8. KNOYDART AND LOCHABER

111

Mountain Biking Adventures:

before the bridge on a path, then R on to Wade's road, keeping R at the end to cross the obvious bridge. It is now 7km to the summit at 547m, the first three on good track, then rough path, rideable when not too steep. There may well be a lot of walking traffic coming down, remember to be courteous. Look back from the summit at the panorama, the Blackwater reservoir and the Mamores, and S the Glencoe mountains. The descent of the steep zigzags of the Devil's Staircase will defeat ordinary mortals, but below them much is rideable. At the bottom I would choose tarmac over the rough Wade's road track, to the Kings House Hotel.

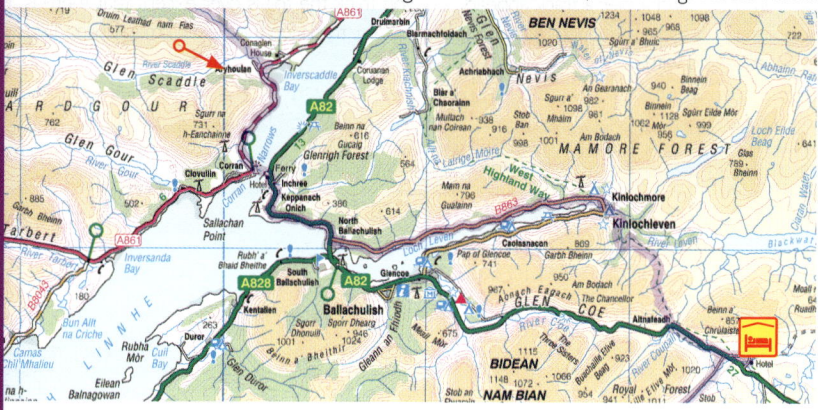

DAY 4.

Start:	Kings House Hotel
Finish:	Taynuilt
Distance:	46km (27miles)
Off-road:	20.5km (12.5miles) 44%
Ascent:	866m (2843ft)
Descent:	1094m (3591ft)
Grade:	M2

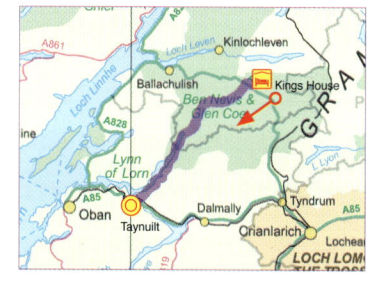

OVERVIEW

A long road descent down mountain flanked Glen Etive leads to 12km of push and ride down the sea loch and an undulating track to finish.

ROUTE

Retrace your route of yesterday to the A82 and cross to descend Glen Etive by a minor road, strewn with camper vans and tents. A km after the road kinks at Invercharnan, cross the Allt nan Gaoirean by bridge, then 800m on, turn L down a

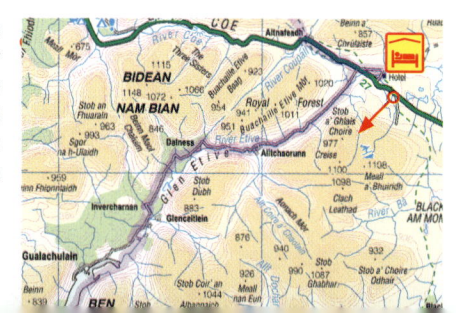

Multi-day routes in northern Britain

track to Colleitir. When the track ends the best option seems to be to follow the walkers' path to Ben Starav by the fence, then cut diagonally right for a footbridge 250m up from the River Etive, all a push. If you are a climber, gaze in wonder at the Trilleachan Slabs. There follows some riding down to and beside the river, but after that the riding is in short bursts till the track in about 10km. There is a path: it leaves the river for a while then follows the loch side, with several significant rivers to ford. After a beach - and we often took to the beaches because of thick bracken - and a pier, a track appears and you think the toil is over, except that there is now significant ascent involved on the undulating dirt track for the next 9km, crossing two major glens and with a forest ascent to finish you off.

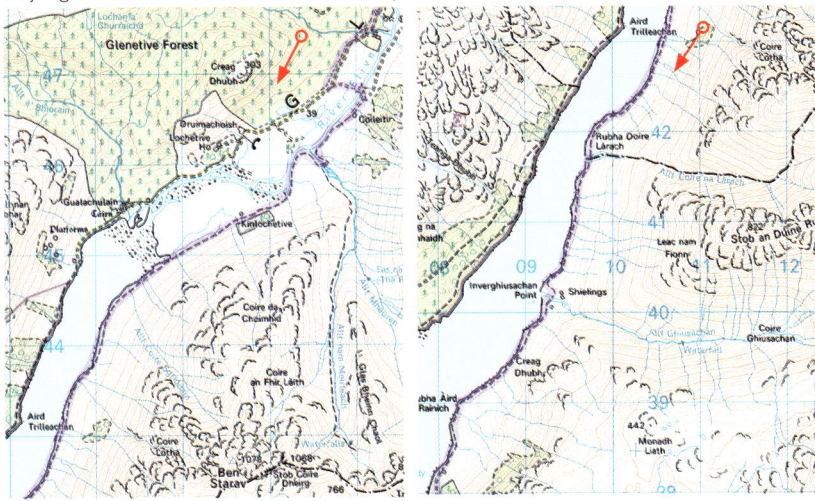

The views up the loch backwards are superb, however. At the road junction in the forest, turn R, and at the Inverawe Smokery turn L to the car park. From here go down the path to the R of the Smokery towards Hugo's Lochan, but turn L just before it to head across boggy meadows to the suspension bridge. There may be difficult gates to negotiate near the lochan. Then follow tracks to the bridge over the railway and on to the A85, and R for Taynuilt.

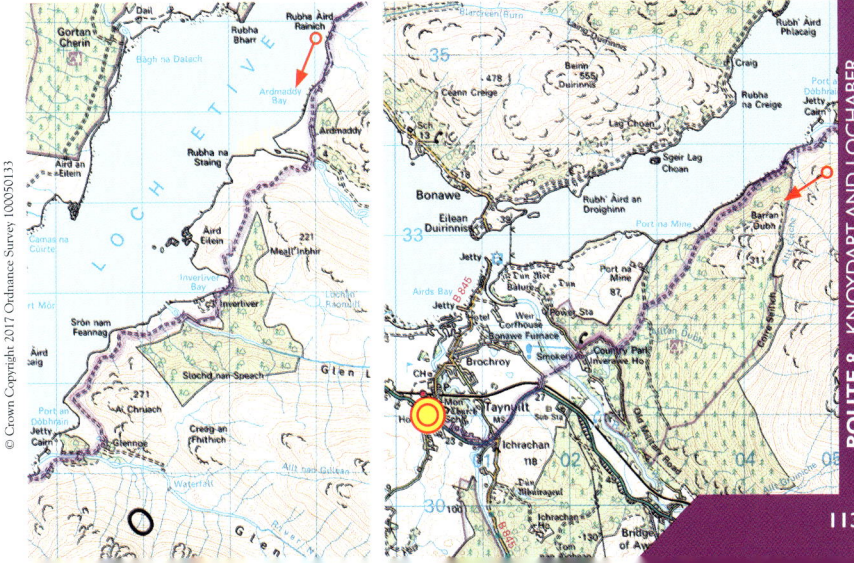

ROUTE 8. KNOYDART AND LOCHABER

113

9. MONADHLIATH CIRCULAR FROM SPEAN BRIDGE

Total route (days):	Three/four days		
Start & Finish:	Spean Bridge		
Total Distance:	239km (148miles)		
Total Off-road (%):	*38.5%*		
Daily distance (km):	*78.5*	*82*	*78*
Daily off-road (%):	*51%*	*45%*	*19.5%*
Ascent:	4688m (15,386ft)		
Crux day grade:	H2		

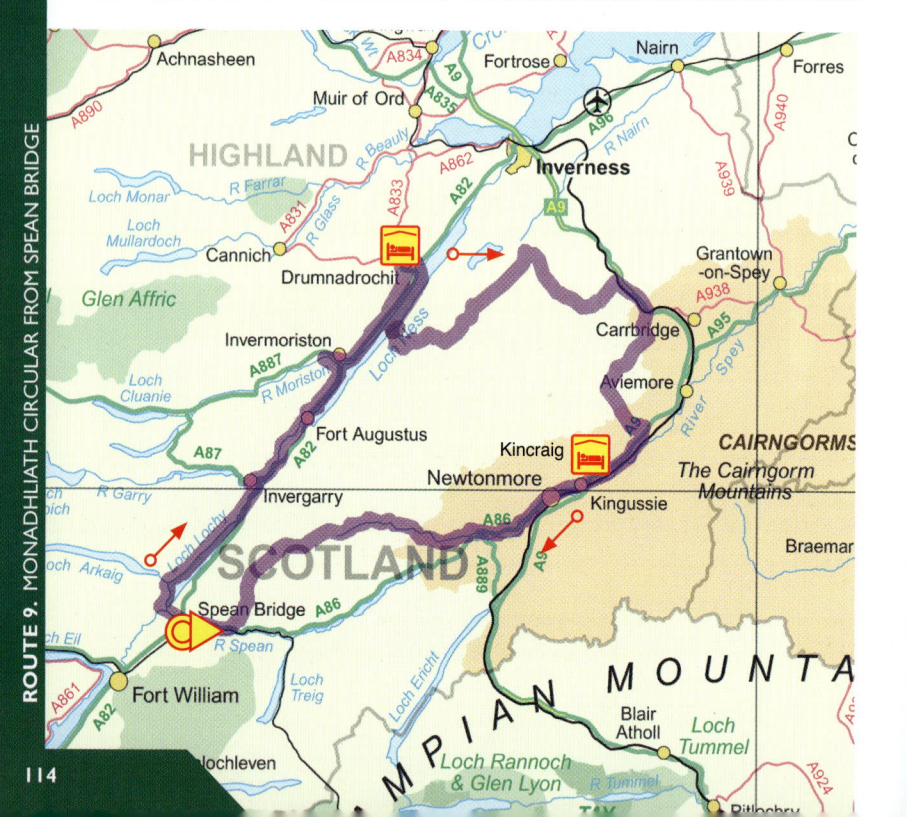

114

Multi-day routes in northern Britain

OVERVIEW

The Monadhliath give black spirits a chance to escape from the promiscuous, extroverted, white spirited Cairngorms to the S. Remote desolation in long meandering glens and moorland passages, visited again with interest in Route 13. The first day avoids the issue by the skirting Great Glen Cycle Route (GGCR), and the last also, by way of the Spey valley to its source, then Glen Roy.

The three day route is dependent on a boat trip. If this cannot be arranged, you must either leave the Great Glen Cycle Route early, at Fort Augustus and follow National Cycle Route (NCR) 78 on minor roads to join this route at Foyers for a 3 day trip or continue on the Great Glen Cycle Route to Inverness, requiring an extra day. At Inverness follow Old Edinburgh Road south from the town centre until it becomes Gen Wades Military Road or take NCR 1 to Clava Lodge then NCR 7 to regain the route Near Tomatin. No details are given of the alternatives.

DAY 1.

Start:	Spean Bridge
Finish:	Drumnadrochit
Distance:	78km (48.5miles)
Off-road:	39.5km (24.5miles) 51%
Ascent:	1877m (6160ft)
Descent:	1910m (6270ft)
Grade:	H1

OVERVIEW

A long day with a lot of ascent, and, bear in mind, the two greatest ascents are near the end. However, much of the day is on good forest track, canal towpath or road, following the Great Glen fault.

INFORMATION

The Great Glen, running from Inverness to Fort William and down Loch Linnhe, is a fault from over 300 million years ago, deepened by glaciers. The Highland hills to the NW have moved NE by 90km or so in that time relative to the Grampian hills in the SE. The Great Glen Way (GGW) as a walking route officially opened in 2002, three years after we did it.

The forests are working ones, so best to observe warnings and any diversions.

There is a tearoom at Invergarry on the route, a café at Invermoriston a little way up the main road W, and many watering holes in Fort Augustus.

Mountain Biking Adventures:

ROUTE

Cross the River Spean and take the A82 W, turning L past the Commando Memorial on the B8004. At Gairlochy, cross the river then the Caledonian Canal, and turn R on the B8005. You are now on the Great Glen Way.

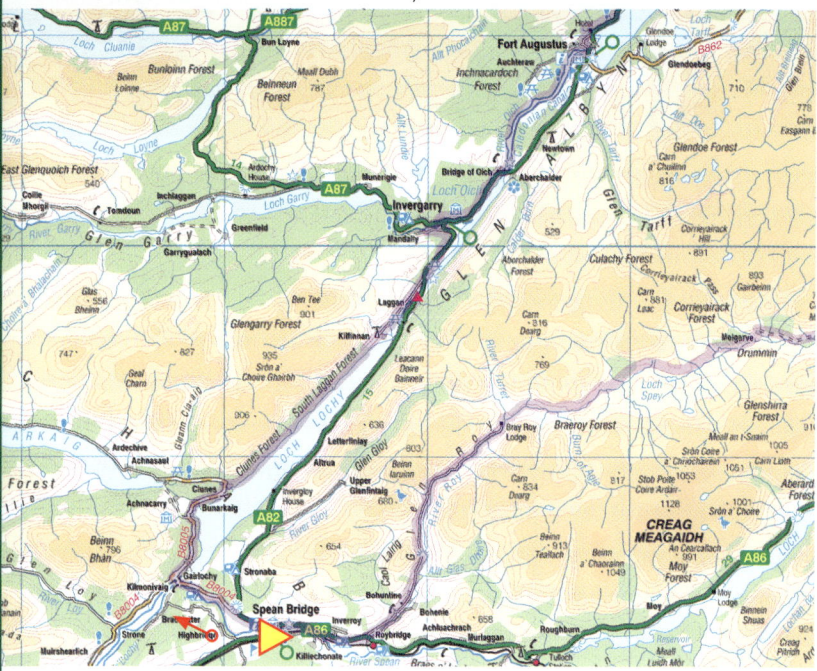

Follow the waymarked route to Laggan, Invergarry, Bridge of Oich, and Fort Augustus. If you have secured a boat across Loch Ness continue on the waymarked Great Glen Way past Invermoriston to Drumnadrochit.

Multi-day routes in northern Britain

Viewpoint above Invermoriston, along Loch Ness. Photo © Lis Burke (cc-by-sa/2.0)

DAY 2.

Start:	Drumnadrochit
Finish:	Kincraig
Distance:	82km (51miles)
Off-road:	*37km (23miles) 45%*
Ascent:	1663m (5459ft)
Descent:	1468m (4818ft)
Grade:	H2

OVERVIEW

Another long day, but less off road. Depends on a boat trip to Foyers. After this view of Loch Ness, today goes over the northern Monadhliath Hills by a little known glen and road, to the Findhorn valley, then over Slochd summit and up the Dulnain valley back into the hills, and over to the Spey valley.

INFORMATION

The 'Grey Mountain Range', N of the Corrieairack pass, SE of the Great Glen and NW of the Spey is mostly moorland, with four Munros to the S, sloping from there NW, long valleys meandering along this slope to the sea. The rock is metamorphic with granite intrusions.

The only chance of refreshment is in Tomatin, slightly N of the route: there is a shop and pub.

ROUTE 9. MONADHLIATH CIRCULAR FROM SPEAN BRIDGE

117

Mountain Biking Adventures:

ROUTE

Take your favoured boat to Foyers. From the pier, cross the river and climb out of Foyers by a minor road. Turn sharp R on the B852. After 2.5km on a 'U' bend turn L on to a minor road, but after a km, at the edge of the wood, turn L on to a track. Follow this round a forest corner along its edge NE to a minor road. Turn R then shortly L on the B862. Nearly 2km later turn R on to a minor road and cross Loch Mhor.

As this veers right to Wester Aberchalder, take the L fork, which soon turns R and L round Easter Aberchalder. Some 350m after the last building keep L through a gate into a wood.

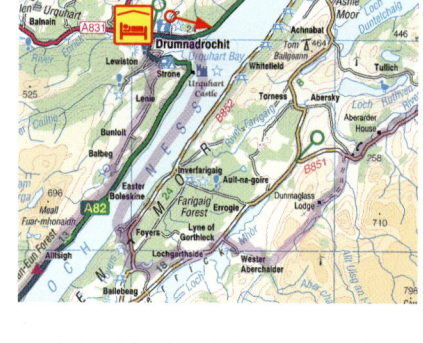

Ride through Conagleann on a good vehicle track, turning N by the boat house at the loch end, round Dunmaglass Lodge, and carry on down the valley on good track to the B851. Turn R and follow it through forest and down the River Nairn valley for 11km. At Woodside, NH678317 turn sharp R on to a minor road connecting to the A9 and the Slochd Mor gap, but which first climbs 250m, then descends to the Findhorn River.

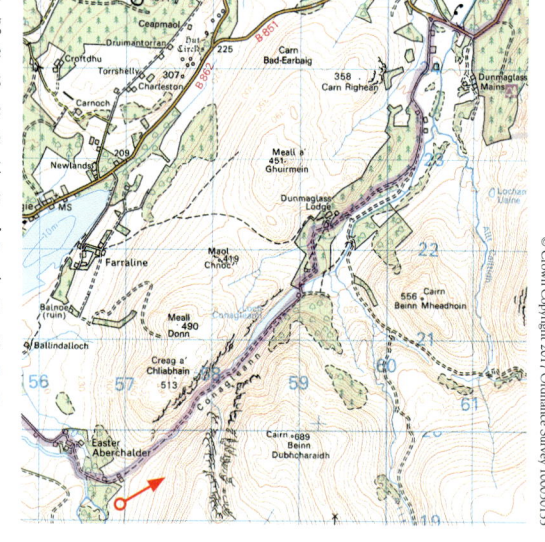

ROUTE 9. MONADHLIATH CIRCULAR FROM SPEAN BRIDGE

© Crown Copyright 2017 Ordnance Survey 100050133

118

Multi-day routes in northern Britain

At the Findhorn Bridge cross it and continue SE on the road. When we did this we got on to General Wade's road over the A9, but it's probably best to continue to where the road joins the A9 and continue on the constructed cycle path of National Cycle Route (NCR) 7, noisy but safe. At the Slochd Mhor Lodge keep S on a forest track, an offshoot of NCR 7, turning R then a quick L on a track as you leave the forest, and keep S then SE on this across to the Dulnain valley. Turn R, up the valley at the first track junction, continuing for 6.5km till a ford crosses the Allt an Tudair; then negotiate a suitable crossing of the Dulnain. There is, or was, a path of sorts on the S bank, whereas keeping on the N bank the track runs out short of the track which takes you S over to the Spey valley. If the river is high, take the bridge a km back. There is now plantation on the S bank, not there when we did it. After 2.5km of possible misery the track S starts by a ford and footbridge. It rises nearly 200m and descends grandly through forest. Keep N of the Allt an Fhearna (not named on 1:50,000 maps) till a clearing, with the forestry buildings seen down to the R, where a path leads down to cross it by bridge. Turn L and round Wester Delfour, to turn right, S, on the main Alvie Estate road. Pass the bungalow and avoid the Lodge to pass under the A9 via a subway to the 'B' road, which leads R shortly to Kincraig.

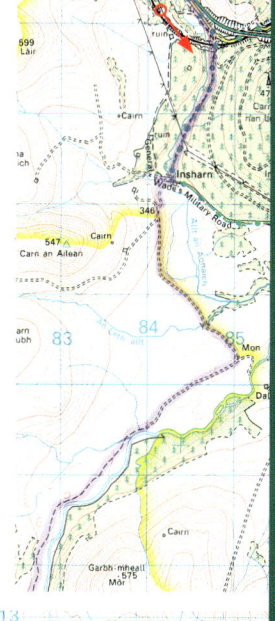

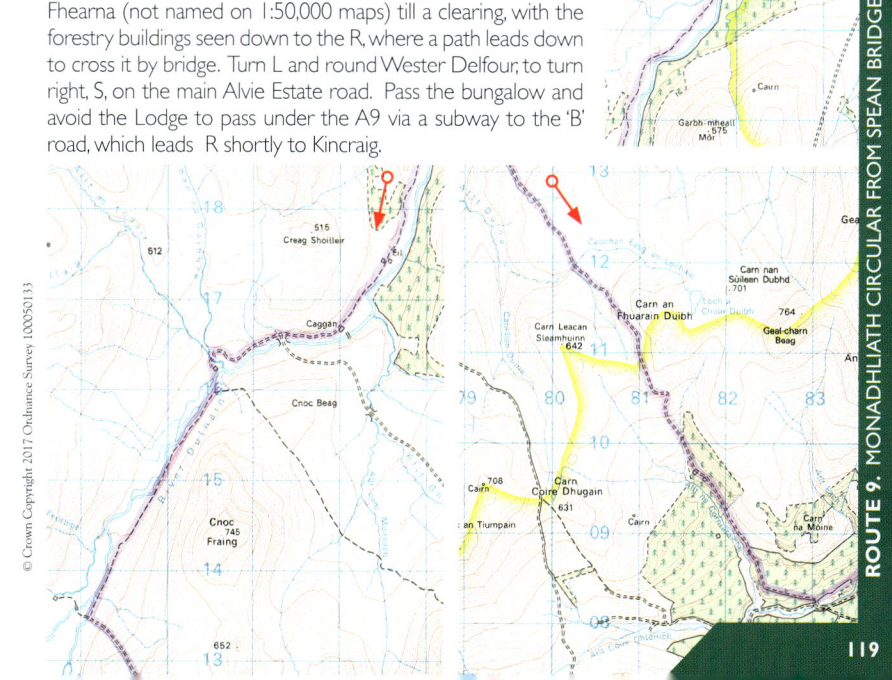

ROUTE 9. MONADHLIATH CIRCULAR FROM SPEAN BRIDGE

119

Mountain Biking Adventures:

River Dulnain crossing.

DAY 3

Start:	Kincraig
Finish:	Spean Bridge
Distance:	78.5km (49miles)
Off-road:	15.5km (9.5miles) 19.5%
Ascent:	1148m (3767ft)
Descent:	1302m (4273ft)
Grade:	M2

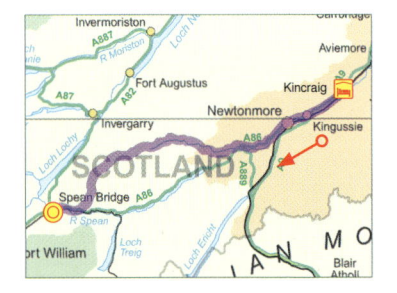

OVERVIEW

Westwards, possibly into the wind, up the Spey valley by road, or by some off road as in the Cairngorm chapters if you're super fit, to its head, then over an often soggy pass to Glen Roy and a long track and road descent. A satisfying off-road traverse of these two glens, although only 19% of the route.

ROUTE 9: MONADHLIATH CIRCULAR FROM SPEAN BRIDGE

© Crown Copyright 2017 Ordnance Survey 100050133

120

Multi-day routes in northern Britain

INFORMATION

Melgarve is now a maintained bothy; when we came through in 1999, whilst in the Laggan shop, we met the lady owner who lived there previously, who, incidentally, told us we were foolish to go over into Glen Roy! A substation is planned near here to connect the power lines to the massive wind farm complex going ahead NE of here, Stronelairg. The Laggan shop is worth stocking up at, and has a 'coffee bothy'.

ROUTE

Take the B9152 (or the minor road round Loch Insh and then B970) to Kingussie then the A86 to Laggan. If you are keen to get off road reverse as much of the latter half of Route 7 Day 2 (pp 93, 94) from Feshie Bridge to Laggan as suits you.

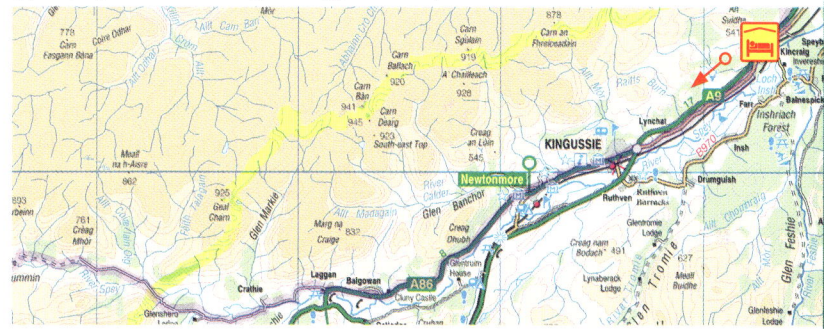

Head W up the minor road from here to Melgarve, 18km gently uphill apart from a steeper 1km after Garva Bridge, appreciating the gentle upper Spey scenery. From here it is the reverse of Route 10, but written forwards here. The vehicle track carries you by bridge over the Yairack, to the locked bothy at Shesgnan, but becomes easy to lose after this until crossing the Shesgnan Burn. It is now distinct and partly rideable, but deteriorates towards the watershed and down to the track beyond Luib Chonnal (open) bothy. The Allt Chonnal caused us some problems, although it had been raining all morning; if very wet it would be impassable. The good track now leads down Glen Roy to the Lodge, where a minor road descends 13.5km to the A86, and a R turn for Spean Bridge. Do look at the admittedly unmissable parallel roads.

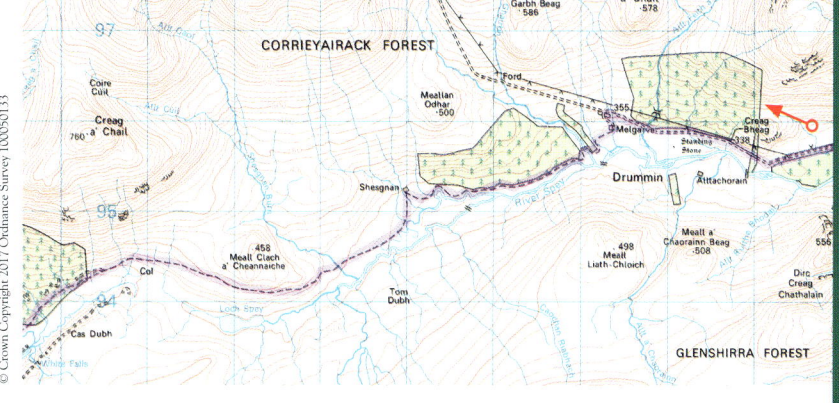

Mountain Biking Adventures:

© Crown Copyright 2017 Ordnance Survey 100050133

The often watery Spey/Roy crossing.

ROUTE 9. MONADHLIATH CIRCULAR FROM SPEAN BRIDGE

Multi-day routes in northern Britain

Near Luib Chonnel, Spey/Roy crossing

ROUTE 9. MONADHLIATH CIRCULAR FROM SPEAN BRIDGE

10. SCOTTISH COAST TO COAST 2: ARDNAMURCHAN TO MONTROSE

Total route (days):	Four days			
Start:	Acharacle, Ardnamurchan			
Finish:	Montrose, Scurdie Ness			
Total Distance:	297.5km (185miles)			
Total Off-road (%):	53%			
Daily distance (km):	58.5	83	84	72.5
Daily off-road (%):	60%	47%	50%	57%
Ascent:	5322m (17,470ft)			
Crux day grade:	H3			

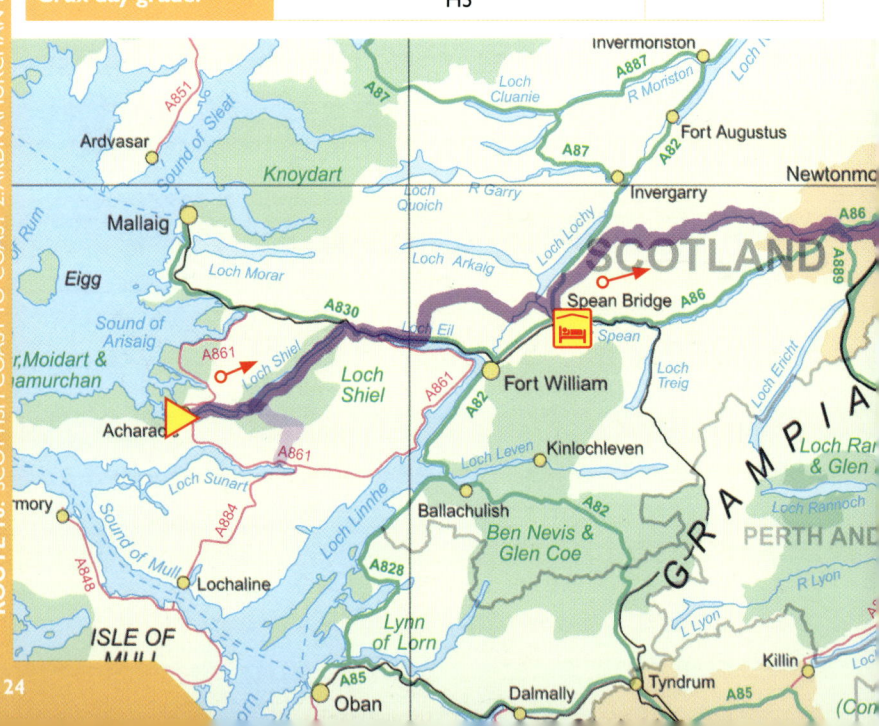

Multi-day routes in northern Britain

OVERVIEW

This route takes the line of least resistance from Ardnamurchan's Atlantic Coast through Lochaber into Speyside, through the Cairngorms and over the Angus Hills, finally delivering you to the North Sea at Montrose. It is not, however, without resistance or adventure. You may start from Ardtoe, which will necessitate a boat ride from Acharacle up Loch Shiel to the pier at Polloch, or remain entirely on land from Strontian. The former is recommended.

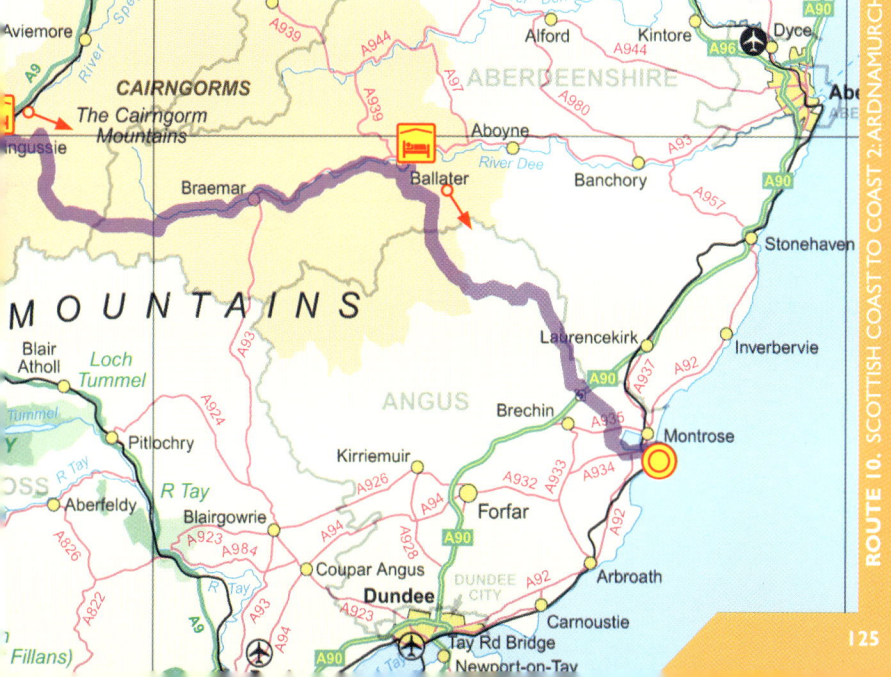

Mountain Biking Adventures:

DAY 1.

Start:	Acharacle
Finish:	Spean Bridge
Distance:	58.5km (36.5miles)
Off-road:	35km (22miles) 60%
Ascent:	1091m (3581ft)
Descent:	1048m (3440ft)
Grade:	E1
Strontian start:	Add 13.5km and 489m ascent

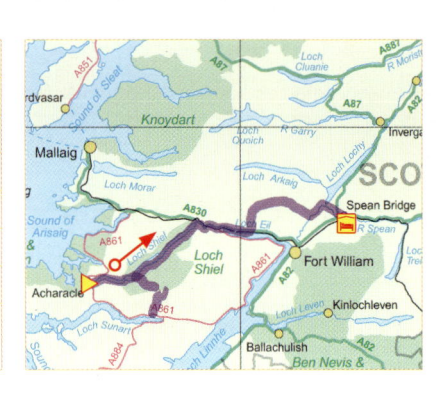

OVERVIEW

An easy start to the trip if the delightful boat trip is taken, the road alternative adds an almost 500m ascent. Both lead to a long forest track by Loch Shiel, and then road and a lonely traverse via forest and moor into Glen Loy, then a short stretch of the Caledonian Canal.

ROUTE

Acharacle Start: Charter a boat to pick you up early from Acharacle from Nick Peake (or Jim Mitchie, though you will need a large party to make this latter cost effective). Ride to Ardtoe on the B8044 the evening before or early in the morning and dip your wheel in the Atlantic (8km return). Once on your boat enjoy the delights of the lower part of the loch, especially as it narrows around Eilean Fhianain at an elbow where mountains begin to rise all around. Possibly too soon you are rounding the headland of Caen na Garbh, and disembarking at the new Polloch Jetty. Go L and follow the good lochside track NW for 18km.

Strontian Start: Dip your wheel in Loch Sunnart and then head up the unclassified road on the RHS of the bridge at the foot of the village, signposted for Polloch and Ariundle. In 1.5km avoid the R turn to Ariundle and follow the un-signposted tarmac road L, N. It climbs steadily and then, after 2km, steeply to a radio mast at 340m. Enjoy zooming down to Loch Doilet and tootle alongside it to the hamlet at Polloch. Cross the bridge and head L beside the flats of the River Polloch before curving through forests and passing the jetty to join the other route.

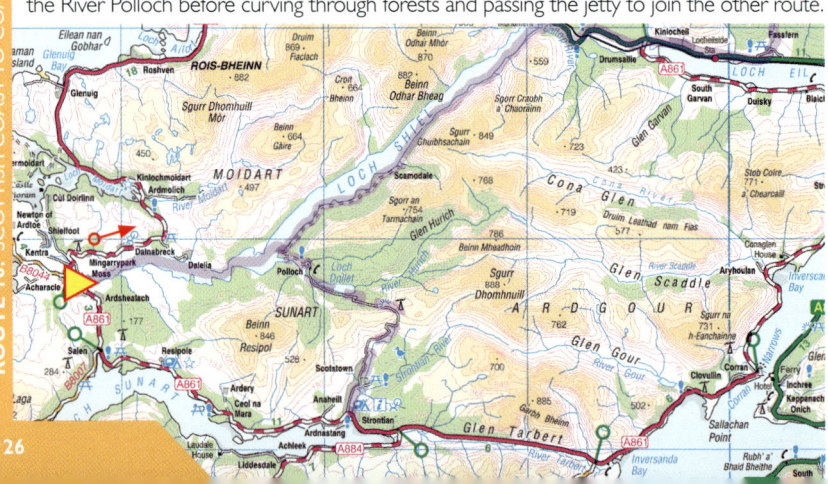

Multi-day routes in northern Britain

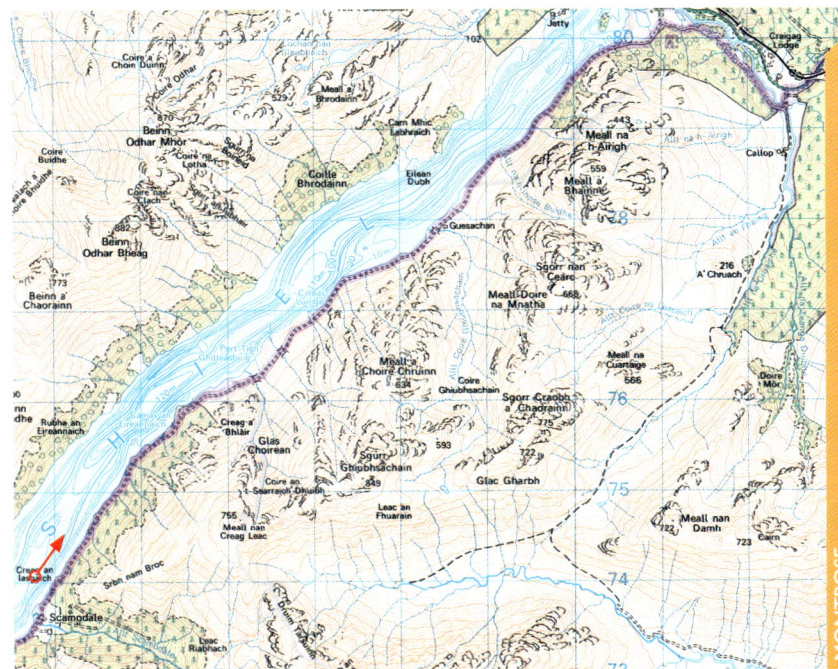

At the Glenfinnan end of the loch marvel at the splendour of Victorian engineering that constitutes the railway viaduct (or engage in Harry Potter sentimentalism according to age/taste). The track bears E at the top of the loch then SW beside the Callop River. Cross this by the bridge at the power station car park and in 200m you are at the A830. Turn R, bear the traffic as best you can and enjoy the scenery for 11km, peeling off L to Fasfern.

Once across the bridge at the centre of the hamlet turn L on a grassy track and follow the An t-Suileag for 2km where the track climbs into a forestry area and joins a much bigger track. Turn L and follow this out of the forestry (which is mostly cut down on your L) and continue N to the bridge just before the isolated building at Glensulaig. Stay on this side of the burn on a grassy track, shown as a path on OS, which goes E for 100m and then curves N. In another 200m ford the burn and follow the track past the buildings to a bridge, not shown on the OS map, and a little further N than the track is shown. The path deteriorates for 2km and some pushing is called for through the watershed, but once in Glen Loy the path is a stony delight until it comes to the tarmac at Achnanellan.

Follow the tarmac E until just past the Glen Loy Lodge (where you can now enjoy accommodation) you issue on to the B8004. Turn R and immediately L (almost straight on) on a track which passes, alongside the Loy, under the Caledonian Canal (you did not misread that). Bear R when you leave the tunnel and in a few metres you will be able to find your way, to your R, up the bank and on to a wide towpath. If you have not done so already, gawp,

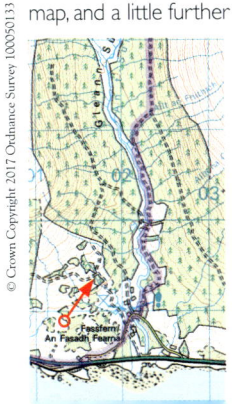

ROUTE 10. SCOTTISH COAST TO COAST 2: ARDNAMURCHAN TO MONTROSE

127

Mountain Biking Adventures:

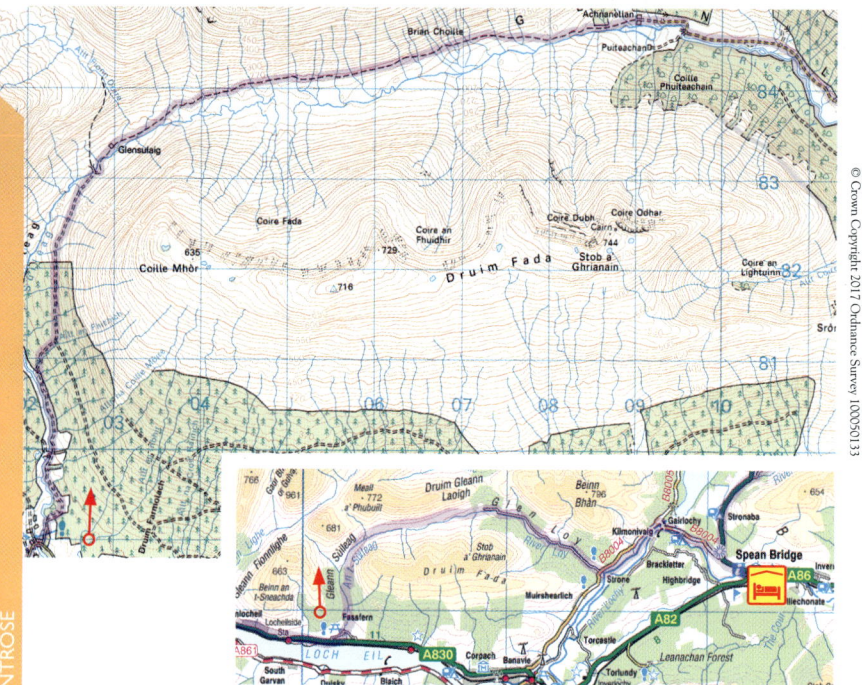

SE at the splendour of 'The Ben' (Nevis) and Carn Mor Dearg in the near distance.

Tootle NE alongside the canal until you come to the swing bridge at Gairlochy. Leave the canal here turning R along the B8006. After 3km join the A82 at the Commando Memorial and glide down to Spean Bridge.

DAY 2.

Start:	Spean Bridge
Finish:	Kingussie
Distance:	83km (51.5miles)
Off-road:	*39km (24.5miles) 47%*
Ascent:	1470m (4824ft)
Descent:	1306m (4289ft)
Grade:	H3

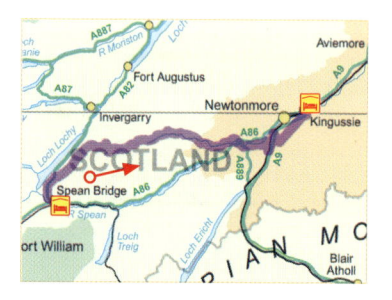

OVERVIEW

A much harder day but with a satisfying if somewhat boggy traverse of the Gloy/upper Roy to Strathspey watershed, finishing with an easy and pleasant moorland path on an Old General Wade's course.

Multi-day routes in northern Britain

ROUTE

Retrace your steps to the war memorial but continue on the A82 for about 4km and then turn R at the signpost to Glen Gloy. In 200m go L on the bridge over the Gloy. The road climbs steeply through a hairpin then more or less contours along the side of the glen until a turning circle and a sign announce 'End of public road'. A good track goes off R to Upper Glenfintaig, but we continue straight on, through a gate, on the slightly grassier track. The track follows the river closely into and then out of forest and then re-enters the forest after about 6km and becomes more easterly. Watch out for the famous 'Parallel Roads', track-scars along the hillside that are the ancient shoreline of a lake dammed by a glacier in the Great Glen.

About 600m into the last forest re-entry the track turns sharply S and then, in a further 250m, crosses a burn. Bushwhack up the burn on its L (N) bank ESE. Where a tributary comes in from the S, the burn continues E for about 50m before turning sharply southwards. At this point continue due E, as best you can, until you emerge from the forest at an indistinct watershed. Continue E until you pick up the line of the Allt a' Chomhlain. Stay on the N bank and follow it, again 'as best you can,' until in just over 1km, it starts to steepen down towards Glen Turret. The ground improves and, though without path, the brave can ride. Once in Glen Turret bear L, bypassing a circular enclosure on your R. Go NE and then N until in about 600m you come to a footbridge over the Turret, about 300m further N than is shown on the map. Cross the bridge and follow the vestige of a track SE until you come to an extensive group of sheilings. The track improves and carries you quickly down to Glen Roy at Turret Bridge.

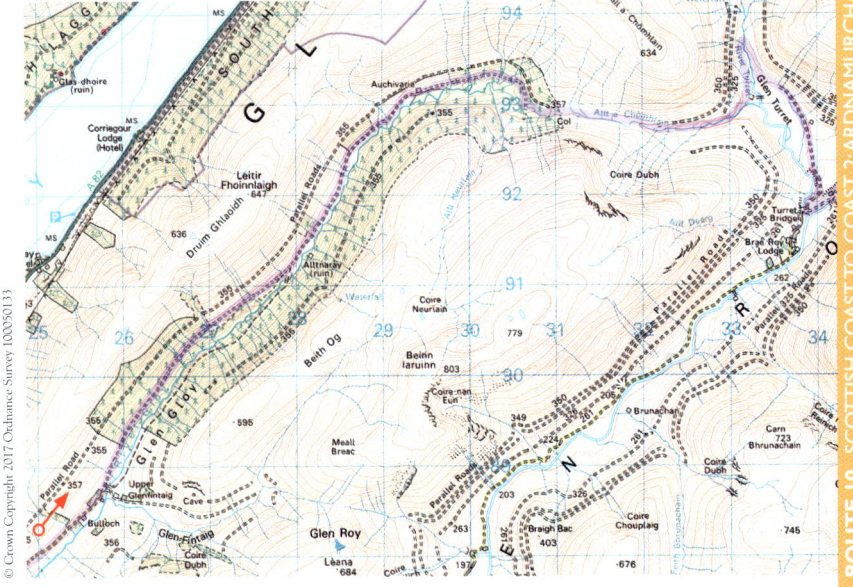

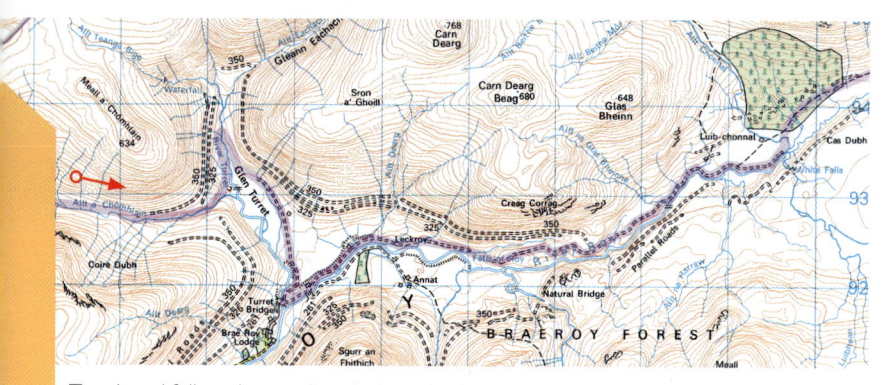

Mountain Biking Adventures:

Turn L and follow the good track along the N side of Glen Roy for 6km. If you're planning to take shelter for lunch at the Luib-chonnal bothy, turn L from the track along an indistinct path to the bothy. Otherwise it may be preferable to stay on the track to its end at the confluence of the Allt Chonnal and the Roy. Enjoy the view of White Falls as the Roy tumbles down from the flanks of Creag Meagaidh. Go N, crossing the Allt Chonnal where you can and continue N till you reach the path heading NE from Luib-chonnal. This river carries a lot of water after rain, and crossing may be difficult. If it looks difficult, think twice because the Shesgnan Burn, which you will meet in 3.5km, can be just as tricky. The path is distinct, but rarely rideable up to the col into Strathspey. In Strathspey it improves slowly until Shesgnan Burn has been crossed. It is easy to lose as you approach Shesgnan Bothy, but improves as you head towards the corner of a forest whence it will carry you quickly to the road at Melgarve. Tootle 13km down to Spey Dam, across the Spey and in a further 3km you are in Laggan, where you may take refreshment at the Laggan Stores, but you may not stop. Now follow Route 7 Day 2 as far as Ruthven Barracks (pp 92/93) then turn L and in a few minutes you will be enjoying the delights of Kingussie.

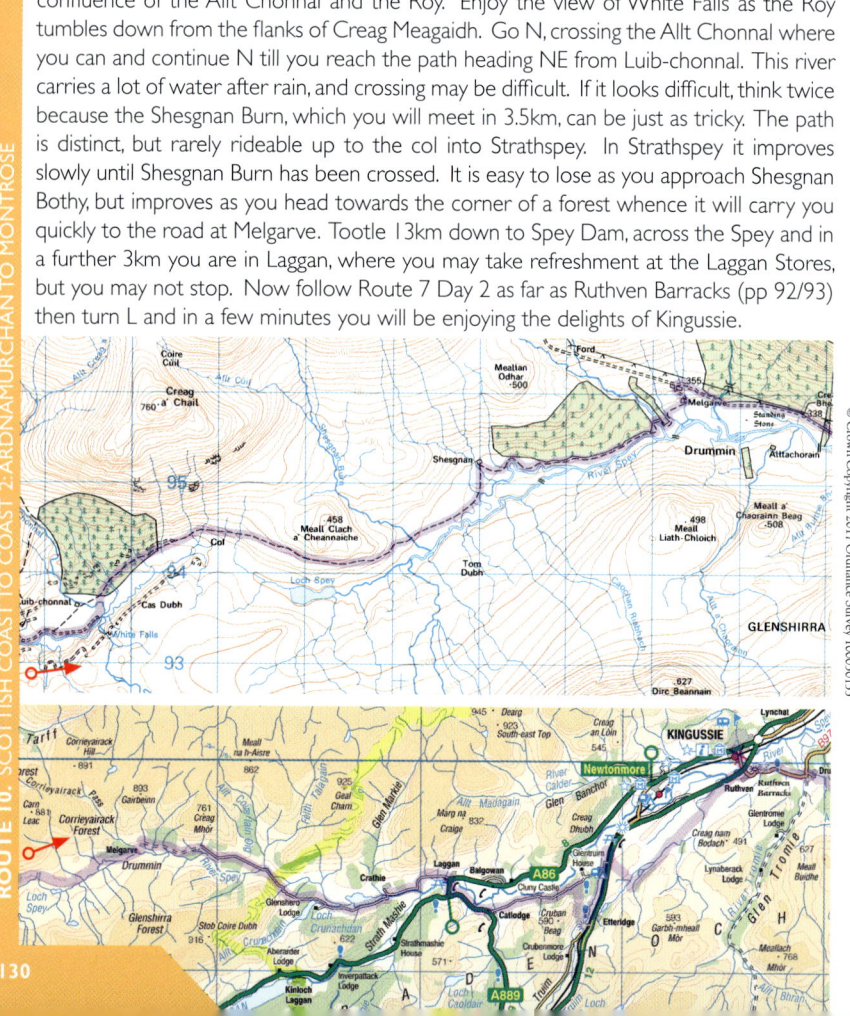

Multi-day routes in northern Britain

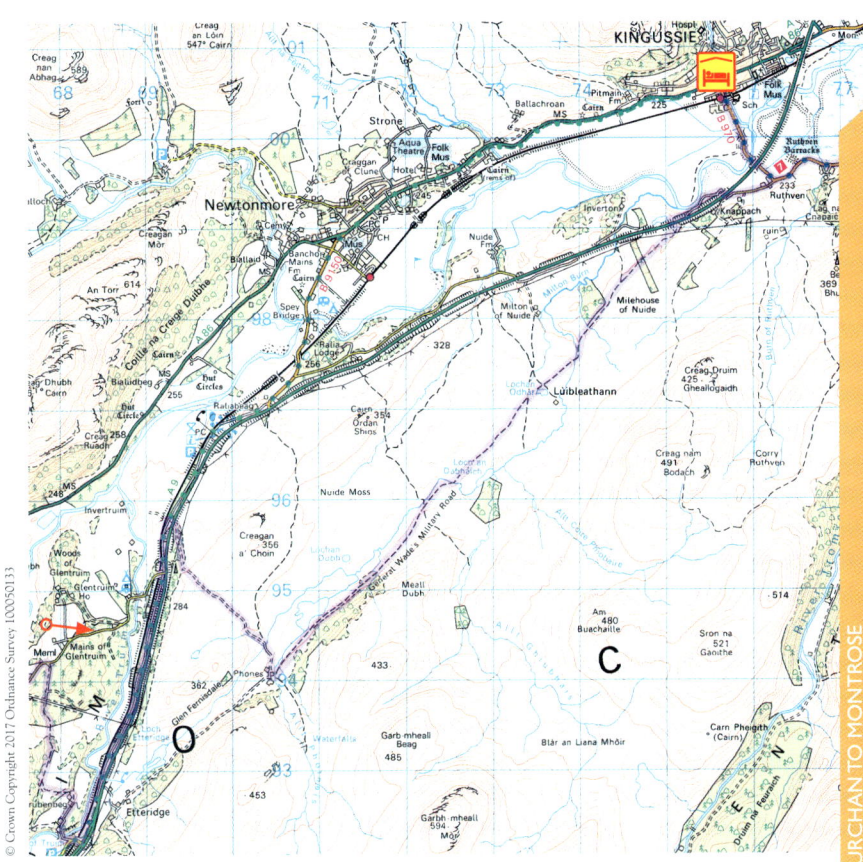

DAY 3.

Start:	Kingussie
Finish:	Ballater
Distance:	84km (52miles)
Off-road:	42km (26miles) 50%
Ascent:	1372m (4505ft)
Descent:	1409m (4624ft)
Grade:	M3

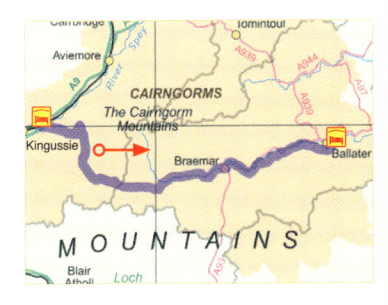

OVERVIEW

Tarmac and forest tracks lead you into Glenfeshie. More tarmac conducts you southwards up this jewel of a strath. Good tracks take you deep into the heart of Cairngorms as the Feshie

ROUTE 10. SCOTTISH COAST TO COAST 2: ARDNAMURCHAN TO MONTROSE

131

Mountain Biking Adventures:

turns sharply E through natural forest below lowering cliffs. Rough, but mostly rideable, paths take you to the high point and traditional luncheon spot at Eidart Bridge from where 1 or 2km of indistinct path take you over the watershed into Glens Geldie and Dee and then out to Braemar on very good paths, tracks and, finally, tarmac. Refreshments here, then road and delightful forest tracks in Royal territory lead to a further road finish.

ROUTE

Retrace yesterday's route over the Spey, under the A9 and past Ruthven Barracks to Tromie Bridge. Turn R into Glen Tromie and after 25m turn L up a track to the hamlet of Drumguish. After just under 500m turn R. Follow this track for 6km as it curves from SSE to NE around Craig Dhubh. It's tempting, at the most southerly point, to take the shortcut by path via Baileguish and Corarnstilmore, but you are unlikely to save time in the bog and the track is a delight.

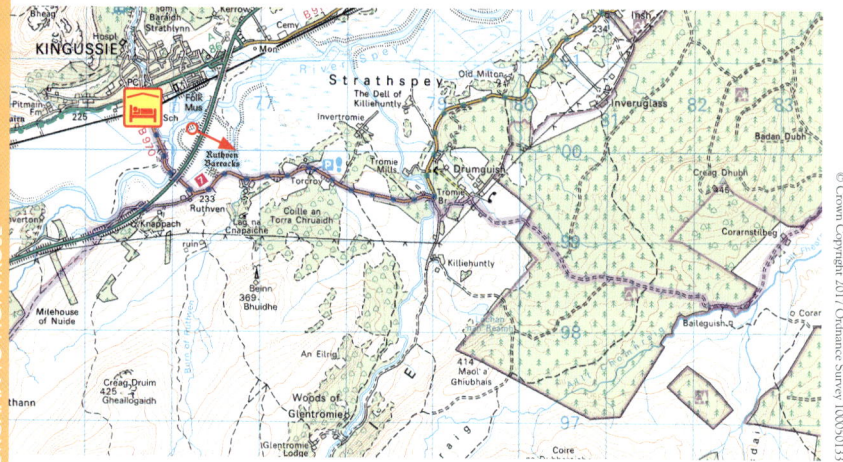

When you meet the tarmac road in Glenfeshie turn R and follow it for 3.5km until a rickety bridge gives you access to the other bank. Follow the delightful path S to meet up with tracks again by the remains of a bridge at Carnachuin.

The bridge at Carnachuin. Now washed away.

Multi-day routes in northern Britain

Follow this good grassy track now as it curves SE. The better track crosses the Feshie at an elbow in the river where the bank is steepest. It's better to stay on the higher, narrow, and in places eroded path if you want to keep your feet dry, rejoining the track after the second crossing.

As the track becomes easterly, it gives way to path, boggy in places. At the 'shelter' (don't expect too much) the path starts to leave the Feshie. Follow the signpost to Eidart Bridge. The path, NE, to this magnificent structure is narrow and easy to miss.

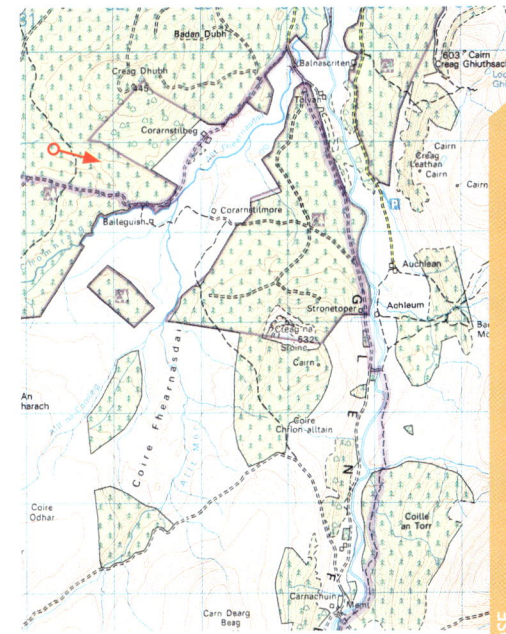

© Crown Copyright 2017 Ordnance Survey 100050133

Ford across the Feshie: one of potentially many. Photo © Jim Barton (cc-by-sa/2.0)

ROUTE 10. SCOTTISH COAST TO COAST 2: ARDNAMURCHAN TO MONTROSE

133

Mountain Biking Adventures:

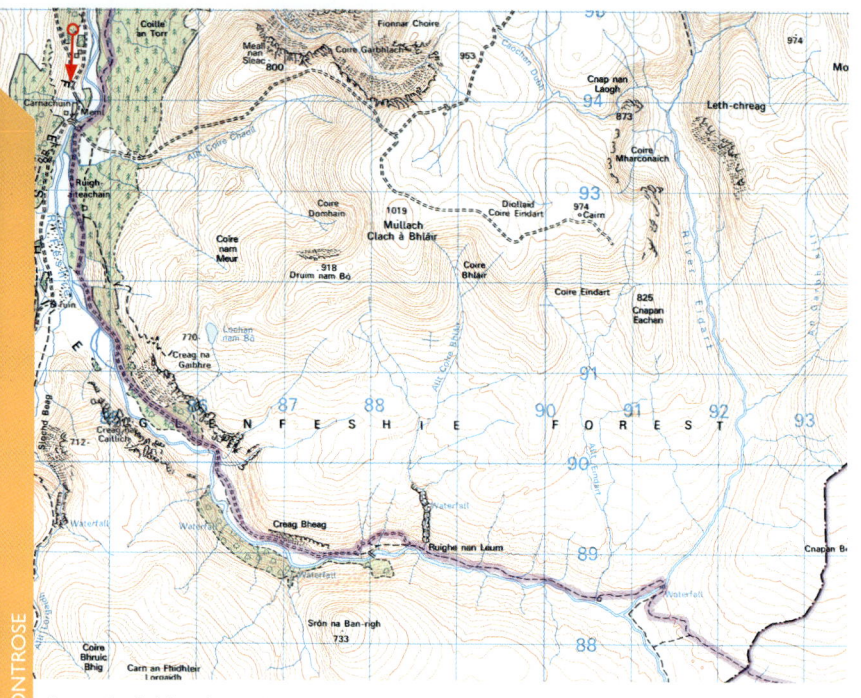

From the bridge the path is very indistinct for 1km, allegedly following a 'C' shape downhill beside the burn and then easterly uphill again. Once it returns to the slightly higher ground it is distinct and a delight to ride for the next 4km along the flanks of Geldie Burn, until it meets the track which takes you via White Bridge into Strath Dee and out, in about 12km, to Linn of Dee.

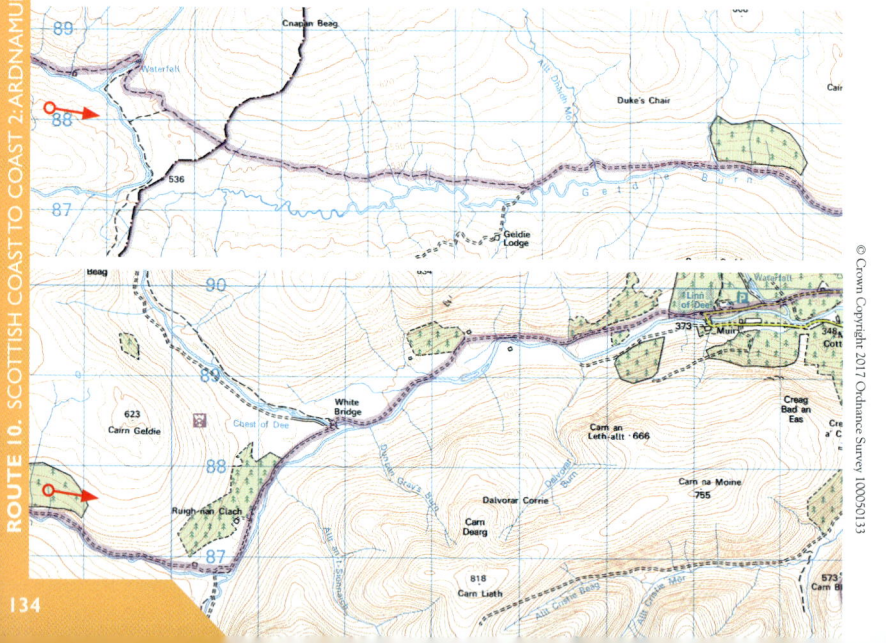

Multi-day routes in northern Britain

Keep L on tarmac through Claybokie to Mar Lodge. Turn R, to pass respectfully through the estate buildings and head towards the magnificent Victoria Bridge. Cross the Dee and take the main road to Braemar.

Take refreshment and continue on the A93 to Bridge of Dee. Immediately after the bridge on the main road, turn R and cross the Dee again on the magnificent Invercauld Bridge into the Balmoral estate. Make sure you call the estate office and seek permission, freely given except when Her Majesty is in residence, or you may be intercepted by young men in black windowed Range Rovers whose suits bulge with muscle and, one imagines, metal.

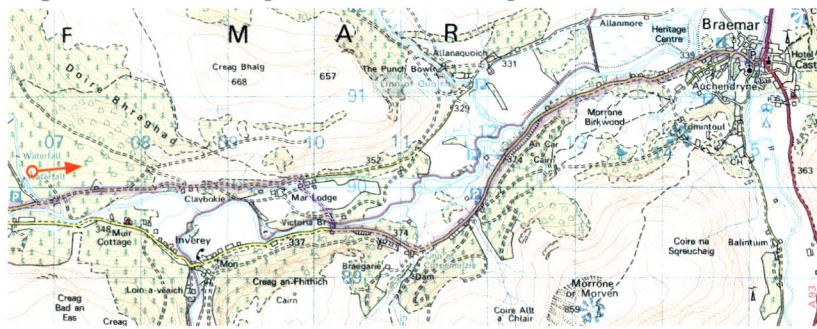

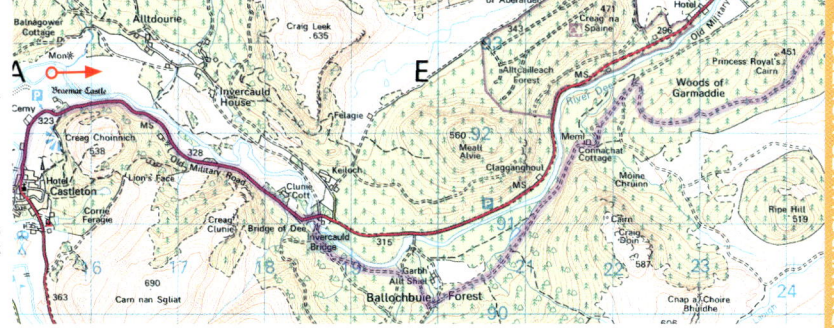

Bear L and turn L again at the fork, avoiding L and R in about 1km, to come to a bridge on your L. Cross the bridge and continue past Connachat Cottage. Take the second R, about a km from the Cottage, and climb up into the Woods of Garmaddy on the track that runs S of Princess Royal's Cairn. Descend joyfully until a bridge on the R crosses Gelder Burn and at the next 'T' junction, in 200m, turn R and follow the track up between Prince Albert's Cairn and Princess Helena's Cairn. At Easter Balmoral pickup the B976 and follow it to Bridge of Muich and in 1 more km, to Ballater.

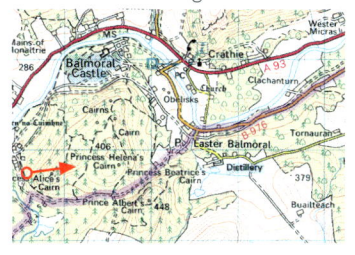

Mountain Biking Adventures:

DAY 4.

Start:	Ballater
Finish:	Montrose
Distance:	72.5km (45miles)
Off-road:	41.5km (26miles) 57%
Ascent:	1389m (4560ft)
Descent:	1585m (5202ft)
Grade:	H2

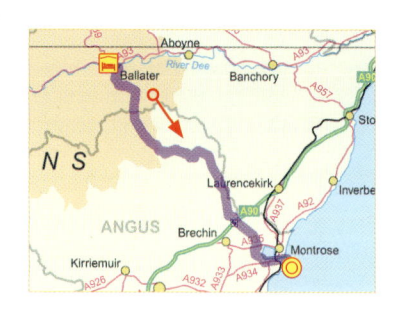

OVERVIEW

Two big climbs over heathery grouse moors, the second to 750m just under the most easterly Munro, Mount Keen, which you can, like two of our group did, shoot up on foot. A rapid descent to the Glens of Angus and a pleasant 20km grassy track/path leads to some road and an impressive lighthouse at the sea.

ROUTE

Retrace yesterday's route to the Bridge of Muick. Just as the road curves toward the bridge take the track on the immediate L of the memorial bench. In 400m turn L and in about a further 150m turn R. The track climbs steeply through forest, and more steeply once it has emerged from the trees up the flank of Craig Vallich. Avoid the first L, which heads for the summit, take the next L by a couple of tiny lochans at a col. Enjoy the retrospective of Lochnagar and the Cairngorm massif before you start to descend through a tight hairpin. Don't get too enthusiastic, because in about 750m you must look out for an indistinct path to the R just after the first burn crossing. Follow this path with difficulty ESE up and over the indistinct ridge of Lach na Gualainn and begin your descent towards

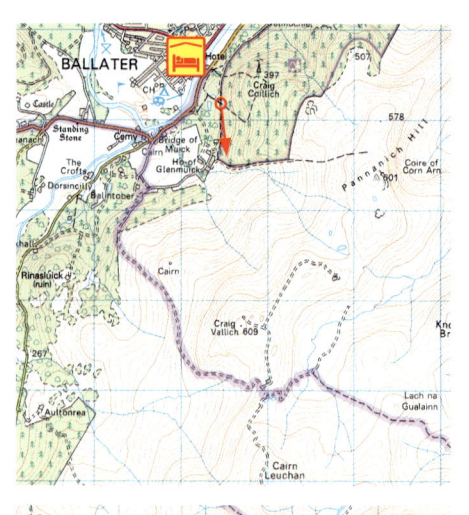

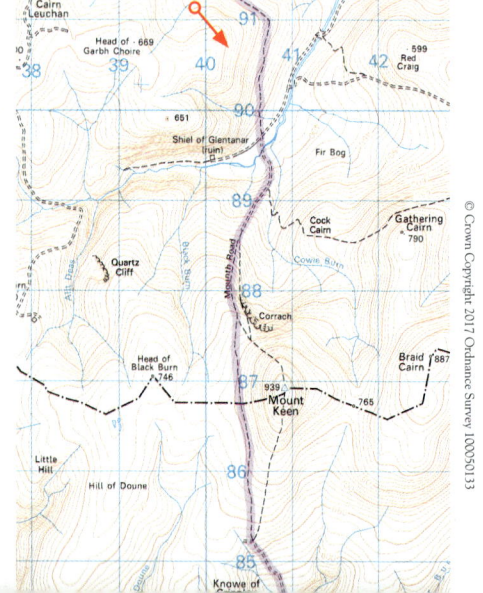

© Crown Copyright 2017 Ordnance Survey 100050133

ROUTE 10. SCOTTISH COAST TO COAST 2. ARDNAMURCHAN TO MONTROSE

136

Multi-day routes in northern Britain

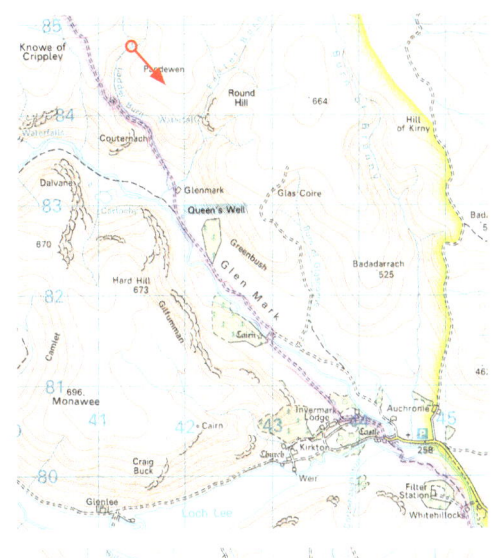

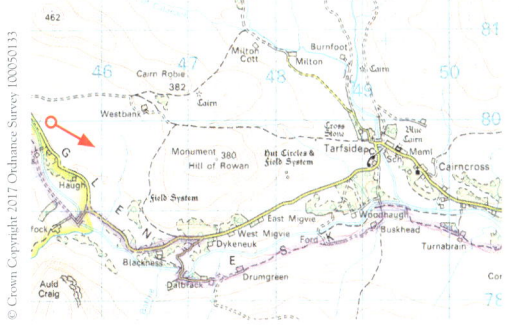

Waters of Tanar and the Mounth Road. The path is steep, narrow and patchy, but many will enjoy it as it hugs the hillside and turns S. At the track, carry straight on, S, and cross the Tanar on a bridge, not shown on the OS map and start your climb up Mount Keen on a good but steep track. The track gets steeper and in 1km deteriorates to a rutted and rocky push. Take the R fork, where it branches and R again in a further kilometre. Here you may remount. Munro baggers might park at the summit of this path and run up Mount Keen.

The reward for your recent grunt work is a fabulous descent on a well-made path/track into Glenmark and to the Queen's Well, providing you don't get too much air on the drainage ditches or miss the hairpins.

If you're in a hurry, you can continue down the L bank of the Mark (which becomes the North Esk after the confluence with Waters of Lee) on the tarmac road to the the B966 just N of Edzell.

The superb track descent to Glen Mark.
Photo © Alan Reid (cc-by-sa/2.0)

Mountain Biking Adventures:

However, on the R bank there is an almost continuous mixture of grassy path and track, well metalled in places, which provides about 20km of a different kind of off-road joy after the exertions and exhilarations of the first part of your day. Continue SE along Glen Mark, crossing the river at the bridge 1.5km from Queen's Well and continue SE again bearing L at the first junction, past Invermark Castle to the head of the tarmac road at a fine bridge. On the nearside of the bridge the path goes off to the R for a couple of hundred metres SE to a footbridge over Waters of Lee. Cross it and continue SE past the filter station and then on good track to cross back just E of Glen Effock. Turn R on the tarmac and follow it for 1.5km to Dykeneuk, taking the first R signposted to Dalbrack and Drumgreen. This road almost doubles back, SW to start with before going S, crossing the Esk and turning E to Dalbrack. As you pass through the farmstead, tarmac gives way to farm track and in another 300m, past Drumgreen, to grassy path. The route continues to hug the Esk, rarely more than 200m from it, on a mixture of grassy path and grassy or well-metalled track for the next 11km, until it turns to tarmac 2km N of Dalbog.

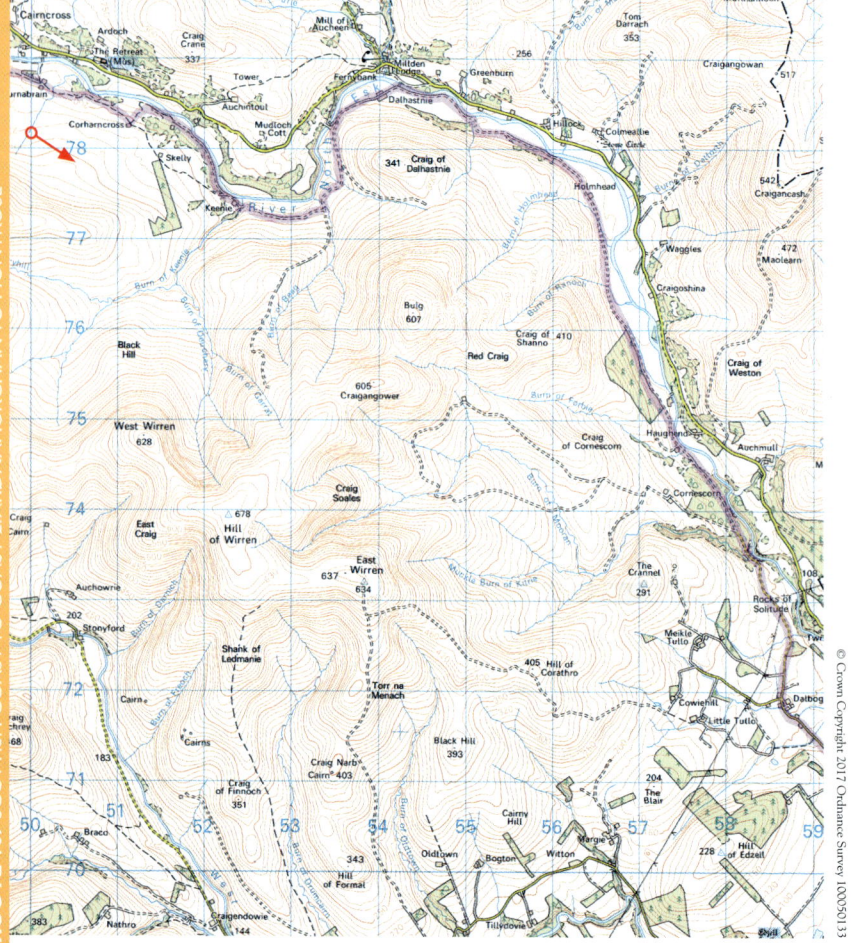

Multi-day routes in northern Britain

Follow the tarmac road S to the B996 and turn right, S, to Edzel, where you will probably be ready for some afternoon tea. Refreshed, continue S for 3km to Inchbare, where turn L for Stracathro. In 1km turn L at the school and then, in 200m, take the next R. Continue SE crossing the A90, turning L and then R again at the next unclassified road. In 4km come to Dun and, soon, the A935. Turn R and then immediately L, following signs to Bridge of Dun. Just past the railway station turn L and follow the minor road around the Montrose Basin to reach the A934. Turn L and at the roundabout in 2km continue straight on for 1km then turn R into Rossie Square, advertised as leading to Lighthouse Road. Tootle along to the lighthouse and, if so inclined, dip your wheel in the North Sea.

Retrace your steps to the big roundabout and turn R for the town centre and railway station.

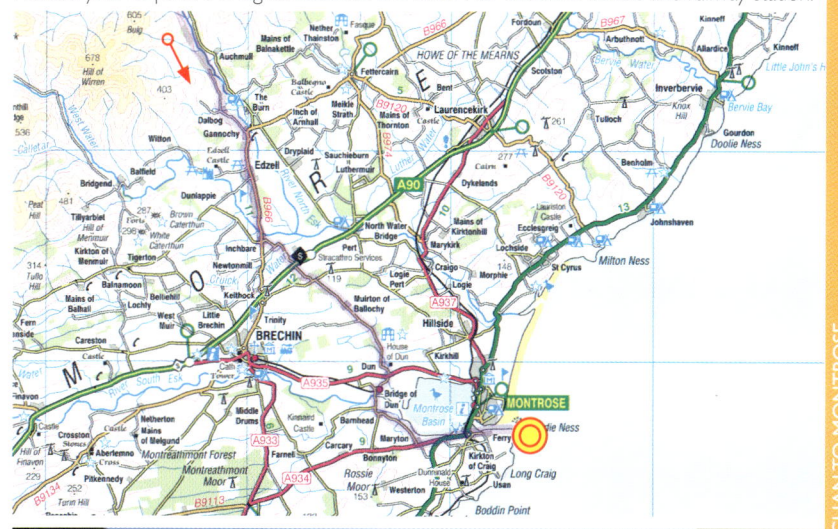

A Feshie crossing.

THE CAIRNGORMS

The Cairngorms are a massive diamond lozenge of granite wilderness enclosed, starting clockwise from Pitlochry, by the A9, the A95, the A939, and the A924.

Skiers play on its northern and eastern flanks. At its heart are the eponymous Cairn Gorm and the magnificent '4000 footers', Ben Macdui, Cairn Toul, and Braeriach. Surrounding these, to the west, south and east is the most remote mass of land in Western Europe.

One pass, the Lairig Ghru, traverses the centre of this wilderness but it is not easily cycled and even if it were, is hard to incorporate in a circular tour. Fortunately, there are many tracks and paths that can be used to circumnavigate the central massive. Four, somewhat overlapping, circuits are presented here, from which a host of variations can be built.

Multi-day routes in northern Britain

11. CAIRNGORM CIRCULAR FROM KINGUSSIE VIA BRAEMAR AND TOMINTOUL

Total route (days):	Three days		
Start & Finish:	Kingussie		
Total Distance:	155km (96 miles).		
Total Off-road (%):	74%		
Daily distance (km):	56	36.5	62.4
Daily off-road (%):	55%	84%	84%
Ascent:	3003m (9856ft)		
Crux day grade:	E3		

Multi-day routes in northern Britain

OVERVIEW

This is the tightest and shortest of the easier routes around the Cairngorms, but delightful nevertheless. The remote Feshie/Geldie watershed leads to the Dee and Braemar, then high grouse moors and Strath Avon. The last day is a classic feast of mountain biking through lowland Cairngorm majesty, including the wondrous natural Caledonian forest of Rothiemurchus.

DAY 1.

Start:	Kingussie
Finish:	Braemar
Distance:	56km (34.5miles)
Off-road:	31km (19miles) 55%
Ascent:	999m (3279ft)
Descent:	901m (2958ft)
Grade:	E3

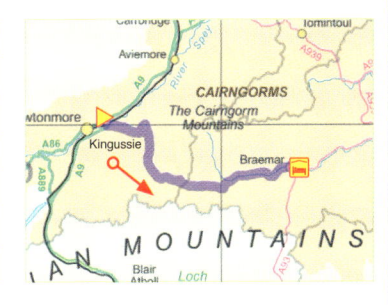

OVERVIEW

Tarmac and forest tracks lead you into Glenfeshie. More tarmac conducts you southwards up this jewel of a strath. Good tracks take you deep into the heart of Cairngorms as the Feshie turns sharply E through natural forest below lowering cliffs. Rough, but mostly rideable, paths take you to the high point, from where 1 or 2km of indistinct path take you over the watershed into Glens Geldie and Dee and then out to Braemar on very good paths, tracks and, finally, tarmac. No refreshment en route.

ROUTE

This day is entirely as for Route 10, Day 3 as far as Braemar (pp 132/135).

Another crossing of the Feshie.

ROUTE 11. CAIRNGORM CIRCULAR FROM KINGUSSIE VIA BRAEMAR AND TOMINTOUL

Mountain Biking Adventures:

DAY 2.

Start:	Braemar
Finish:	Tomintoul
Distance:	36.5km (23miles)
Off-road:	31km (19miles) 84%
Ascent:	987m (3240 ft)
Descent:	987m (3240 ft)
Grade:	E3

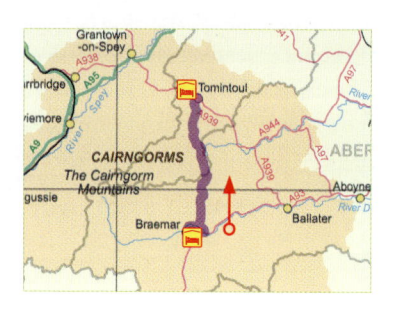

OVERVIEW

Excellent tracks punctuated by about 2km of delightful singletrack through big mountain country, grouse moors to start, then the long Strath Avon

ROUTE

Take the A93 East towards Ballater for about 4km. Pass Invercauld Bridge on your R and in about 200m turn L. Bear L through hamlet of Keiloch and then, in 1400m bear R to take the track which climbs steeply under the flank of Craig Leek. Follow this track for 10km. Fabulous views of the Dee Valley and the end of Beinn a Bhuird reward the climb up past Invercauld. Easier cycling 'contours' round to the flanks of Culardoch, where the track steepens considerably. From the summit there is a tremendous downhill into Glen Gairn, continue down the Glen for just over a km and cross the River Gairn by bridge. In about 600m turn L amidst several lochans. The Loch Builg path goes off to the R in about 400m, just before locked gates.

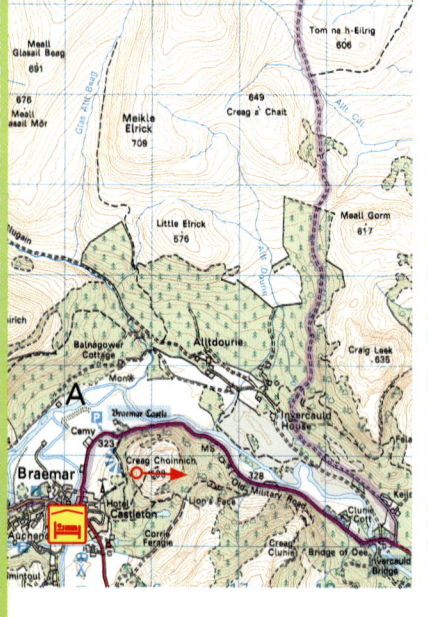

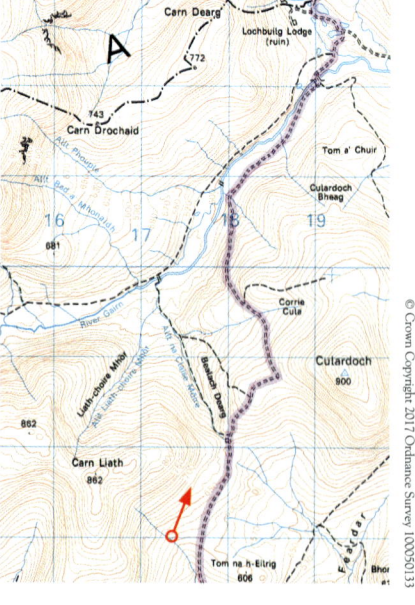

ROUTE 11. CAIRNGORM CIRCULAR FROM KINGUSSIE VIA BRAEMAR AND TOMINTOUL

© Crown Copyright 2017 Ordnance Survey 100050133

144

Multi-day routes in northern Britain

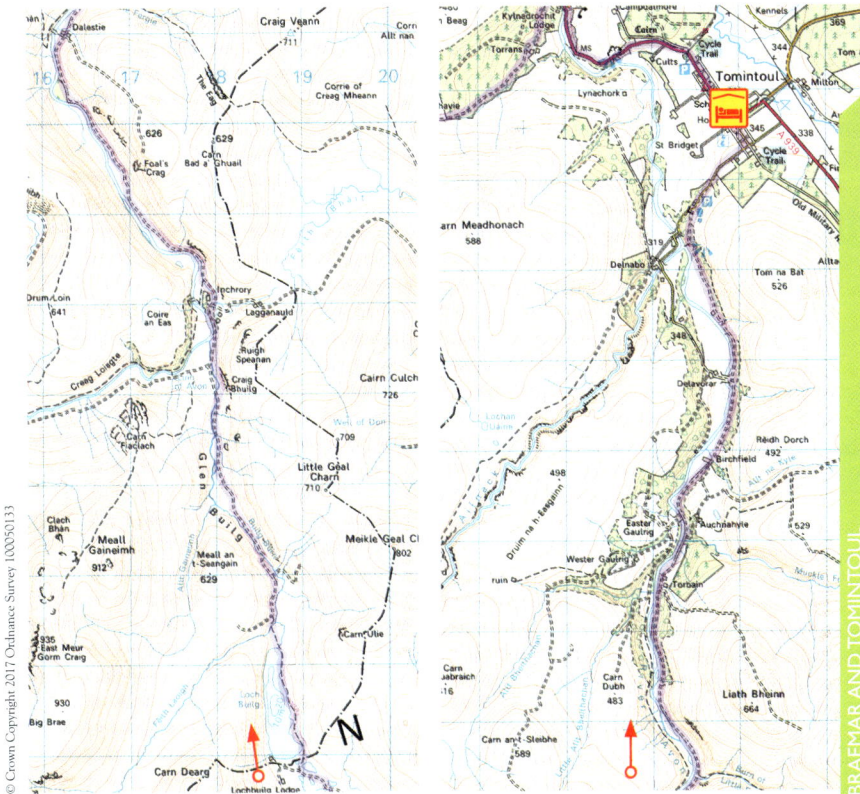

Though indistinct for the first couple of hundred metres, this soon becomes a well-defined and delightful singletrack switchback beside the loch.

Singletrack by Loch Builg.

ROUTE 11: CAIRNGORM CIRCULAR FROM KINGUSSIE VIA BRAEMAR AND TOMINTOUL

145

Mountain Biking Adventures:

About 300m after Loch Builg the path meets a track which carries you 16km N to Tomintoul, first by the River Builg which you must ford twice. The River Avon joins majestically from the L and you continue on its R bank until you meet the minor road 1km from Tomintoul. Turn R here and then first L to come to the centre of the village.

Strath Avon.

DAY 3.

Start:	Tomintoul
Finish:	Kingussie
Distance:	62.5km (39miles)
Off-road:	*52km (32.5miles) 84%*
Ascent:	1017m (3339ft)
Descent:	1125m (3692ft)
Grade:	E1

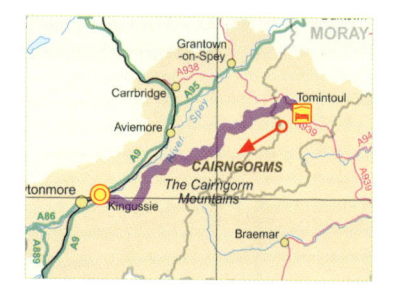

OVERVIEW

Magnificent – almost no need to put a foot down – romp into Strath Nethy and through the marvels of the Rothiemurchus natural Caledonian forests.

Nevertheless the route is complicated, and the description necessarily long. Because of its quality, two of the three other routes share this day.

ROUTE

Leave Tomintoul on the A939 N until, in a couple of kilometres, you come to Bridge of Avon. In 150m after the bridge, a track to the L turns back sharply. Take it and climb steeply through woodland, keeping to the L when it forks in about 500m. In about 2km the track turns sharply R to the N, and drops into Glen Brown at the start of small forest. A patchy path follows the

Multi-day routes in northern Britain

Glen SW between the river and the forest edge on the L. After about 1km, look out for a track on the opposite bank of the Brown and ford it at any convenient place. The track fords the unnamed tributary of the Brown in 200m and then rises more steeply to meet a better track. (This latter area is not well represented on the OS map.) Turn R, ford the burn again and begin a long and steady climb westwards. From the summit, enjoy the descent towards Dorback Lodge, perhaps not letting rip as much as you could, so you can enjoy the views of the Cairngorms in front of you.

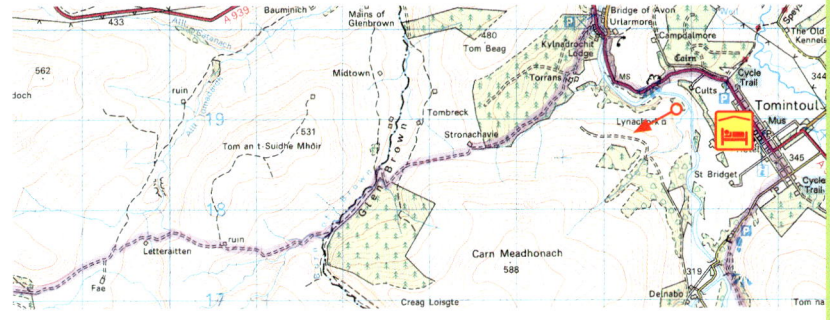

About 300m before the Lodge, carry straight on, avoiding the L fork. This slightly poorer track brings you out on the tarmac in Strath Nethy just W of the Lodge. Follow the tarmac for 1km to Ballintuim and turn L here just after a thin strip of woodland on the L. About 100m down the track, bear L again to miss the farm along a track shown on the OS map as a path, and again L, about three quarters of the way along the strip of woodland. About 300m after the end of the woodland bear L on the slightly less distinct track (cutting off the corner as shown on the map) SE and then E then S again to meet the Dorback Burn. Ford the burn and pick up the heathery path, more or less due S.

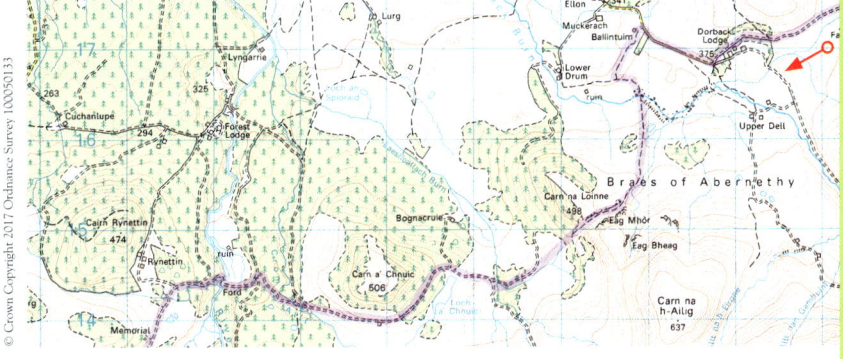

After 1km the path curves to the SW and passes through a small defile, the Eag Mhor. After the defile it continues SW, first through woodland and then through scrub (not shown on the map). It becomes more distinct after about 300m and enters another patch of woodland. The path fords Faesheallach Burn and, after 50m emerges into more open ground and on to a very good track. Follow this W for 2.5km, avoiding turns to L and R until, at a crossroads, you go straight on and descend steeply to ford the River Nethy. Go W for 600m, (ignoring a track in from the R) and, at the next junction turn L to head SSW to Ryvoan Bothy and thence out by improving, but increasingly busy, tracks to Loch Morlich.

Mountain Biking Adventures:

Ryvoan Pass.

Whatever time of day it is, take appropriate refreshment at the Glenmore Shop Cafe and Restaurant. Go down the steps at the LHS of the cafe, and head for the loch. Follow the path S about 100m from the shoreline. Eventually you will come to a wooden bridge over the river, which is about 250m from the loch. Go S for 150m, turn L, then turn R in another 100m. Cross a minor stream and continue until you meet a better track running W along the southern edge of Loch Morlich. Follow this, hugging the loch and ignoring two L turns until you come to a large forestry road at NH956093. Turn L and follow this track for 1km, where a well signposted, but still easy to miss, path goes off to the R to the Cairngorm Club Footbridge. Cross the bridge and in 200m turn L. The next 'T' junction, in about 2km, is the track around Loch an Eilein. The shortest route is to turn L and when, at the southernmost part of the loch, the path departs from the shore, turn L by Loch Gamhna. (If you have time, go right round Loch an Eilein in either direction. It is a treat.)

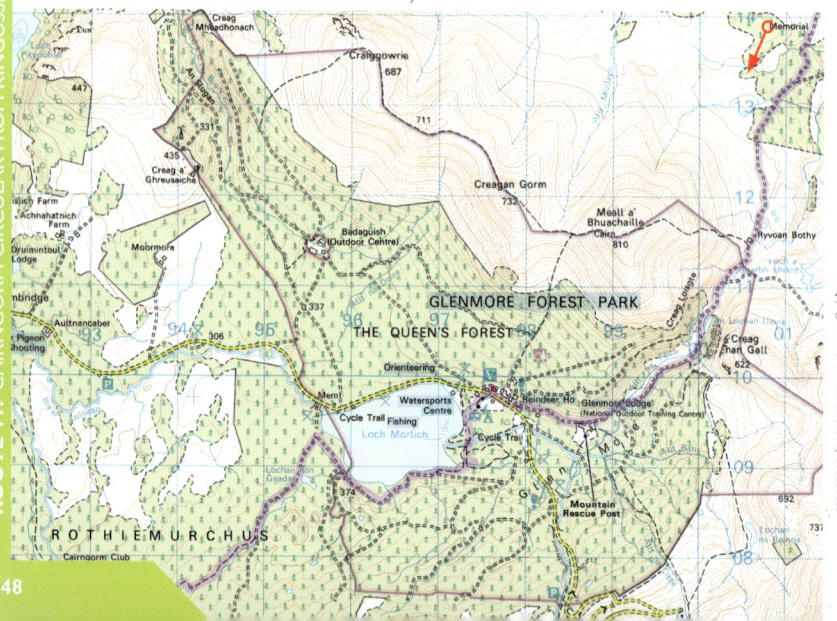

ROUTE 11. CAIRNGORM CIRCULAR FROM KINGUSSIE VIA BRAEMAR AND TOMINTOUL

148

Multi-day routes in northern Britain

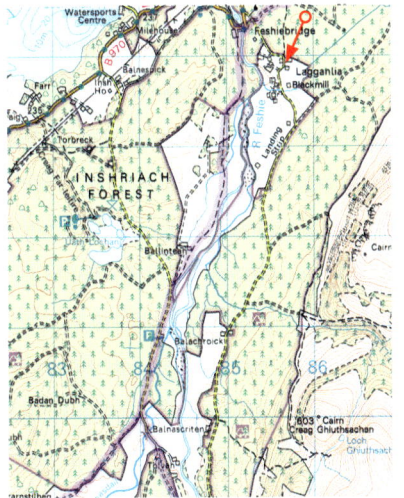

Continue SSE, (avoiding the path that goes around Loch Gamhna) on this entertaining singletrack, until by a small hut you come upon a forest track. Follow this for 2km to a crossroads at NH863055, where turn L. At the next 'T', in 1km, turn R and follow the track down to Feshie Bridge. Cross the Feshie, take the first L, S on a track by some dwellings. This soon becomes a path. Follow it southwards to Ballintean. Here a bizarre detour, not shown on the map, takes you around the curtilage and eventually delivers you on to the tarmac road down Glen Feshie. Turn L, and after about 1500m you will find yourself at the track you came in on Day 1. Reverse your route to Kingussie.

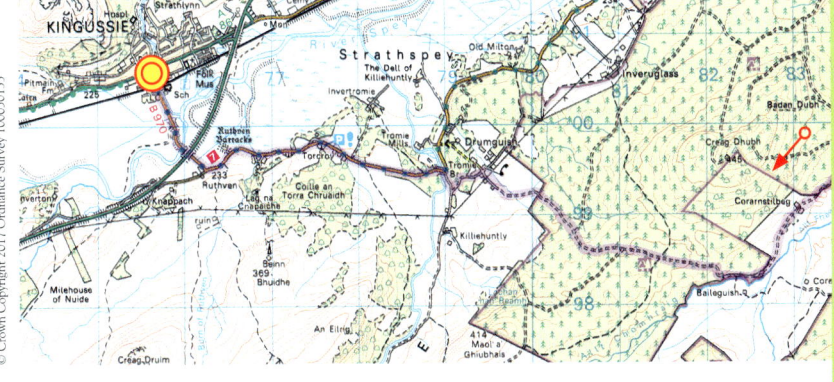

ROUTE 11. CAIRNGORM CIRCULAR FROM KINGUSSIE VIA BRAEMAR AND TOMINTOUL

149

12. CAIRNGORM CIRCULAR FROM BRAEMAR VIA AVIEMORE AND BLAIR ATHOLL

Total route (days):	Three days		
Start & Finish:	Braemar		
Total Distance:	204.5km (127miles)		
Total Off-road (%):	60%.		
Daily distance (km):	76.5	83.5	45
Daily off-road (%):	83%	48%	43%
Ascent:	3881m (12,739ft)		
Crux day grade:	H2		

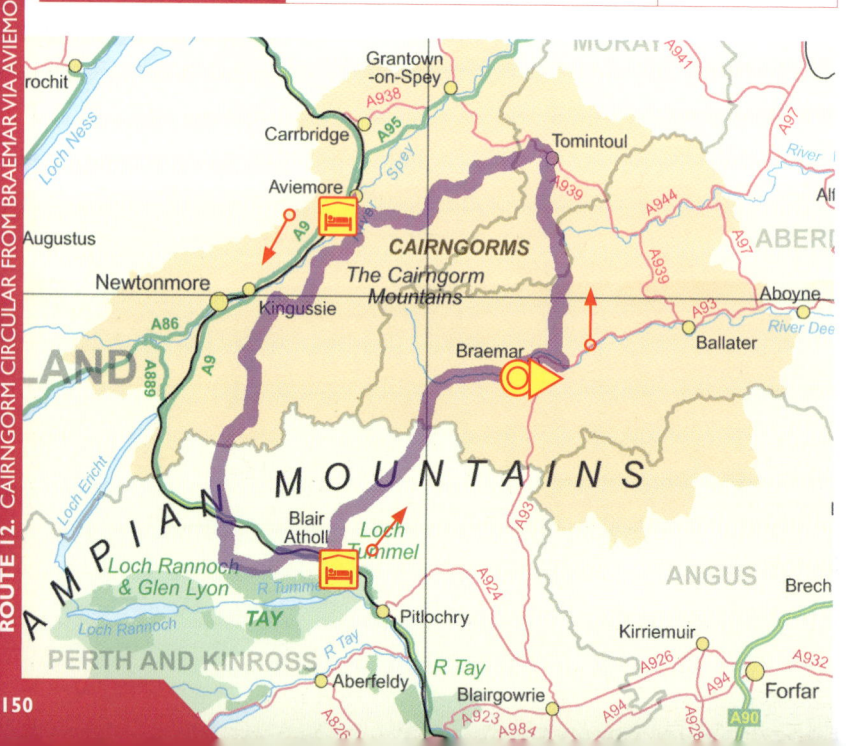

Multi-day routes in northern Britain

DAY 1.

Start:	Braemar
Finish:	Aviemore
Distance:	76.5km (47.5miles)
Off-road:	63.5km (39.5miles) 83%
Ascent:	1703m (5591ft)
Descent:	1824m (5986ft)
Grade:	H2

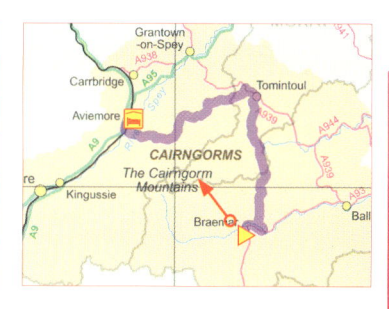

OVERVIEW

This day incorporates Day 2 and the Abernethy Forest section of Day 3 from Route 11. Lunch available at Tomintoul, and afternoon tea at Loch Morlich.

ROUTE

From Braemar follow Route 11 Day 2 to Tomintoul and Route 11 Day 3 as far as the Cafe at Loch Morlich (pp 144 -149). Cross the road from the cafe and take the purpose-built and signed cycleway to Aviemore, noting that it leaves the roadside into the forest at one point and also crosses the road later. Enjoy an evening of tourist entertainment in the restaurants and pubs.

Feith Laoigh crossing.

ROUTE 12. CAIRNGORM CIRCULAR FROM BRAEMAR VIA AVIEMORE AND BLAIR ATHOLL

Mountain Biking Adventures:

DAY 2.

Start:	Aviemore
Finish:	Blair Atholl
Distance:	83.2km (51.5 miles)
Off-road:	39.5km (24.5miles) 48%
Ascent:	1247m (4093ft)
Descent:	1328m (4358ft)
Grade:	M2

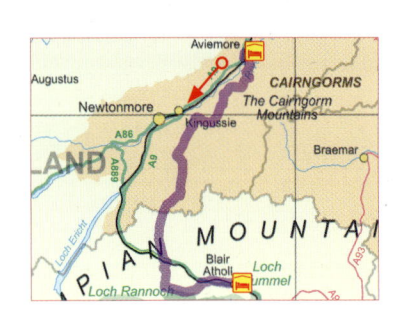

OVERVIEW

Marvellous forest rumble, big through-strath between mountains, one last climb on tarmac, and delightful minor roads to supper. No refreshment en route without taking detours.

ROUTE

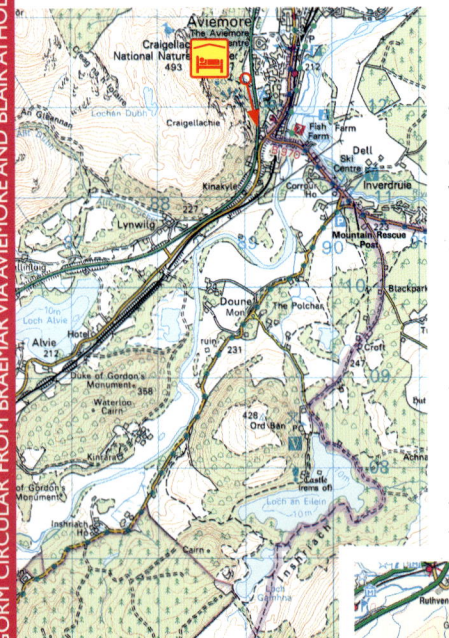

Head S on the B9172 and turn L on to the B970 at the edge of town. Take the second R, after about 2km, signposted for Tullochgrue and Black Park. Follow this for about a km until the tarmac sweeps L. Carry straight on on a well-metalled track, and in 1500m you will find yourself at the at the Loch an Eilein picnic place. Go around the loch in either direction. If you have time, go right round again until you end up at the southernmost point where the path by Loch Gamhna goes off to the S. Here you pick up the Rothiemurchus half of Route 11, Day 3, and follow it to the Glenn Tromie road, 200m S of Tromie Bridge. Turn L and follow this road as it hugs the river S for 14km, passing Loch an t-Seilich and then Gaick Lodge. The tarmac ends at the dam, but a well-metalled track continues to the Lodge from where a good, but rough, track continues for 1.5km to a junction. Turn L, ford the Allt Gharbh Ghaig and continue W to Loch Bhrodainn. The track continues beside the loch, deteriorating somewhat as you leave the water behind, for

ROUTE 12. CAIRNGORM CIRCULAR FROM BRAEMAR VIA AVIEMORE AND BLAIR ATHOLL

© Crown Copyright 2017 Ordnance Survey 100050133

152

Multi-day routes in northern Britain

2km SW until you meet the outfall stream from Loch an Duin. Cross this where you can, and seek out the indistinct path SSW on the W side of the loch. This soon improves and becomes mostly rideable. From the end of the loch the path drops toward Edendon Water. You will see a good track on the other side of this river. Cross where you can and take the track S (L).

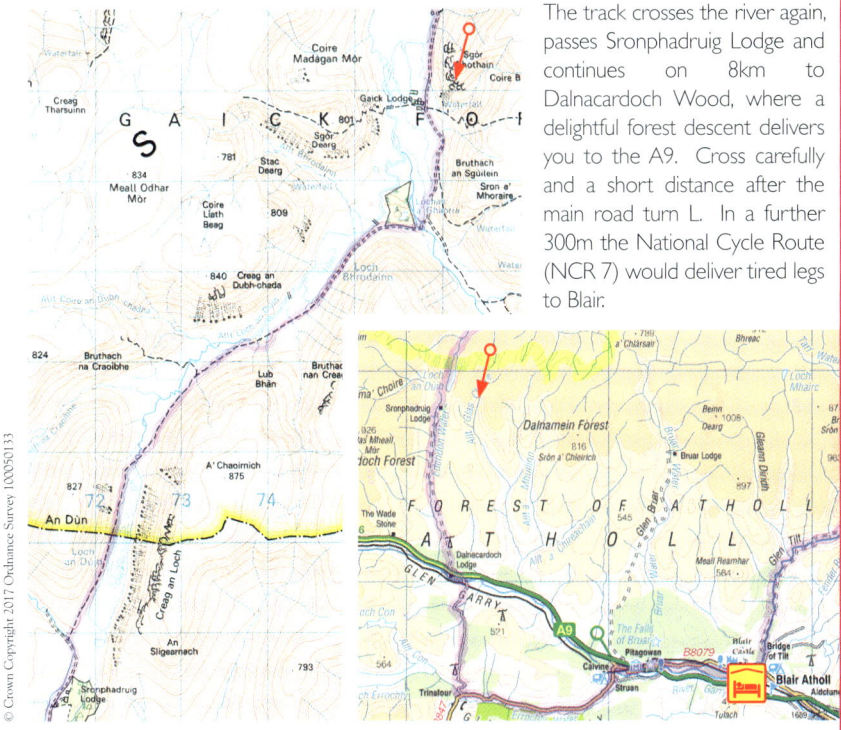

Loch an Duin.

The track crosses the river again, passes Sronphadruig Lodge and continues on 8km to Dalnacardoch Wood, where a delightful forest descent delivers you to the A9. Cross carefully and a short distance after the main road turn L. In a further 300m the National Cycle Route (NCR 7) would deliver tired legs to Blair.

ROUTE 12. CAIRNGORM CIRCULAR FROM BRAEMAR VIA AVIEMORE AND BLAIR ATHOLL

© Crown Copyright 2017 Ordnance Survey 100050133

153

Mountain Biking Adventures:

We, however, bear R and follow the Wade's Road signposted to Trinafour for fabulous views back at the Cairngorm massif. At Trinafour turn L for 7 low traffic kms along the B847. Under the railway, a R turn delivers you back on to the NCR 7, which takes you to Blair Atholl in a further 8km.

DAY 3.

Start:	Blair Atholl
Finish:	Braemar
Distance:	45km (28miles)
Off-road:	19.5km (12miles) 43%
Ascent:	932m (3058ft)
Descent:	728m (2390ft)
Grade:	E3

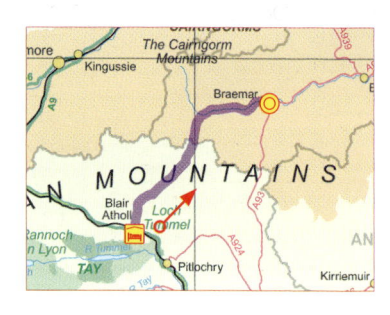

OVERVIEW

Straight up Glen Tilt and straight down the other side. A classic walk or ride through the Southern Cairngorms, lovely woods initially, then a defile and the lightly wooded Caledonian Pine area of Deeside to finish. Wholly rideable for the brave. No refreshment.

ROUTE

From the E side of Bridge of Tilt, go N on the minor road to Old Bridge of Tilt. Turn L and cross the bridge and in about 200m turn R on to a well-metalled track which comes back sharply on itself through woodland. It soon drops to the Tilt, crosses it and then follows the valley NE for 15km.

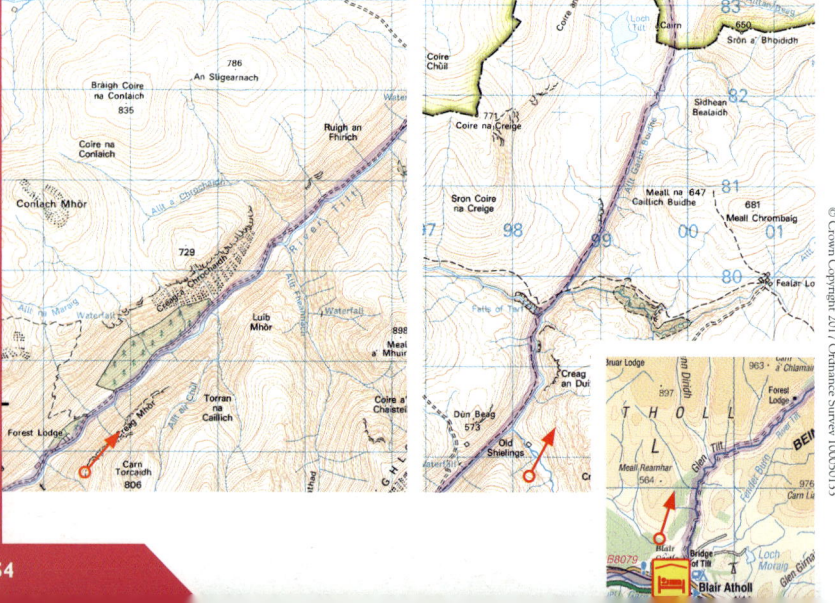

ROUTE 12. CAIRNGORM CIRCULAR FROM BRAEMAR VIA AVIEMORE AND BLAIR ATHOLL

154

Multi-day routes in northern Britain

As the track begins to rise away from the river, another branches off to the R and soon deteriorates to a path. You leave the glaciated U-valley, and enter a steep defile. The path is good, but the drop to the R is not good in places, and you may wisely choose to push at these times. In just over 2km you reach the Falls of Tarf. In another 5km the defile starts to open out to a broad watershed and soon you are enjoying the descent to the ruined Bynack Lodge. In about 0.5km there is an easy ford of the Allt an t-Seilich, which you recross at a bridge in a further 0.5km. Some 200m after this you must ford Geldie Burn. This can be a challenge and sometimes should not be attempted. Across the Geldie, turn R and head along good tracks to Linn of Dee to pick up Route 10 Day 3 to Braemar (pp 134).

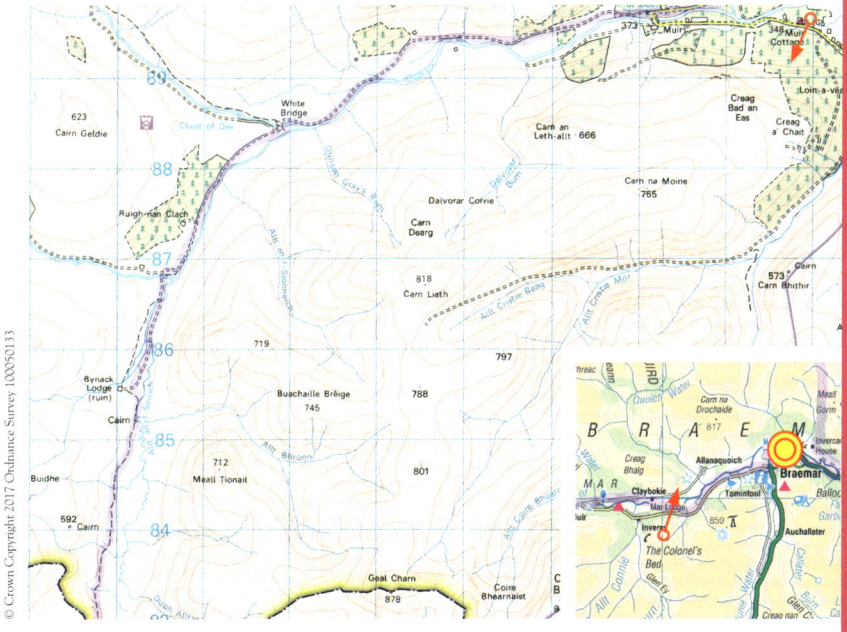

The broad watershed.

ROUTE 12. CAIRNGORM CIRCULAR FROM BRAEMAR VIA AVIEMORE AND BLAIR ATHOLL

155

13. CAIRNGORM AND MONADHLIATH CIRCUIT FROM BLAIR ATHOLL

Total route (days):	Four days				
Start:	Blair Atholl				
Finish:	Kinloch Rannoch/Rannoch Moor Station				
Total Distance:	249km (155miles).				
Total Off-road (%):	62%.				
Daily distance (km):	58	61.5	62	68	
Daily off-road (%):	75%	57%	55%	63%	
Ascent:	5016m (16462ft)				
Crux day grade:	H3				

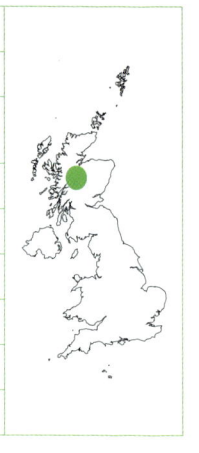

Multi-day routes in northern Britain

OVERVIEW

A big route through both the heart and more peripheral areas of the National Park. Day 2 ascends twice to over 750m and involves crossing the river Avon which, if high, would require retreat or a detour of 5 or 6km around Loch Avon with still no guarantee of a safe crossing. Day 3 involves lots of bushwhacking in high wild country. Both are remote.

The route as described is a 'C' rather than a complete circuit. You can descend from the train/sleeper at Blair Atholl and rejoin it at Rannoch Moor. The authors stayed at Kinloch Rannoch and arranged transport to Blair on the first morning.

DAY 1.

Start:	Blair Atholl
Finish:	Braemar
Distance:	58km (36miles)
Off-road:	43.5km (27miles) 75%
Ascent:	1423m (4672ft)
Descent:	1223m (4013ft)
Grade:	M2

OVERVIEW

A deviation from Glen Tilt round the remote glens S and E of the mighty Beinn a Ghlo and over a high col, to join the Tilt (route of Day 3, Route 12) just before half way. Some good riding.

ROUTE

Take the minor road from the E side of Bridge of Tilt in Blair Atholl towards Old Bridge of Tilt. Go straight on following signs for Glenfender and Monzie. The road is steep. Avoid turns to L and R and follow the tarmac to Loch Moraig. Here, at a gate and cattle grid, it becomes a well-metalled track. Carry straight on for 1700m, continuing to rise, though less steeply. Take the less distinct, and easy to miss, path off to the L about 300m after the summit. This is rough and deteriorates to singletrack in about 1km and descends to a burn.

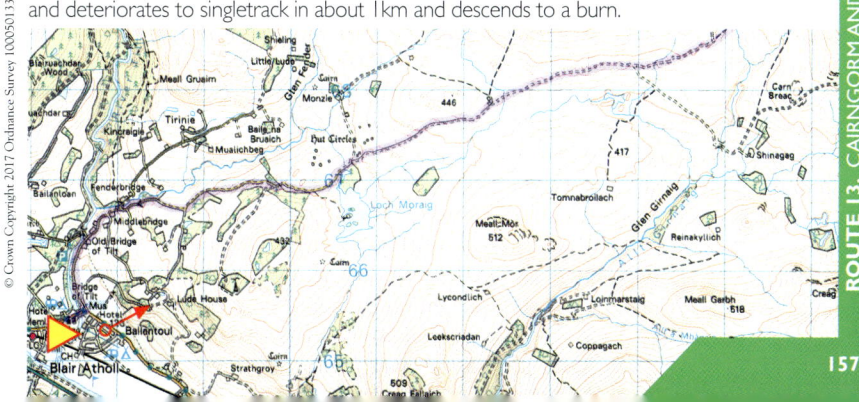

ROUTE 13. CAIRNGORM AND MONADHLIATH CIRCUIT FROM BLAIR ATHOLL

157

Mountain Biking Adventures:

Avoid L turns which are unmarked on the map. Across the burn the path is easy to lose as you rise steeply on to the shoulder of Sron na h-Innearach. Don't worry, just keep going (pushing) up ENE until you come to the much better path coming up from the south. Turn L. This is now mostly cycleable singletrack which, after 3km, just over the watershed, gives way to a good track. Follow the track NE and then trending SE, and enjoy the descent to Daldhu.

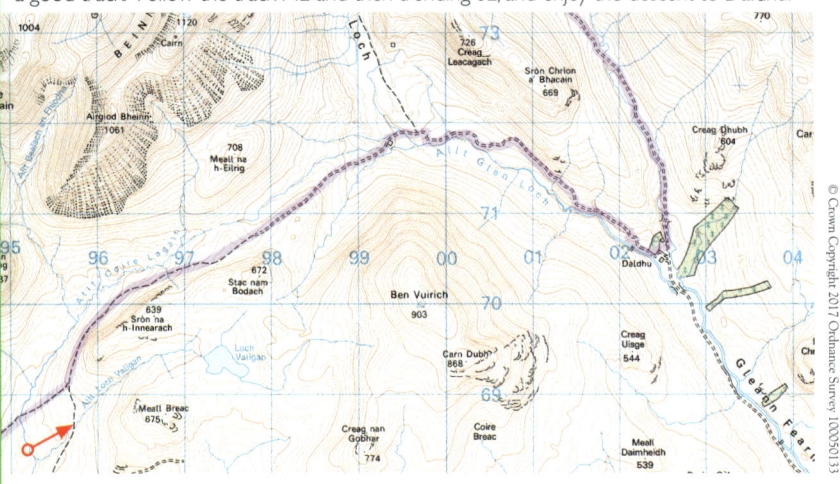

At the 'T' junction 100m or so beyond the buildings, turn L and go N on the well-made track to Fealar Lodge. The track rises steadily beside the Allt Fearnach then more steeply to the col at its end. It drops slightly over a couple of kilometres into Gleann Mor and then contours at about 550m altitude above the Allt a Ghlinne Mhoir and its tributary the Allt Feith Lair (Fealar) to this remotest lodge and farmstead. About 50m before the lodge, cross a bridge and pass through a gate. Where the track passes the lodge keep round to the L as it doubles back in front of a row of farm buildings. Keep going SW, aiming for a gate about 40m past the end of buildings. This admits you to a delightful singletrack. Follow this roughly westwards for 2km until it drops you steeply into the upper reaches of Glen Tilt about 500m N of the Falls of Tarf. Cross the river and take the good path, R, NW. Your way is now as Route 12 Day 3 (pp 154/155) as far as Linn of Dee and then as Route 10 Day 3 (pp 134/135) to Braemar.

Above the watershed Glens Girnaig/Loch. Carn Liath of Bein a Ghlo in mist.

ROUTE 13. CAIRNGORM AND MONADHLIATH CIRCUIT FROM BLAIR ATHOLL

Multi-day routes in northern Britain

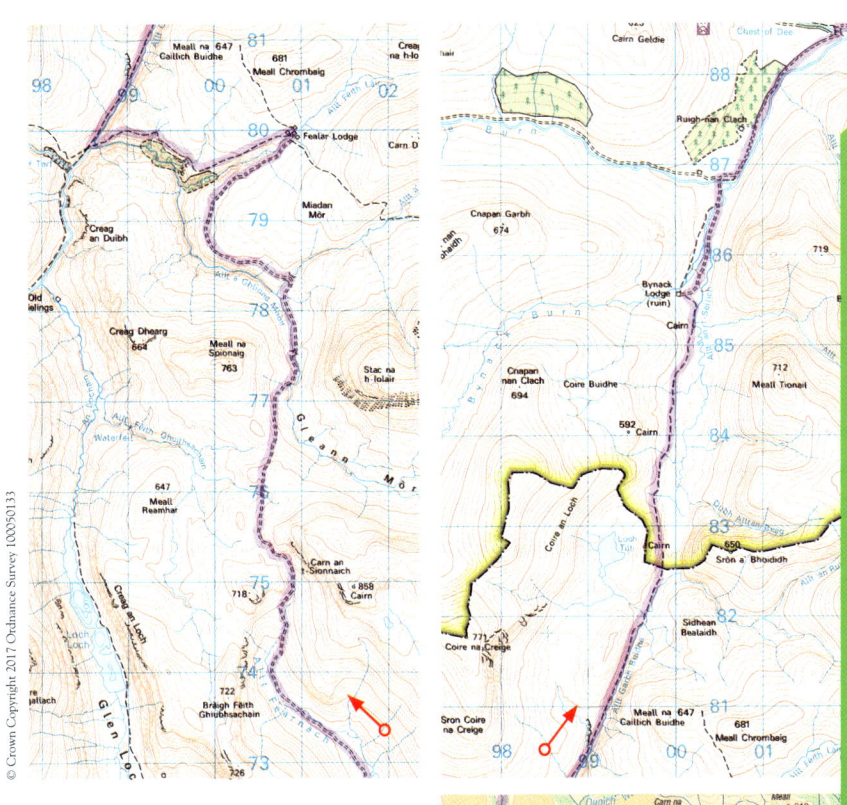

DAY 2.

Start:	Braemar
Finish:	Carrbridge
Distance:	61.5km (38miles).
Off-road:	*35km (22miles) 57%*
Ascent:	1174m (3855ft)
Descent:	1249m (4099ft)
Grade:	H3

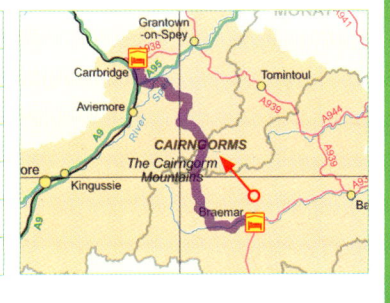

ROUTE 13. CAIRNGORM AND MONADHLIATH CIRCUIT FROM BLAIR ATHOLL

159

Mountain Biking Adventures:

OVERVIEW

The big mountain day, with a scenic approach up Glens Lui and Derry through Caledonian Pine Forest to another of the great N/S Cairngorm passes, Lairig an Laoigh. A good technical descent eventually, and more good riding through Abernethy Forest.

ROUTE

Leave Braemar on the minor road towards Lynn of Dee until, in 5km you reach, and cross, Victoria Bridge, and go up through the estate buildings to the minor road on the other side of the Dee. Turn L and look out for an un-signposted and unprepossessing R turn on to a track just after crossing the Lui Water. Take this track for about 5km to Derry Lodge.

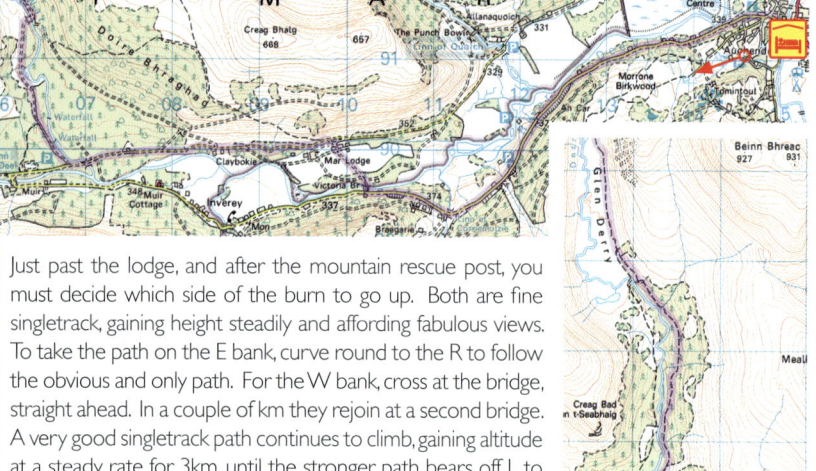

Just past the lodge, and after the mountain rescue post, you must decide which side of the burn to go up. Both are fine singletrack, gaining height steadily and affording fabulous views. To take the path on the E bank, curve round to the R to follow the obvious and only path. For the W bank, cross at the bridge, straight ahead. In a couple of km they rejoin at a second bridge. A very good singletrack path continues to climb, gaining altitude at a steady rate for 3km, until the stronger path bears off L to Coire Etchachan. Take the less distinct path, which steepens and becomes quite rough – a push for almost all – N to Laraig an Laoigh. Enjoy the magnificent views both ways and continue N, cycling where you can, which is not very much, down into Glen Avon.

Ascending on the E side of Glen Derry.

ROUTE 13. CAIRNGORM AND MONADHLIATH CIRCUIT FROM BLAIR ATHOLL

160

Multi-day routes in northern Britain

Approaching the Avon crossing.

Cross the Avon at the stepping stones, though don't expect to keep your feet dry except in the driest summer. And be prepared to accept that the river cannot be crossed. Continue NNE on a fair, but rocky path past Lochan a Bhainne to come to the shoulder of Bynack Mor. A short but steep push brings you out on to a broad plateau on the eastern flank of this magnificent hill. The path is now surprisingly good and easy to cycle into Coire Odhair before rising again to almost 800m. Enjoy the views of the Cairngorm mountain massif, then prepare yourself to drop 250m in barely a km on the magnificent technical descent into Strath Nethy. Cross the Nethy by the footbridge and continue on the track WNW for 1.5km. At the next junction turn R. The well made but occasionally rocky path rises to Ryvoan Bothy and continues on easier ground to enter Abernethy Forest. Follow it for 3km and take the second L track to Forest Lodge. (If you come to the Nethy again, you've come too far!) In another 1.5km go straight on at a crossroads and turn L in about 100 m. Follow this track W for 1.5km, ignoring both L and R turns, to where it curves NW to meet tarmac in a further 500m.

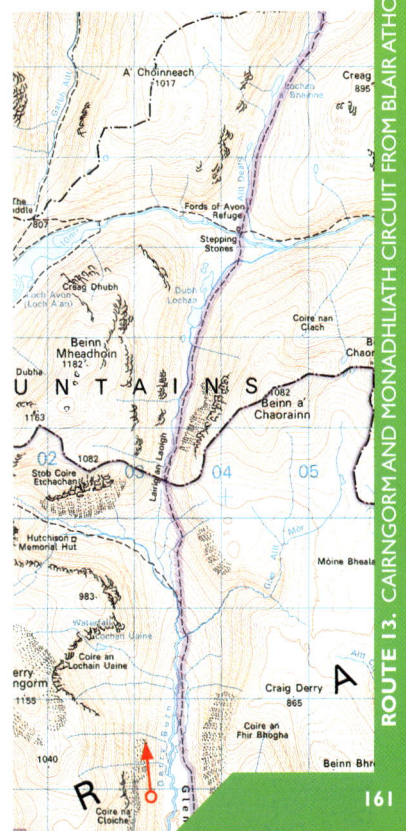

ROUTE 13. CAIRNGORM AND MONADHLIATH CIRCUIT FROM BLAIR ATHOLL

161

Mountain Biking Adventures:

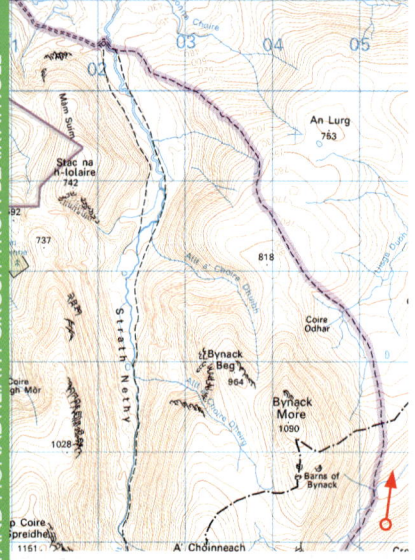

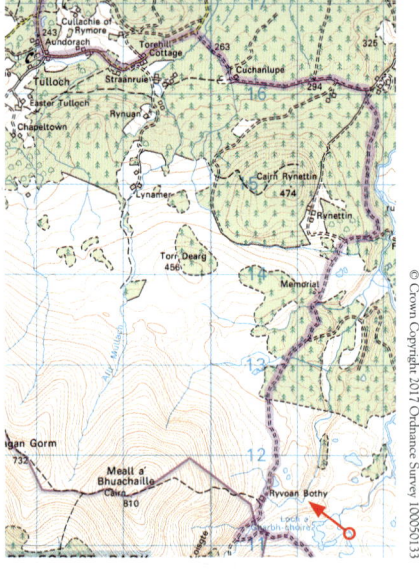

The descent from Bynack More to the Nethy.

Follow the tarmac road W then N, ignoring several turns L until you come to a 'T' junction. Follow signs, L, for Loch Garton and Boat of Garton. In about 1km you will pass the Osprey Centre at Loch Garton which is well worth a visit. In another 1.5km you arrive at the B970, turn L and in one more km turn R on the minor road to Boat of Garton.

Across the Spey, go under the railway, turn L then first R to go W, to follow National Cycle Route (NCR) 7 towards the A95. At the main road turn L and R quickly, to follow NCR 7 again through pleasant forest tracks to Carrbridge, although if you've had enough climbing, take the road.

ROUTE 13. CAIRNGORM AND MONADHLIATH CIRCUIT FROM BLAIR ATHOLL

© Crown Copyright 2017 Ordnance Survey 100050133

162

Multi-day routes in northern Britain

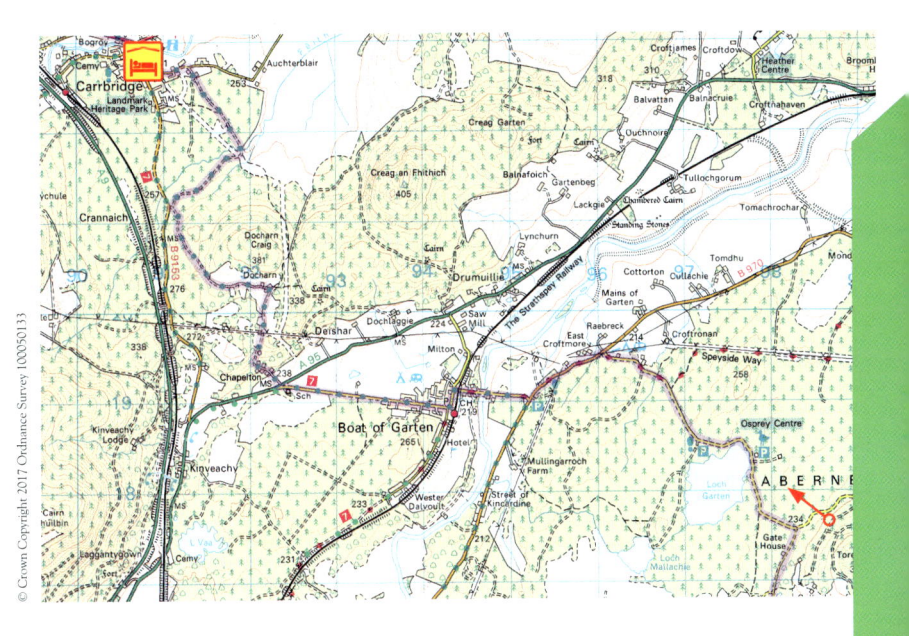

DAY 3.

Start:	Carrbridge
Finish:	Laggan
Distance:	62km (38.5miles)
Off-road:	*34km (21miles) 55%*
Ascent:	1242m (4078ft)
Descent:	1242m (4078ft)
Grade:	H3

OVERVIEW

A long, remote, through route of the Monadhliath, using the Findhorn valley and ascending to 870m, before a good, but relatively short, descent by track down the Markie valley. A tough peaty bushwhack with many minor up and downs for 6 to 7km makes this a big and serious day.

ROUTE

From the centre of the village take Station Road (signposted 'Station and Dalnahaitnach'). Follow NCR 7 via Sluggan Bridge and the Slochd Summit for 14km to Findhorn Bridge. Cross the bridge and take the first L, signposted to Garbole and Coignafearn. Follow this to where the tarmac runs out in 16km at Coignafearn (Old Lodge). Cross the Allt Calder and go straight on, on a well-metalled track, to pass Coignafearn Lodge on your R. Continue SW,

ROUTE 13. CAIRNGORM AND MONADHLIATH CIRCUIT FROM BLAIR ATHOLL

163

Mountain Biking Adventures:

ignoring a L turn at 300m but, in a further 4km, at NH652122, turn L, across the river on a bridge, and take the more southerly track. This curves SSW and climbs, steeply in places, until in a further 4km it ends in a turning circle. A vestige of a path continues in the same direction, but you are soon bushwhacking. Follow the path as best you can, contouring for 2km until, after crossing the third side stream from the R, you find yourself on the banks of the Abhainn Cro Chlach. Hack along the stream, splashing through it as you must for another 1400m, where it trends more southerly. At the next confluence, after about 500m, at NH622043, take the L fork and follow it as it trends SW to a low col between Beinn Odhar to the R and Sneachdach Slinnean on your L. Briefly enjoy the respite from the mire whilst admiring the magnificent views back down Glen Findhorn and forward into the gorge of Red Burn.

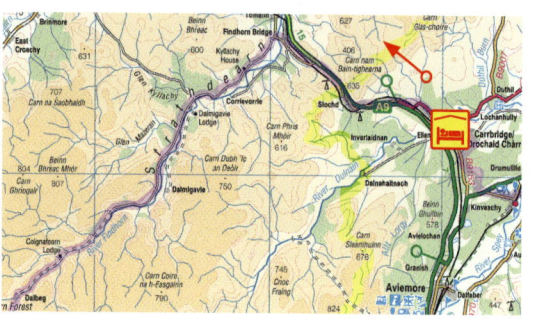

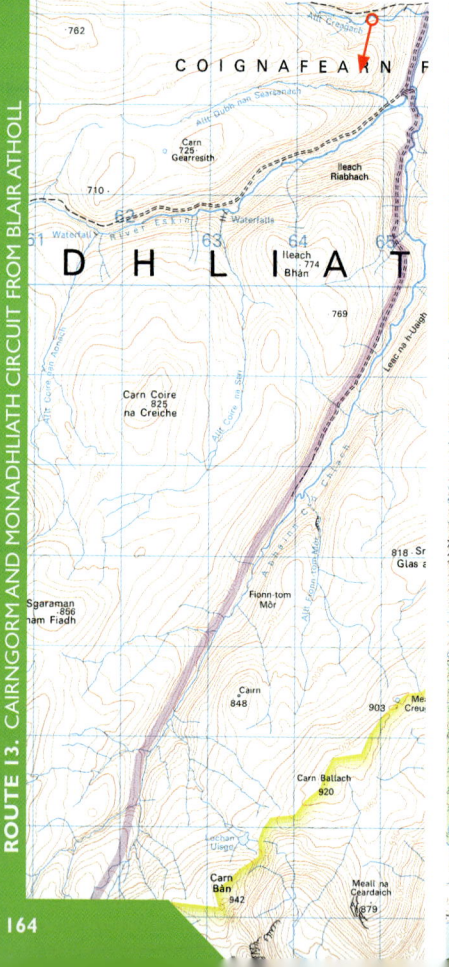

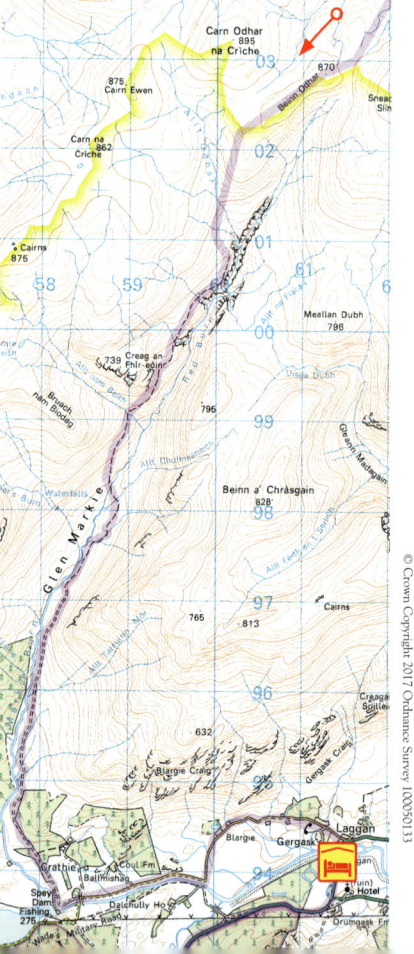

ROUTE 13. CAIRNGORM AND MONADHLIATH CIRCUIT FROM BLAIR ATHOLL

© Crown Copyright 2017 Ordnance Survey 100050133

164

Multi-day routes in northern Britain

Make your way R for 300m to the summit of Beinn Odhar on much better ground and then proceed SW, keeping to the high ground until the nose between Red Burn and Allt Odhar becomes more pronounced. Direct yourself SSW, riding where you can down the ridge towards a point on the Allt Odhar some 2 to 300m NW of the Red Burn Ravine. In poor visibility be particularly careful to skirt the ravine to the W. Cross Allt Odhar and, very shortly, the tributary coming in from your R. The OS map shows a path rising to a point about 250m to the S of this. Find it if you can. It seems to come and go, but becomes very definite about halfway between the two next streams in from the R. If you're not exhausted, and perhaps you should be, enjoy the descent along this delightful path down to Glenn Markie.

Descent to Glen Markie.

Once across the Markie Burn by a relatively new bridge at NH 588983, the path is again less good, but in less than a km gives way to good track. Follow it until in about 3.5km, under Spey Dam, it turns sharp L and in 250m meets tarmac. Continue to Laggan and seek out your bed and well earned dinner.

DAY 4.

Start:	Laggan
Finish:	Kinloch Rannoch/Rannoch Moor
Distance:	68km (42.5miles)
Off-road:	42.5km (26.5miles) 63%
Ascent:	1177m (3862ft)
Descent:	1230m (4037ft)
Grade:	M3

Mountain Biking Adventures:

OVERVIEW

A pleasant route up a valley (which may be soon – 2016 - spoiled and, possibly, tracks changed, by hydro works), leads to some very good singletrack between mountains of the Ben Alder group, then some 4km of bushwhack leads to track and road to finish either E or W.

ROUTE

Leave Laggan on the westbound A86. Don't be tempted by the Wolftrax mountain biking centre. After 8km, at an impressive track turn L, signposted Gallovie Farm. In 200m cross the River Pattack, and in another 300m turn L and go up through Gallovie Farm. Keep going S for 2km then turn R across the Pattack again. In 700m recross, L, and continue southwards for 7km until you reach Loch Pattack. Turn R along the S shore of the loch and, just as you leave it, turn L, and S again towards Culra Lodge.

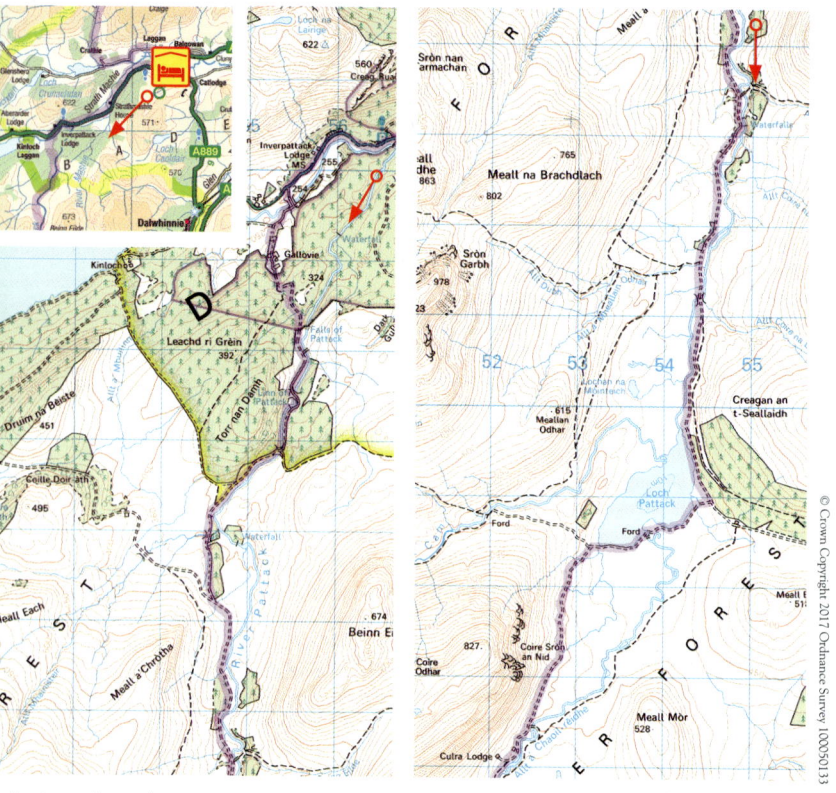

As the main track curves up towards the lodge, stick with the narrow track/broad path which carries on SW close to the river. Follow this superb path, gradually gaining altitude towards the Bealach Dubh for 3.5km. A steep 0.5km takes you up to the col, where fabulous views open up of Loch Ossian and the Lochaber mountains. The path continues contouring comfortably around the corner of Ben Alder via the Bealach Cumhann and descends delightfully, in 4km to Benalder Cott. Watch out for drainage ditches, scientifically designed to cause snakebite punctures.

Multi-day routes in northern Britain

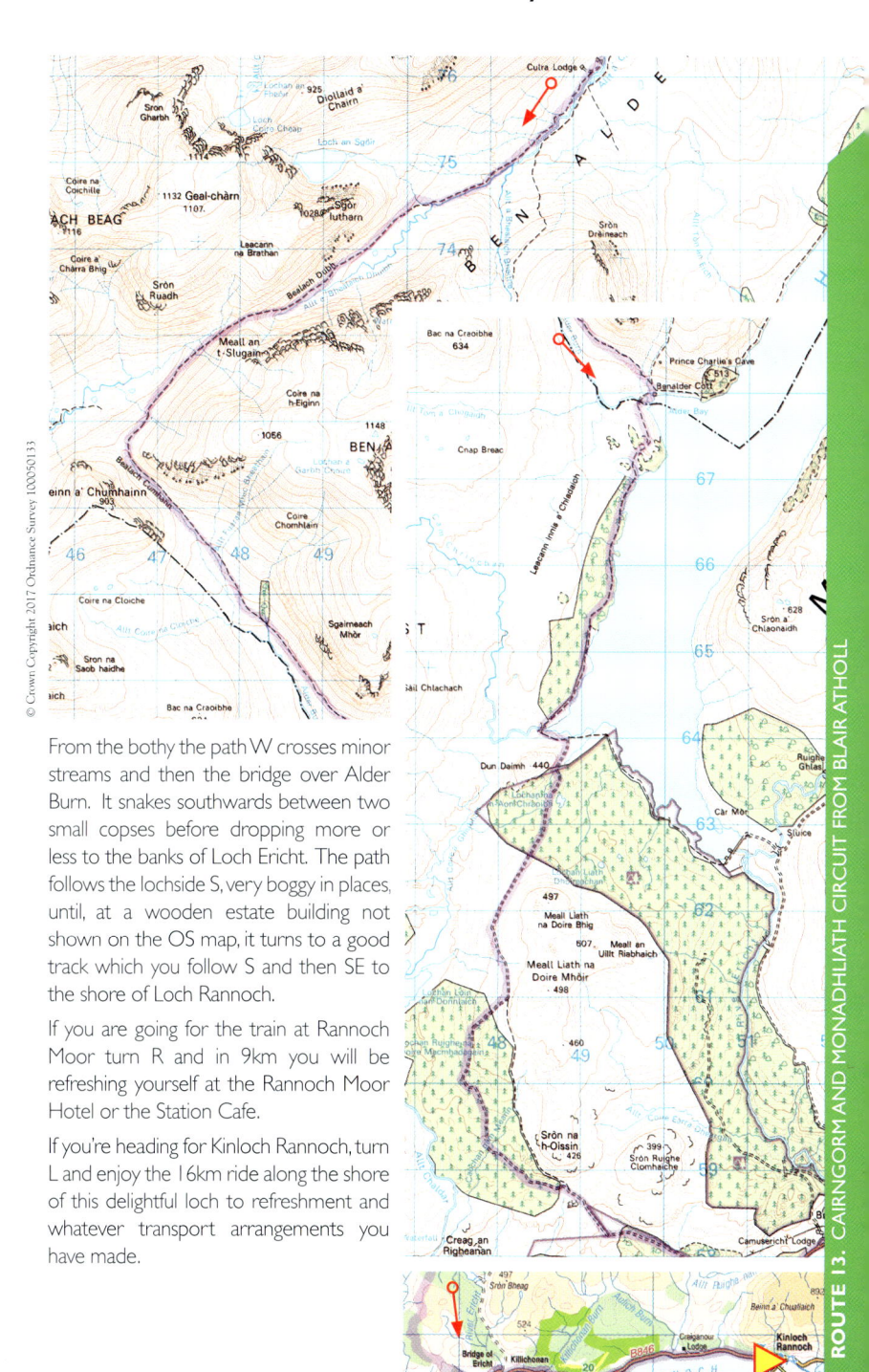

From the bothy the path W crosses minor streams and then the bridge over Alder Burn. It snakes southwards between two small copses before dropping more or less to the banks of Loch Ericht. The path follows the lochside S, very boggy in places, until, at a wooden estate building not shown on the OS map, it turns to a good track which you follow S and then SE to the shore of Loch Rannoch.

If you are going for the train at Rannoch Moor turn R and in 9km you will be refreshing yourself at the Rannoch Moor Hotel or the Station Cafe.

If you're heading for Kinloch Rannoch, turn L and enjoy the 16km ride along the shore of this delightful loch to refreshment and whatever transport arrangements you have made.

ROUTE 13. CAIRNGORM AND MONADHLIATH CIRCUIT FROM BLAIR ATHOLL

167

14. CAIRNGORM CIRCULAR FROM BALLATER, VIA TOMINTOUL, KINCRAIG AND BLAIR ATHOLL

Total route (days):	Four days			
Start & Finish:	Ballater			
Total Distance:	238km (148miles)			
Total Off-road (%):	62%.			
Daily distance (km):	53.5	49.5	62	73
Daily off-road (%):	52	86	74	42
Ascent:	5448m (17,880ft)			
Crux day grade:	H3			

Multi-day routes in northern Britain

OVERVIEW

In many ways, now a variation on the theme, this route explores the eastern end of the national park, adds interest to the southbound leg from Glen Spey to Glengarry, and has a right Royal treat at the end.

DAY 1.

Start:	Ballater
Finish:	Tomintoul
Distance:	53.5km (33miles)
Off-road:	28km (17.5miles) 52%
Ascent:	1816m (5960ft)
Descent:	1673m (5490ft)
Grade:	H2

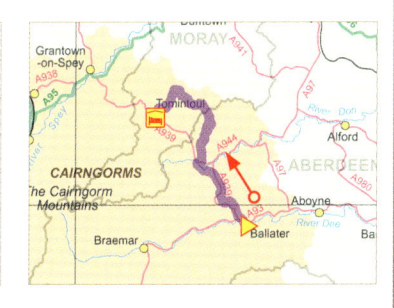

OVERVIEW

A remote feel to today over the eastern Grampian moors, with three big off-road ascents, all pushing for mortals. Some good descents make up for this. A hard day.

ROUTE

Leave Ballater on the A93 towards Braemar. About 0.5km from the edge of town, just before Bridge of Gairn, take the minor road to the right signposted to Lary. In 4km the tarmac ends at the homestead of Lary. Pass the buildings to your R, go through the gate marked 'No unauthorised vehicles beyond this point' and turn L on a well-metalled track to the farm at Inverenzie. Cross Glenfenzie burn and keep to the track as it bears sharply S and then, after passing a few more farm buildings, curves round W and continues along the bottom edge of the wood. Just out of the wood bear R and climb steadily, ignoring turns to R and L until you arrive at the A939 which, unfortunately, you must follow for 3.5km N (R).

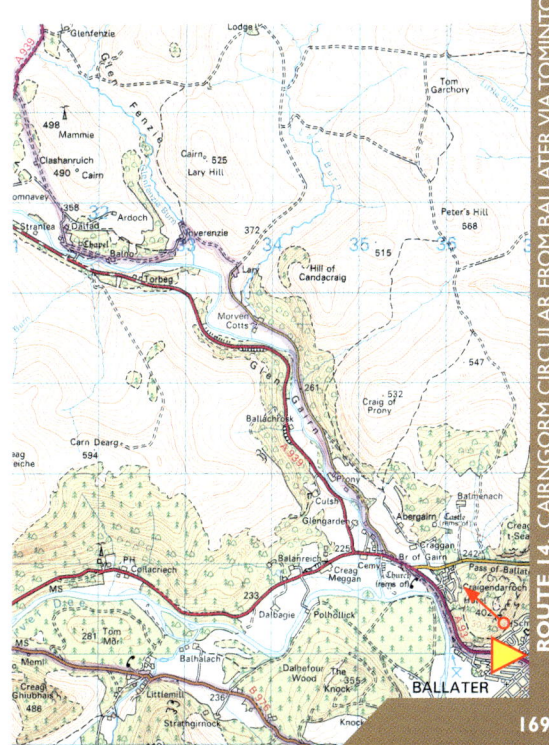

ROUTE 14. CAIRNGORM CIRCULAR FROM BALLATER, VIA TOMINTOUL, KINCRAIG AND BLAIR ATHOLL

169

Mountain Biking Adventures:

Some 300m after the summit, as the road starts to steepen, take the track to the L, signposted 'Public Footpath of Old Military Road to Cock Bridge.' Follow it NW until, in 3.5km, you rejoin the A939 just east of Cockbridge. Turn R, and in 1km turn L where two tracks come down to the road at the same point. Take the second, rightmost non-tarmac track through a gate to the R, and once through the gate keep R on the better track. Climb and climb, first by the burn on your R and then across a broad shoulder to Cairn Vachich. Enjoy the views of the Cairngorm massif, and the more gentle whisky country all around. The track goes a few metres W of the summit and then begins to descend (shown on the OS map as a path) before a final zigzag to the bothy at Sheil.

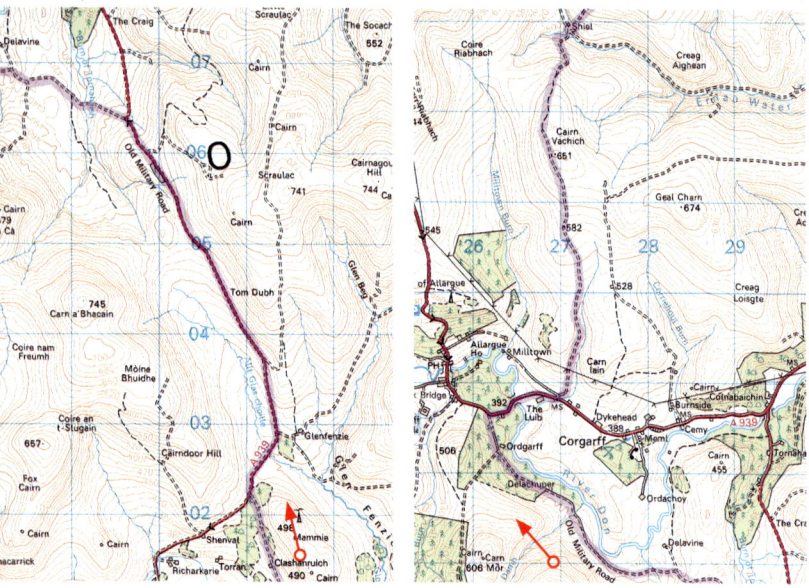

Go up the hill, sharply back to the R to start with, climbing over The Socach, enjoying the similar views and descent, turning L after a km, down to Long Moss. Turn R and descend gently for 1km before following the track to the L and climbing through the valley of the Allt na Caillich. In about 400m after the climb steepens, where a distinct track comes in from the R, your path goes L, NW, distinct at first but then fragmenting as it climbs steeply to the sharp col between Dun Muir and Meikle Geal Charn. Push.

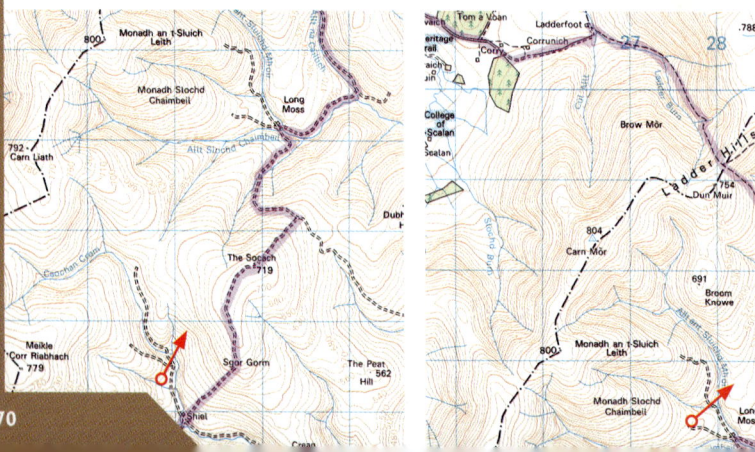

Multi-day routes in northern Britain

At the col continue NW and descend equally steeply into the valley of the eponymous Ladder Burn, probably walking until you have crossed the stream coming in from the R. Enjoy the rest of the grassy singletrack down to Ladder Foot and follow the better track W to Chapeltown. Turn R on the minor road and follow it for 4km to Knockandhu. At the B9008 turn L for Tomintoul.

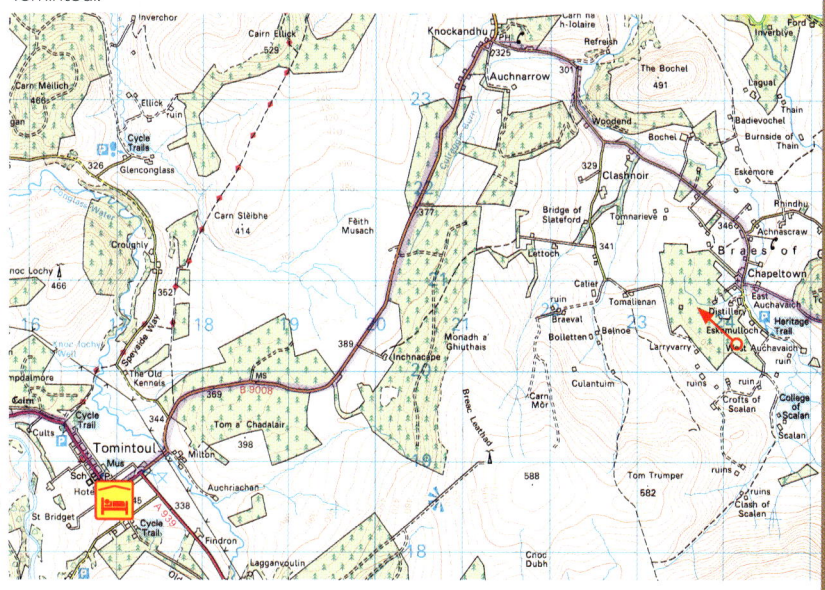

DAY 2.

Start:	Tomintoul
Finish:	Kincraig
Distance:	49.5km (31 miles)
Off-road:	42.5km (26.5miles) 86%
Ascent:	876m (2874ft)
Descent:	993m (3258ft)
Grade:	E1

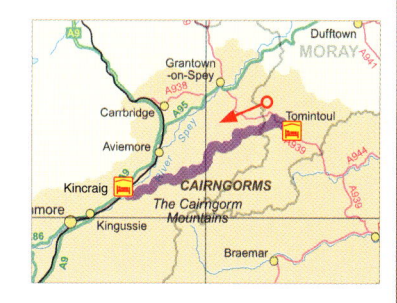

OVERVIEW

A lovely, easy day after yesterday's exertions, and superb riding once more through the ancient and peaceful Caledonian Forests.

ROUTE

Follow Route 11 Day 3 as far as Feshie Bridge (pp 146/149). Cross the bridge on the B970 and follow it W for 1.5km until you take the R turn signposted for Kincraig.

Mountain Biking Adventures:

An easy track in Rothiemurchus Forest.

DAY 3.

Start:	Kincraig
Finish:	Blair Atholl
Distance:	62km (38.5miles)
Off-road:	46km (28.5miles) 74%
Ascent:	1452m (4766ft)
Descent:	1543m (5064ft)
Grade:	H3

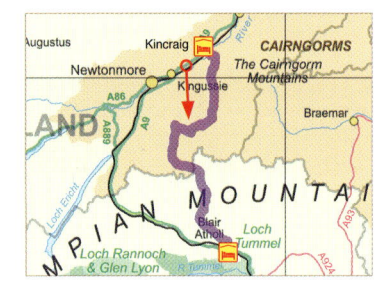

OVERVIEW

A long route S through the range, using three valleys, Feshie, upper Tromie, and Bruar, with big ascents between them. Remote, with 2km pathless and featureless at 700m.

ROUTE

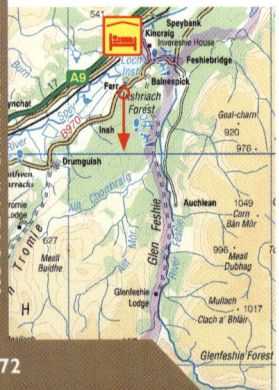

Reverse your journey from the village to Feshie Bridge. Just before the bridge take the first L, S on a track by some dwellings. This soon becomes path. Follow it southwards to Ballintean. Here a bizarre detour, not shown on the map, takes you around the curtilage of the big house, but through everyone else's front garden, and eventually delivers you on to the tarmac road down Glen Feshie. Turn L, follow the tarmac road up the glen for 12km past Glenfeshie Lodge, where it becomes a track, apparently heading for the gash of Slochd Beag at the foot of the glen. At a ruin, Ruigh Fionntaig, bear R

Multi-day routes in northern Britain

and ford a small burn. Take a last look back at the Feshie sweeping magnificently E, regret that you are not following that route (10) today, but promise yourself that you will, heave a sigh of relief that your route is not up the Slochd Beag and continue up the good track, SW, through a steep narrow pass and descend past the Lochan an t-Sluic.

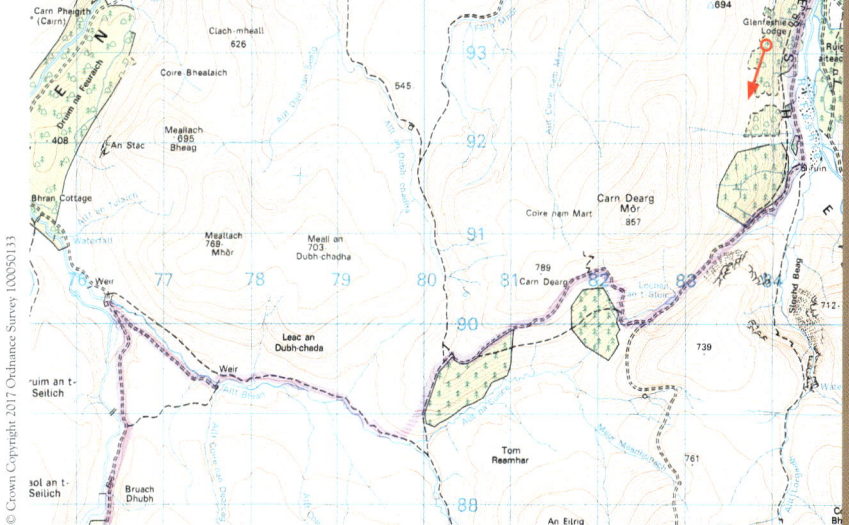

Bear R at the fork about 300m after the lochan and continue R, northwards in front of a forestry plantation. If you're keen, look out for the indistinct track, L, that takes you through the middle of the forest on a firebreak and returns to the track in 2km. Otherwise, grin and bear it and make the 100m climb on the track for the pleasure of zooming down the shoulder of Carn Dearg to the next patch of forest. The track stays tight round the upper, northern, boundary of this forest until, just after a turning circle, it heads northerly and the southern path you're looking for becomes indistinct. Stay close to the edge of the forest and descend on grass as best you can to get to its W-most point. The map shows a path S from here to a junction in the burns and then coming back WNW. It's better to take a bearing SW and hack across the heathery ground for under 0.5km until you pick up the path patchily cycleable WNW alongside the Allt Bhran. Follow it for 2km to the weir. Cross it here and take the track NW for just over 1km into Glen Tromie. (The enthusiast may cut off the corner by taking the path WSW from the weir.)

The descent to Glen Tromie.

ROUTE 14. CAIRNGORM CIRCULAR FROM BALLATER, VIA TOMINTOUL, KINCRAIG AND BLAIR ATHOLL

173

Mountain Biking Adventures:

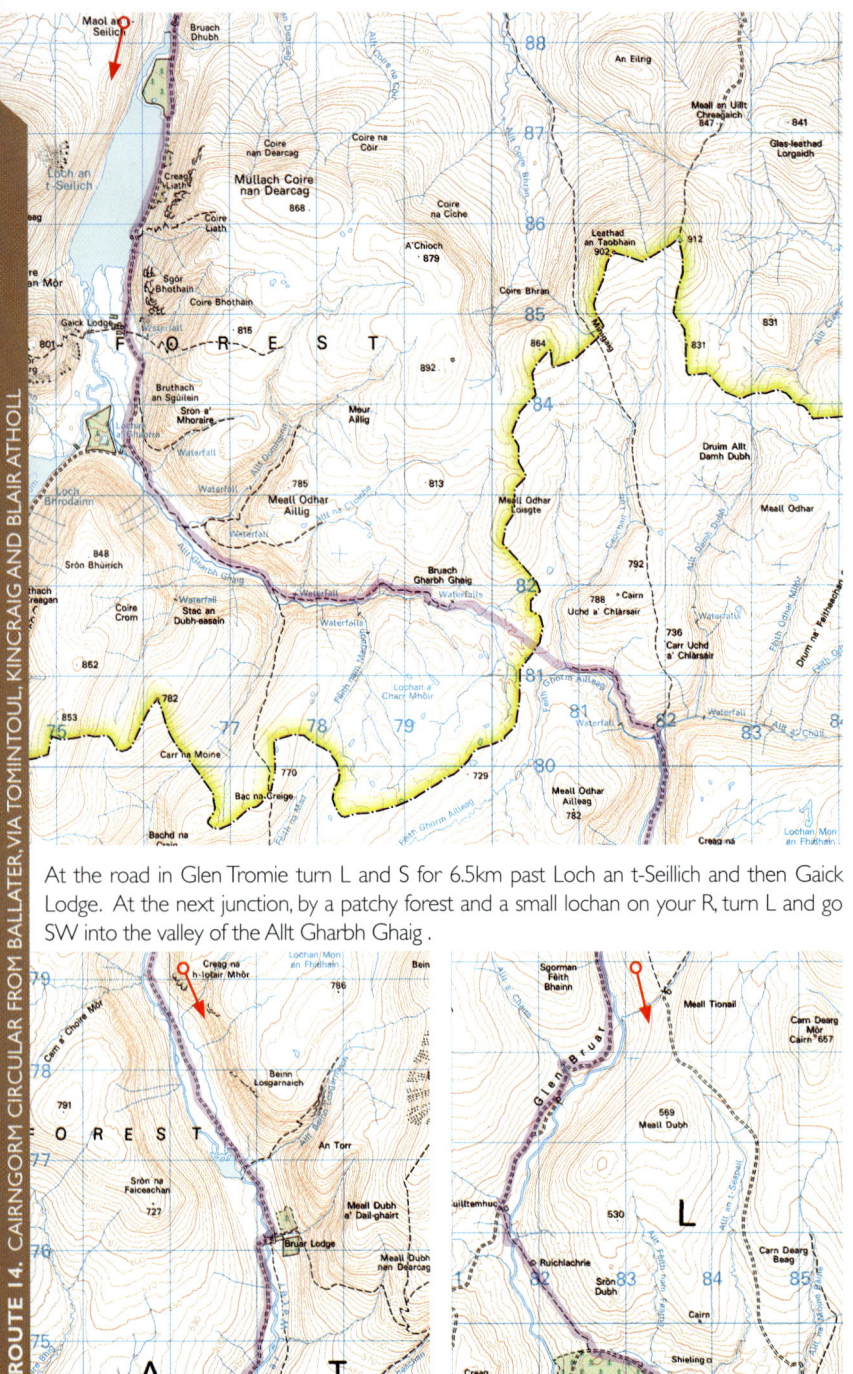

At the road in Glen Tromie turn L and S for 6.5km past Loch an t-Seillich and then Gaick Lodge. At the next junction, by a patchy forest and a small lochan on your R, turn L and go SW into the valley of the Allt Gharbh Ghaig.

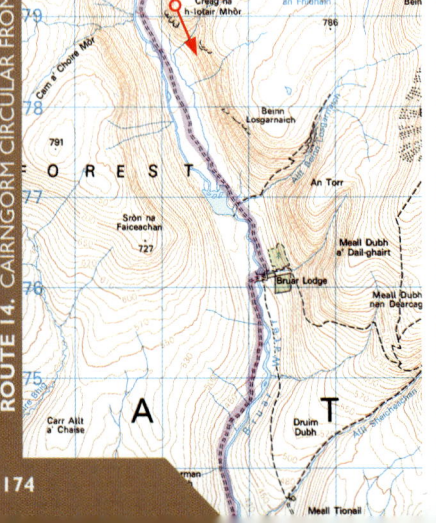

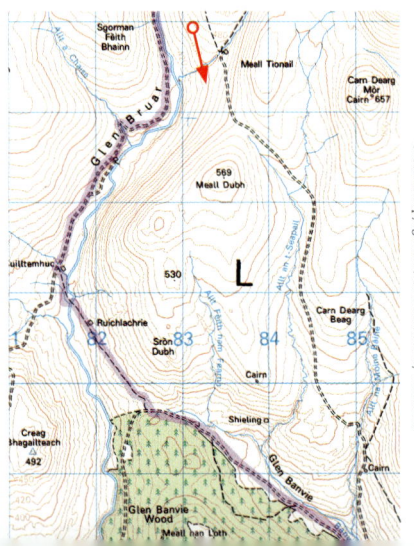

ROUTE 14. CAIRNGORM CIRCULAR FROM BALLATER, VIA TOMINTOUL, KINCRAIG AND BLAIR ATHOLL

© Crown Copyright 2017 Ordnance Survey 100050133

174

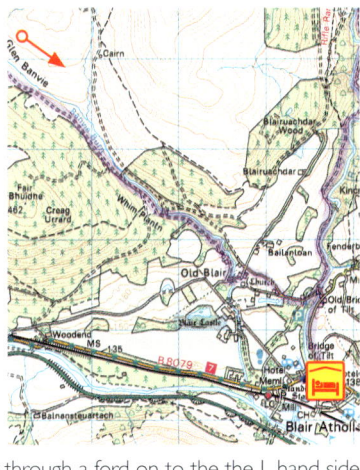

Multi-day routes in northern Britain

A good track continues much further into the valley than is shown on the OS map but eventually, ignoring turns to L and R, the route becomes due E, the valley becomes steep and tight and the path becomes, for 2km, a difficult push/carry. As the defile opens out by two small waterfalls the path ends and the wasteland begins. Take a bearing ESE until, from just across the watershed you can see down into the cut of the Feith Ghorm Ailleag. Head for the confluence of this burn and the Caochan Lub coming in from the N. From their junction a good path rises which hugs the edge of the valley round into Glenn Bruar in a further km. The path is easily rideable, but the runouts, in case of a fall to the right, are dire. Once in Glen Bruar a good track takes you S, past the lodge, for 10km to Cuilltemhuc. Here, a L turn takes you on a less good, but very distinct track down beside the river, through a ford on to the the L hand side of the valley, to rise past Ruichlachrie to the edge of Glen Banvie Wood. Turn L here and enjoy the delightful descent by Banvie Burn to Old Blair. Turn L and cross the bridge and, 200m through the hamlet, turn R on the minor road to Old Bridge of Tilt. Cross the bridge and take the R hand turn down to Blair Atholl.

DAY 4.

Start:	Blair Atholl
Finish:	Ballater
Distance:	73km (45.5miles).
Off-road:	30.5km (19miles) 42%
Ascent:	1304m (4280ft).
Descent:	1235m (4054ft)
Grade:	E2

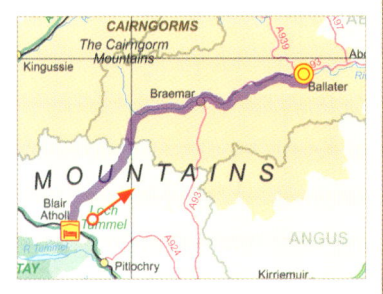

ROUTE

Take the Glen Tilt/Geldie/Dee Route, Day 3 of Route 12 to Braemar, then the second part of Route 10, Day 3 to Ballater.

The push up the Allt Gharbh Ghaig.

ROUTE 14. CAIRNGORM CIRCULAR FROM BALLATER, VIA TOMINTOUL, KINCRAIG AND BLAIR ATHOLL

175

15. DALWHINNIE TO DUNKELD

Total route (days):	Four days			
Start:	Tulloch, Glen Spean			
Finish:	Dunkeld			
Total Distance:	235.5km (146miles)			
Total Off-road (%):	70%			
Daily distance (km):	55	52	70	59
Daily off-road (%):	91%	60%	61%	80.5%
Ascent:	3882m (12,741ft)			
Crux day grade:	M3			

176

Multi-day routes in northern Britain

OVERVIEW

A further two day visit to the Cairngorms, with a new approach day through 'Monarch of the Glen' country. Lots of lovely forest track, good singletrack, lochs and no need to put a foot down. Needs more planning to start: theoretically it could be done by train start and finish, but as accommodation is sparse around Tulloch, we took a taxi (several obliging operators) from Dunkeld to Dalwhinnie, where a bunkhouse offered us good basic accommodation, and again from there to Tulloch next morning.

DAY 1.

Start:	Tulloch, junction on A86 at NN342809, or Railway Station
Finish:	Dalwhinnie
Distance:	54.5km (34miles)
Off-road:	49.5km (31miles) 91%
Ascent:	1021m (3350ft)
Descent:	870m (2854ft)
Grade:	E2

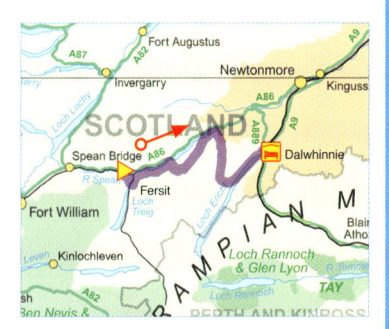

OVERVIEW

An easy day on mainly good forest tracks, with only the initial 5km on tarmac. Open aspects alongside Lochan na h-Earba and up Glen Pattack break the enclosure of the forest. Plenty of time to visit the Distillery for a tour at the finish.

INFORMATION

The magnificent micro-granite cliffs of Binnean Shuas, opposite Lochan na h-Earba, presents the climb 'Ardverikie Wall' to you, made famous by 'Classic Rock'. Ardverikie House itself, an upmarket wedding venue, was Glenbogle House in the BBC's 'Monarch of the Glen', with much of the filming done both here and up Glen Pattack. There is a major hydroelectric scheme approved (2016) for Glen Pattack, which will no doubt disturb its tranquility for some time and may involve a dam.

Dalwhinnie Distillery is worth a visit, the last tours are 1700hrs in summer, 1630hrs September, 1600hrs October. Tasting obligatory. No tearooms en route.

ROUTE

Head down the minor road to Fersit, pass through the farm and make a rectangular excursion on the track to enter the forest. Continue on the track for 9.5km, avoiding all L turns, to Torgulbin. Cross the river and follow it round, then E to a junction. Turn R and cross the moor to the secluded sandy beach of Lochan na h-Earba, following the E bank of the lochan, then its

ROUTE 15. DALWHINNIE TO DUNKELD

177

Mountain Biking Adventures:

lesser twin. Continue on the E of the outflow river then cross to Ardverikie House, turning R just before it and joining Loch Laggan side. Follow the track nearly to Kinloch, turning S as the track veers N, to climb over a hill through, then by, the forest.

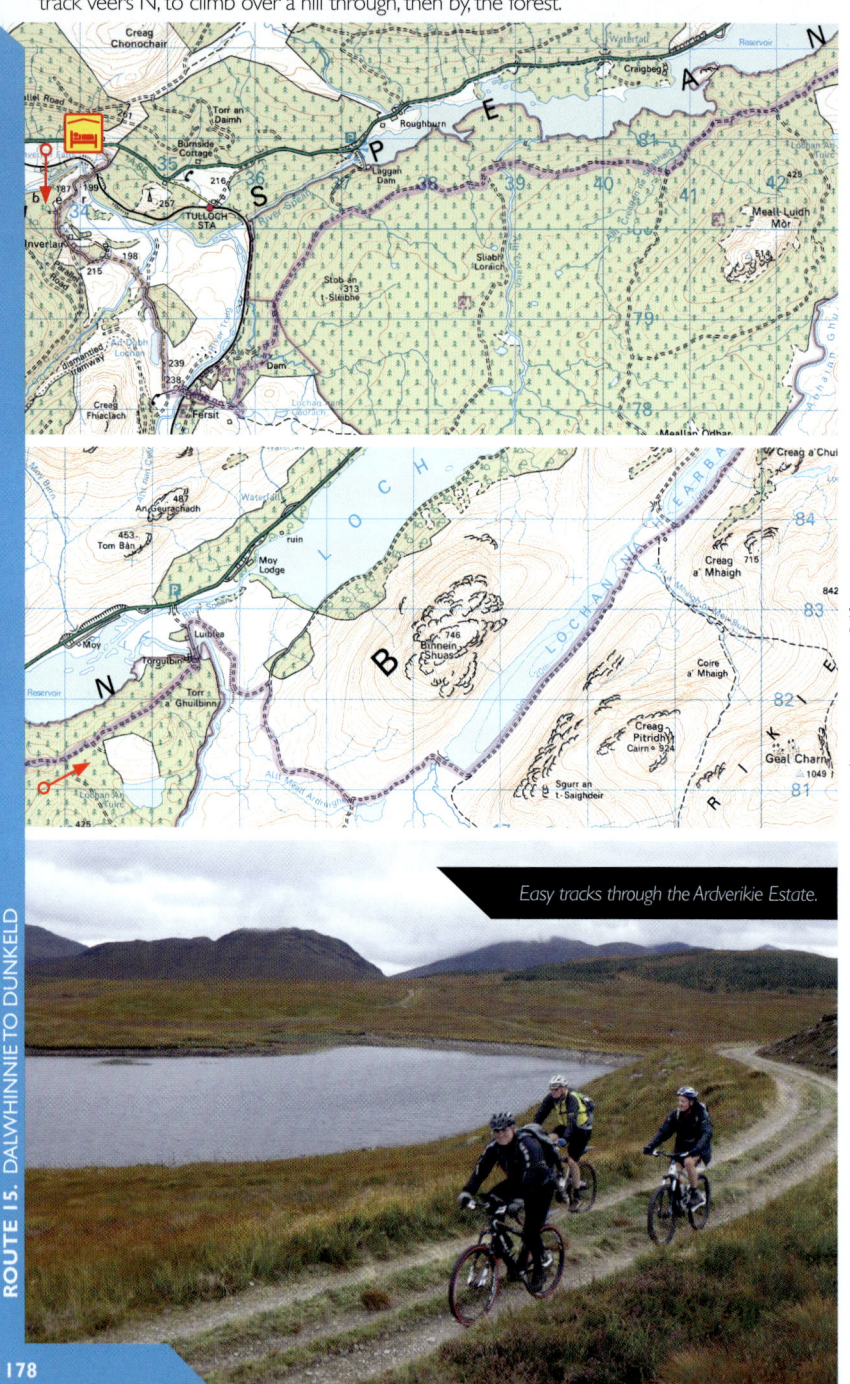

Easy tracks through the Ardverikie Estate.

ROUTE 15. DALWHINNIE TO DUNKELD

© Crown Copyright 2017 Ordnance Survey 100050133

178

Multi-day routes in northern Britain

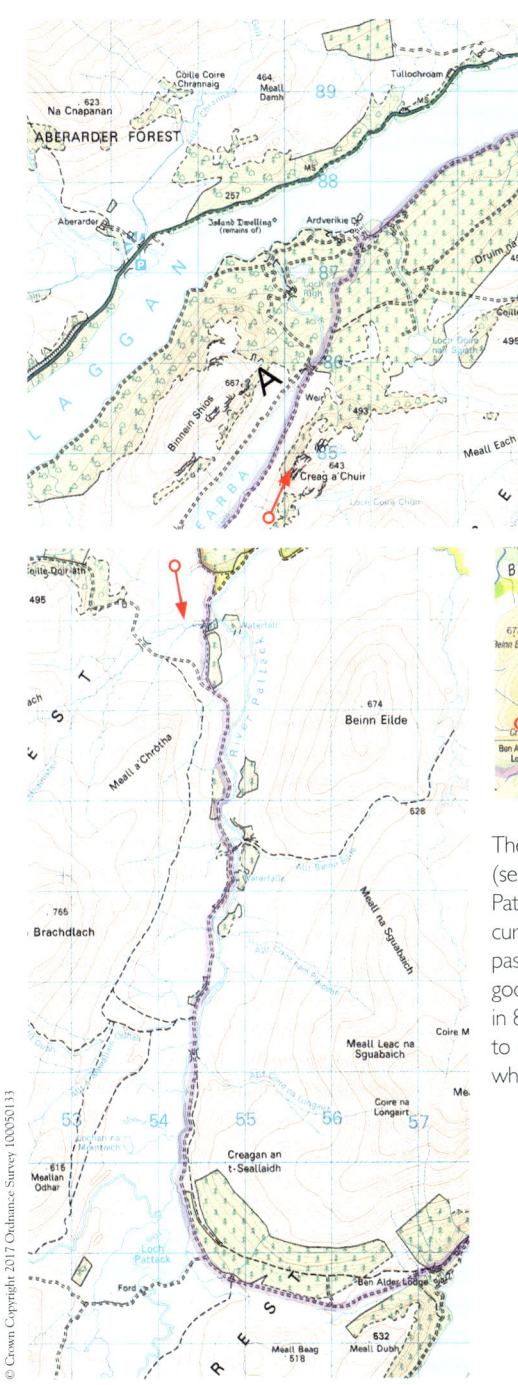

The good track snakes up Glen Pattack (see Information), but towards Loch Pattack gets distinctly boggy. It then curves round and descends gently to pass above Ben Alder Lodge. Still a good track, now by Loch Ericht, it leads, in 8km, to the Dam, where continue N to cross the railway and head for the whisky!

ROUTE 15. DALWHINNIE TO DUNKELD

179

Mountain Biking Adventures:

DAY 2.

Start:	Dalwhinnie
Finish:	Aviemore
Distance:	52km (32.5miles)
Off-road:	31km (19.5miles) 60%
Ascent:	536m (1760ft)
Descent:	678m (2224ft)
Grade:	E1

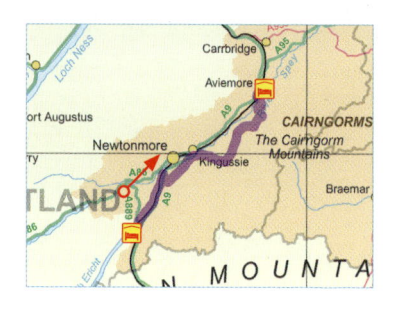

OVERVIEW

An easy day with the delightful, flat General Wade's path/track to start, some easy forest paths and the perennial favourite singletrack from the Inchsriach Forest to Loch an Eilein.

INFORMATION

In 2017 a pass under the A9 is promised from near Crubenbeg to Etteridge, straightening things out. General Wade's road has an original bridge on it, but the original drainage has gone. He made no culverts. The gaunt Ruthven Barracks was built in 1760. Just past the barracks is the Insh marshes RSPB Reserve, alas with no tearooms, any refreshments are off route at Kingussie and Kincraig.

ROUTE

Go N on the A889, turning R after the distillery and railway line on to an unclassified road, and take this for 8km. As it joins the A9, turn off L on a constructed cycleway. Then follow Route 7 Day 2 (pp 93), using the off road options, to Feshie Bridge. Here, take Route 7 Day 3 (pp 94/95), untill the track junction in the forest E of Loch an Eilein, NH905077. Turn L here and continue round the loch, to turn R off the road a km past the picnic site at Milton Cottage. The track goes past Lochan Mor (not named on OS map), and 400m past it veers L on a path which emerges on the B970 at Inverdruie. Go L 100m then R, to drift into Aviemore.

Cairngorm Club Footbridge, Rothiemurchus.

Multi-day routes in northern Britain

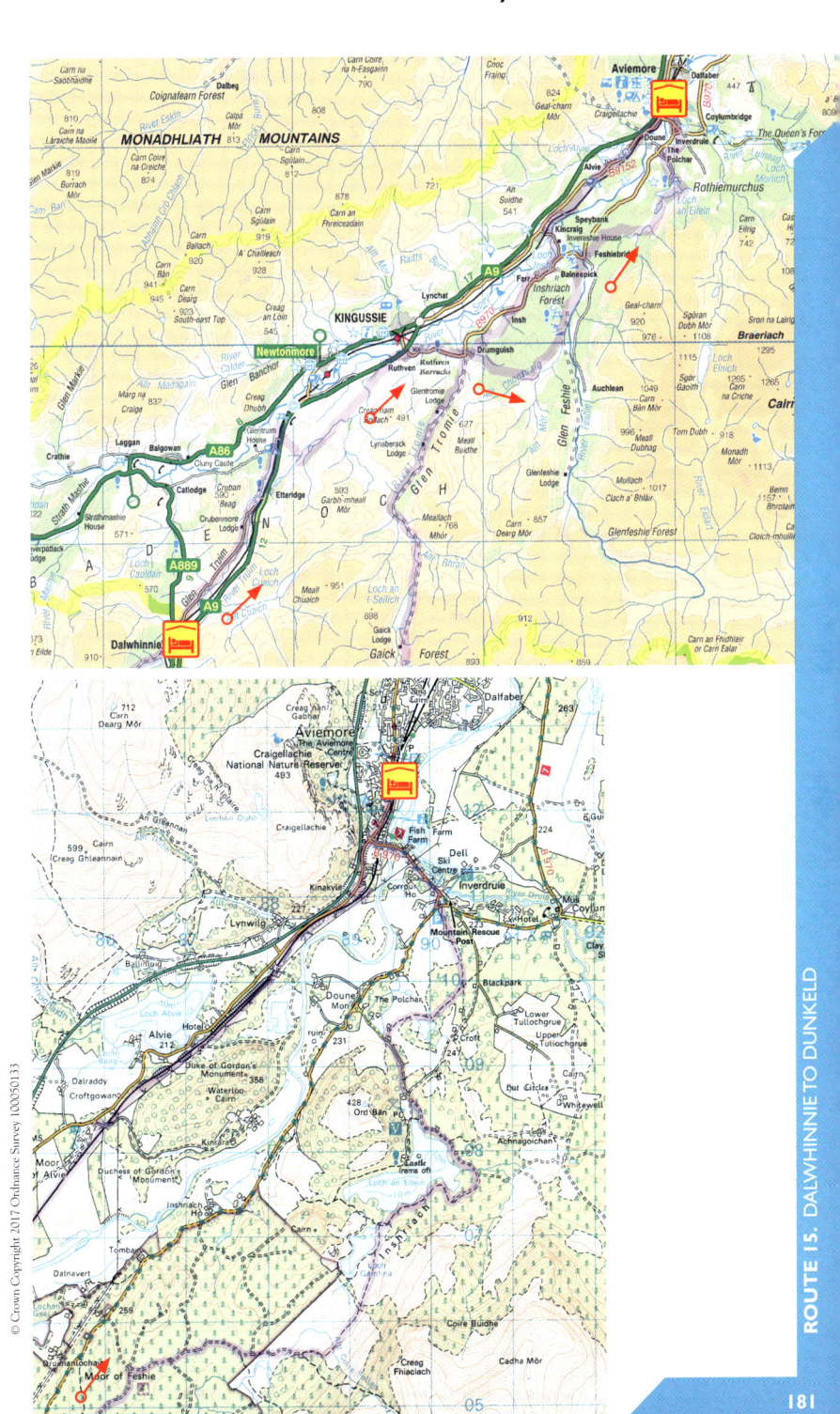

ROUTE 15. DALWHINNIE TO DUNKELD

181

Mountain Biking Adventures:

DAY 3.

Start:	Aviemore
Finish:	Blair Atholl
Distance:	70km, (43.5miles)
Off-road:	40km, (24.5miles) 61%
Ascent:	1011m (3318ft)
Descent:	1090m (3579ft)
Grade:	M3

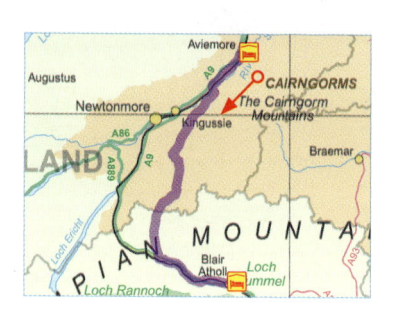

OVERVIEW

A return up the Spey Valley to Tromie Bridge via the specially made Badenoch Way and some road, then a magnificent through route through the Cairngorms as for Route 12, Day 2. This involves 16km of road up Glen Tromie, before some rough singletrack and tracks to the A9 in Glen Garry. The Trinafour road loop adds 6.5km and about 240m ascent, but no tearooms.

INFORMATION

Loch Insh is a major centre for watersports, with an Outdoor Centre, which even boasts a dry ski slope. The Gaick Estate, of 20,000 acres, was bought by the Dutch billionaire, Anders Povlsen, in 2013. He is now (2016) the second largest private landowner in Britain, owning more than the Queen. Mr Povlson says he 'is not the owner, more the custodian', and is demonstrating rewilding and woodland regeneration on his other estates.

ROUTE

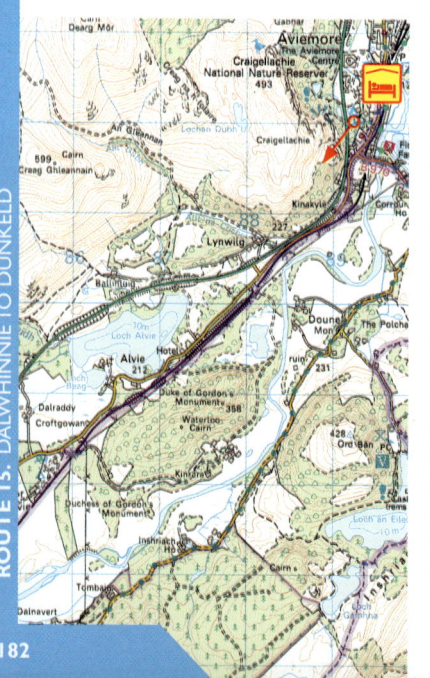

Head S out of Aviemore, and 600m after the roundabout turn L on to the Badenoch Way. This hardcore surfaced path follows the railway, after passing under it. It recrosses under the line twice to enter the Dalraddy Holiday Park briefly. Past Speybank it enters an oak and birch wood on a bank above the Spey, and exits at Kincraig. We suggest taking the roads, L from here round Loch Insh to the B970, R here and 3.5km later turn L on the signed Badenoch Way, rather than diverting into Inshriach Forest again for more off-road. The track passes by Inveruglass and comes out at the crossroads you traversed yesterday. Cross this to the road and turn L up Glen Tromie. Now follow as for Day 2, Route 12 (pp 152/153). At the A9 the same choice as Route 12 exists, more ascent up for a good retrospective view, or down the National Cycle Route track to Calvine, then road.

Multi-day routes in northern Britain

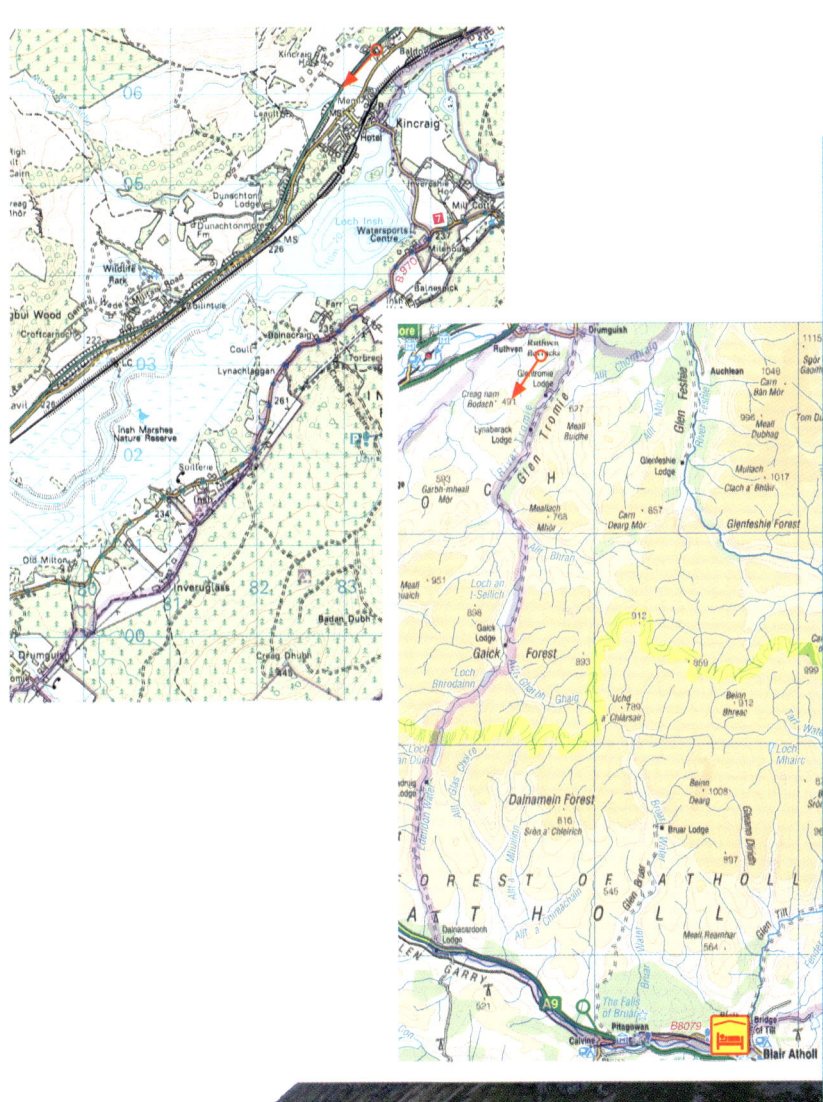

Crossing the Allt Gharbh Ghaig.

ROUTE 15. DALWHINNIE TO DUNKELD

183

Mountain Biking Adventures:

DAY 4.

Start:	Blair Atholl
Finish:	Dunkeld
Distance:	59km (36.5miles)
Off-road:	47.5km (29.5miles) 80.5%
Ascent:	1314m (4313ft)
Descent:	1392m (4570ft)
Grade:	M2

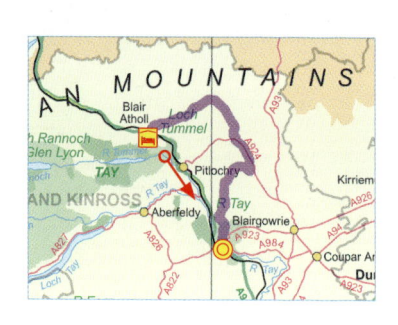

OVERVIEW

An ascent of 450m on road, track, then path with some pushing, leads to a good singletrack descent.

A road section leads to a moorland track and path ascent and a long lovely descent on a good track home.

INFORMATION

Do not be tempted by what appears to be a more direct route from Straloch through Kindrogan Wood and subsequent moorland on a track indicated on some maps. The track shown from Mains of Enderby does not exist and the going gets foul. No refreshments en route.

ROUTE

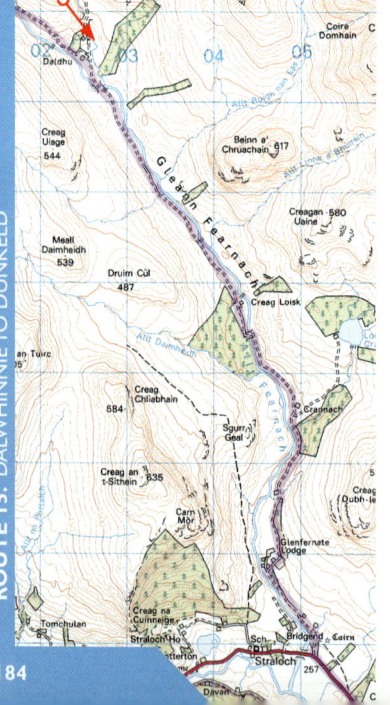

Start as for Route 13 Day 1 (pp 157, 158), untill Daldhu in Gleann Fearnach, where turn R down the Glen on a good track for nearly 8km to the A924. Turn L here for nearly 5km to Kirkmichael, turn R over the bridge then L on a track marked the Cateran trail. After 3km and just before Dalvey, turn sharp R and go NW on a track between plantations, across a moor and W alongside a forest. About 1.5km after the forest corner, and 400m after a kink in the track, a path, not on some maps, turns off R at NO046576 and goes SW then S, over a low pass, through a wall and S to the L of a small plantation, to lead down and curve W to join a good Landrover track at the N end of Lochan Oisinneach Beag. Turn R and keep L at the next junction, and enjoy a rather good descent of nearly 18km to the end.

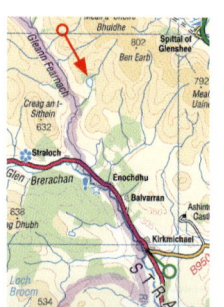

© Crown Copyright 2017 Ordnance Survey 100050133

ROUTE 15. DALWHINNIE TO DUNKELD

Multi-day routes in northern Britain

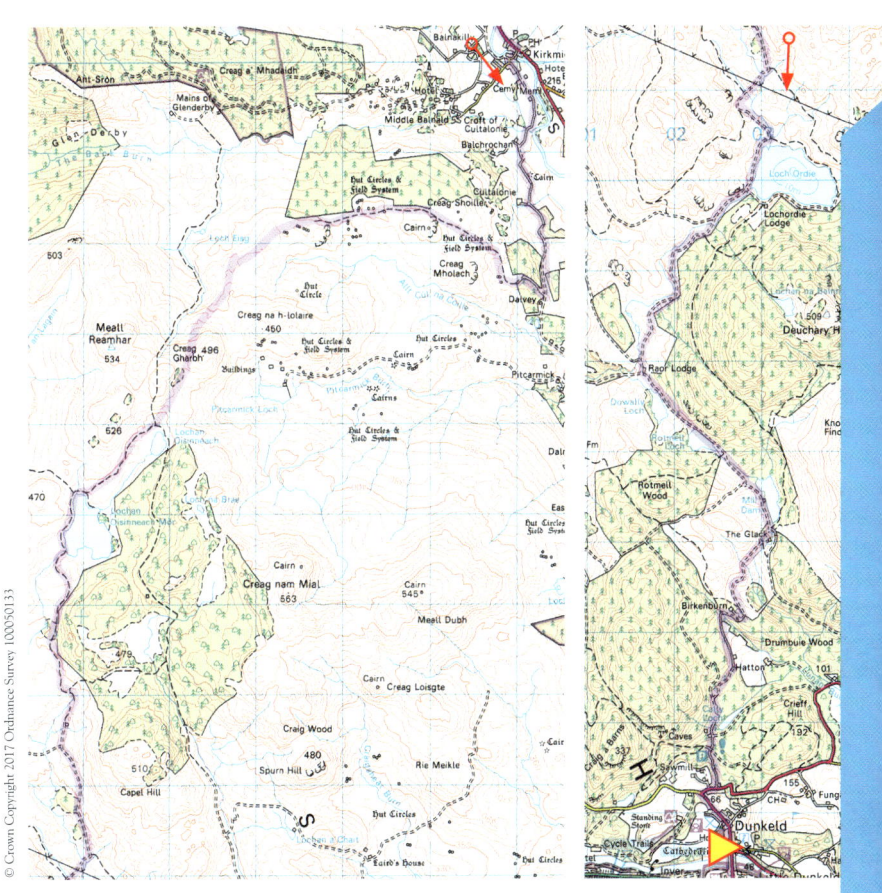

At Lochan Oisinneach Mor take the L junction, then, at the next junctions, keep R, L, then R, leading to Loch Ordie. Here go on the R of it, then R at its westernmost end, to follow the Dowally Burn to Raor Lodge. Turn L here uphill, go past two lochs, and 500m further on take a L to Mill Dam and on to circumnavigate Birkenburn. Turn L, S past this and down to Cally Sawmill and the A923, turning R for Dunkeld.

Lochan na h-Earba beach. Stop!

ROUTE 15. DALWHINNIE TO DUNKELD

185

16. PERTH TO FORT WILLIAM

Total route (days):	Four days			
Start:	Perth			
Finish:	Fort William			
Total Distance:	259.5km (161.5miles)			
Total Off-road (%):	61%			
Daily distance (km):	77	85.5	62.5	35
Daily off-road (%):	55%	65%	60%	69%
Ascent:	5259m (17,260ft)			
Crux day grade:	H3			

Multi-day routes in northern Britain

OVERVIEW

Day 3 needs planning well in advance for the Loch Etive boat trip. At present, 2017, the Nature Cruise company we used has finished (retired), and there is also no ferry to Bonawe. The company owner is trying to sell it, so there is a possibility that it may be available in 2018. If this cannot be arranged, travel by road over the Connel Bridge to Bonawe, either by taxi or cycling (25.5km, 540m ascent), then a good access track leads in just over 13km and with 400m ascent, to where our route starts. An extra day, or an early start, taxi and being supermen/women? Also, see Information, Day 3, re supper arrangements.

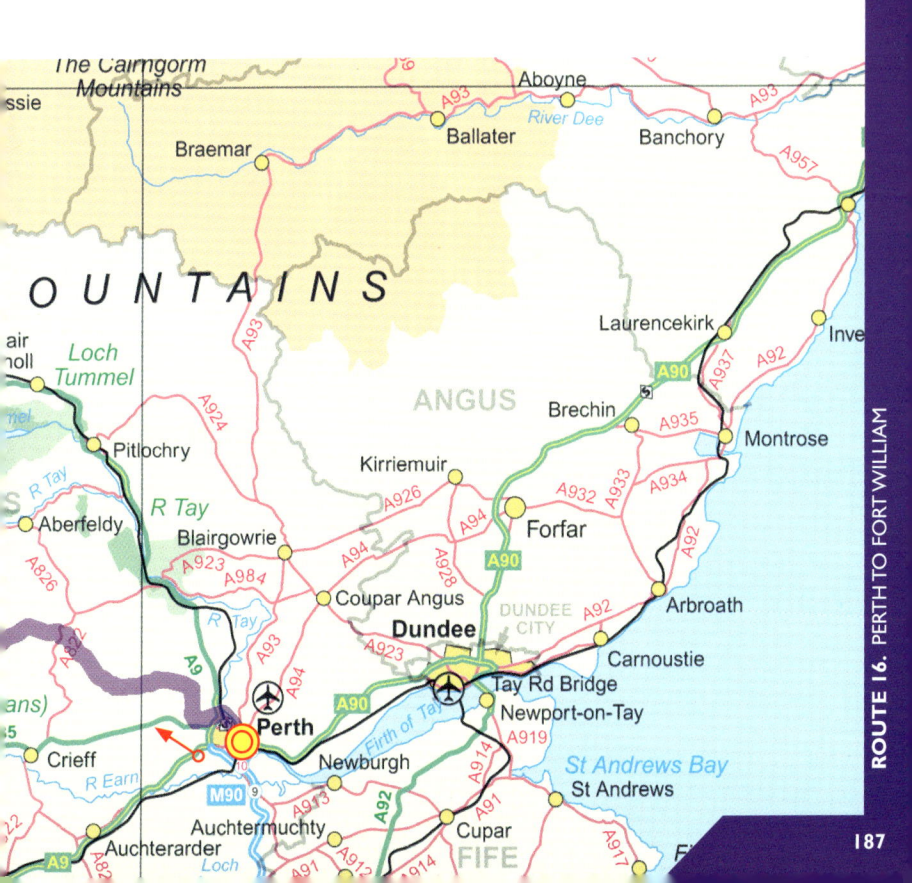

Mountain Biking Adventures:

DAY 1.

Start:	Perth
Finish:	Killin
Distance:	77km (48miles)
Off-road:	42km (26miles) 55%
Ascent:	1570m (5155ft)
Descent:	1463m (4802ft)
Grade:	M2

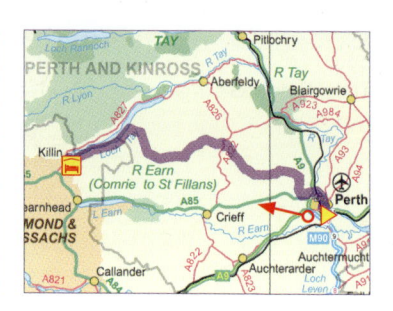

OVERVIEW

A short cycleway by the Tay leads to a road section gently ascending Glen Almond. Three, mostly tracked, moorland passes, progressively decreasing in height and rejoining the Almond in its upper reaches, leads to Loch Tay and an undulating road to Killin.

INFORMATION

Those who haven't had enough exercise on arriving at Loch Tay can ascend back to 560m, keeping on the Rob Roy Way from Ardeonaig. The farmer used to object to MTBs using the path section, however, and the descent is nothing special, on forest tracks. Refreshments only at the Ardeonaig Hotel, who let us have tea outside, but sheltered.

ROUTE

From the city centre get on to the waterfront, Tay Street, and head N towards West Street Bridge which carries the A85 over the Tay. About 50m S of the bridge there is a signed path 'NORTH INCH' and Sustrans National Route 77. Take it, under the bridge, keeping R at the golf club. Follow it through parkland on the river's edge and keep following it as it curves round on to the S bank of the Almond, crossing this river at Almond Bank.

ROUTE 16. PERTH TO FORT WILLIAM

© Crown Copyright 2017 Ordnance Survey 100050133

188

Multi-day routes in northern Britain

Head N on minor roads through Pitcairngreen, noting its unusual (for Scotland) village green, and 2.5km later turn L on to the B8603. This gradually ascends, rejoins the Almond valley, and in 11km delivers you to a hairpin bend opposite Milton Farm. Turn R here on a track and quickly L to Morningside. Negotiate the yard and cross the Old Shanacher Burn, then start on a long track ascent of grouse moorland to a pass, and a good descent to Girron and the A822.

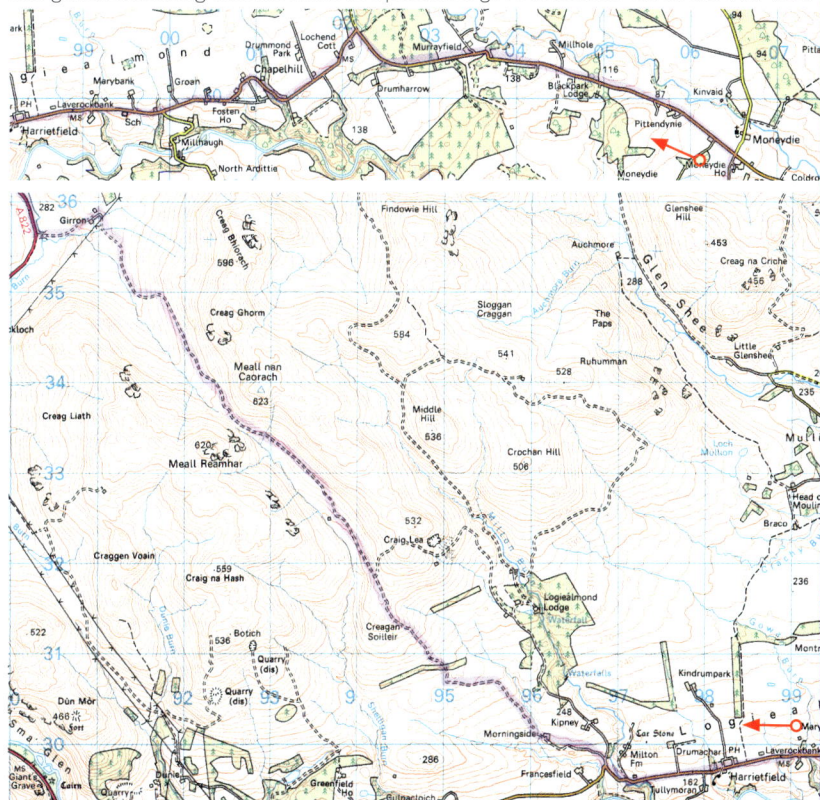

The moor track from Glen Almond.

ROUTE 16. PERTH TO FORT WILLIAM

189

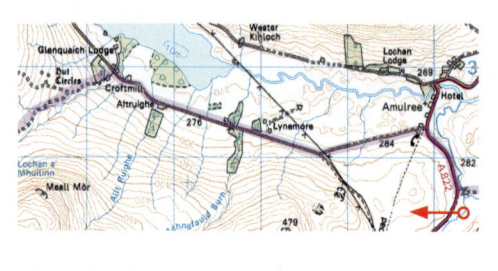

Mountain Biking Adventures:

Turn R, and L in 800m, and follow the road for nearly 4km to Croftmill. You are now on the Rob Roy Way (RRW), till Loch Tay. Turn up the vehicle track, becoming a boggy path by Loch a' Mhuilinn, faint in places. Over the tight pass of Glen Lochan descend on the R of the burn into a gully and across a wooden bridge over the Glenshervie Burn. Follow the RRW L then R round the barns of Auchnafree, then down by track to the Almond and follow this upriver for 6km to a dam. Soon after this, the track ends and a rough quad track continues, then a poor path. At Dunan, an active grouse shooting lodge, an access track leads N in a short distance to the watershed, the lowest of the day, then descends, with a few fords for interest, to Loch Tay. Be sure to to cross the burn where it turns W near Tullichglass, to the S bank. The road to Killin by Loch Tay is pleasantly wooded, but undulating and 16km long. The last 2km could be avoided by taking a forest track bypassing Auchmore.

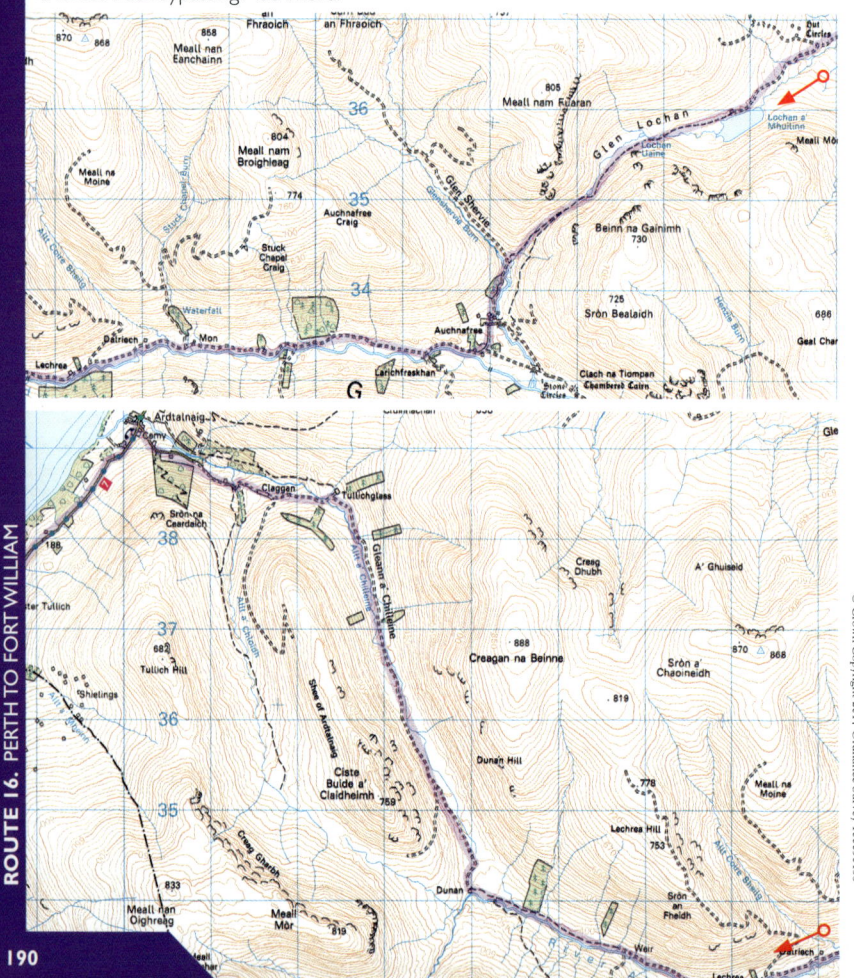

Multi-day routes in northern Britain

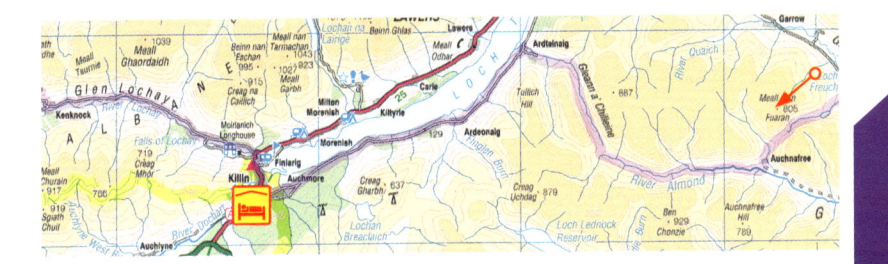

DAY 2.

Start:	Killin
Finish:	Taynuilt
Distance:	85.5km (53miles)
Off-road:	*56km (35miles) 65%*
Ascent:	1923m (6312ft)
Descent:	2012m (6604)
Grade:	H3

OVERVIEW

A hard day with a lot of ascent, starting with some road, then track, a hotel for lunch then some very good biking and increasingly good mountain scenery, to finish along a sea loch on a good but hilly track.

INFORMATION

The Lochay to Lyon hydro road was reported in 2013 to have deteriorated very badly. Hydroelectric is much in evidence today, as in much of the Highlands. The first power station you see is across Loch Tay, at Finlarig, fed from the dam west of Ben Lawyers by a pipe with a fall of over 400m. The biggest energy output is from the Lochay station, which you pass. This is fed by the river and by pipeline from Cashlie. The massive pipe visible by Kenknock Farm carries water from the Rivers Lochay and Dochart catchment, south over the hill, to Loch Lyon, the stations being at Lubreoch, by the dam, and Cashlie down the Glen.

Refreshments are at the Bridge of Orchy and Inveroran Hotels.

ROUTE

Head N on the A827 and turn L up Glen Lochy after the eponymous bridge. A road section of 11km then gently rises up Glen Lochay to Kenknock Farm, after which turn R up the hydroelectric road and grind up a 300m ascent, then lose most of that descending to Glen Lyon. There is now a choice of tracks along Loch Lyon;

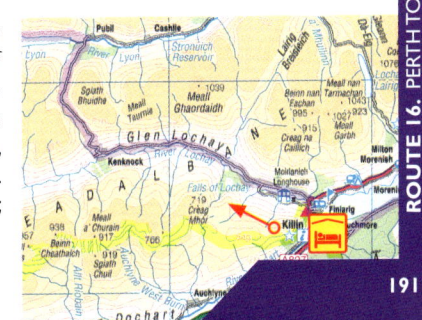

ROUTE 16. PERTH TO FORT WILLIAM

191

Mountain Biking Adventures:

a new track on the S, or an improved track on the N. The southern one looks good from satellite and aerial imagery, and if chosen, you need to turn L just after the start of the forest on the R and follow it round the end of the loch, and ford the Abhain Ghlas, which could be tricky if river levels are high. Carry on N for 1.5km, then E to join the northern track. We used the northern track, sketchy at the time towards the W, but now looks to be good from satellite and aerial imagery. Below the dam, take the second track L after the river and climb, keeping W. A ford with huge 'stepping stones' crossing the Allt Caillich could be a problem in very wet periods. Just before the end of the loch, branch R uphill on a track/path into Strath Tarabhan. After fording the river at the watershed, keep to the track hugging the Allt a'Chuirn and descend the glen, negotiating some interesting fords. A km after passing under the Fort William Railway line, cross the bridge over the Allt Kinglass and continue on the track, the West Highland Way, to Bridge of Orchy. The track is mostly grassed over worn cobbles.

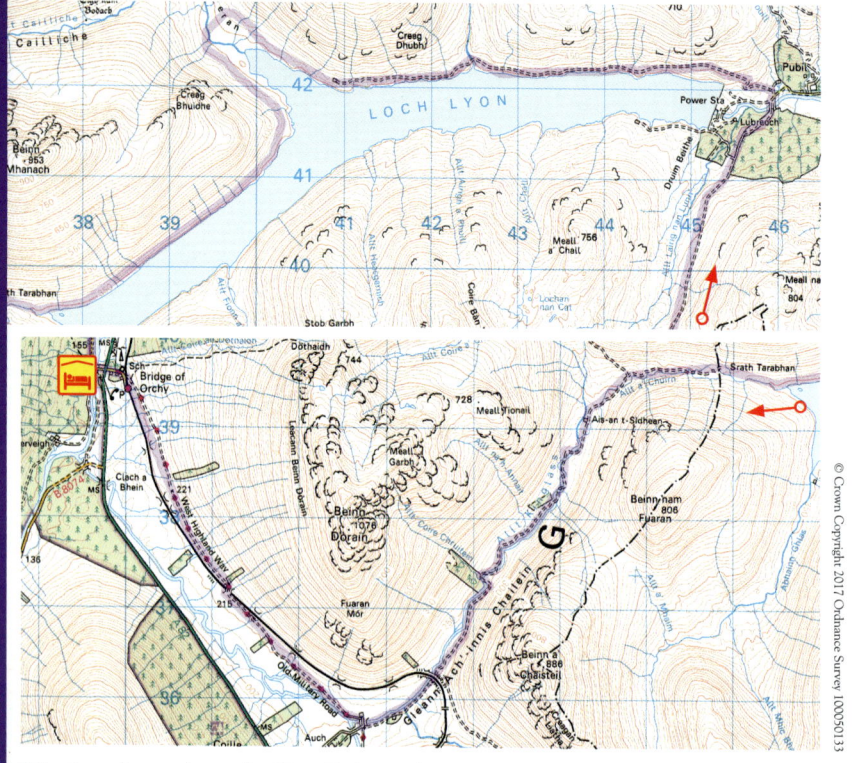

Take the quiet road over the River Orchy to Victoria Bridge, then turn W on a track after the bridge. Keep on the track via Clashgour. The direct path starting by the river is not good. Ford the tributary (old maps show a bridge, imagery does not now), and in 200m the main river, where there are stepping stones. Carry on the track to ford a southern tributary. If the water level is intimidating, cross the first tributary and back up it till a path goes W through the forest and, in 500m, over the main river by a bridge. The track is now rough but rideable, and down to another River Kinglass, becomes interesting as it crosses some bare rock. Fording the Kinglass River seemed easier to us than using the poor bridge. After this the path is poor, but soon becomes a track which descends speedily all the way to Loch Etive.

Multi-day routes in northern Britain

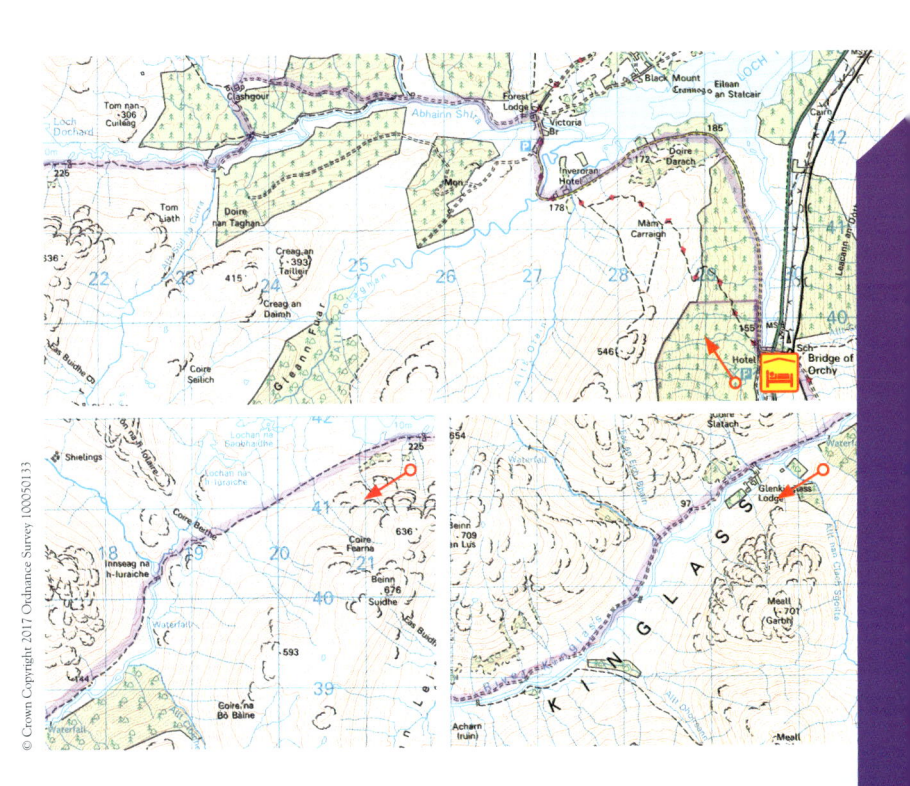

© Crown Copyright 2017 Ordnance Survey 100050133

The granite slabs before Glen Kinglass.

ROUTE 16. PERTH TO FORT WILLIAM

193

Mountain Biking Adventures:

At the 'T' junction turn L to cross the Kinglass and for the next 9km a good dirt track takes you up and down, crossing two major glens and with a forest ascent to finish you off. The views up the loch backwards are superb, however. At the road junction in the forest, turn R, and at the Inverawe Smokery turn L to the car park. From here go down the path to the R of the Smokery towards Hugo's Lochan, but turn L just before it to head across boggy meadows to the suspension bridge. There may be difficult gates to negotiate near the lochan. Then follow tracks to the bridge over the railway and on to the A85, turning R for Taynuilt.

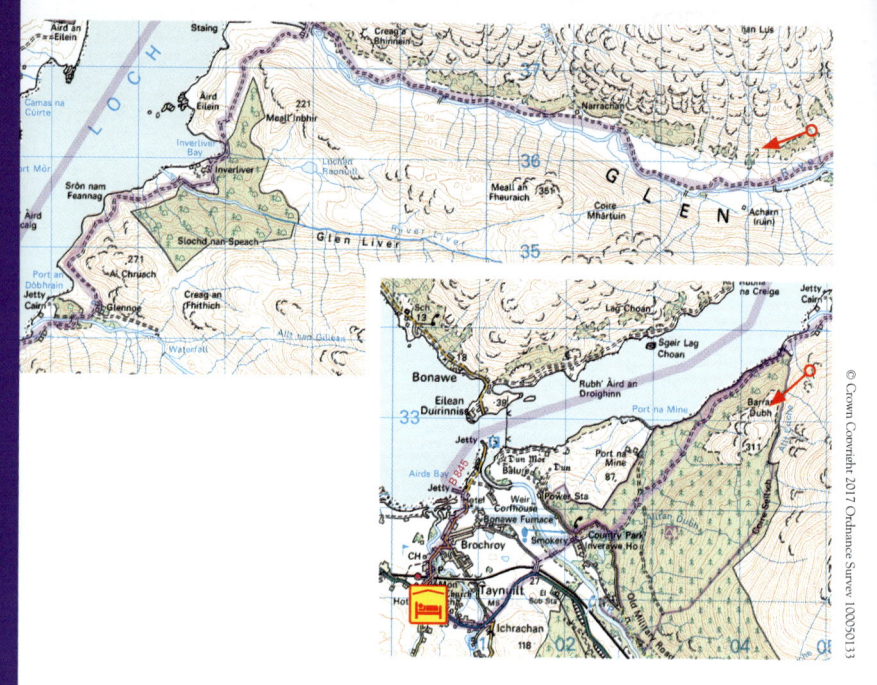

© Crown Copyright 2017 Ordnance Survey 100050133

DAY 3.

Start:	Taynuilt
Finish:	Loch Ossian Youth Hostel
Distance:	62.5km (39miles)
Off-road:	37.5km (23miles) 60%
Ascent:	1186m (3983ft)
Descent:	798m (2620ft)
Grade:	H3

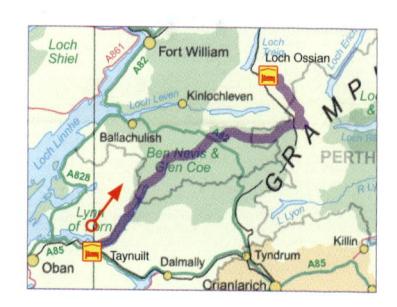

ROUTE 16. PERTH TO FORT WILLIAM

194

Multi-day routes in northern Britain

OVERVIEW

Assuming a boat can be hired up Loch Etive, a journey of about an hour, and giving an opportunity to view the superb mountain scenery near the head, this still gives a long, hard day, with rough sections immediately you land, and across the peat bogs of Rannoch Moor. The alternatives are detailed in the main 'Overview'. The final 13km of what was a rough track is now a dirt track with some ascent, to get to the rather wonderful, isolated YHA.

INFORMATION

Loch Ossian Youth Hostel now has a small shop selling 'Beyond the Beaten Track' ready meals and snacks. Best to check they have these and what they are. We brought all our provisions, including beer and whisky, on a prior visit, as the shop wasn't there then. This had to be brought in from Corrour Station, 1.6km away by track. But note all non-biodegradable rubbish has to be taken away, although our remaining whisky was welcomed then by the manager! There is a licensed restaurant at the station as well, last orders 8pm. The 'eco' label for the hostel indicates composting toilets and a reed bed filter. Hot showers are also now installed, pah, you're having it easy.

The track from near Rannoch station was an old drover's road, part of The Road to the Isles, and the Corrour Old Lodge was temporarily, last century, a (very successful!) isolation hospital. The track has been upgraded (2015), to allow cables from the hydro schemes to supply the whole Ossian estate. Kings House Hotel and Rannoch Station offer refreshments, the latter before 4.30pm in summer only, but Tel 01882 633247 to possibly arrange a later arrival. Watch out for a Hogwart's Express.

ROUTE

Alighting at the pier at Barrs (NN 076397) after an hour's nautical sight-seeing in your chosen boat, bear R, away from the buildings and pick up a fairly good track which soon curves left, NW, leaving the poor coastal path. Follow the track for 400m until you find a track, R. This track, which you follow for about 5km, is, at once obvious, raised like a dike for a km or so, and then almost disappears but it is consistently hard going, rocky and grassy. (One wonders if it is a 'parallel road' feature like those found in Glen Gloy.)

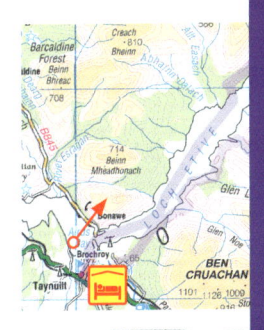

The track by Loch Etive.

Mountain Biking Adventures:

Where it ends, and is succeeded by a faint path, look up to your L to see the magnificent granite Trilleachan slabs. In a further km, you arrive at a large jetty and the tarmac road near the head of the loch, probably with some relief.

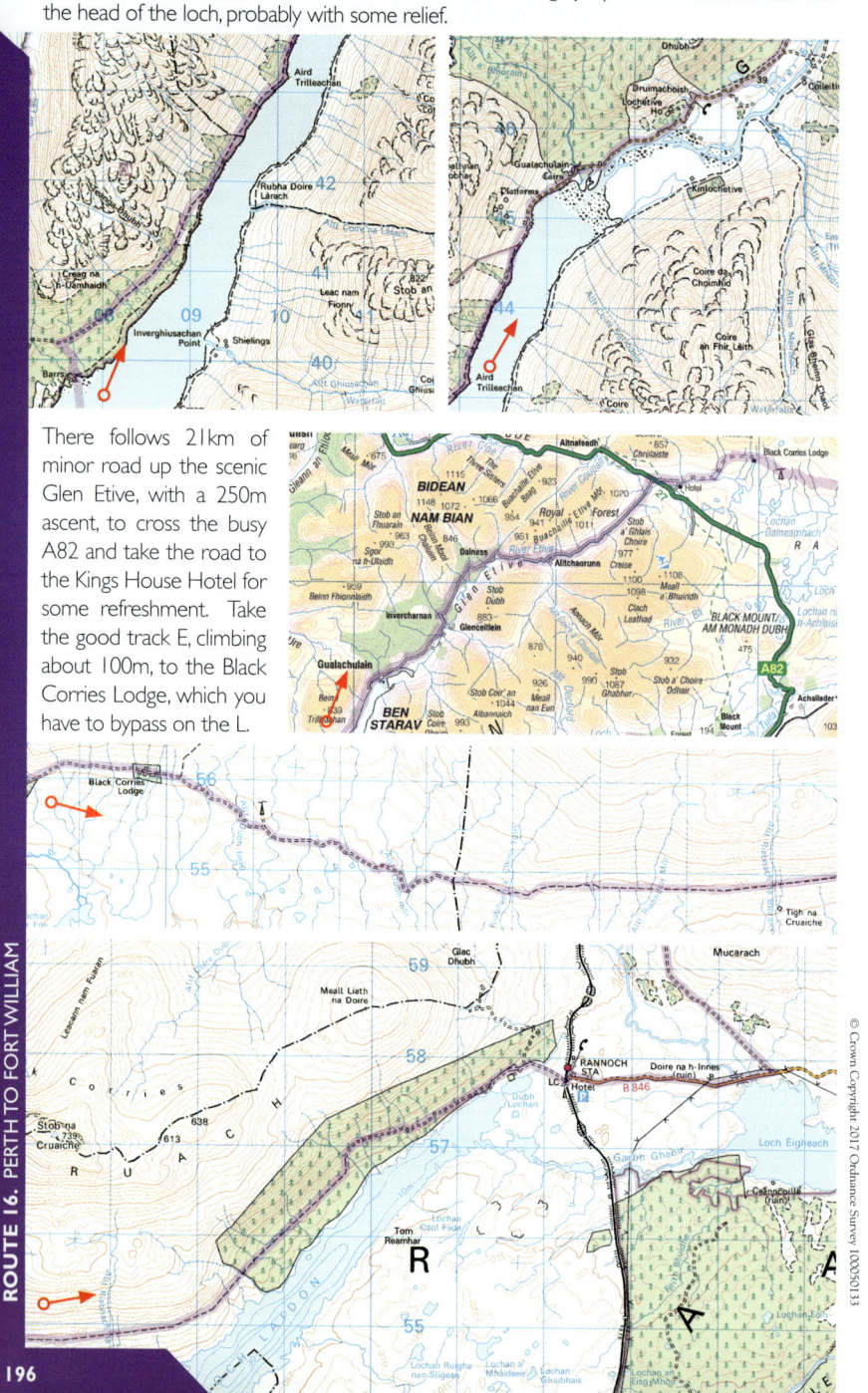

There follows 21km of minor road up the scenic Glen Etive, with a 250m ascent, to cross the busy A82 and take the road to the Kings House Hotel for some refreshment. Take the good track E, climbing about 100m, to the Black Corries Lodge, which you have to bypass on the L.

ROUTE 16. PERTH TO FORT WILLIAM

© Crown Copyright 2017 Ordnance Survey 100050133

196

Multi-day routes in northern Britain

The track remains rideable for 5km, then stops, and what follows is hard work across peat groughs. We've seen one source from the '90s which alleges 'much is rideable'. Afraid not. Follow the electricity poles, pushing and carrying until you reach a large turning circle in an area of harvested forest (still shown on the map as Forest). This good track continues for 5.5km through the forest to Rannoch Station and its delightful tearoom.

Look at the time: there are 16km to go still, mostly on good track, though with nearly a 300m ascent to the midpoint. If no time for tea, head E on the road till opposite Loch Eigheach, then turn L on a good track, recently improved. After about 3km there is a new bridge over the Allt Eigheach, and the improved dirt track goes all the way home. If you delight in river crossings ignore the bridge and take the double ford in about 200m. The track climbs and passes the lonely Corrour Old Lodge ruins, and just after it starts to descend you fork L at Peter's Rock, with its explanatory plaque, and descend to the lovely Loch Ossian.

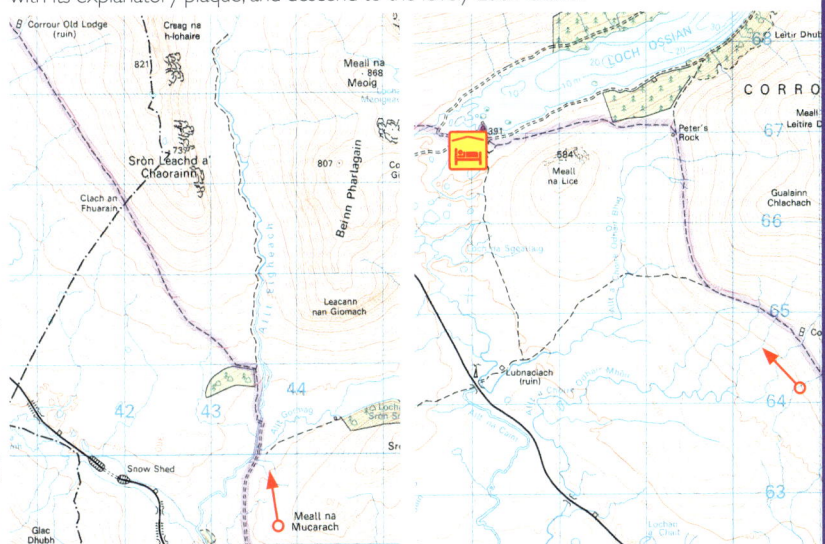

Enjoying the bogs near Loch Ossian.

ROUTE 16. PERTH TO FORT WILLIAM

197

Mountain Biking Adventures:

DAY 4.

Start:	Loch Ossian Youth Hostel
Finish:	Fort William
Distance:	35km (21.5miles)
Off-road:	24km (15miles) 69%, although could be 100%
Ascent:	580m (1905ft)
Descent:	962m (3157ft)
Grade:	M2

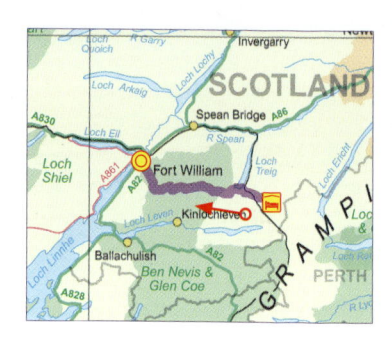

OVERVIEW

The fording of the Abhain Rath after 13km at Luibelt would be impossible in really wet weather, better then to take the track past Loch Ossian and on to Glen Spean, or the train. A short section of track leads to a partly rideable track through gloriously wild, remote glens. We easily spotted an eagle here. A short rocky carry leads to a road or forest track descent home. A splendid short day to finish.

INFORMATION

An interesting small dam at the watershed prevents the water of Nevis capturing the southern upper branch of the Abhain Rath, bound for hydropower via Loch Treig. There is a bothy at Meanach, opposite Luibeilt, which is now a ruin.

ROUTE

Take the track E, soon forking R towards Loch Treig. Pass under the rail line, after which a good descent leads to the loch. Turn L and follow the head of the loch round to Creaguaineach Lodge. Here take the far, N, bank of the Abhain Rath past Staoineag at least as far as Luibeilt (both on the opposite side).

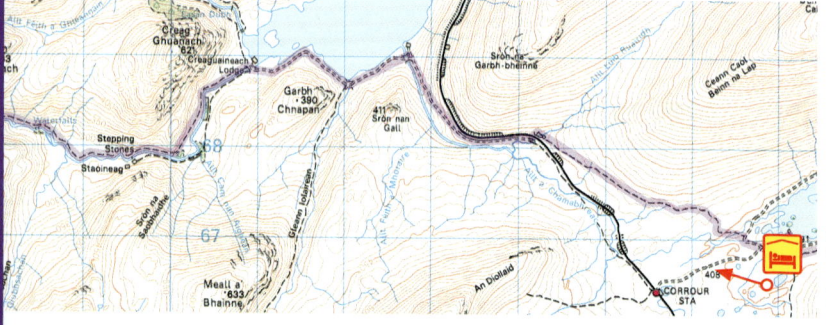

The path tends to fade in places, occasionally boggy, but then often rideable grassy riverbank. If the water is low, cross at Luibeilt and take the poor grassy, boggy track along the S bank as far as Tom an Eite, the small tump at the watershed. If you elect not to cross, continue on the even less distinct N bank path as it rises imperceptibly up to the watershed.

Multi-day routes in northern Britain

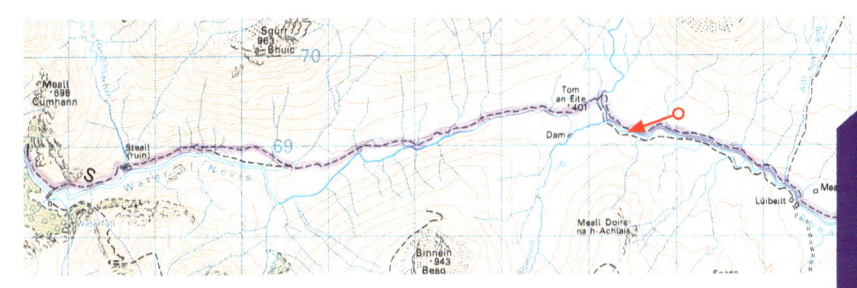

Whichever side you choose there is a potentially serious crossing just before Tom an Eite, where the two main tributaries bring water from the Grey Corries to the N and the Mamores to the S. Continue, partly riding, gently down upper Glen Nevis. Once past Steall ruins and a footbridge, the glen opens out a little, and you are now into a busy tourist area, with walkers coming up the impressive Nevis Gorge to view the splendid Steall falls.

Descending Glen Nevis before the gorge.

A good path leads to the gorge, which is a walk and carry. Join the road and cruise the 11km down the glen to the Fort, although you could do the last 8km in the Nevis Forest on tracks all the way from Achriabhach, with minimal initial ascent.

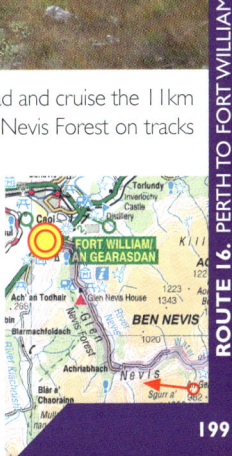

ROUTE 16. PERTH TO FORT WILLIAM

199

17. ENGLISH COAST TO COAST, WHITEHAVEN TO SUNDERLAND

Total route (days):	Four days			
Start:	Whitehaven			
Finish:	Sunderland			
Total Distance:	224km (139miles).			
Total Off-road (%):	67%			
Daily distance (km):	60.5	47.5	56	60
Daily off-road (%):	77%	60%	35%	95%
Ascent:	5554m (18,228ft)			
Crux day grade:	H3			

200

Multi-day routes in northern Britain

OVERVIEW

This route was thrust upon us by one of our group in 2004. He claimed to have got it from MBR, but cannot confirm that now, neither can we, having tried to get back copies and contacting MBR directly. The start is the same as many recorded coast to coasts, e.g. Tim Woodcock's, but deviates to Ennerdale, and the last day is also well recorded.

Two days of superb scenery passing through the centre of the Lake District, with some extended pushing and carrying, lead to the Pennines. Crossing here close to the highest point, Cross Fell, the Pennine Way is briefly joined, with a mixture of grouse moorland and post-mining landscape leading through the spine to Weardale. The last day is a dedicated cycle route, downhill or flat after a steep pull out of Stanhope, with the finish by the tidal Wear and a rejuvenated Sunderland.

Mountain Biking Adventures:

DAY 1.

Start:	Whitehaven west pier
Finish:	Ambleside
Distance:	60.5km (37.5miles)
Off-road:	46.5km (29miles) 77%
Ascent:	2003m (6574ft)
Descent:	1943m (6379ft)
Grade:	H3

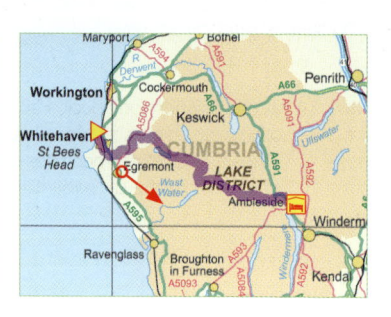

OVERVIEW

A hard day! An easy lead in via a railway cycle path, then two hard push/carry ascents through the heart of the Lake District, the superb scenery just about counteracting the walking (unless you're an expert and very fit), an infuriating carry/push down the Rossett Gill path and at last some biking, with the classic Loughrigg Terrace to finish, if you have the energy to take in the view.

INFORMATION

Whitehaven was developed by the Lowther family in the 17th century as a port to export the local coal. The other major such ports at the time were Sunderland and Newcastle, which gives some symmetry to this expedition. It was a planned, grid town, and the most complete Georgian town in Britain, really quite different! The coal mines were sometimes going out (under) the sea, the last one closing in 1986. The new marina was built in the '90s. The Lake District's details have been extensively documented elsewhere, but I can't help telling that you pass close by the two crags where British climbing really started, Pillar Rock, and The Napes on Great Gable, and both will be in view for some time on your pushes, and also Gimmer Crag, a classic venue, high up on the L down Mickleden.

The two major pubs at Wasdale Head and the Old Dungeon Ghyll Hotel will inevitably be greeted with joy. There's not much else to refresh you en route, although you may be lucky at the isolated Black Sail Youth Hostel with some tea if you chat the warden up.

ROUTE

After visiting the lighthouse at the far end of the harbour return to the marina at West Strand and turn L into Quay Street. Pick up the blue signs for the C2C Sustrans National Cycle Route 71. Follow the signs, and on the outskirts this takes the old railway track, now tarmacked, round Cleator Moor and by Rowrah. After Rowrah keep on the C2C/NCR 71, turning L onto a minor road, then R at Lamplugh School and straight on through Kirkland. At the next T junction turn R and leave the Cycle Route go through Croasdale and on to Bowness Knot car park by Ennerdale Water.

Multi-day routes in northern Britain

Here a good forest track leads gradually upwards beyond the lake for 8.5km to the wonderfully isolated Black Sail Youth Hostel. Continue for 350m up the track then cross the River Liza by a bridge and climb steeply up by the Sail Beck, some carrying being required for at least one rock step. Two thirds of the way up the path deviates away from the beck and soon reaches the pass. The next 1.5km drops you 400 m and is a technical descent, particularly as it steepens to cross Gatherstone Beck. Path "improvements" by stone slabs in 2015 have altered the path somewhat. Down in Mosedale a straightforward track leads through some fords down to Wasdale, and refreshments for most. Note there are no public toilets at the Hotel, but some kiosk ones by the car park 400m down the road.

Tony near Black Sail Pass.

Leaving Wasdale Head, the path visible up the side of Great Gable.

Mountain Biking Adventures:

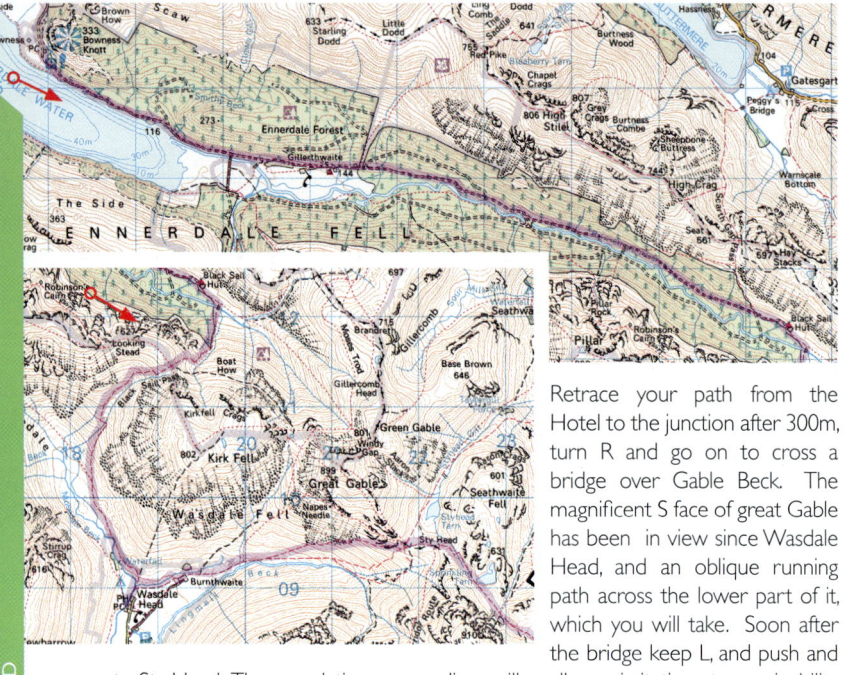

Retrace your path from the Hotel to the junction after 300m, turn R and go on to cross a bridge over Gable Beck. The magnificent S face of great Gable has been in view since Wasdale Head, and an oblique running path across the lower part of it, which you will take. Soon after the bridge keep L, and push and carry upto Sty Head. The superlative surroundings will quell your irritation at your inability to ride. At Sty Head continue on the clear path easterly round some impressive low rock outcrops, then south-easterly up past Sprinkling Tarn, with the imposing cliffs of Great End on your R, then past Ruddy Gill on the L to Esk Hause, a definite crossroad of paths. The riding is technical, and we mostly pushed. Now a descent looms, with some rideable sections, to the N of Angle Tarn, then a short push to the col S of Rossett Pike, and an infuriating descent to the S of Rossett Gill, which may be rideable for experts by the Gill lower down. Certainly you can ride easily after the bridge over Stake Gill, a good track leads to the back of the Old Dungeon Ghyll Hotel, where most will take some refreshment. The impressive mass of Gimmer Crag up the L hillside coming down Mickleden is worth scanning, the obvious line of "The Crack" splitting the NW face.

Near Esk Hause, looking to the Langdale Pikes.

Multi-day routes in northern Britain

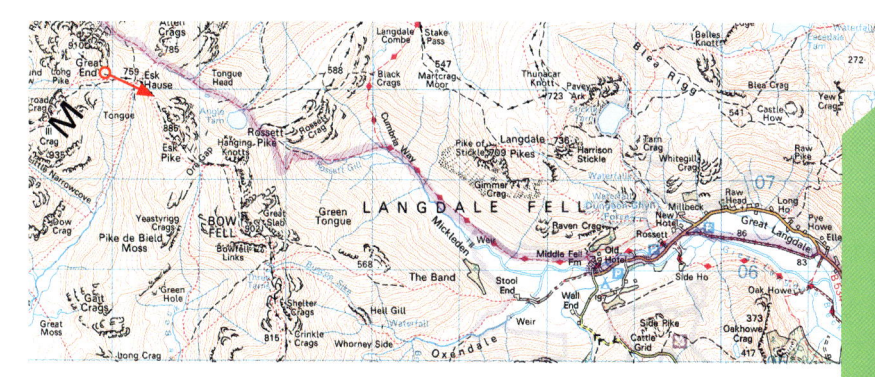

Take the road from here for a km and turn R through the car park opposite the New Dungeon Ghyll (Stickle Barn), where a byway track leads direct across the valley to join the main road a km from Chapel Stile. Turn first L in the village, past the church and on up the minor road, past the Youth Hostel and down to a road junction, past which take the Bridleway R, which becomes Loughrigg Terrace, good riding if the walkers have all gone home, likely at the hour you'll be here. Continue by Rydal Water, but at the wood you must go R up the bank onto a track which takes you over to Pelter Bridge, where the main road leads to Ambleside. A long but spectacular day.

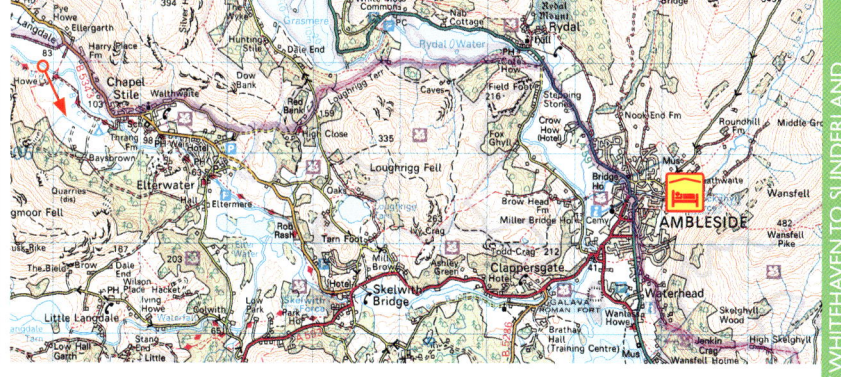

DAY 2.

Start:	Ambleside
Finish:	Culgaith
Distance:	47.5km (29.5miles).
Off-road:	28.5km (18miles) 60%
Ascent:	1484m (4872ft).
Descent:	1393m (4573ft)
Grade:	M2

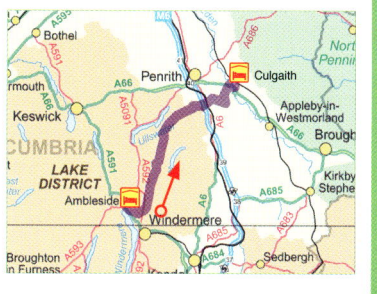

Mountain Biking Adventures:

OVERVIEW

The gem of Skelghyll Wood leads on to a long sometimes boggy valley upto a big push onto the Kentmere Round ridge. Good riding mostly then along High Street with a long grassy descent and 19km road to finish.

INFORMATION

High Street is a roman named route twixt forts at Ambleside, (quite near the Lake, unobtrusive low remains), and Brougham (Penrith). Summer fairs took place here in the 18th and 19th centuries, including horse racing; it seems Appleby Fair has taken over from this windy venue.

There is a café/stores in Askham, at the crossroads, and also a café in the courtyard of Lowther Castle, the house and grounds of which have recently started to be renovated, the latter with some interesting features. Entrance free for the café.

ROUTE

Go S from the centre of Ambleside on the main road and turn L up Old Lake Road, and as it descends to the main road turn L again up Skelghyll Lane. Ignore several L turns to properties, but after the wall on the L ends take the L fork up, over a beck and steeply up through the wood. Leaving the wood a good view of the Southern Lakes enfolds. Continue up onto Robin Lane, now a track, round the fell and down to the Troutbeck road by the Post Office. Turn L and quickly R, steeply, down a road to join the main Kirkstone Pass road. Turn L, then, after the church, R into Limefitt Caravan Park.

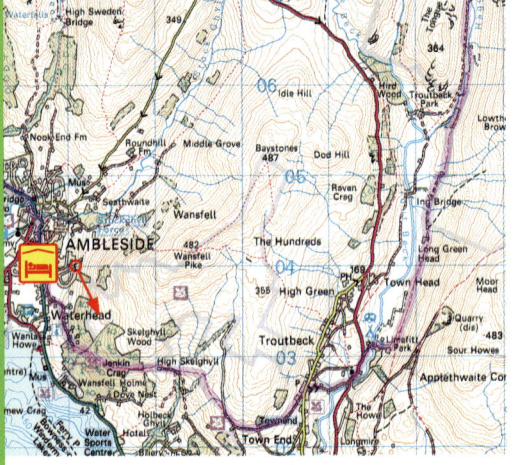

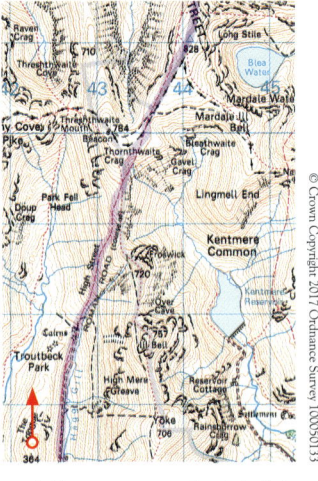

Cross the Trout Beck and head directly up the hillside through the caravans, going L to join a Bridleway heading N. This takes you down into, then up the main valley, to the R of the Tongue up the Hagg Gill valley for 5km, where a long push starts upto the main path of the Kentmere round, continuing on this but keeping northerly when it goes R for Mardale Ill Bell. On High Street normal service should be resumed: descend to the Straits of Riggindale and ascend a short distance, turning R at an obvious junction. This takes you round Rampsgill head, after which fork L to High Raise.

Multi-day routes in northern Britain

The group on High Street summit.

Fairfield and Dove Crag from High Street.

Now there is a good 9km undulating ride down to Ketley Gate on Askham Fell, with the last 3 to 4km being a lovely fast descent on grass. Take care to turn L before Loadpot Hill, not R, otherwise navigation is straightforward, and you can go over the tops or round as you wish.

ROUTE 17. ENGLISH COAST TO COAST; WHITEHAVEN TO SUNDERLAND

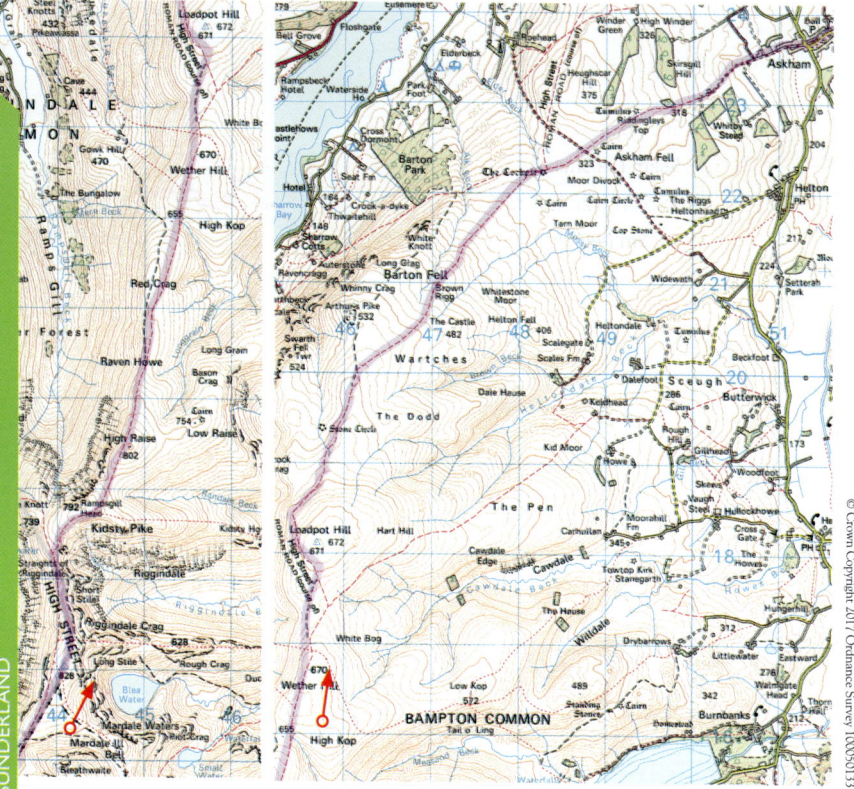

Mountain Biking Adventures:

At the plateau of Askham Fell, however, a mass of paths exist and care is required to find the Bridleway which leads down to Askham. Go straight through the village, cross the Lowther and continue straight on, forking L at GR531243, then L onto the A6. Over the M6 turn R and go for 2.5km to join a road where part of Whinfell Forest lies ahead. Turn R on it and L in Cliburn, climbing up past the Centre Parcs complex and down towards the A66, where the road turns to the R before a "T" junction, turn L here and pass under the "new" dual carriageway. At the old road turn R, and a short way after crossing the Eden turn and up to Culgaith.

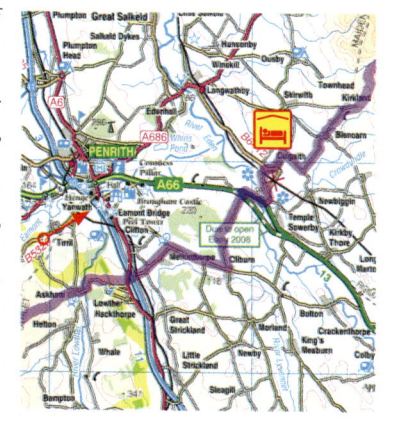

ROUTE 17. ENGLISH COAST TO COAST, WHITEHAVEN TO SUNDERLAND

© Crown Copyright 2017 Ordnance Survey 100050133

208

Multi-day routes in northern Britain

DAY 3.

Start:	Culgaith
Finish:	Stanhope
Distance:	56km (34.5miles)
Off-road:	19.5km (12miles) 35%
Ascent:	1359m (4460ft)
Descent:	1303m (4278ft)
Grade:	M2

OVERVIEW

Another big ascent, 500m on a good track, crests the Pennines, followed by a longer track descent to Garrigill. A short ascent out of the village leads to a 10km bleak Pennine road, always above 400m, then an old mine track goes over the hill to Weardale and an easy ride on roads to Stanhope.

INFORMATION

Virtually all of today's route is in the North Pennines Area of Outstanding Natural Beauty, the UK's second largest AONB. The moorland scenery is a result of centuries of farming and mining, mainly for lead. 40% of the UK's upland hay meadows are in it. The Pennine Way, Britain's first National long distance path, is joined alongside Cross Fell, the Pennines' highest Fell, and followed to Garrigill: pity the poor walkers on the hard surface of a one-time corpse road. Greg's Hut, at the path's summit, is a famous bothy and converted mine workers cottage, and a frequent overnight venue on the Pennine Way, worth a look inside.

The George and Dragon in Garrigill is the only watering hole till Weardale, but has intermittently shut, currently (2016) open. If asking for "tea" in Upper Weardale, best to add "a pot of..." or they'll think you mean supper/dinner.

ROUTE

Take the minor road NE out of Culgaith and turn R after a km, then L after a longer km to Blencarn. Turn L at the second junction in Blencarn, to Kirkland, and follow the beckside road to Kirkland Hall. Here join the Bridleway going NE, which becomes a bit of a push till it evens out along the northern shoulder of Cross Fell and joins the Pennine Way. Now it is all rideable, although stony, along and down to Garrigill.

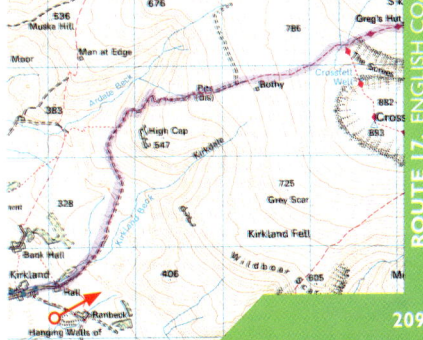

ROUTE 17. ENGLISH COAST TO COAST, WHITEHAVEN TO SUNDERLAND

209

Mountain Biking Adventures:

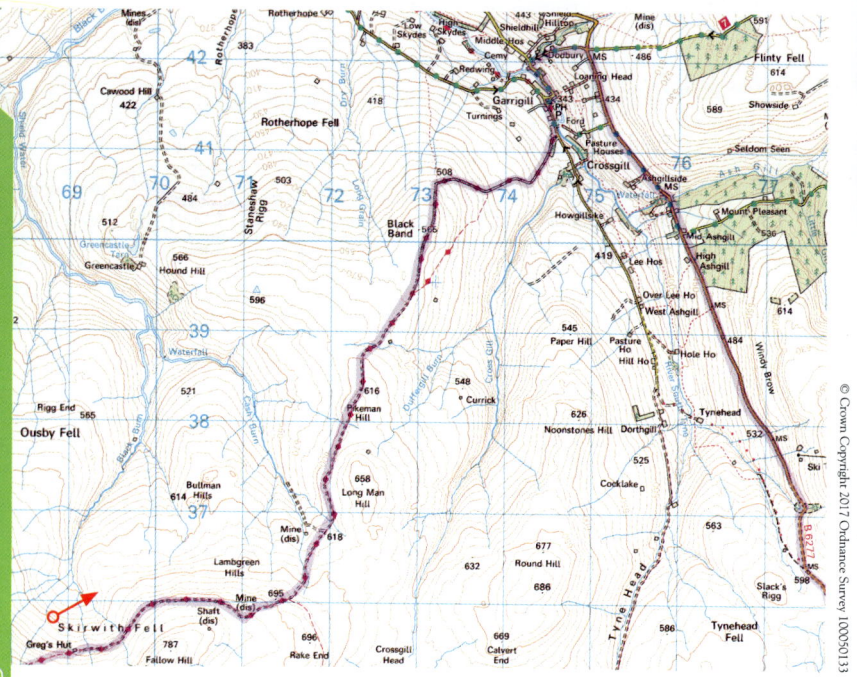

To get to the B6277, either go N on the E bank of the South Tyne and turn first R up a minor road, very steep to start, or, if not fed up with pushing or if you're superman or woman, ascend the Bridleway from the village direct. Take the B6277, the main road from Teesdale to Alston, S. It climbs to 597m after 6km, then contours around the head of the Harwood valley for another 4km where turn L up an old mine track at GR813351. This takes you over to Weardale, joining a minor road on the way down. Turn R down the main A689 for 12 easy km to Stanhope, or carry straight on at Daddry Shield on a minor, quieter but more undulating road to cross the Wear just before Stanhope.

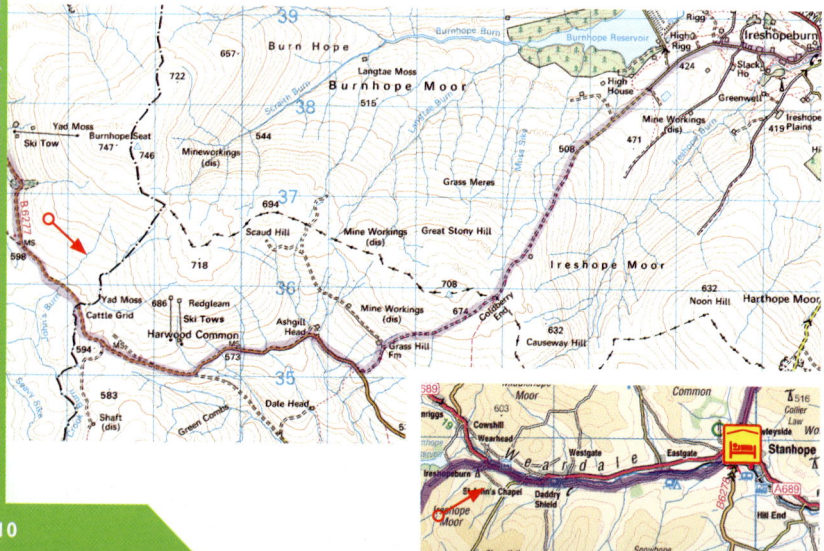

ROUTE 17. ENGLISH COAST TO COAST, WHITEHAVEN TO SUNDERLAND

DAY 4.

Start:	Stanhope
Finish:	Sunderland north pier
Distance:	60km (37.5miles)
Off-road:	57km (35.5miles) 95%
Ascent:	708m (2326ft)
Descent:	916m (3006ft)
Grade:	E1

OVERVIEW

A stiff road climb followed by a gentle downhill on old railway routes with some urban off road bits, coming to the sea via the Wear and the Stadium of Light.

INFORMATION

This is part of Sustrans National route 7, most of it taken over from the Consett and Sunderland Railway which closed in 1985. This was Britain's first commercial railway, serving the lead mines in the hills, and bringing limestone and coal to the steel works. Sustrans commissioned many art works along the route, most made of steel, commemorating the areas industrial heritage. The grandest, which is unplaqued, is "Terris Novalis", just before Consett. This 7m high stainless steel sculpture of a theodolite and an engineer's level pays homage to Consett's Iron Company, a huge, high quality steel works closed in 1980. It is the work of Tony Cragg, and erected in 1996. Other notables are a huge King Cole of stone/brick near Chester-Le-street and a maze by Andy Goldsworthy near Leadgate, representing the underground routes of the Durham coalfield, which you cycle the edge of.

There's the Jolly Drovers pub by the maze, various watering holes at Beamish centre just off the route, and a café in the Washington Wildlife Centre.

ROUTE

Go N up the B6278 from Stanhope, signposted C2C NCR7 for 3km, a climb of 230m, and turn R on a track 300m after the summit, unsignposted, but blocked by rocks to vehicular traffic, which connects to an old railway track leading L to join the Waskerley Way at Parkhead Station. If you miss or don't fancy this track keep on the B6278 for 2 km until a waymark R turn, just before the road begins to rise again, takes you to Parkhead.

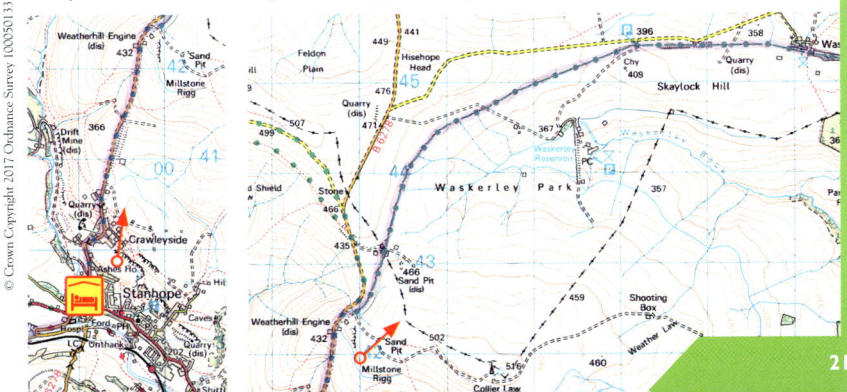

Mountain Biking Adventures:

The hard work is now over. Follow the waymarked C2C/N7 downhill all the way (nearly), past Consett, Stanley, Beamish Park, and Chester-le-Street to the Stadium of Light in Sunderland, enjoying the sculpture and maze, and the social history and industrial archaeology as you go. Admire the Stadium of Light, continue past the University until the waymarked route brings you to The Marina. Follow the promenade round and onto the pier if that is your end point, or the beach and the North Sea.

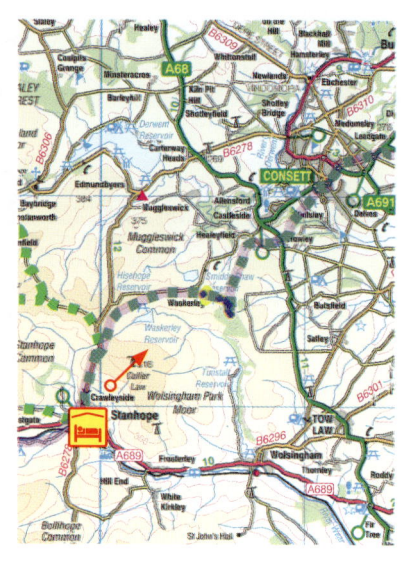

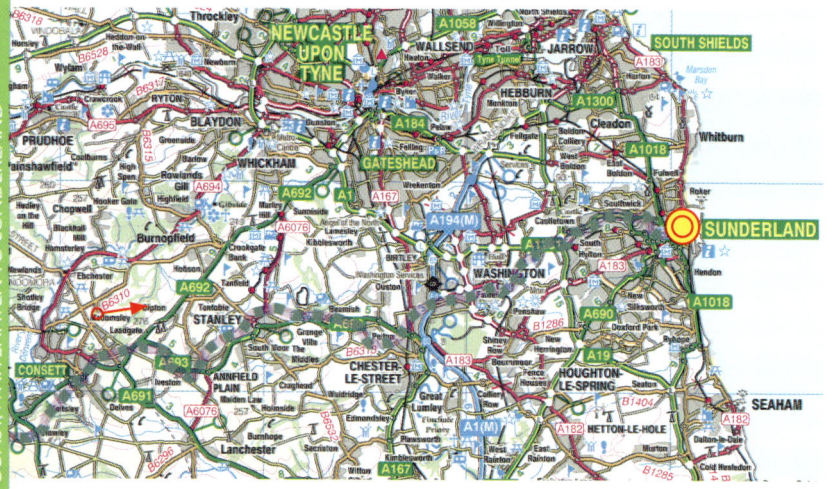

Multi-day routes in northern Britain

The end. Sunderland beach.

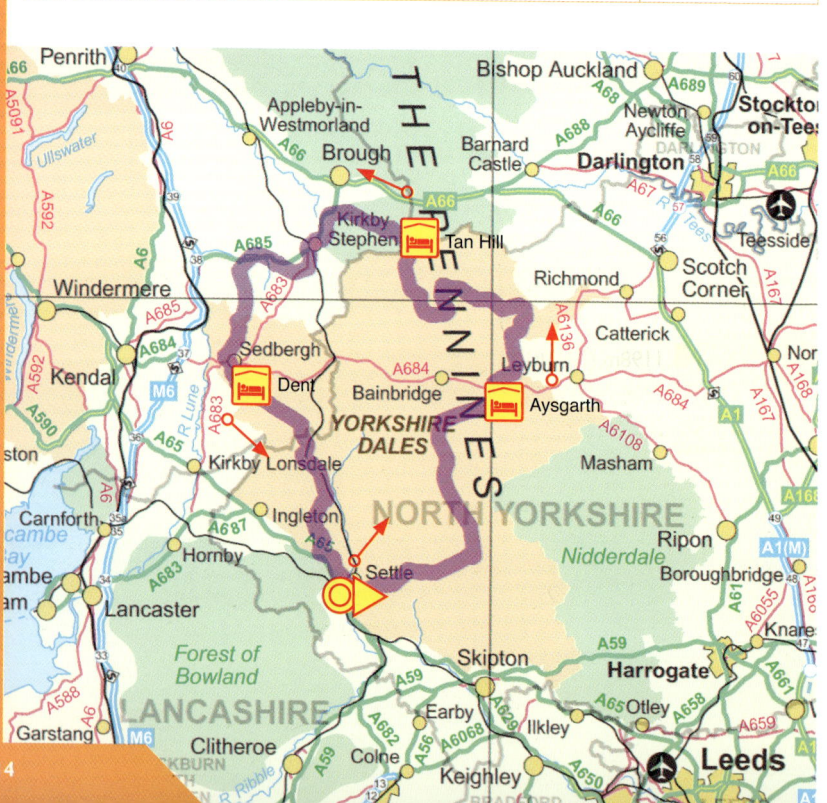

18. DALES CIRCULAR FROM SETTLE

Total route (days):	Four days			
Start & Finish:	Settle (or on to Lancaster on the last day)			
Total Distance:	183.5km, (114 miles). Circular: 26.km (16.5miles) extra to Lancaster Station			
Total Off-road (%):	62%			
Daily distance (km):	48.5	45	56.5	34 or 62 if going on to Lancaster Station
Daily off-road (%):	61%	69%	27%	66%
Ascent:	4887m (16,040ft)			
Crux day grade:	M1			

ROUTE 18. DALES CIRCULAR FROM SETTLE

214

Multi-day routes in northern Britain

OVERVIEW

The circuit goes well from Settle, accessed by train, but could finish at Lancaster with better connections, and where I live!

Excellent Dales scenery with limestone crags and terrain; atmospheric post-industrial landscape in Swaledale, including part of MBR's top 20 trails in the UK 2014; the highest inn in Britain; the grassy Howgills with a splendid descent; lovely Dentdale; and then part of the PBW on the last day. Biking on limestone turf is a joy, although tracks are more slithery when wet.

INFORMATION

The 'Dales' is the area of the Yorkshire Pennines where glaciation has cut into the massif through millstone grit and sandstone, forming wide 'U' valleys in the underlying limestone, separated by flattish moors of bog and heather on the less permeable rocks.

The pale grey limestone gives these dales their characteristic stone walls, field barns and charming villages, in places similar to how the Vikings laid them out, which make them different from the large dales further north. Hay meadows with rampant wild flowers impress in June.

The ravages of mining are evident in places, particularly Swaledale.

DAY 1.

Start:	Settle
Finish:	Aysgarth
Distance:	48.5km (30miles)
Off-road:	29.5km (18.5miles) 61%
Ascent:	1198m (3931ft)
Descent:	1140m (3743ft)
Grade:	E1

OVERVIEW

Classic Dales Scenery. A steep pull out of Settle leads to the straightforward Stockdale Lane passing through stunning limestone country. This is the southern limb of the Settle loop of the PBW. Mastilles Lane, another limestone lane, leads across and down to Wharfedale, where roads up the long dale lead to a bit of a push up a moorland track then a long descent into Wensleydale.

ROUTE 18. DALES CIRCULAR FROM SETTLE

215

Mountain Biking Adventures:

INFORMATION

Settle is serviced by trains from Leeds and Bradford, and from Carlisle by the famous, if not express, line. From the Lancaster main West Coast line there is a branch to Giggleswick, a mile S by road, although with an infrequent service. It is a busy market town, particularly on Tuesdays, market day.

Stockdale Lane is in the line of the Mid-Craven fault, which fractured the Great Scar Carboniferous Limestone around 300 million years ago and raised it up on the N side to 900m, although it has eroded since. The crags around Attermire are thus formed by it. To the S it is millstone grit and looks (and feels underfoot or wheel) completely different.

Mastilles Lane was a Roman road, and indeed our route goes right through a square Roman 'marching fort', best seen on Google Earth. Later it was a drove road, used to take sheep from Fountains Abbey to summer pastures as far as the Lake District.

Aysgarth is famous for its three falls on the Ure, pretty impressive after heavy rain. The best view of the upper fall is actually from the bridge, of the others involves a walk downstream. Less well known is an Edwardian rock garden in the main village, and the fact that the churchyard of the 12th century St Andrew's is probably the largest in England.

There is a pub in Kilnsey, and pubs and tearooms in Kettlewell, Starbotton and Buckden.

ROUTE

From the station go up Station Road to the main road in the centre, turn R up Chapel Street. This leads to the briefly cobbled Victoria Street. Keep L at the first junction and R at the next, signed 'The Pinfold 150 yrds' and 'Pennine Bridleway'. At Black's Plantation a track, Lambert's Lane, goes L, and at a R and quick L on the minor road, becomes Stockdale Lane, metalled to Stockdale Farm. Here the limestone track goes N round the farm, marked for the PBW.

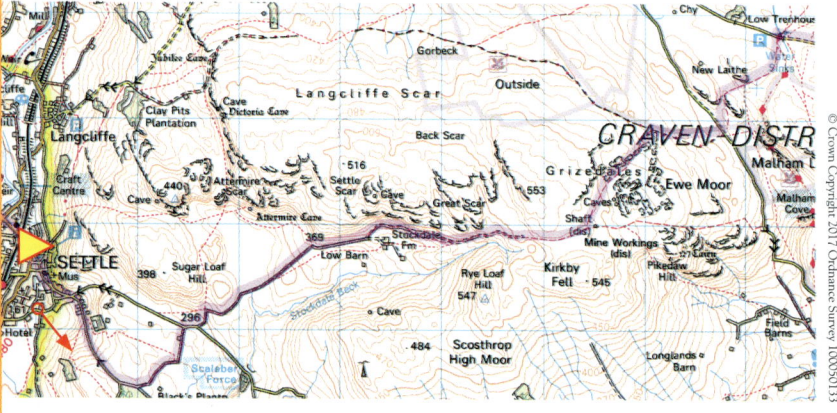

© Crown Copyright 2017 Ordnance Survey 100050133

Just before Nappa Gate, SD875640, turn L and follow the PBW track through gated fields, with Malham Tarn visible straight ahead. At an improved track turn R to Langscar Gate, then L for 50m on the minor road, and take a bridleway R. After nearly 400m this takes a right angled turn to the R and curves down to the minor road by the Malham Tarn outflow stream.

Turn R to Street Gate and on to the wide Mastilles Lane, taking care at the fast descent at Kilnsey Moor. This leads to Kilnsey and the Tennant Arms.

ROUTE 18. DALES CIRCULAR FROM SETTLE

216

Multi-day routes in northern Britain

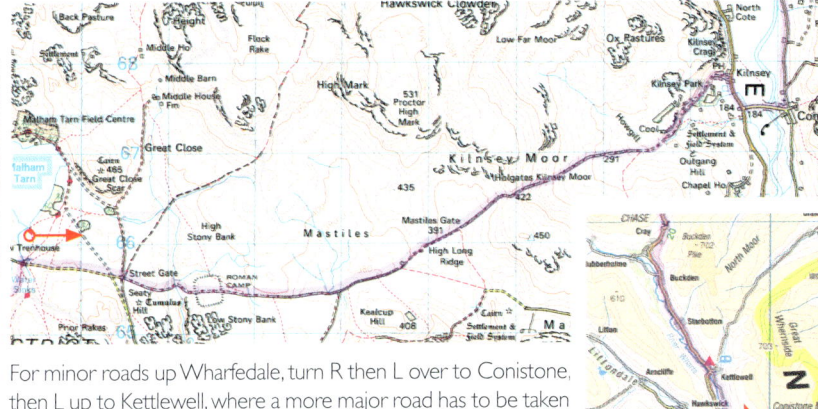

Mastilles Lane.

For minor roads up Wharfedale, turn R then L over to Conistone, then L up to Kettlewell, where a more major road has to be taken to Buckden. Through the car park at the N end of Buckden, a bridleway leads up through a wood and along to join the road again above Cray, then, after a steep short ascent, turn L up Gilbert Lane at spot height 419m. This track is rideable, although steep in places, up to and across Stake Moss. As the track starts to descend, fork R, signed Carpley Green, and just after the second subsequent gate, fork R on to the signed bridleway 'Thoralby'. A thin, but definite path leads to the R of a cairn where it joins a wider track. Unfortunately, soon after, the track has been 'improved' (2015) in places. Keep on this obvious main one. After crossing a beck (Skellicks) carry straight on (L) at the signed bridleway junction, eventually reaching a good walled track with an excellent unimproved descent to Thoralby. Here, turn L, and continue straight on at the main road junction to take the first turn R off the road on to Eastfield Lane, leading to a 'B' road by Bishopdale Beck. Turn L here, unfortunately up a steep short hill, then L on the 'A' road to the first part of Aysgarth village.

ROUTE 18. DALES CIRCULAR FROM SETTLE

217

Mountain Biking Adventures:

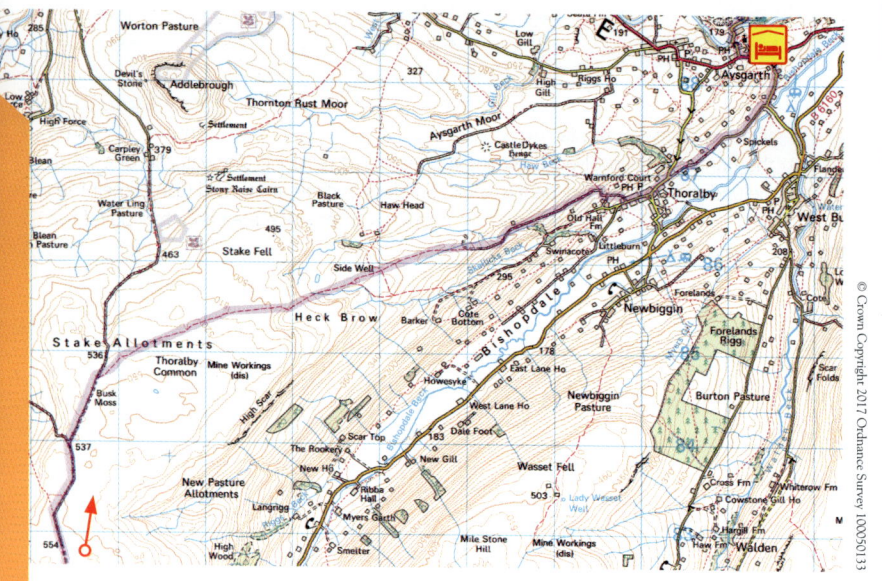

If your accommodation is in Aysgarth West then you might want to keep on the 'B' road from Thoralby to Aysgarth, although there are a few 'up' chevrons.

DAY 2.

Start:	Aysgarth
Finish:	Tan Hill
Distance:	45km (28miles)
Off-road:	31km (19.5miles) 69%
Ascent:	1521m (4994ft)
Descent:	1207m (3963ft)
Grade:	M1

OVERVIEW

Some pushing due to steepness over the grouse moors to Swaledale. Up this Dale and its northern flank through interesting country ravaged by lead mining, leads to a delightful ride by the Swale in its upper reaches, before some possibly muddy pushing up part of the PW to Tan Hill.

INFORMATION

Bolton Castle, giving the village its name, was built in the 14th century, and was torched by Henry VIII as its Baron Scrope did not support his religious reforms. Mary, Queen of Scots, resided there for six months.

Multi-day routes in northern Britain

Reeth is a market centre for the area, and used to be the hub for Swaledale lead mining. This started before the Romans, although they appreciated the value in these hills, and in the peak of a 250 year period, the mid 1800s, there were a thousand miners living in Reeth. The galena ore containing lead occurs in veins, initially these were dug into vertically, to form 'bell pits', seen as circular holes. Later, horizontal levels were dug, helped by explosive technology. Hushes, such as the Bunton one, involved damming a stream and releasing the water in one go to expose the underlying rocks and identify veins. Smelting, such as at the Old Gang Smelt Mills, involved simple heating, which removed most remaining trees in the area, and then peat from the moors was used. The residue from all these processes is toxic from the lead, and remains so, causing the characteristic large barren spoil heaps.

The Tan Hill Pub was built for miners working locally (it used to be surrounded by miners' houses), but now depends on passing trade, like the Hell's Angels party of 250 or so that we once encountered and gatecrashed for a drink. There are full facilities in Reeth, and a café just off route at Keld.

ROUTE

Take the road down to the Ure and its falls, and up to Carperby. Turn R and continue towards Castle Bolton, but turn L 300m before the turn to it, up a bridleway. This soon joins the minor road, which turns a right angle by the castle. Turn L, 100m after the bend, up a track leading up and over the ridge of Black Hill. The bridleway is marked as taking a separate course from the track for a distance, which I would ignore. A short down on the track and over Apedale Beck leads to another rocky incline to Greets Hill, where go R at a junction to the summit cairns. A gate on the R leads on to a rocky and technical track following the fence on the L and descending to a minor road. Keep on down this and at a right angled bend keep straight on, down a thin bridleway path through heather, veering L very quickly at the next junction, and being careful to turn sharp R just before the Gill, continuing down on a dirt track to join the road which leads to Grinton and Reeth.

From Reeth take the main road up the Dale, forking R just after Healaugh on to a minor road, then again R on to a gravel track after 200m. Ignore a 'Private

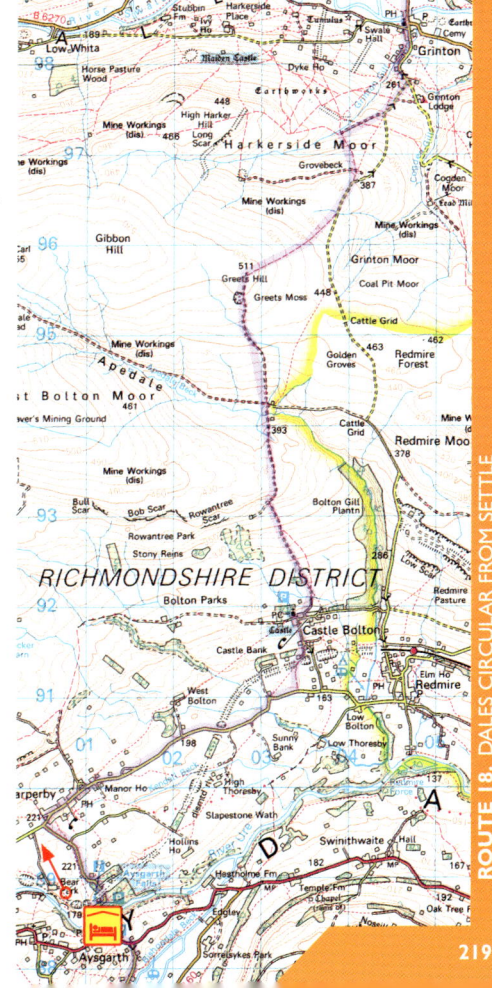

Mountain Biking Adventures:

Land, no vehicles' sign here, as it is a bridleway. Past this, a wood is entered, and the track goes R, through a metal gate. After the second gate the grassy, steep track goes diagonally up the hill to the L. This will be a push for maybe 400m. At a branch in the track a sign suggests a R fork, carry straight on. A bit boggy now. A small gate indicates the path descent to Bleaberry Gill. The far bank is also a short push up steps. At the top the obvious, but thin, track through the heather is not on the line of the bridleway on the map, but soon leads to Surrender Bridge, where a gravel track leads up the valley past the ruined and atmospheric Old Gang Smelting Mills. Fork L at Level House Bridge (the second bridge) and go up and through the moonscape of spoil heaps to a junction at SD947014, where a decision has to be made: a technical rocky descent through Bunton Hush boulder field; or a longer, but initially easier, descent to the R. If you're superman or woman, and come out the other side of the Hush at a signed crossroads, take a singletrack diagonally down to Gunnerside Beck and go up alongside it, the track now rock strewn, and pass to the R of the derelict buildings. The easier R descent curves N, but note the mapped bridleway at SD941022 does NOT exist. Possibly the best way down is to go L at a small cairn 300m after the signed path to Keld, through heather on a thin path which curves round L and comes out on the bridleway down to the Gill. Turn R, N, up this and turn L down the obvious path to the bridge (the bridleway on the opposite bank N of here is awful).

Upper Swaledale before Keld.

Multi-day routes in northern Britain

Turn L up a rocky track, boggy where it levels out. After Botcher Gill Gate there is a short climb then a good descent, curving R above Swaledale to join a minor road, which is taken to Ramps Home Farm, continuing as a good track. The next 2km up the Swale valley are glorious, both scenically and under wheel.

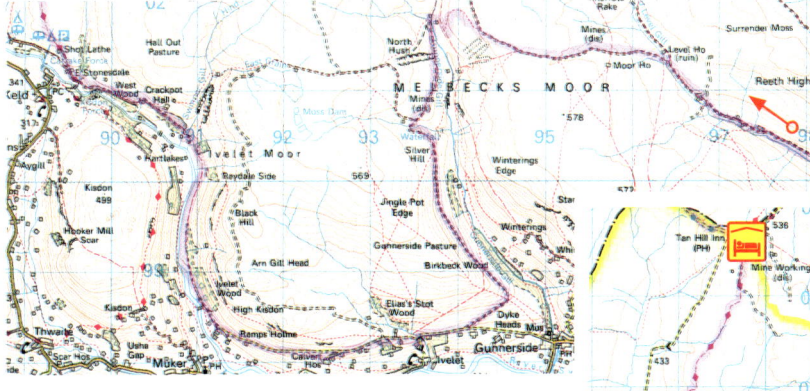

At the junction with the PW, if desperate for a drink, descend to the bridge and then a push and a lane lead to Keld and the café. Otherwise turn up the PW track and push to East Stonedale, carrying on up the hill on the well blazed PW path, boggy in places, and rideable till past Lad Gill when a push will be needed. The last 500m is on an old mine track to Tan Hill.

DAY 3.

Start:	Tan Hill
Finish:	Dent
Distance:	56.5km (35miles)
Off-road:	25km (15.5miles) 27%
Ascent:	1336m (4385ft)
Descent:	1722m (5651ft)
Grade:	M1

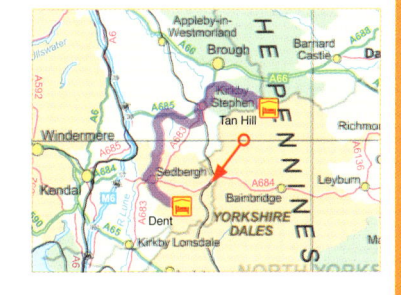

OVERVIEW

A short bushwack near the start leads to minor roads descending to Kirkby Stephen. The described route bypasses the town on a disused railway track, now a 'Poetry Path', then ingenuously circumnavigates the busy main road to the M6, to the start of a major off-road route S through the Howgill Fells, to the highest point thereof and a great descent, finishing off down a fast and safe last 2km.

ROUTE 18. DALES CIRCULAR FROM SETTLE

221

Mountain Biking Adventures:

A better way to bypass the main road would be to take minor roads to the start of the Smardale railway path NY739082, and follow this lovely, and becoming classical, route to Newbiggin-on-Lune. However, this is owned by the Cumbria Wildlife Trust and they have an archaic policy of 'no cycling on reserves'. Therefore, I cannot formally give this as part of my route, though they have a local 'turn a blind eye policy', which means that polite passing of walkers will get you through.

INFORMATION

The Poetry Path is part of the railway path restored by the Northern Viaduct Trust just after the millennium. Twelve poems, celebrating the life of hill farmers by relating to their calendar, are engraved on local sandstone blocks. The idea arose following the Foot and Mouth outbreak which devastated this area in 2001. The railway line was over Stainmore, carrying coke from South Durham to the iron works in Barrow-in-Furness, and iron on the return journey. It closed in 1962.

The Howgills differ geologically from the terrain so far, the bedrock being Silurian grit or slate, most of which is hidden under grass. The valleys are steep sided and the tops rounded domes.

Sedbergh is dominated by its public school, built in 1525, but is also England's only book town, Hay-on Wye being half in Wales. Thus bookshops abound.

Dent is a lovely, relatively quiet 'Western' Dales village, having its own brewery a few miles up the valley which owns the George and Dragon. Opposite this pub, on the cobbled street, is a granite memorial stone to Adam Sedgwick, Dent's famous son, one of Geology's founders.

There are full facilities in Kirkby Stephen, just off route, and in Sedbergh, and pubs in Ravenstonedale.

ROUTE

Go W downhill on the Brough road and, after 4km, look out for a bridleway sign at NY869091. Go L down a short boulder field, then pathless rough grass. At the bottom follow above Potter Syke, finding a quad track by a wooden plank bridge just after the bend in the Syke. Follow this, then aim on a branch rightwards for the corner of the main plantation, with young trees in 2016. A green track leads beside this then disappears, you have to somehow descend to the river and ride on grass by a barn, to ford the Belah by a gate. Follow the wall 'up and over', then over two Stowgills and up a muddy track in front of Wrenside Farm to join the farm track, which shortly becomes metalled.

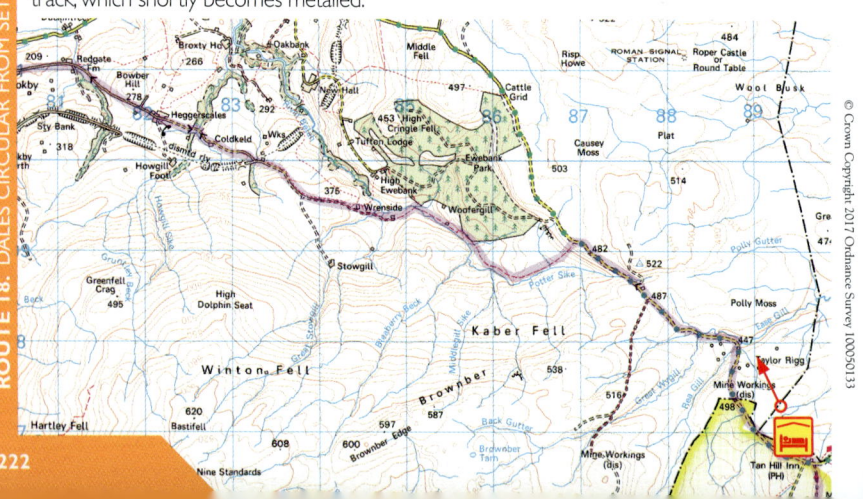

Multi-day routes in northern Britain

Follow the road to Winton, taking care to go straight on down a narrow road just past Rookby, and turn L in the centre, then L at the fork after 250m, which takes you through Hartley, and shortly after a L turn in the road and a short hill, to a disused railway via a steep ramp on the R. This leads S for 1.6km, past the poems referred to in INFORMATION, and an information hut on the R some way down, to the River Eden, where a path on the R leads to a steel 'Millennium' bridge, with a dramatic view of the falls of the Eden. The path leads up to a road through a gate, go straight across this and along Station Road to the main A685, where turn L for 100m and fork L off the main road by a small parking area and park. This minor road leads to Halfpenny House, an old drovers' road name, turn R here up a purpose built cycle and footpath to Kirkby Stephen Station.

A quick R and L and you're back on the busy A685 but only for a short distance: fork L on the A683 then again L on a minor road after a short while. After a L hand bend turn R through a gate up a signed bridleway. This leads to a wall and passes alongside it, and then, via several possible tracks, over R to the long straight wall, following this to the 'Tommy Road'. Turn R then L at the A683 for a km, forking R off it on a minor road to Ravenstonedale.

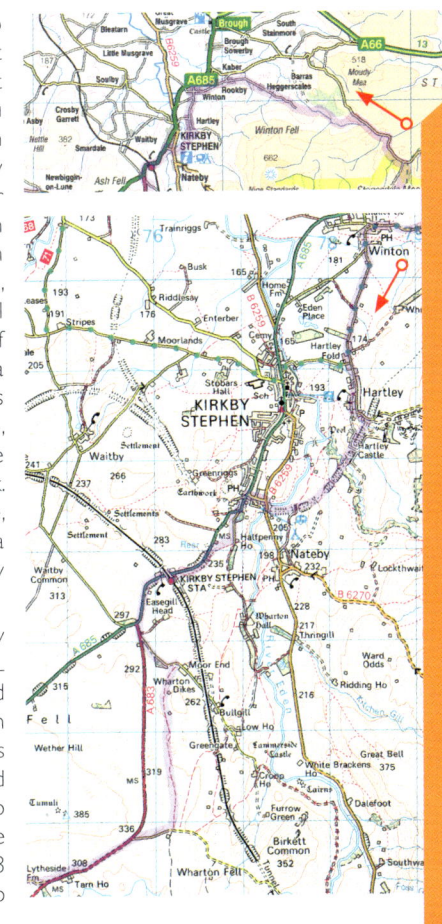

So far, the route from Kirkby Stephen has been avoiding the main road to the M6, the A685, as much as possible: here you have to decide either to get on it for 3.5km to the Bowderdale turn, or to take it for a short while and detour through Newbiggin-on-Lune and then N through Wath, or gain the Weasdale road via a bridleway starting at NY716044, then joining the main road via a bridleway going N through the Weasdale nurseries or a minor road N at NY699042, although this third alternative seems a trifle excessive in view of what's to come.

The Bowderdale path.

ROUTE 18. DALES CIRCULAR FROM SETTLE

223

Mountain Biking Adventures:

Turn down to Bowderdale off the A685 and L up a track just after its beck. This leads up into the Howgills, but make sure to turn L on to the bridleway path about 1.5km after leaving the road. This is rough, but rideable, for 4.5km up lonely Bowderdale, until forced off to push diagonally up the long slope on the R to the Calf at 676m. Technically, the bridleway curves away from the ridge near the top and then doubles back S. From here it's a good track to Calders, turning R here and down steeply then rising gently to pass alongside Arant Haw.

A superb descent on a path through safe grassy terrain awaits you, turning L at SD658937; be careful not to descend L too soon at an obvious, but inferior, path before this, SD662942.

Your descent ends above Lockbank Farm, through which you head to a road, taking you down to Sedbergh for tea.

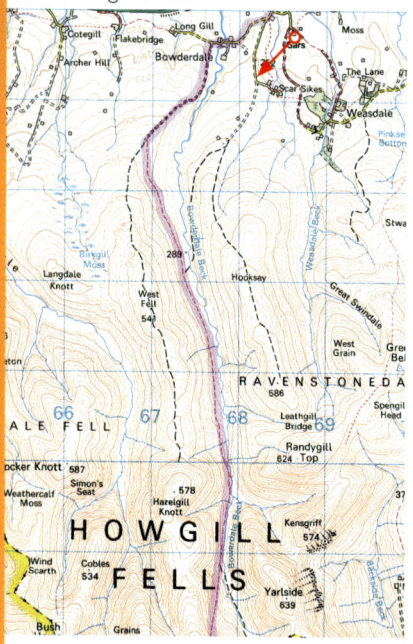

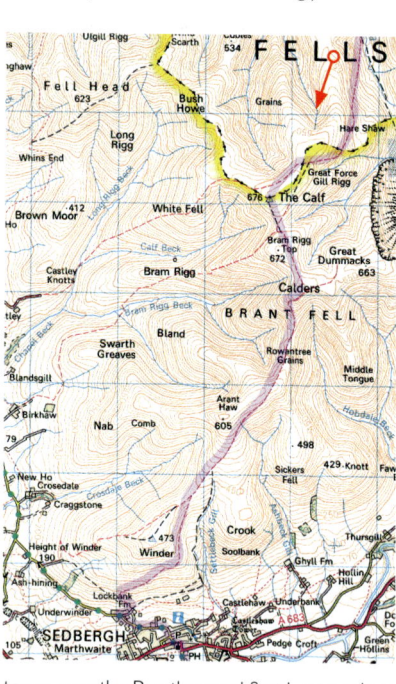

Take the 'B' road signposted to Dent S from the town, over the Rawthey and first L up a minor road, then soon R and, after 100m, turn L up the Dales Way bridleway. Follow this over the shoulder of Long Rigg, down to the Dent road again by a splendid gate on the R, straight across the road down a track to the River Dee, where the map suggests you ford it, but to keep feet a bit drier, go over the footbridge on the right. At the minor road turn left for Dent.

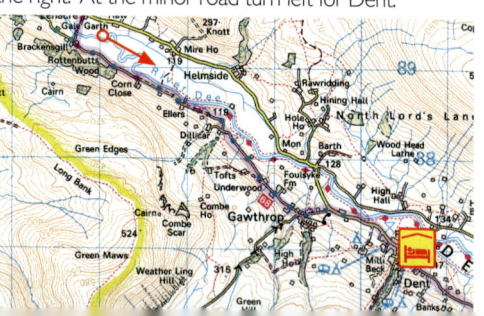

Multi-day routes in northern Britain

DAY 4.

Start:	Dent
Finish:	Settle or Lancaster. Both via Austwick
Distance:	Settle: 34km (21miles) Lancaster: 62km (38.5miles)
Off-road:	Settle: 22.5km (14 miles) 66% Lancaster: 17.5km (11miles) 28%
Ascent:	Settle: 832m (2732ft) Lancaster: 1040m (3413ft)
Descent:	Settle: 822m (2699ft). Lancaster: 1160m (3808ft)
Grade:	E1

OVERVIEW

A rough track goes high over and round the N ridge of Whernside, down to Ribblehead and down that Dale, the last major one visited on this trip. A few km of lovely limestone riding on part of the PBW leads to lesser known Crummackdale, with easy lane/track riding through two delightful hamlets, Wharfe and Feizor, and a short limestone turf stretch to a road finish.

INFORMATION

The Craven Way over Whernside's N ridge is thought to be an old drovers' road and then a packhorse route. The 24 arched Ribblehead Viaduct carries the Settle to Carlisle line, the last main line to be built in Britain, from 1869-1876. The marshy ground needed concrete 25 feet below ground level for each pillar. A large shantytown existed in the land N and E of the viaduct, further information given on a board by the track. More than 130 men died here, mainly of smallpox, typhus and cholera, and most were buried in the nearby Chapel-le-Dale churchyard. The Blea Moor tunnel is over 2km long and took five years to build. Rock was winched up seven shafts sunk from above, the rock deposited in obvious mounds, and three of the shafts remain for ventilation.

ROUTE

At the George and Dragon take the R fork out of Dent, and the L one just over a km on, and a R fork after Mill Bridge. In 250m up the hill, take the bridleway on the L, which turns immediately R and heads up the shoulder of Whernside. This is a push of over 200m ascent on sandstone based track, after which the youthful will be able to ride on round the end of the shoulder, nicely named the Boot of the Wold, and now on a better surface of limestone or its turf.

As it descends, the tourist pedestrian route to/from Whernside joins from the R so be careful not to mow down inattentive groups of walkers. Just past the Bleamoor Sidings buildings the main track becomes a path, so you must turn R under the railway on to a bridleway track to Winterscales, then L past this on a metalled road to Gunnerfleet Farm. Here, turn L over the beck to a track that leads under the magnificent Ribblehead Viaduct to Ribblehead.

Mountain Biking Adventures:

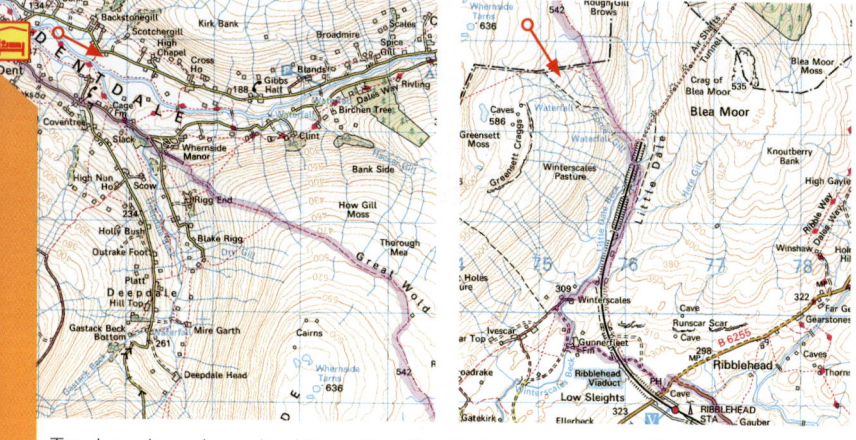

Turn L on the main road to Hawes, then R at the bottom on the B6479 towards Horton-in-Ribblesdale. After 3.5km turn R up a bridleway track marked as the PBW, turning R at the junction and on past the farm track on the R, over a stream, and through a gate. Here the track turns L, S, and climbs gently on gradually improving limestone turf. Follow the wide grassy track with PBW signs to guide you, past the three peaks junction at Sulber, then Sulber Gate, forking L 750m after the Gate at a signpost 'Crummack'. A pleasant grassy track leads down to the farm, where a metalled farm track heads down the valley.

If you're heading for Lancaster and in a hurry, continue down Crummack Lane to Austwick, otherwise fork L at the first junction on to a track and negotiate the ford or take the bridge, and on along the walled path to Wharfe. Here there is another choice: to follow the PBW to Settle by carrying straight on to the road to Helwith Bridge, turning right opposite Dry Rigg Quarry to Stainforth and up to Upper Winskill before the descent to Settle; or to go S in the 'centre' of the hamlet on a track to the main road, R and L after 100m up the track of Wood Lane. After 1km take the L turn at a crossroads, and at Meldings Barn, after crossing a beck, turn L to Feizor. At this, the second delightful hamlet of the day, turn L and first R up a bridleway signed Stackhouse. This becomes a wide grass track with good riding to the road at Buck Haw Brow, although you must fork R at the top of the hill at a sign not quite pointing to 'Buck Haw Brow'. Turn downhill on the old main road to Settle.

On the Pennine Bridleway near Sulber Gate.

ROUTE 18. DALES CIRCULAR FROM SETTLE

226

Multi-day routes in northern Britain

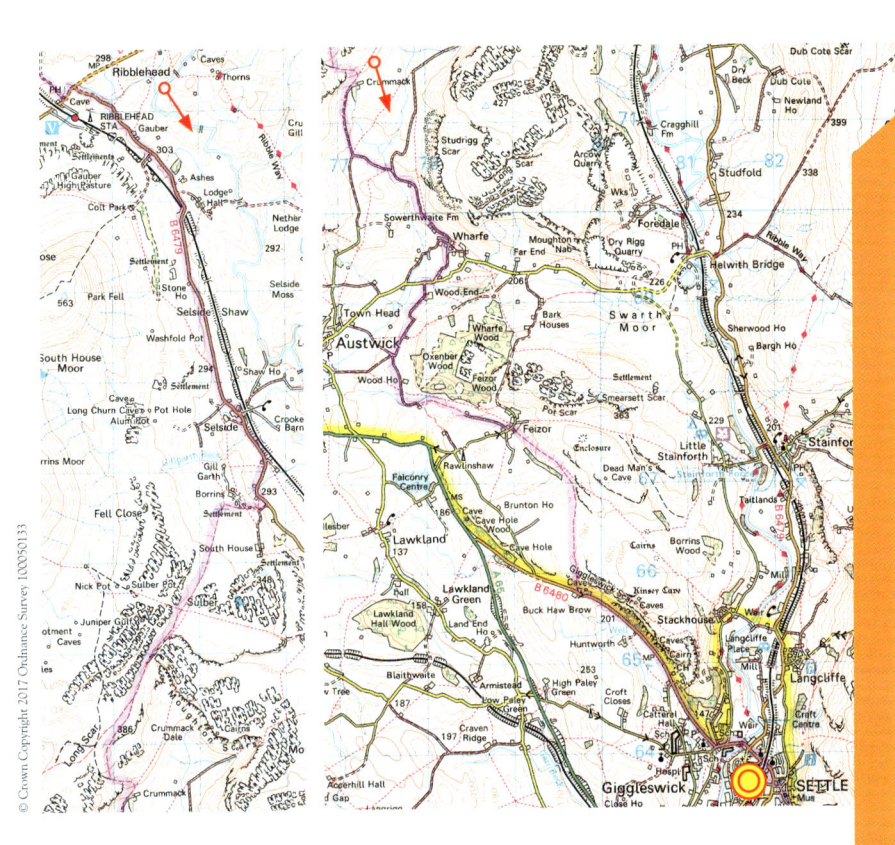

AUSTWICK TO LANCASTER.

If you've sneaked some lunch at the Gamecock, turn R at the junction just down from it, then L after 200m on a quiet lane leading to the busy A65. Cross this by a L and immediate R, and 2km further, fork R to pass under a railway. Turn L immediately and carry on to Keasden crossroads, over which you are now on Mewith Lane, a quiet, pleasant and undulating-down road that, after about 10km, leads to a 'T' junction. Turn R and shortly L, then keep on the 'main' road to Wray village. At the 'T' junction in the centre turn L and after 2km turn L on the main A683 road to Lancaster. The cycle path to Lancaster is indicated on the L as the River Lune comes close to the road, a few hundred metres from Bullbeck picnic site, but you have to cross the road to a gate to gain it. This leads past the scenic Crook of Lune to Lancaster.

ROUTE 18. DALES CIRCULAR FROM SETTLE

227

19. HIGH CUP /TEESDALE CIRCULAR

Total route (days):	Four days			
Start & Finish:	Lancaster			
Total Distance:	231km (143miles).			
Total Off-road (%):	37%			
Daily distance (km):	69	53.5	49.5	58
Daily off-road (%):	26%	36%	34%	53%
Ascent:	4850m (15,920ft)			
Crux day grade:	M1			

Multi-day routes in northern Britain

OVERVIEW

This route was designed to have no carries and an easy start, due to illness, but turned out to be rather good! Days 2 and 3 based on the Pennine Way (PW), and Day 4's off-road is all on the Pennine Bridleway (PBW). As Days 3 and 4 are southerly, a spell of mild weather would make this much pleasanter. Hard road ascents on Day 3 and, possibly, Day 4.

DAY 1.

Start:	Lancaster
Finish:	Orton, Cumbria
Distance:	69km (43.5miles)
Off-road:	18km (11.5miles) 26%
Ascent:	1477m (4848ft)
Descent:	1248m (4098ft)
Grade:	E1

OVERVIEW

An easy start on canal towpath, enjoying the splendid view of Lakeland across Morecambe Bay from this elevated position, then a jaunt to the coast; undulating side roads round Kendal to Borrowdale (the less famous one); good off road involving a push up 150m, down to Tebay, then Orton.

INFORMATION

The handsome viaduct at the start was finished in 1797, but cost so much that there was nothing in the pot to connect the Lancaster canal to a southern system, hence it is isolated.

Arnside and Silverdale are in an Area of Outstanding Natural Beauty, noted for its limestone pavements and woods in an out of the way position, but unfortunately, you only sample a little of it close up on the track around the Knott. At the narrow end of the funnel of Morecambe Bay, there is a significant tidal bore.

Tebay is a grey railway village, most of its working inhabitants now employed in the popular and independent motorway services nearby, but Orton is more interesting, with its 13th century church with a whitewashed tower, a welcoming pub with sheds for bikes and a factory (and café) for handmade chocolates.

Shops, pubs and cafes in Arnside, after that two more pubs en route near Kendal but none then till Tebay.

ROUTE 19. HIGH CUP /TEESDALE CIRCULAR

229

Mountain Biking Adventures:

ROUTE

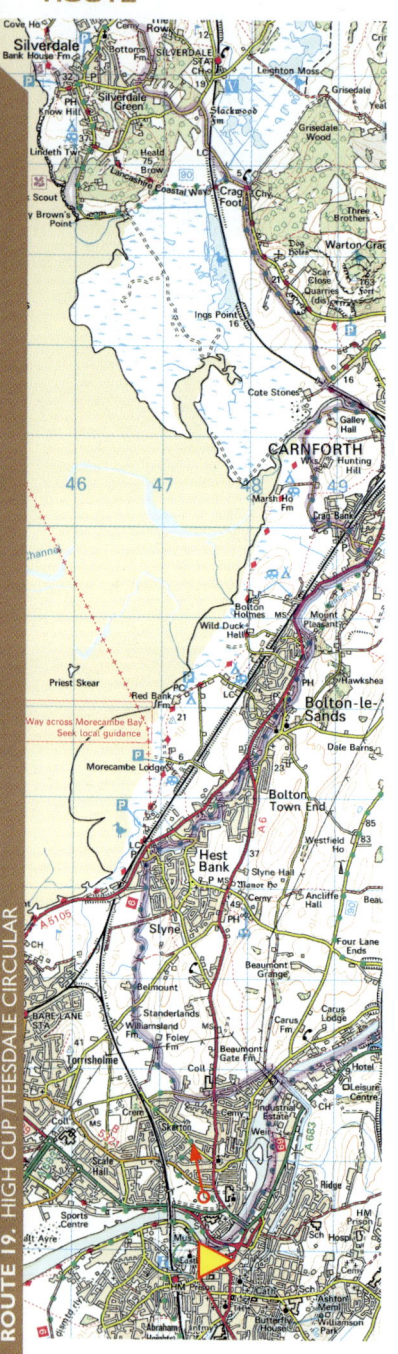

If coming by train, the Luneside cycle path is found by exiting the Station via the northbound platform, turn R on a road then straight ahead at the corner on a track by a field, turn R under the railway line at the end and immediately L.

At the Aquaduct, a ramp leads from the cycle path up to the S side of the canal, where turn L and have a pleasant ride to Carnforth, avoiding the dogs.

At Bridge 127, Thwaite End Bridge, pass through a small gap just the other side to the busy A6. Cross this and go down Crag Bank Road, join Longfield Drive, and carry on round the curve through saltmarshes. As you reach the River Keer, cross it by a narrow footbridge and continue up a track by the Carnforth rail sidings. Cross over the railway line at the top and turn L on the road.

After the level crossing turn L at the 'T' junction, then first R, Bottoms Lane. At the end turn L then quickly R on Cove Road, and follow this with coastal views till opposite Arnside Tower. Here, pass through a gate, L, for a little pleasant off-road on a track, up through two more gates and down N to join New Barns Road, follow this round to Red Hills Road and L at the main Silverdale Road to go down to Arnside Promenade.

Pass along the Promenade and round to pass under the railway (To Barrow) L, and on till just after the next bridge, over the River Bela, where take a L. Do not follow the dog-leg of the Cumbria Coastal Way, but after the right angle turn keep straight on to Heversham, crossing the A6 again.

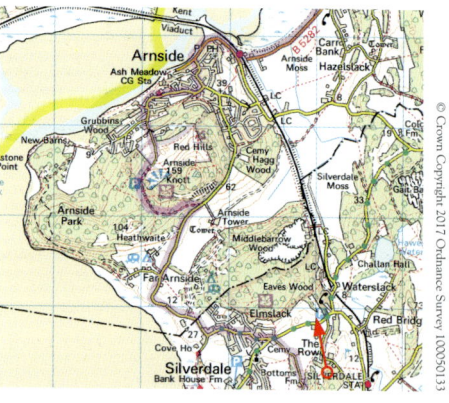

Multi-day routes in northern Britain

Up a short hill to Woodhouse, turn L here, on to cross a canal and N to Crosscrake junction, straight on up the hill to turn first R and cross the busy A65 by the Punch Bowl pub. The quiet road opposite passes along the S side of the Helm, a very popular jaunt for Kendalians and their dogs. A sting in the lane's tail awaits near the main road junction, where turn L then R by the Station pub.

This minor road takes you, via a short dog-leg at the A684, to the A685 near Meal Bank. Turn R on to the main road, and first L down the hill, but in almost 200m, turn R down a rough track taking you over the River Mint and up to a 'T' junction. Turn R, over the hill to Patton Bridge, by the E side of Whinfell Tarn, and up the E side of the Mint valley.

A short way past Ashstead Farm, take the track N through a gate as the road turns W. This leads up to the A6, where after a short ride onwards (much quieter now than at Carnforth), turn R at the next corner on a track down to Borrowdale, and carry on down the valley. The 160m ascent up to the col from Low Borrowdale on a mostly grassy track/path is definitely worth it on a good day, as the descent is good, on a grassy path till a track takes over after a tributary of Roundthwaite Beck.

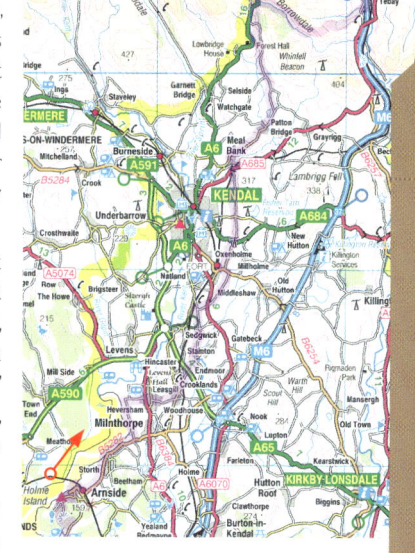

Descending to Roundthwaite.

Cross the beck again on the road at Roundthwaite and go N, fork R at the next junction, under the M6, and as the road ends, under the mainline railway and via a path to a footbridge. Over the River Lune, turn R on a path to join a track, then road to Tebay, where, if you're really thirsty, the Cross Keys is on the R, but it is only a ten minute pedal on an undulating road N to Orton and the George, so it makes little sense.

ROUTE 19. HIGH CUP /TEESDALE CIRCULAR

Mountain Biking Adventures:

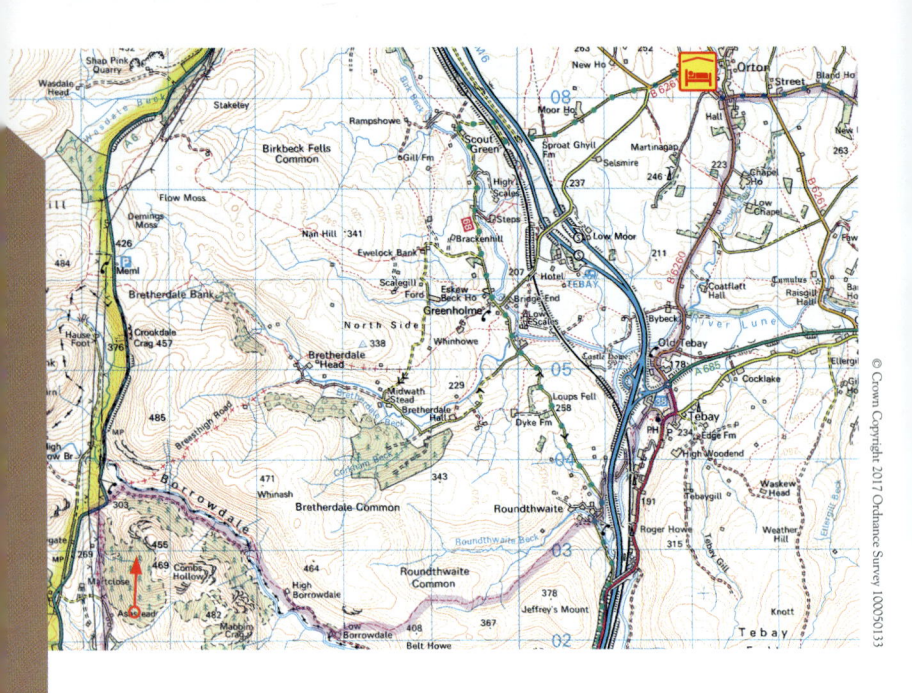

DAY 2.

Start:	Orton
Finish:	Middleton-In-Teesdale
Distance:	53.5km (33.5miles)
Off-road:	19km (12 miles) 36%
Ascent:	1141m (3745ft)
Descent:	1141m (3745ft)
Grade:	E1

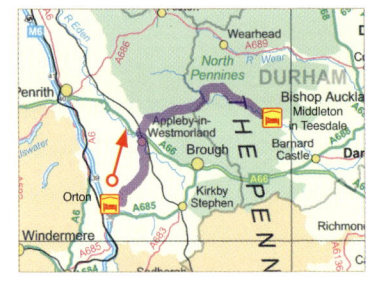

OVERVIEW

The short off-road over the limestone of Great Asby Scar and alongside the wondrous spectacle of High Cup, make up for the relatively long distance on road. Deviations to view Cauldron Snout cataract and High Force can be made on this touristy day. A short stretch some way before High Cup Nick is not rideable. Taking in some geological information about High Cup the night before is recommended, as it is too complex to detail here.

INFORMATION

Appleby, which was the county town of Westmorland before Cumbria engulfed it in 1974, has the only shops and cafes en route till Teesdale, although the Stag at Dufton does lunches till 3pm. It is an attractive town with a good Tourist Information Centre: it sells my books!

Multi-day routes in northern Britain

The Langdon Beck Hotel is an interesting place to stop for refreshments.

Birkdale Farm is at 470m (1550ft altitude), which must be one of the highest farms in Britain. You certainly don't get habitations at this altitude on the western side of the Pennines. It survives by being part of an environmental scheme helped by the Northern Uplands Moorland Regeneration Project, combining the management of sheep and grouse shooting.

The area around Cow Green used to be rich in rare Alpine type flora, drowned when the Reservoir was built in 1970 for the industries of Teesside. The sheep have seen to the rest of the flora, but a small enclosed area to the R of the track by the reservoir has flowers such as the alpine bistort in summer. The reservoir itself merely regulates the flow of the Tees, water being extracted downstream.

To visit High Force, a 500m walk, pay at the shop by the Hotel car park. Bowlees Visitor Centre beyond that has much local information and an exhibition gallery. Middleton itself is an attractive and interesting old market town, a lead mining centre in the early 19th century, when The London Lead Mining Company moved its northern headquarters there. The Forresters is a pleasant French restaurant and worth a visit to cap this excellent tourist day!

ROUTE

Head E, initially on the B6261, for 2km, to turn L up Knott Lane, a stony track. Through the gate a short climb leads to a grassy track, after the next gate turn R along the bridleway signed Great Asby. This leads delightfully down through limestone scenery and is over, all too soon, at the road leading to the village.

Keep on the main road to Burrells and then Appleby. The bridleway up a field by the corner at Broadmire Plantation doesn't look attractive.

Cross the Eden in Appleby and turn L up the main street, under the Settle to Carlisle railway and busy A66, to follow signs to Dufton.

Just past a dip on the entrance to Dufton, turn R on a track, which is now the PW, really the theme of this adventure. It is a good track till the gate at NY722250, although the gradient may make you occasionally descend if you're as old and feeble as we are.

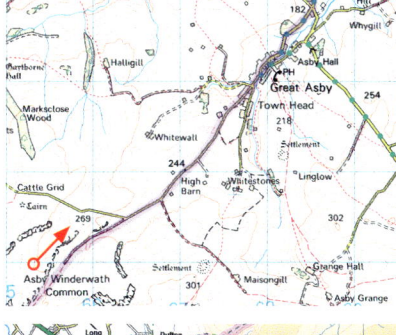

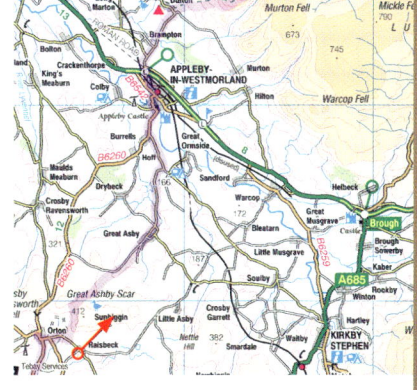

Mountain Biking Adventures:

The rough stretch is around 1.5km before the Nick, but soon relents to lovely limestone turf where you can relax and enjoy the view. Past the Nick the path gets a little muddy but is still good, but after the footbridge over Maize Beck at NY768267 it soon becomes a push uphill. At the top it now joins a recently made (2014) track, which leads rapidly and non-technically down to Birkdale Farm.

Onto grass by the Nick of High Cup.

Multi-day routes in northern Britain

Press on to cross the River Tees below Cow Green Dam, and continue on the metalled track to the road junction at NY817308 then turn R to Langdon Beck. From here it's an easy road down Teesdale to Middleton.

DAY 3.

Start:	Middleton-in-Teesdale
Finish:	Hawes
Distance:	49.5km (30.5miles).
Off-road:	17km (10.5 miles) 34%
Ascent:	1218m (3998ft)
Descent:	1218m (3998ft)
Grade:	M1

OVERVIEW

Based on the legally cycleable parts of the PW, which are all rideable apart from uphill grunts. Steep road ascents occur near the start and finish, the latter, Buttertubs Pass, is a Yorkshire classic. Refreshments are at Tan Hill pub, and cafes at Keld and Thwaite.

INFORMATION

'God's Bridges' abound in this northern limestone country, natural bridges over streams.

For Tan Hill information see Route 19.

Keld is a lovely hamlet sporting a café and various accommodations, usually all booked as it is a busy junction 'twixt the PW and the very popular Coast to Coast walks.

The steep Buttertubs Pass is a classic, used on the 2014 Tour de France, and also a Top Gear favourite. It is named after a series of cool limestone potholes into which passing farmers are said to have dipped their produce on hot days in passing. Crossing this without stopping will give you a lot of satisfaction.

Smile as you career past the Simonstone Hotel, scene of the 'Clarkson steak' fracas.

Hawes is a surprisingly busy town all year round, having a large Farmers' Auction Market and Wensleydale Creamery with tours, Wensleydale cheese tastings and a café and shop.

Accommodation is abundant but usually almost fully booked, beware.

ROUTE

Cross the Tees on the main road and follow this for just over 1km until you reach the Tees Railway path on the R. Take this for 1.5km, over your second River Lune of the trip, and be careful to get on to the road at NY964236, to take this SW.

Mountain Biking Adventures:

The easiest way over from Lunesdale to Baldersdale is the minor road turning S at NY932213, turning R again in Baldersdale at the 'T' junction. Turn L down the dam track and L again before it, snaking down to cross the River Balder.

Once over the River Balder, go through an iron gate and up the track to Clove Lodge. Go down then along the road past the lodge, turning R off it at the second signed bridleway, to trudge up the definite, but thin, path rideable from the top of Peatbrig Hill.

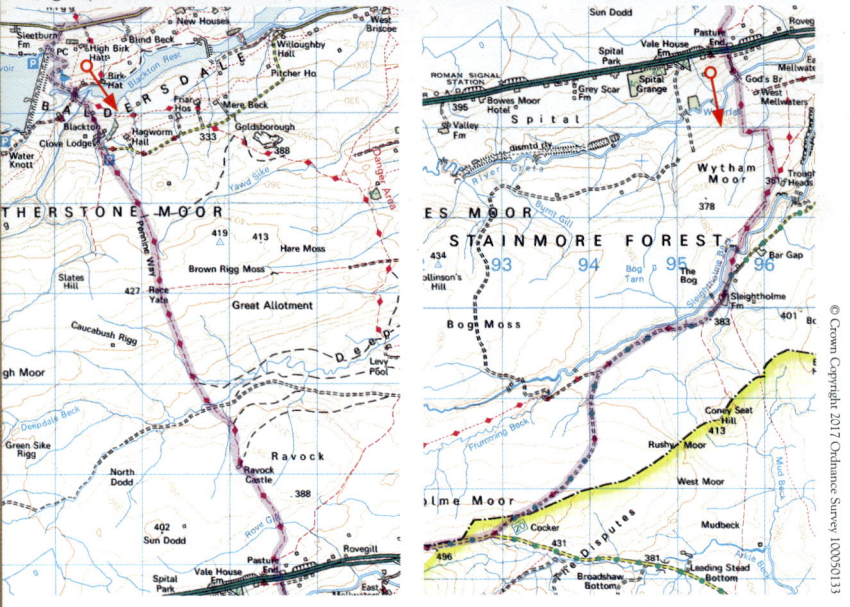

After Deepdale Beck, (interestingly a plethora of Gills, Strands and Sikes around also) be careful to cross Duckett Sike as per the map, rather than going up a better looking track on the W side, marked 'Duckett Sike'. Another down and slight up leads to the very busy A66, but a deviation R leads thankfully to an underpass. It is tempting, on the other side, to cycle diagonally down the field to the visible house, but better stick to the bridleway.

A gate to the L of the house leads through to God's Bridge, across which you go up the R side of the wall ahead, to another gate. Through this turn L alongside another wall, then R, following the line of the bridleway, indicated with a few marker posts.

Above Trough Head Farm turn R by the signpost, to follow a wall, and after 400m turn L through a gate in it. Follow the path parallel to the wall over rough fields till opposite the point where Sleightholme Beck takes a bend to the L, when go to the edge and find a clear wide grassy path down to the beck and cross it by a footbridge. Follow the PW signs through three fields to the road and turn R to Sleightholme Farm.

The road passes through a gate and becomes a track, which you stay on, forking L at the first junction (straight on leads to the quagmire of the PW), to the 'B' road from Arkengarthdale to Tan Hill, which involves a steep sting in the tail near the inn.

From here it's a good bit of biking due S from the Inn, on a good track to start with, although it gets somewhat muddy lower down if conditions are wet. It's down, however, and leads to excellent views of Swaledale.

Multi-day routes in northern Britain

Escaping a Hell's Angels party at Tan Hill.

At East Stonedale Farm, carry straight on, then R at the next fork to curve down to the footbridge across the Swale and go steeply up to a track leading shortly to Keld.

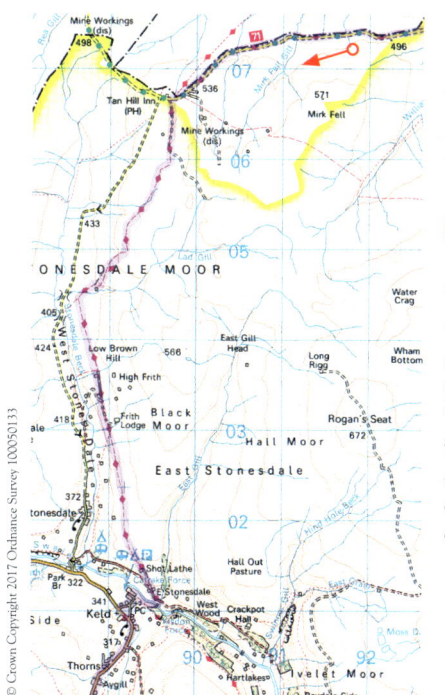

Go up through Keld village, noting the information room on the way up, to join the 'B' road, and turn L to Thwaite, after which fork right for an increasingly steep ascent over Buttertubs Pass, and down a good descent to Hawes with a few dog-legs lower down.

ROUTE 19. HIGH CUP/TEESDALE CIRCULAR

237

Mountain Biking Adventures:

DAY 4.

Start:	Hawes
Finish:	Lancaster (cycle path/ Lune aqueduct junction)
Distance:	58km (36miles).
Off-road:	30.5km (19miles) 53%
Ascent:	1001m (3286ft)
Descent:	1234m (4049ft)
Grade:	M1

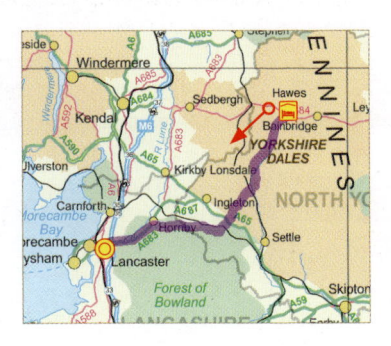

OVERVIEW

A stiff ascent by track or road leads to a long easy descent off-road, then lovely limestone paths on the PBW over from Ribbledale to Clapham, a pleasant minor road undulating downhill to the Lune valley and a finish on a cycle track. Every metre cycleable.

INFORMATION

Gayle, another gorgeous hamlet, has a working sawmill powered by a water turbine installed in 1879, although it started life as a cotton mill.

The Cam fell track has controversially been 'improved' in recent years to accommodate the frequent heavy timber lorries serving the extensive plantations of Cam Fell and upper Langstrothdale.

Ling Gill is a National Nature Reserve, access to which is not encouraged, although not forbidden. It is tricky to traverse in any case (on foot) and it is advised to carry a kitchen surface spray and rub your footwear before entering, to protect the rare White Claw Crayfish. I am not making this up.

The gated wooden Far Moor Bridge over the Ribble is rather splendid, and of a prize-winning novel design, made of Scottish larch. Note here, and at the railway bridge, the stone mounting blocks for horses, although I have never seen a horse on the PBW.

Clapham is a busy walking and caving centre, with several cafes and the New Inn. The tunnel was built in Victorian times to allow Thwaite Lane to go under a track on a new embankment from Ingleborough Hall, and so keep the plebs from seeing them in their carriages en route to the Show Cave and Trow Gill.

Mewith Lane is a designated cycle route, part of the Morecambe to Bridlington 'Way of the Roses'.

ROUTE

From Hawes centre take the B6255 W, forking L at Cam Road, the good track 1km from the edge of town. Climb, gently at first, and then with more difficulty, as the track gets steep and rocky towards the top. You are joined by the PW about half way up, and return briefly to tarmac just after Dodd Fell Hill.

Multi-day routes in northern Britain

Alternatively you would not be disappointed by the road climb to Fleet Moss, another Yorkshire classic. Go W up the main street and turn L to Gayle, past the Creamery. Press on up the minor road, the stiff ascent being, unfortunately, near the top.

After the track from Bainbridge has joined, the road takes a right-angled L turn, but you carry straight on, still on a minor road, till the above PW route joins, and soon after it becomes a good track.

At Cam End, the timber lorries go R to the main road, but you follow the PW and PBW signs L down a good track past Ling Gill.

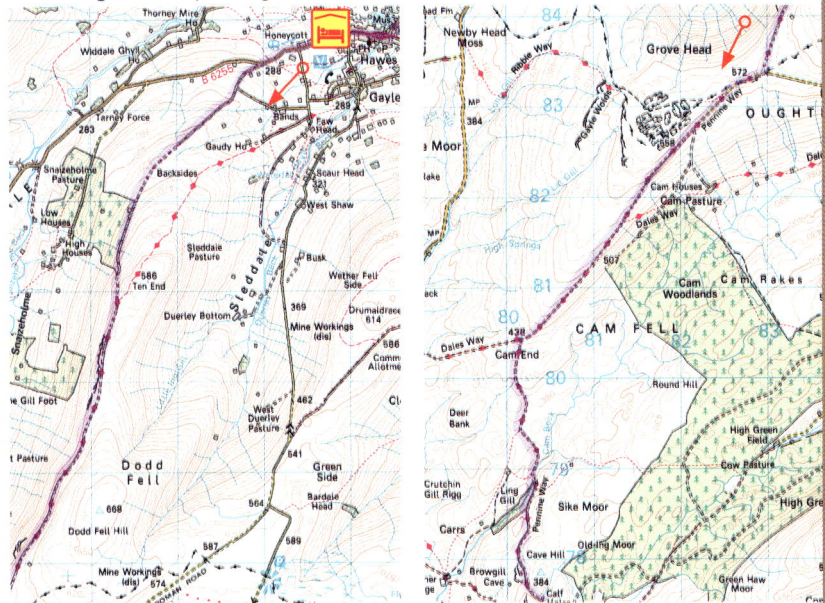

Carry on down and up the track to High Birkwith Farm, where the track becomes road, and on to turn R down the PBW, marked as such at a gate at SD802760. This leads down to the Ribble and along to the new (and hence not on maps) gated wooden Far Moor Bridge. Over this the track curves round to pass under the Settle to Carlisle line.

The new PBW bridge over the Ribble.

ROUTE 19. HIGH CUP /TEESDALE CIRCULAR

239

Mountain Biking Adventures:

As the track nears the main road, it leads up to it L. Cross here and go up the track opposite, turning R at the junction, and on past the farm track, over a stream, and through a gate. Here the track turns L, S, and climbs gently on gradually improving limestone turf. Follow the wide grassy track with PBW signs to guide you, past the three peaks junction at Sulber and on to Long Scar, where signs guide you R, down through gates towards the trees of Trow Gill, to join the top of a stony track. A fast descent leads to a sharp, rough ascent, which could catch you unawares, having not dismounted so far. Turn R at the junction and down to Clapham through the tunnel, a sign before which urges you to dismount, although the ground is good, just take it slowly and you will be OK.

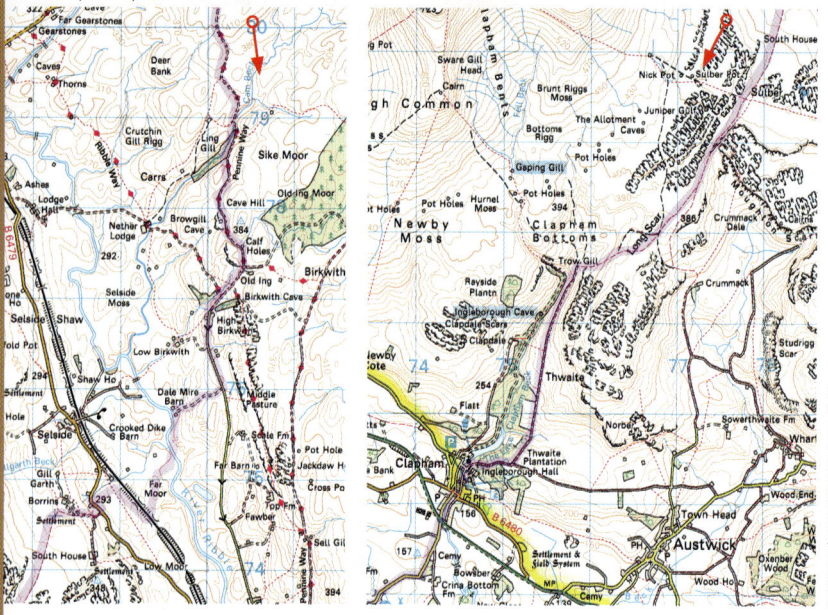

Having taken refreshments, go over the bridge opposite the New Inn and turn L, going alongside Clapham Beck to cross the busy A65. There is an underpass although I've never needed it.

Keep going to Clapham Station junction, straight on here under the railway line, keeping R after the Wenning Bridge. An uphill stretch leads to Keasden crossroads, where turn R on Mewith Lane, a quiet, pleasant and undulating down road, which in about 10km leads to a 'T' junction. Turn R and shortly L, on the 'main' road to Wray village.

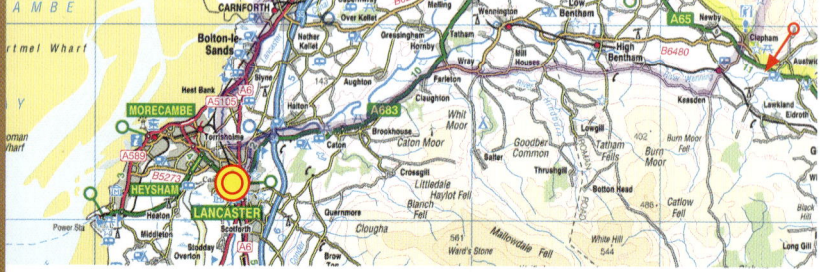

Multi-day routes in northern Britain

At the 'T' junction in the centre turn L, and after 2km turn L on the main A683 road to Lancaster. The cycle path to Lancaster is indicated on the L as the River Lune comes close to the road, a few hundred metres from Bullbeck picnic site, but you have to cross the road to a gate to gain it. This leads past the scenic Crook of Lune back to the start and Lancaster.

High Cup Nick.

Lovely single track through Great Asby Nature Reserve.

20. GREAT CHALK CHALLENGE, EASTBOURNE TO PRINCES RISBOROUGH

Total route (days):	Four days				
Start:	Eastbourne				
Finish:	Princes Risborough/Goring on Thames				
Total Distance:	398km (212miles)				
Total Off-road (%):	71%				
Daily distance (km):	102	102	91	**103/70**	
Daily off-road (%):	85%	61%	76%	77/86%	
Ascent:	6816m (22,370ft)				
Crux day grade:	H1				

242

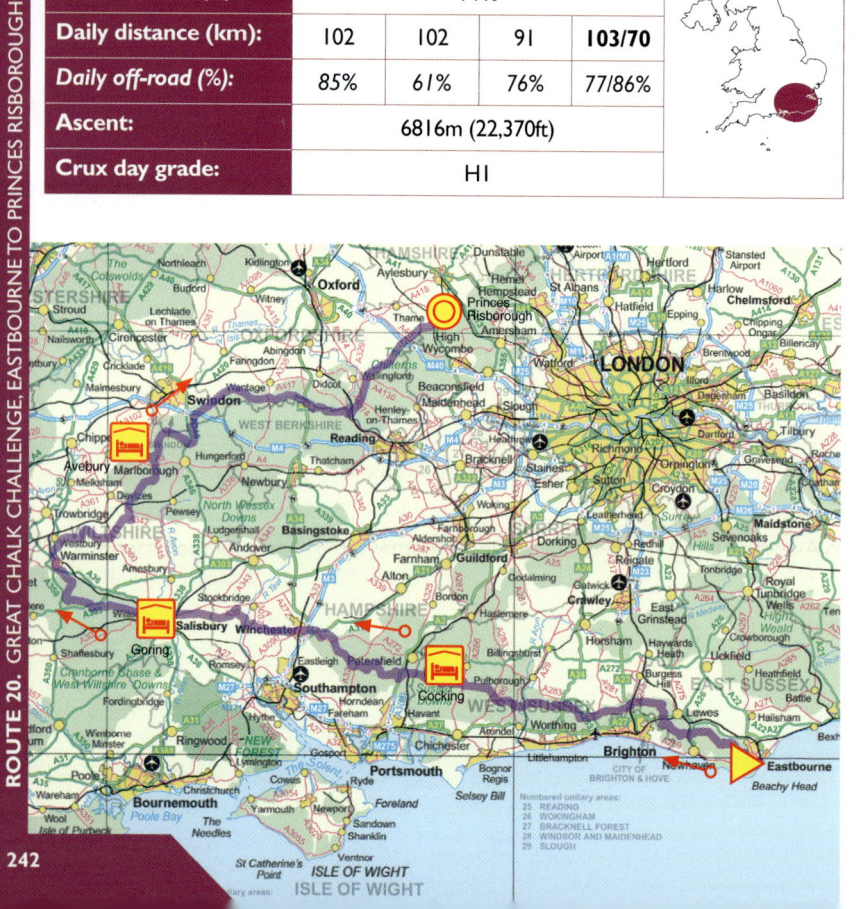

OVERVIEW

This route is unusual on two counts. It has to be acknowledged that it is not really that much of an adventure. One is rarely more than a km from tarmac or habitation, and the vast majority of it is along established trails where the key navigational technique is 'follow the waymarked path.'

Nevertheless, it's the biggest undertaking in our book in distance and ascent by a fair margin. It is very substantially off-road yet there is no need to put a foot down. It has a delightful arc around a substantial area of bucolic southern England and both the start and finish can be easily gained by train from London or the Midlands.

The majority of the route is so well described in the Official National Trail Guides to the South Downs Way and the Ridgeway and the accompanying maps, published by Harvey, that no further guidance is given here on these sections.

Both the South Downs Way and the Ridgeway are marked with the National Trail acorn symbol plus a coloured arrow. Yellow arrows indicate footpaths upon which bikes are not permitted. Bridleways, restricted byways, and byways upon which bikes are permitted, are indicated by blue, purple, and red arrows respectively.

Unlike many of the other routes you cannot go far wrong, but there are many, many more opportunities to do so and the use of a GPS with preprogrammed route is highly recommended, simply to save time.

The way is saturated in history: neolithic highways and centres; Iron Age fortresses; Roman roads and citadels; Saxon and Norman churches; agricultural oddities like dew ponds.

It begins in Eastbourne, and the first day and a half follow the South Downs Way (SDW) bridleway to Winchester. (As an aside, the SDW is a fabulous, if monstrous, day out for the fit and committed.) The second part of the second day follows, as best as possible, the line of a Roman road from Winchester to Old Sarum at Salisbury. The line then curves northerly round the boundary of the Salisbury Plain military training area before picking up Wans Dyke and the Wessex Ridgeway to Avebury. From the fabulous stone circle there, the Ridgeway then carries you ENE to Goring on Thames where you may get trains to London and the Midlands or go on for another 33km of wooded track, thick with red kite, to Princes Risborough where there are also good rail services to Birmingham and London.

Mountain Biking Adventures:

DAY 1.

Start:	Eastbourne
Finish:	Cocking
Distance:	102 km (64miles)
Off-road:	87km (54.5miles) 85%
Ascent:	2521m (8274ft)
Descent:	2466m (8094ft)
Grade:	H1

OVERVIEW

A series of about a dozen sharp climbs to 200m and descents to almost sea level interspersed with flattish higher-level sections on delightful chalk bridleways and byways. Plenty of pubs and village shops.

ROUTE

From the town centre follow Grove Road and then Meads road SW until Carlisle Road is taken to the R. Follow Carlisle Road more westerly for about 300m, where fork R on to Paradise Drive. In a further 200m take the track that comes out on the corner of Paradise Drive and Link Road.

Climb steeply and follow the waymarked path for 98km until you come onto tarmac, briefly, at Hill Barn, grid reference SU 879166. To avoid the A286, turn R and follow the bridleway down to Cocking where there is a delightful pub and a handful of B&Bs.

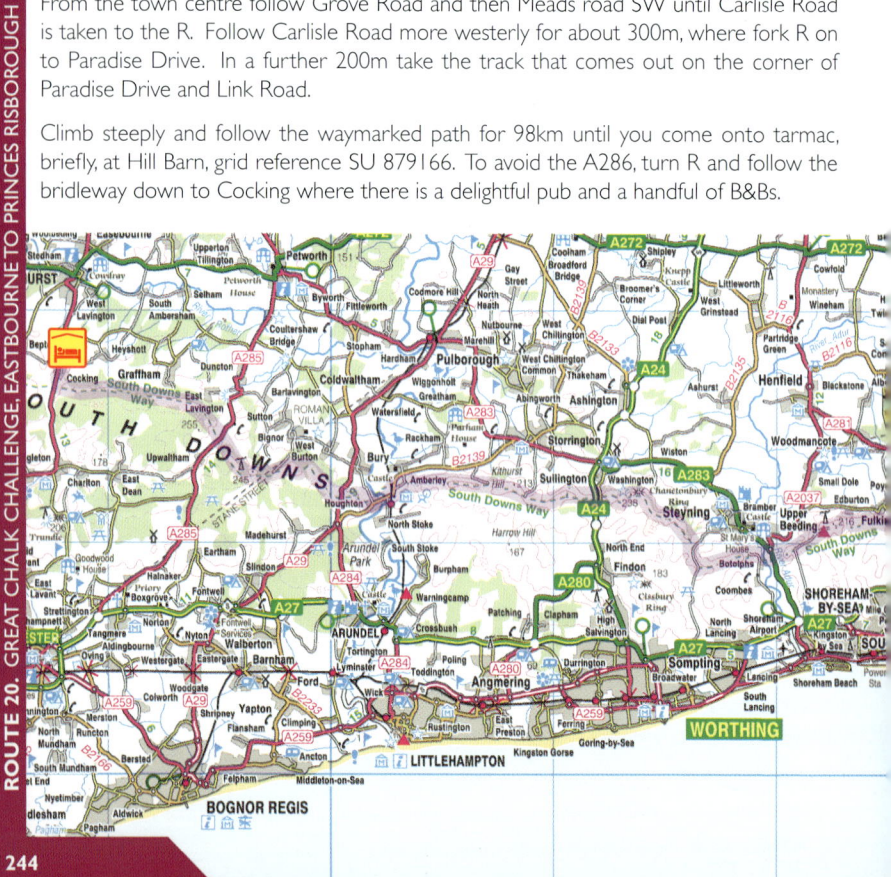

Multi-day routes in northern Britain

A wide chalk trail.

ROUTE 20. GREAT CHALK CHALLENGE, EASTBOURNE TO PRINCES RISBOROUGH

245

Mountain Biking Adventures:

Shadows lengthening at the end of a long day.

DAY 2.

Start:	Cocking
Finish:	Salisbury
Distance:	102 km (64miles)
Off-road:	62km (39miles) 61%
Ascent:	1903m (6246ft)
Descent:	1903m (6246ft)
Grade:	H1

OVERVIEW

More delightful chalk ridge riding interspersed with more steep ascent and descent until Meon Valley is passed, and there is a little more of a meander into Winchester. From Winchester the line of an ancient road is clung to as best as you can, westwards on minor roads, byways and bridleways.

ROUTE

From Cocking village centre take the A286 S for about a km and rejoin the SDW at Hilltop, or take Crypt Lane to Crypt Farm and then the continuing bridleway to cut off the corner and meet the SDW near the Cocking Down tumulus. Follow the waymarked path to Winchester where, if you haven't eaten already, you will be very ready for some lunch.

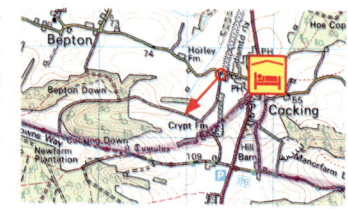

Multi-day routes in northern Britain

Take in the magnificent Cathedral and return to the High Street and follow it W until it becomes Romsey Road, the B3040. Continue W until you meet the aptly named Sarum Road on the R. The line of this Roman road is clear on the OS map. Sometimes it is a minor tarmac road or byway and you can take it. At others it is a footpath so you must seek a way around. Start by taking the tarmac for 6km, turning L on to a track labelled 'Monument'. Amuse yourself at this bizarre commemoration of a horse called 'Beware Chalk Pit', and continue on bridleways, byways and minor roads of your choice through the villages of Kings Somborne, Houghton, Broughton, Middle Winterslow until at Windmill farm, 50m S of Dunstable Corner, a very straight but rather overgrown track takes you directly towards Old Sarum.

South Harting from the SDW.

ROUTE 20. GREAT CHALK CHALLENGE, EASTBOURNE TO PRINCES RISBOROUGH

247

Mountain Biking Adventures:

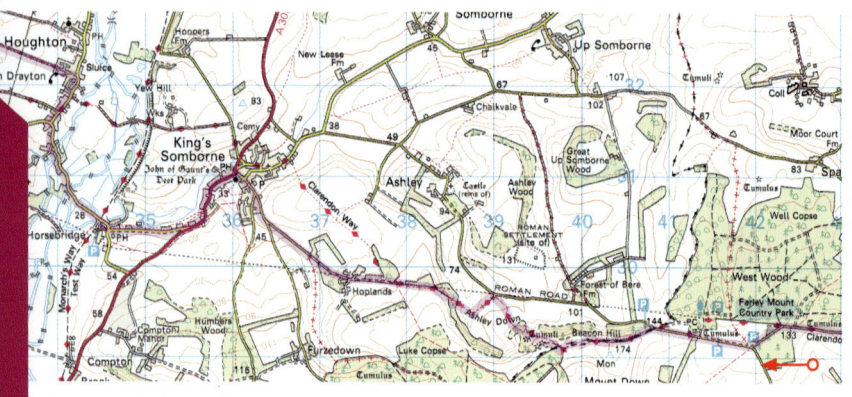

Our route is shown in the maps, but a 'line by line' description would be tiresomely long. You may choose to stick to the minor roads.

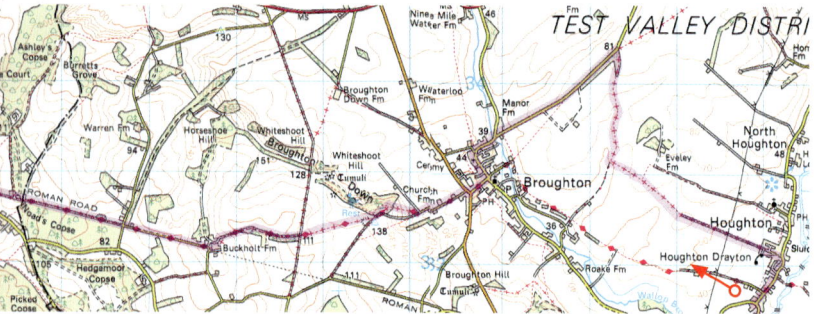

Where the Roman road issues on to the A30, go straight across along Old Malthouse Lane, until you cross the railway line at a double roundabout on the A338 and go L into Spire View. Where this road emerges into Old Castle Road, turn R and in about 200m you reach the ancient Roman fortress of Old Sarum. To get to Salisbury town centre, head S on the A345 or pick up one of a choice of cycleways.

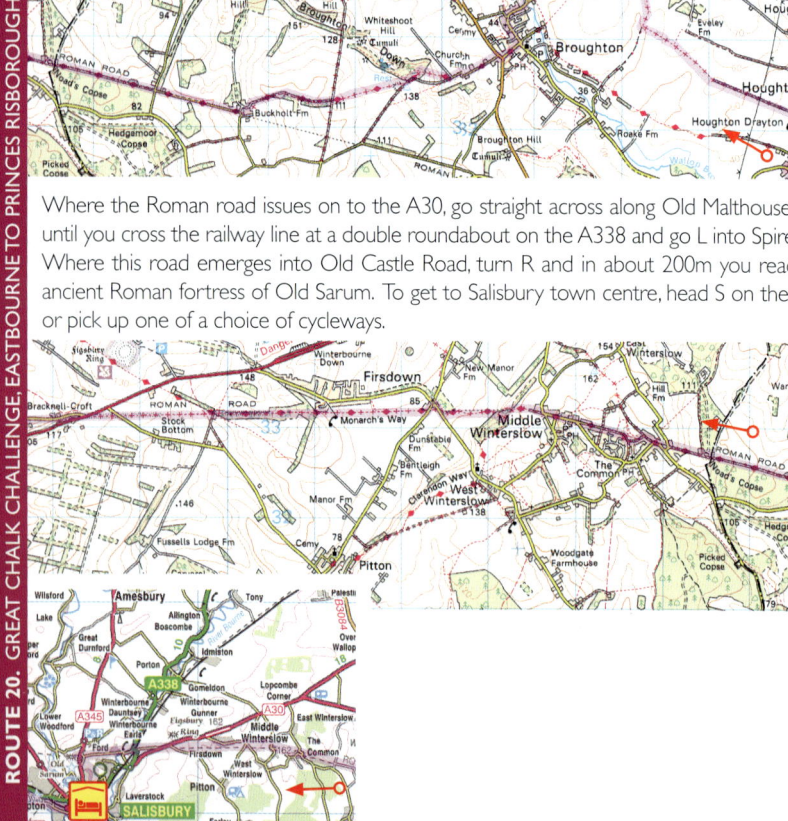

Multi-day routes in northern Britain

DAY 3.

Start:	Salisbury
Finish:	Avebury
Distance:	91km (57miles)
Off-road:	69km (43miles) 76%
Ascent:	1120m (3675ft)
Descent:	1020m (3348ft)
Grade:	H1

OVERVIEW

Delightful Wessex countryside, mostly on good byways, often delightfully wooded, above the Wylye valley to Warminster. Then slightly higher level open track around the western and northern perimeter of Salisbury Plains' Imber firing range before heading N and linking up with Wansdyke and the beginning of the Ridgeway.

ROUTE

Take National Cycle Route 24 W from the city centre for 3.5km. At the A3094 turn R, and in a few metres turn L on to the A36, follow this to the roundabout with the A30 and turn L on to it. It turns L at the roundabout and bears round to the R through the centre of Wilton, becoming West Street and then, at a L hand bend, becomes Shaftesbury Road. Just around the corner turn R by The Bell pub. In a little way go under the railroad and, at the corner with The Hollows, take the track between them heading due W. Climb steadily, sticking to the byway that heads slightly northerly and then westerly again through the middle of the mature Grovely Wood on the quaintly and aptly named First and Second Broad Drive.

Grovely Wood.

ROUTE 20. GREAT CHALK CHALLENGE, EASTBOURNE TO PRINCES RISBOROUGH

249

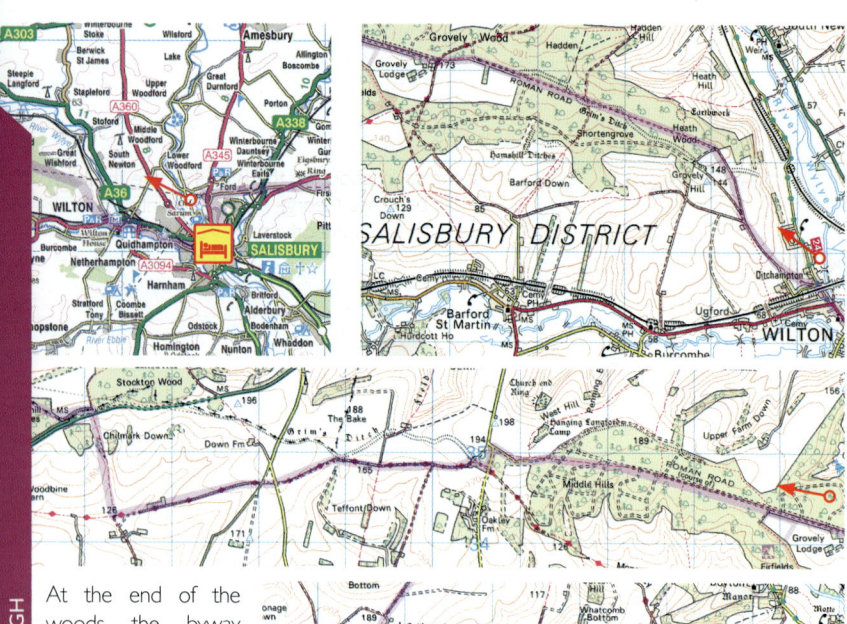

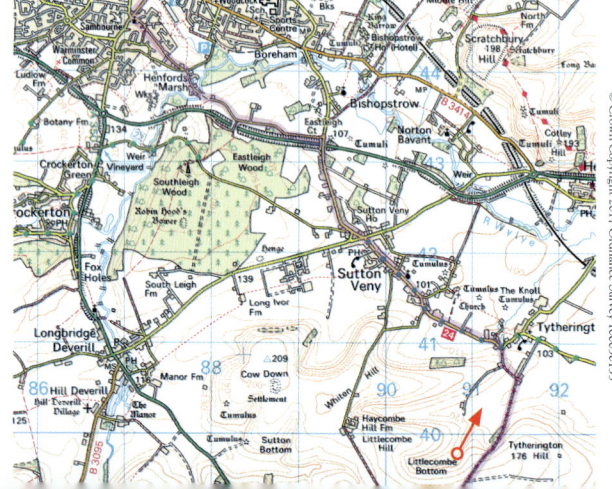

Mountain Biking Adventures:

At the end of the woods the byway does a L and then quickly bears R. Follow this track, also called Ox Drove, for about 4km, avoiding all track and tarmac deviations to L and R until at ST 964 343 you turn R, N. Climb steeply to the A303 and cross it with care. Just after entering the woods at the other side turn L and then bear R for 1km, turning R and then soon L at the next track. Continue broadly W for 4.5km through the delightful broadleaf forest. On emerging from the forest the track bears L for 200m and then sharp R. In just under 1km you arrive at the end of a long thin wood with

ROUTE 20. GREAT CHALK CHALLENGE, EASTBOURNE TO PRINCES RISBOROUGH

© Crown Copyright 2017 Ordnance Survey 100050133

250

Multi-day routes in northern Britain

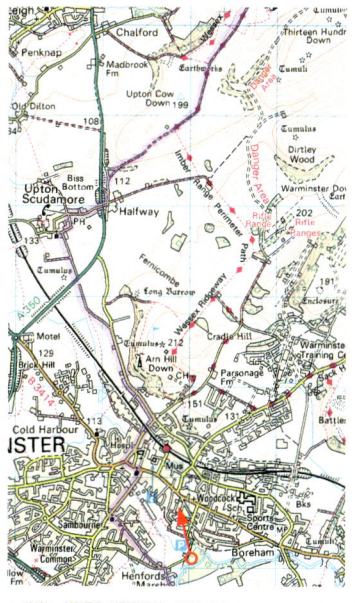

track down each side. Take the R hand track, keeping R at the next small copse, N, for 4.5km to the hamlet of Tytherington. Turn L here, and wend your way on minor roads, broadly NW, to the centre of Warminster.

At the roundabout on the B3414 where the High Street becomes George Street, turn into Portway and head NW under the railway and then bear L as your way becomes Westbury Road. In just over 1km take the L hand 'no through road' to Upton Scudamore, crossing the A350 with care. At the village go R and R again at the Angel Inn. In a little way, cross the A350 again by bridge and bear L and soon R at another 'no through road' sign. Climbing steeply, the tarmac soon gives way to track and this is the start of the Imber Range Perimeter Path, also designated 'White Horse Trail' and 'Wessex Ridgeway'.

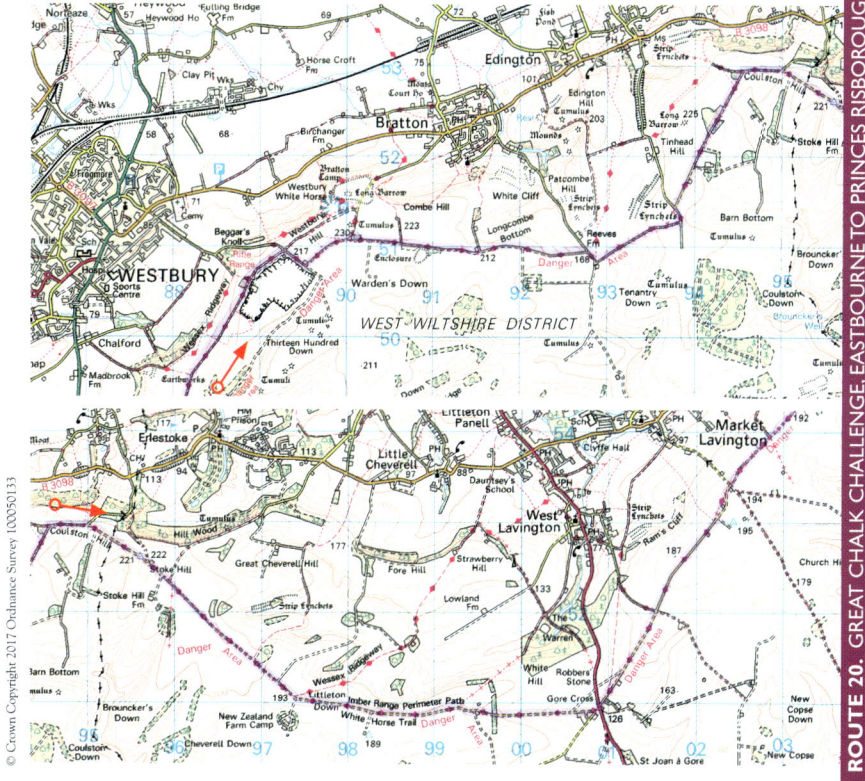

Mountain Biking Adventures:

Follow it, for 24km, until just beyond Urchfont Hill where a tarmac road drops steeply to the N and continues just E of Urchfont village, crossing the B3098 and coming out on to the A342 opposite a small housing development called Ostler's Yard.

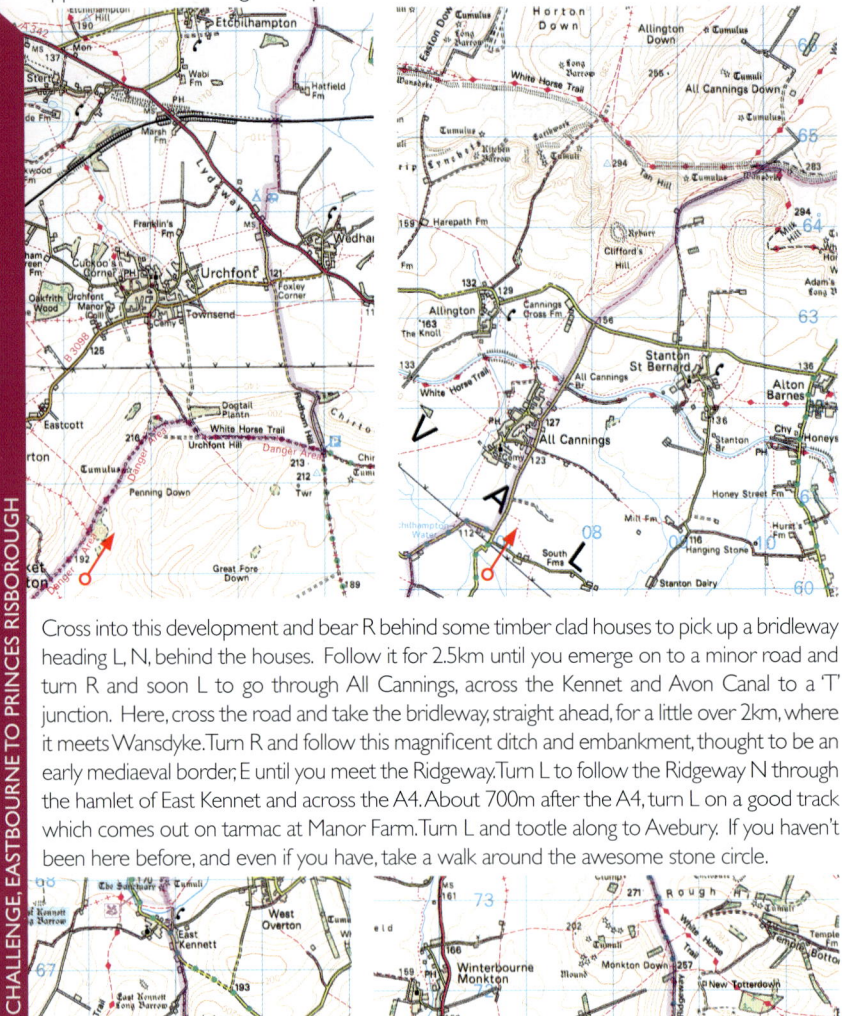

Cross into this development and bear R behind some timber clad houses to pick up a bridleway heading L, N, behind the houses. Follow it for 2.5km until you emerge on to a minor road and turn R and soon L to go through All Cannings, across the Kennet and Avon Canal to a 'T' junction. Here, cross the road and take the bridleway, straight ahead, for a little over 2km, where it meets Wansdyke. Turn R and follow this magnificent ditch and embankment, thought to be an early mediaeval border, E until you meet the Ridgeway. Turn L to follow the Ridgeway N through the hamlet of East Kennet and across the A4. About 700m after the A4, turn L on a good track which comes out on tarmac at Manor Farm. Turn L and tootle along to Avebury. If you haven't been here before, and even if you have, take a walk around the awesome stone circle.

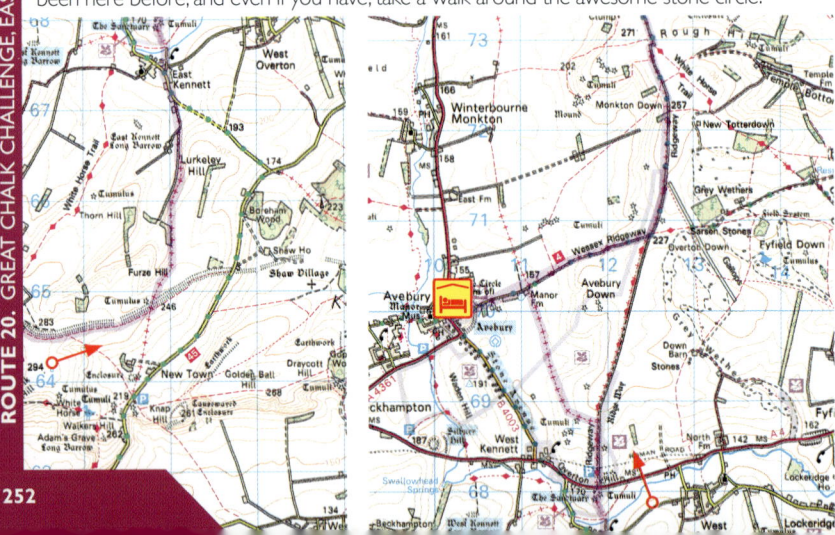

252

Multi-day routes in northern Britain

DAY 4.

Start:	Avebury
Finish:	Princes Risborough/Goring on Thames
Distance:	103/70km (64/43miles).
Off-road:	78/59km (49/37miles) 77/86%
Ascent:	1273/900m (4178/2954ft)
Descent:	1313/1000m (4309/3282ft)
Grade:	H1/M1

OVERVIEW

A magnificent, high-level, chalk track, with much less up-and-down than the SDW, but also less opportunity for refreshment. Take a good packed lunch and plenty to drink if you do not want to accept a significant diversion. A good day out on its own, and, if you go the full distance to Princes Risborough, a big day after everything you have done to get here!

ROUTE

From the Red Lion pub in the centre of the village, cross the A4361 and take the tarmac road, ENE, that you came in on, until you rejoin the Ridgeway after 2km. Turn L and follow the waymarked track, 68km, to Goring on Thames, where you can get trains to Birmingham and the north, and Reading and the south, east and west.

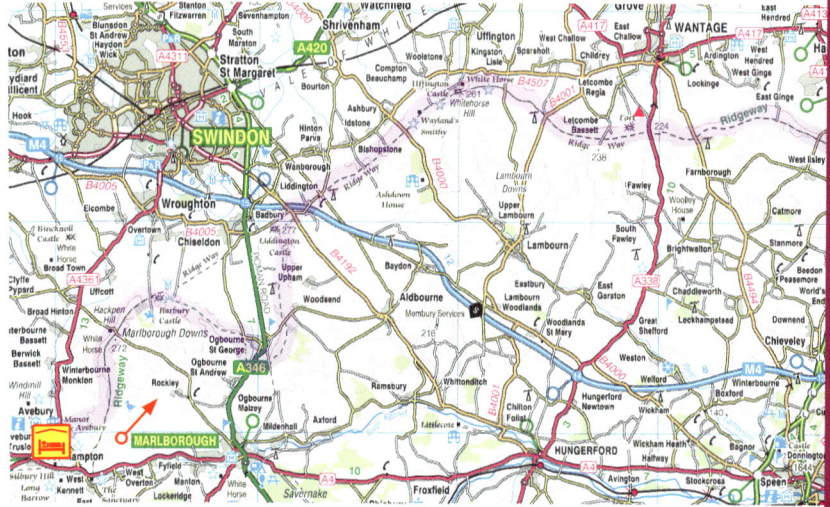

Enjoy your view of the Thames from the bridge, because, if you are continuing, you must leave the Ridgeway for little way now, in the interest of alacrity, clarity and lack of contention. It's not clear which, if any, of the next section along the Thames bank is open to cyclists.

ROUTE 20. GREAT CHALK CHALLENGE, EASTBOURNE TO PRINCES RISBOROUGH

253

Mountain Biking Adventures:

Go through the centre of Goring, with plenty of opportunity for refreshment, and turn L on the B4009 just after the railway bridge. After about 0.75km turn R into Elvendon Road and in a further 500m branch L into Ickneild Road. This minor road follows the line of the Ickneild Way, clearly marked on the OS map. Follow the Ickneild Way on minor roads and bridleways until, about 1km after the delightful Ickneildbank Plantation, the Ridgeway rejoins your track.

Follow the waymarked track, mostly wooded, mostly straight on, beneath the Chilterns' escarpment until you emerge on tarmac near Bledlow. Follow the road signs to Princes Risborough and the station.

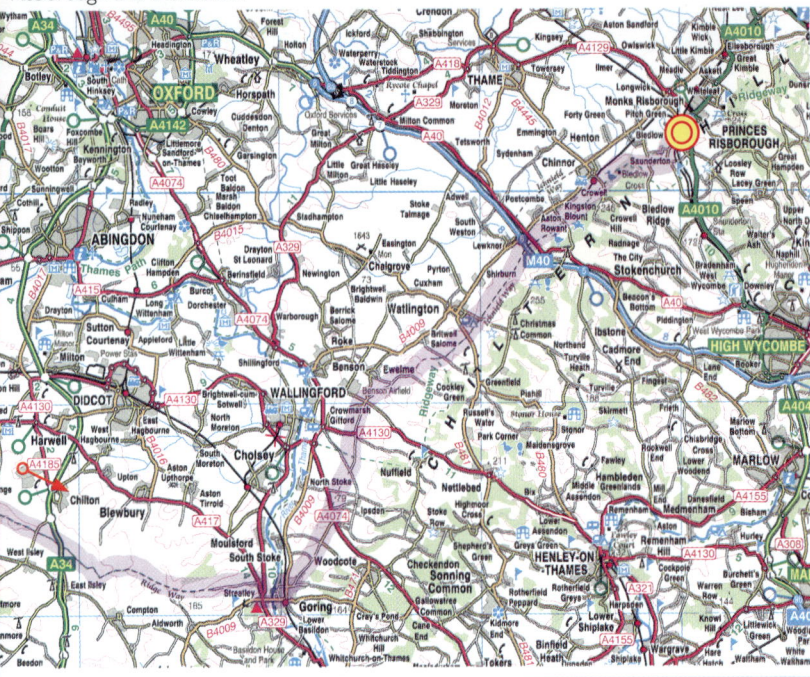

On the Ridgeway.